A Year in the Life of
Somerset County
Cricket Club

CONTENTS

FOREWORD

Andy Nash, Chairman of Somerset County Cricket Club, is a basket case, and Roy Kerslake our President is unquestionably certifiable. However, I confess that when it comes to the game of cricket, I should be taken away by men in white coats ... and I don't mean umpires.

Somerset is everyone's second county, probably because we make a habit of coming second in the County Championship. We did once manage to come equal top, and even then the authorities found a way of taking the trophy away from us.

With *A Year in the Life of Somerset Country Cricket Club*, Andy Nash brings to life the day-to-day problems a modern county chairman has to tackle. He must balance the books, deal with inflated egos on and off the field, and dutifully follow the team around the county circuit, wondering if we might be relegated or, finally, be anointed as county champions. And as Andy points out, three wins or three losses in a row can determine in which direction you will go. Andy also describes having to deal with a visiting touring side, selecting overseas players, arranging the fixture list for county matches, CB40 games and sell-out crowds for the T20 matches, not to mention buying graveyards, working with the local council and having to cope with the problems of rain stopping play – an occurrence over which he has no control, but will often decide if you make a profit or a loss at the end of the season.

But it's the account of the behind-the-scenes, day-to-day workings of the club that makes this book captivating, not only for Somerset supporters, but also for those who consider cricket to be a religion, not a sport.

Mind you, the ending is weak. Somerset come second again.

Jeffrey Archer
Fan

ACKNOWLEDGEMENTS

Many people have contributed to this book – far too many to mention all by name. I must though give special thanks to: Richard Walsh and Richard Latham for their outstanding and regular contributions to the Somerset County Cricket Club website's news section; 'Dave' of *SCCC News*; Mike Robinson, Alan Lockyer, Alexander Davidson and Mike Williams for their very generous gift of so many wonderful photographs which light up several sections; and all the writers whose articles I have featured throughout the journal.

I have made every effort to gain permissions for the use of the sources quoted in the text, but sometimes without success. If the reader can shed any light on those which I have been unable to attain then please contact The History Press directly.

INTRODUCTION

Somerset County Cricket Club is an institution in the West Country. The club was formed, after lunch, at Seaton Cricket Club in Devon following a match between the Gentlemen of Devon and the Gentlemen of Somerset in August 1875, and ever since has lit up countless summers with the characters and contests which make a county cricket club the special entity that it is. I've been privileged to be 'on the bridge' of the Club since 2004, when I was appointed Deputy Chairman to Giles Clarke CBE. In 2008, following Giles' elevation to the chair of the ECB I was elected to succeed him and have enjoyed – for the most part anyway – all that this has entailed. I've forged many friendships in the club and across the game and from the office I hold I'm extremely fortunate to be able to view the game through a rare lens. As Chairman I meet people of all ages playing, managing, developing and supporting this great game from all over the world and it struck me that it might be of some service to record events from this vantage point for all those who share my love of our club, and also perhaps the game of cricket in general. What follows is a chronologically organised journal of 2012 and the many events of note and colour which have yet again woven a rich tapestry for members and supporters to savour. Chairing a professional cricket club is akin to being the captain on a ship permanently on the edge of mutiny! There are of course many elements which make up the crew and they all live in perfect harmony while successive victories are notched up; but as someone once observed, any sports team is only ever three consecutive losses away from a crisis in which factions appear, disagreements are magnified and the blame game begins in earnest. Another county CEO recently reminded me that at any one time in the season roughly half the clubs are in compete disarray as they tussle with all their demons in the lower half of a table. Somerset isn't immune from setbacks and challenges of the management kind; but I do think we've a certain durability born out of decades of suffering and overcoming existential threats – none more so perhaps than the Shepton Mallett episode in 1987. However, even this pales compared to our *annus horribilis* in 1885 when we only won one of six first-class matches despite fielding twenty-six players and three of the defeats were amongst our ten heaviest of all time. We were unable to even field a full side for the fourth fixture and so we were stripped of our hard won first-class status at the end of the season. We had to play second-class cricket for five seasons before being readmitted in 1891. We've managed to hang on since.

I hope you enjoy the year's journal, which comprises events and happenings involving a great many folk who came within Somerset County Cricket Club's orbit in 2012, that I've had the privilege to witness either first hand or indirectly, and while I've done my best, I'm quite certain my account will fail to do it justice.

JANUARY

SUNDAY, I JANUARY. LONDON

A new year dawns and eventually my thoughts are drawn to bridesmaid's apparel! Somerset CCC in 2011 once again over-achieved on the pitch by finishing in the upper echelons of the County Championship and also reaching *both* domestic one-day finals for the second year in succession; but for the second year in succession we also managed to lose both finals, hence the wedding aphorism. Our season still finished on a high as, against all the odds, we made it through to the semi-finals of the Champions League T20 in Chennai, India, where we were narrowly beaten by the competition's ultimate winners the Mumbai Indians. No disgrace there; but losing five (we made the T20 final in 2009 as well) domestic one-day finals on the trot really, really hurts. So, let's dare to think, maybe THIS is the year! In common with all Somerset members and supporters, and many other supporters because our very public agonies have made us many cricket fans' second favourite club; I pray that it is.

TUESDAY, 3 JANUARY. ADELAIDE, AUSTRALIA

Alfonso Thomas is a very gifted cricketer and a great character. With his family he's a charismatic and popular presence in our club. He has become an international tour de force in the T20 format and this year is going to play in three continents in the next three months!

ALFONSO HELPS STRIKERS TO VICTORY – Somerset County Cricket Club Site

The Somerset bowler helped his side climb to second place in the Australian Big Bash. Alfonso Thomas helped Adelaide Strikers get back to winning ways when they beat Brisbane Heat by 31 runs with two overs to spare in the Big Bash T20 competition out in Australia earlier today (Tuesday).

Opting to bat first at the Gabba in Brisbane, the Strikers posted 166 for four from their 20 overs, with Thomas not required to bat.

The Somerset vice captain bowled the first over when the Heat replied, which went for 15, including two 6's by Matthew Hayden. His next over, which was the third of the innings went for just 7 runs and included the wicket of the host's captain Peter Forrest.

Thomas returned to bowl the 18th over, the last of the match, during which there was a run out and from which he conceded only 4 runs as the Heat were dismissed for 135.

The Somerset bowler ended with the impressive figures of three overs, one wicket for 26 runs.

The Adelaide Strikers have now won two of their four matches and are currently second in the eight team table, behind Hobart Hurricanes who have played the same number of games and won them all.

Thomas and the Adelaide Strikers are next in action when they travel to take on Perth Scorchers on Sunday January 8th.

MONDAY, 9 JANUARY. THE COUNTY GROUND

Nowadays players are on annual salaries. Gone are the days of them window cleaning or driving lorries over the winter! A lovely vignette of how poorly rewarded professional cricketers were was of an ex-player being told his pension accumulated while playing for Somerset was £240. He said, 'That's not going to go terribly far in a month, is it?' He was duly corrected: 'I'm afraid this is the value of your entire pension pot!'

SOMERSET STEP UP THEIR TRAINING PROGRAMME AHEAD OF NEW SEASON – SCCC Site

With a little over twelve weeks until the 2012 season gets underway, the Somerset players begin their first full week of training tomorrow (Monday) after returning from the Christmas break.

Reflecting on the first few days back Andy Hurry the Somerset Head Coach said: 'We had a brief squad meeting with the guys first thing on Wednesday and there is certainly a bit of pre-season atmosphere about the place returning from the break, which is really good.'

Looking ahead to the coming weeks Andy said: 'The boys have now stepped up their skills programme which is integrated into their excellent physical training programme they are undertaking in the gym.'

'However now they are doing a lot of one-to-one sessions, as well as two structured squad skills sessions; one is on cricket intelligence and developing their awareness of how to play smarter cricket, and the other is on squad fielding, looking to reinforce our strength in that area.'

Regarding those players who are currently away playing cricket, people like Max Waller, Nick Compton, Jos Buttler, Pete Trego and Alfonso Thomas, the Head Coach said: 'It's great for the lads who are overseas playing cricket because it can be a long winter working indoors. For the guys who have got the opportunity to go overseas it is very exciting and a great experience as well.'

Andy added: 'At the end of this month we are hopefully sending James Hildreth and Arul Suppiah over to India to attend the Spin Clinic in Pune and we are just finalising arrangements for that.'

With the new campaign creeping ever closer there is no time like the present to join Somerset CCC, and membership can cost from as little at £129, providing you sign up before the end of January.

To become a member of Somerset CCC for the coming season click the membership box on this page and join on-line at any time, telephone 0845 337 1875 between 9am and 5pm Monday to Friday or call into the Main Office in the Andy Caddick Pavilion at the County Ground.

DUBAI, ENGLAND V ICC XI

George Dockrell burst onto the scene at the age of 17 with some sparkling displays at the T20 World Cup in 2010 as the tournament's youngest player. Somerset supported Cricket Ireland by playing there during the Troubles under Brian Rose's captaincy. We've enjoyed a strong relationship ever since and these contacts brought young George into our orbit. I travelled back from Chennai with George following the CL T20 last October and got to know him better. He's a very bright and shrewd young man, who is enjoying the development of his cricket career as well as pursuing his studies at Trinity College in Dublin. He's now a fixture in the Irish ODI side and I'm sure in time will develop into a formidable spinner of the red ball too.

THURSDAY, 12 JANUARY. THE COUNTY GROUND

We've enjoyed a terrific relationship with Kieron Pollard since 2009, but unfortunately he's unavailable for the 2012 T20. We are determined to win the T20 and qualify again for the CL T20, so the highest calibre alternative was sought. Brian Rose has produced some substitute here. The reaction was phenomenal and our site crashed for the first time following his announcement!

SOMERSET SIGN CHRIS GAYLE FOR TWENTY20 – SCCC Site

Somerset County Cricket Club are delighted to announce that they have signed West Indian all-rounder Chris Gayle as their second overseas player for the 2012 Twenty20 Cup competition.

Brian Rose, the Director of Cricket said: 'We are delighted to have been able to sign Chris for this season; he is a tremendously exciting player and one of the people who would get into any World T20 XI.'

'Chris is a tremendous all-rounder; his batting is outstanding, he bowls and can open the attack with his off spinners and he is also a brilliant fielder, so we are absolutely delighted.'

Kieron Pollard, who has been such a great player for Somerset in previous seasons, is unable to return in 2012 due to the West Indies tour to England.

Chris Gayle said: 'I am delighted to be heading to Somerset this summer, they are a great club and hopefully I can make a key contribution to their T20 campaign this year.'

Gayle, who is a left-handed batsman and right-arm spinner, has an impressive record in all formats of the game. He plays his domestic cricket for Jamaica and captained the West Indies between 2007 and 2010.

In Twenty20 cricket Gayle has played in 20 matches for his country in which he has scored over 600 runs at an average of 32.47, including 34 sixes and a top score of 117 against South Africa in 2007. This was the first-ever T20 century and is still the highest individual innings at international level in this format of the game. In these games he also captured 12 wickets at a cost of 21.16 and has an economy rate of 7.29.

Gayle's talents have been in great demand in Twenty20 and he has appeared for Kolkata Knight Riders and Royal Challengers Bangalore in the Indian Premier League, for Western Australia Warriors and Sydney Thunder in the Australian Big Bash, as well as Matabeleland Tuskers in the Stanic Bank 20 Series in Zimbabwe.

In all Twenty20 cricket Gayle has played in 85 matches, hitting almost 3,000 runs, including 195 sixes and has an average of 39.58, as well as taking 47 wickets at 31.19 with an economy rate of 7.47.

WEDNESDAY, 18 JANUARY. ADMIRALTY HOUSE, LONDON

Marcus Trescothick (known as Banger because of his lifelong love of sausages) is a living legend at Somerset. The Keynsham-born batsman was among guests at an event hosted by Deputy Prime Minister Nick Clegg yesterday to mark the achievements of the Time to Change programme, run by charities Mind and Rethink Mental Illness, to end the stigma and discrimination faced by people with mental illness.

There are so many stories which attest to his outstanding qualities both as a cricketer and also as a person. His battles with mental health have been well documented and all I would add is to underline the admiration and respect we all feel for the way he has selflessly managed his problems – always finding time for others he can help. A Kent member wrote to me at full wattage in 2009 following our matches at Canterbury and Colchester. Apparently he had asked Marcus, having seen him in the park, to say hello to some lads playing cricket. The point of his letter was not just that Marcus spoke to them, but that he joined in the game for a couple of hours, passing on advice and encouragement! The following day he played a masterful innings against Essex, smashing a double ton to the astonishment of all who witnessed it. The Kent member's letter signed off with the point that maybe Marcus should practise in the park more often!

SATURDAY, 21 JANUARY.

Somerset's improvement on the pitch since our double wooden spoon in 2006 owes much to the development of a number of home-grown young players. Our age-group structure, Academy and Cricket Board have received attention and investment and subsequently have conspired to produce a conveyor belt of talent who have developed and prospered. Two young men forced their way through to our first team squad in 2009 where their array of special talents became evident pretty quickly. Jos Buttler and Craig Kieswetter have now broken through into Team England squads and the whole West Country is justifiably proud of them. There are a number of others whose skills and characters have been honed on the playing fields of the West Country and who are set to follow in their footsteps.

Craig and Jos have today both been named in the fifteen-man England Lions squad for their five match one-day series against Sri Lanka 'A' which begins next Friday.

Their Tour schedule is as follows (all matches 50 overs a side):

Friday, 27 January: Sri Lanka 'A' v England Lions (Dambulla)

Sunday, 29 January: Sri Lanka 'A' v England Lions (Dambulla)

Tuesday, 31 January: Sri Lanka 'A' v England Lions (Welagedera)

Friday, 3 February: Sri Lanka 'A' v England Lions (Colombo)

Monday, 6 February: Sri Lanka 'A' v England Lions (Colombo)

MONDAY, 23 JANUARY. LORD'S
ECB MEETING TO DISCUSS THE MORGAN REVIEW

Few subjects create as much heated debate as the domestic structure and the fixture list of cricket in England and Wales. A county club is a broad church of interests, and I have witnessed many foam-flecked arguments in favour of the first-class game, while at the other end of the spectrum lie those for whom the future is all about the more easily digestible T20. Both camps, and others, testify that their argument alone commands the sunlit moral high ground. The reality is that the domestic game and the counties need both the red- and white-ball formats to survive and prosper. Looked at commercially, the first-class game is the greatest money-spinner as it is the most important element of the media rights package sold by the ECB to broadcasters every four years. It underwrites the game in England and Wales, and a proportion of the proceeds is distributed to all eighteen counties annually and guaranteed in an Memorandum of Agreement which is used as evidence of future income and against which the counties borrow money. However, this distribution of approximately £1.6m annually is nowhere near enough to sustain a county cricket club. If ever counties are to be weaned off the ECB's teat and on to solids, we must embrace the commercial benefits of limited-overs cricket. The debate will rage on, and I compare it to trying to solve a Rubik's cube while wearing a blindfold and taking instructions from a room full of onlookers!

ECB MEETS WITH FCCS AND MCC TO DISCUSS MORGAN REVIEW
– ECB Site

ECB met with representatives of all 18 First Class Counties and the MCC today to discuss the recommendations made in the Morgan Review earlier this month.

The ECB's Board were keen to provide the First Class Counties and MCC with an opportunity for dialogue on the detailed recommendations contained in the Morgan Review.

The discussions were wide ranging and constructive and all the views expressed will be reported back to the ECB Board by Gordon Hollins, MD Events and County Business, at its next meeting in March. The meeting received feedback that the Review provided a constructive template for the First Class game. In particular the counties welcomed the strengthening of the First Class Cricket department.

Key discussion points included:

·the importance of domestic one day cricket being scheduled on Sundays

·the benefits of LV=County Championship matches being played in divisions of eight and ten

·assessing the relative commercial and cricketing benefits of the forty and fifty over formats in the Clydesdale Bank competition

After attending the meeting at Lord's, Guy Lavender the Somerset Chief Executive said: 'The opportunity to discuss the Morgan Review recommendations collectively with other FCCs was invaluable and I am sure these discussions will help to steer the eventual decisions taken by the ECB Board.'
    The Chief Executive added: 'There was widespread support and collective determination to ensure we have a vibrant domestic game, with a surprising amount of consensus around a number of key issues.'

TUESDAY, 24 JANUARY. THE COUNTY GROUND

Today we fell foul of the cat's-cradle of laws and rules which now govern whether a player who is not a British passport holder may be granted a visa to play cricket in England. Roelof van der Merwe became a big favourite with his teammates, colleagues and supporters while we were in the CL T20, but because Cricket SA didn't renew his one-day contract he could not get the UK visa he needed. Very frustrating for all concerned, but Brian Rose pulled another rabbit out of the hat! We announce today that we've signed South African all-rounder Albie Morkel, in place of Roelof van der Merwe, to play alongside Chris Gayle in this season's T20 Cup competition.

WEDNESDAY, 25 JANUARY. THE COUNTY GROUND. THE 2011 GENERAL COMMITTEE MEETING

SCCC's governance hinges on the club's General Committee. Apart from having the club's CEO and elected Honorary Officers it also has the elected representatives of the eight regional areas which serve the membership all over the South West of England.

SOMERSET COUNTY CRICKET CLUB AGM

Somerset CCC is a members' club and this is one major reason why the club has been around since 1875. The membership are represented in eight Area Committees and these in turn elect and appoint representatives onto the club's General Committee. A simple but effective constitution seems to preserve in aspic the DNA which makes the club work. We are effectively a blend of volunteers and executives who combine to be accountable and take the necessary decisions to make the club tick. Crucially, all profits/surpluses which remain after tax can be reinvested directly into the club. Once a year, as with most other companies and organisations, an AGM is held where members can hold to account those of us attempting to run the club. We routinely get over 200 members attend and we do our best to inform and occasionally entertain them.

SOMERSET HOST WELL ATTENDED AGM – SCCC Site

Almost 250 members attended the Somerset CCC Annual General Meeting that was held in the County Room on Wednesday evening.

David Gabbitass the Vice Chairman of SCCC took the chair and opened the meeting with a message from Roy Kerslake the Club President, who is currently in Australia.

Andy Nash the Chairman of SCCC gave a full report, which included a resume of the Club's achievements both on and off the field. The Chairman then outlined the core objectives before moving onto the future aims which included the County Ground achieving Category B status to enable Somerset to host international matches.

The Chairman also talked about the Morgan Review which raised a number of questions from the members present.

Brian Rose the Director of Cricket talked about the playing side of the Club and stressed that his primary aspiration was still to win the County Championship. The future of the Club looked bright particularly in the light of the success that a Somerset team including many younger players had enjoyed playing in the CB40 games against Essex and Durham and out in the Champions League, when several of the senior players were missing.

Alex Tetley the Hon Treasurer talked about the Club's finances and reported on one of the most successful financial years in the Club's history, which included an increased turnover of 12½% on the previous year.

Four members of the committee were returned unopposed – Richard Parsons (North Somerset and Bristol), David Gabbitass (Devon and Cornwall), David Pope (Bath and Wiltshire) and Brian Dawe (Taunton).

The meeting concluded with the presentations of Honorary Life Membership to Andrew Moulding, who retired from his post of Cricket Development Manager in 2011 after 16 years in post and David Gabbitass, who has been a great servant to the Club for many years.

The AGM closed just before 9.15pm.

Reflecting on his first AGM, the Chief Executive Guy Lavender said: 'As a member's Club the AGM is the most important single annual event we hold. Last night's AGM was very well attended by Members, the Committee and all of the playing and coaching squad there were available. It was a great opportunity to reflect, look to the future and answer some excellent questions posed by Members.'

(See p.318)

TUESDAY, 31 JANUARY. THE COUNTY GROUND

Membership is cricket's version of football's season tickets. It is a vital though declining (as a proportion of total income) form of income and cash flow. We put a big effort into trying to retain existing members and attract new ones. At present our membership is rising gradually above the 6,000 level, with people joining from all over the West Country and a smaller number from the Somerset diaspora scattered to all four corners of the Earth.

Today is the last day when 2012 memberships can be purchased at the early buyer's discount, so quite a push is on via our online media and mail-outs to boost recruitment.

FEBRUARY

THURSDAY, 2 FEBRUARY.

Our disabled men's team are superb and have won their national competition three times in the last five years. They are a credit to our club, and Jon Tucker the skipper needs to share the secrets of how to cross the line in finals with Banger!

KIERAN COSENS OFF ON ENGLAND DISABILITY XI FIRST EVER OVERSEAS TOUR – SCCC Site

Somerset's Kieran Cosens is off on the trip of a lifetime when he flies out to Dubai in the near future after being selected for the first tour ever undertaken by the England Physical Disability Cricket squad.

All rounder Cosens is Somerset born and bred and currently lives in North Petherton with his wife and young family. He has been involved with the high performance squad right from the time it was first established at the end of 2010 and is relishing the prospect of playing cricket for his country.

'We have only played friendlies up until now, so the first serious matches we play will be against Pakistan out in Dubai, which is also the first ever England PD XI international tour. It's good to be involved with something right from the start and I am very excited.'

Kieran, who is slightly paralysed down the right side of his body as a result of suffering a stroke when he was born, is no stranger to cricket because his father plays, and he became involved when was a pupil at Kingsmead School in Wiveliscombe.

'I have also been playing cricket for the Somerset Disabled team for 12 years now and have played in the team that has recently enjoyed a great run of success.'

The England PD XI tour to Dubai is for two weeks and during that time they will play their Pakistan counterparts in two T20 and four ODIs.

'Its great and I just can't wait. It's the opportunity of a lifetime and I intend to grab it with both hands and take every chance I get.'

How much training was involved in playing at this level?

'Because it's a high performance squad it's like any other England team, they don't take it easy on you because you have got a disability, so there is a lot of fitness and trying to find the time to do it all is sometimes quite difficult, but I know it will all be worth it.

'I train with the rest of the England PD squad one weekend every month, but in between there is a lot of fitness work to do and we get regularly tested when we are together.'

Kieran has also received a lot of help and coaching from Dan Hodges, who is something of a legendary figure in Somerset cricketing circles.

'I also owe a lot to Dan Hodges because he has been my coach ever since I started playing cricket and has helped me out a lot with my coaching. We talk most days and he is proper chuffed with what I have achieved.'

The Somerset all rounder is being sponsored by Millichamp and Hall the batmakers, who are based at the County Ground and Irwin Mitchell Solicitors.

'I am very grateful to both my sponsors and their help is very much appreciated. I can't thank them enough.'

Kieran, who sets off for Dubai the second week in February added: 'Hopefully this will be the start of a long international career and something that me and my family can look back over and be proud of.'

SATURDAY, 4 FEBRUARY. HOME

An email exchange with our club President, Roy Kerslake, who is wintering in Perth WA with his family. Roy has been President for eight years, and he and his wife Lynn are the most terrific ambassadors for the club. Along with his love of cricket he has a very fine mind and an in-depth understanding of the game forged in the crucible of professional cricket. He has been a constant source of wise counsel to me since I became Chairman. His only weakness I've identified is his misplaced support of lowly Torquay Utd! We compare thoughts on a number of issues and in particular the progress of the invigorated Big Bash. Roy confirms what we've all read – it was extremely well supported, dwarfing attendances for recent first-class and ODI matches. The tickets for the final sold out in just fifteen minutes, apparently. This success holds portents for the future of the domestic game in England and I expect the issue to gain more awareness, and the debate to heat up, as the 2012 season progresses and T20 aficionados realise our own tournament has been cut back from eight home matches to just five because it hasn't proved sufficiently popular!

SUNDAY, 5 FEBRUARY. BANGLADESH

It's not often that twins break into the same team, but the pride of North Devon, Craig and Jamie Overton, have graduated through our Academy to represent England at Under-19 level. Both are likely to play in the forthcoming U19 World Cup later this year.

CRAIG OVERTON ENJOYS SUCCESS ON ENGLAND UNDER 19s TOUR – SCCC Site

England Under 19s may have lost their seven match 50 over one day series against their Bangladesh counterparts five games to two, but Somerset Academy youngster Craig Overton has certainly acquitted himself very well.

The 17-year-old all rounder, who hails from North Devon and attends West Buckland School, played in six out of the seven matches and enjoyed success with both bat and ball.

Craig ended in fifth place in the batting averages, scoring 113 runs at an average of 22.60, with a best of 36.

With the ball the right arm medium fast bowler, who opened the attack, sent down 36.1 overs. He ended as joint third highest wicket taker, claiming seven scalps at a cost of 28.28 each and fourth best in the series averages for the England Under 19s.

Commenting on the youngster's tour Jason Kerr the Academy Director said: 'Without feedback from the England camp it looks as if Craig has had a very productive series. One that has been challenging both on and off the park. Trying to sit exams and compete in a one day series on foreign soil isn't easy.

'Craig will have learnt a great deal during the 7 match series, he's been given lots of responsibility. Opening the bowling in the majority of the games and batting in the middle order. Contributing in all the games will give him huge confidence as he prepares for this coming summer. We look forward to seeing him at the Academy sessions this week.'

MONDAY, 6 FEBRUARY. GRAZE BAR AND RESTAURANT, QUEEN'S SQUARE, BRISTOL

One of my pals at university in Swansea was Dick Edmonds. Dick is a sports nut and through living and working in Cheddar for many years has become a naturalised Somerset fan. He was diagnosed with oesophageal cancer in November last year. This is one of the most difficult types of cancer and his prognosis isn't good. Dick was a very popular student at college – with a dry sense of humour formed in the crucible of a West Midlands childhood. Being a Coventry City fan, he says, he's also well used to suffering and so is well equipped to cope with the stresses and strains inflicted by cancer! Another mate from those happy days, Andy Mason, got in touch and we talked about what we could do to support him. Dick, Andy and I met in December at the County Ground and toured 'back-stage' at the County Ground. It also turns out Dick, while teaching at Cheddar, was schoolmaster to one Joseph Buttler and he knows Jos and his family extremely well! Dick's eldest son Mike was best man at Jos' elder brother's wedding last year! Andy and I decide to try to reconvene our group of pals from uni and although we've not met as a complete group since graduation in 1978, true to form, having been hunted down via social media networks, they all turn up from all over the UK to meet Dick for an evening in Bristol. Dick has a great time and we decide to meet every month to support him on his challenging journey through chemotherapy and help him in his battle with this awful disease. We also plan to hold some of our monthly get-togethers at SCCC over the season. I also decided to dedicate this book to him, because if cricket is a metaphor for life then Dick personifies better than anyone else I know the qualities that you will need to make the journey. It is his amazing stoicism and fortitude in the face of overwhelming odds that has kept us all turning up every month to be with him.

TUESDAY, 7 FEBRUARY. TAUNTON

Alfonso Thomas (Fons) was back in Taunton briefly before jetting off to South Africa on Monday evening on the next stage of his whirlwind winter T20 tour. This is a good illustration of how the advent of T20 has given professional cricketers more opportunities to play the game year round and enrichen themselves in the process.

He has had a brief respite from travelling in the Southern Hemisphere to catch up with his family and teammates after playing for Adelaide Strikers in the Australian Big Bash.

•••

We've also heard the news today that Jos Buttler and Craig Kieswetter (Bagel) have been selected for the England squads to play in the forthcoming ODI and T20 series against Pakistan in Abu Dhabi and Dubai. Another great opportunity for this duo to further their England careers.

FRIDAY, 10 FEBRUARY. THE GREYHOUND, STAPLE FITZPAINE. SUPPER WITH WAYNE AND BELINDA KIESWETTER

Somerset is renowned as a friendly and family-orientated club. Craig and his brother Ross both attended school in Somerset and quickly became settled in the county. Linda and I first met Wayne and Belinda when we were on a trip to Cape Town, where they have a home, and we have become good friends since. I was lucky to be with Wayne to see Craig achieve his maiden first-class century at Taunton in 2009.

Meanwhile, in Bangladesh, Pete Trego captained the Sylhet Royals in their opening match of the Bangladesh Premier League on Friday, but his side was blown away by future Somerset T20 teammate Chris Gayle, who smashed a 44-ball unbeaten century to see the Barisal Burners to a ten-wicket victory.

Pete, batting at number three, went to the wicket after 8 balls with the score on 10 and remained at the crease until the final over before he was eventually third man out with the total on 157.

The County Ground favourite finished with 62 off 54 balls, which included seven fours and one six as the Royals posted 165 for four off their 20 overs.

However, when Chris Gayle walked out to open the innings he proceeded to blast ten sixes and seven fours on his way to an unbeaten 101 as the Burners reached 167 without loss in 13 overs.

SATURDAY, 11 FEBRUARY. LINCOLN, NEW ZEALAND

Women's cricket is gaining popularity quickly, and Somerset County Cricket Club has built upon the success we had in hosting the Women's T20 World Cup in 2009. One of our most successful players is Anya Shrubsole, and today she was very much brought to the fore as England women managed a 181-run victory over New Zealand Emerging XI at the Oval in Lincoln in the first warm-up game of their tour ahead of the ODI and T20 series against New Zealand. England posted 292 for nine from their 50 overs, captain Charlotte Edwards making 123, which included 17 boundaries before she retired.

WEDNESDAY, 15 FEBRUARY. DUBAI

Andy Hurry (Sarge) came to cricket via the Royal Marines and has established himself on the circuit as an outstanding coach. Justin Langer labelled him the best he had ever worked with – praise indeed. Others have spotted Sarge's talents and this is the second occasion he's been invited by Andy Flower to join up with Team England overseas. It's great experience for our First XI coach and can't do his long-term prospects in the game anything but good.

ANDY HURRY LINKS UP WITH ENGLAND COACHING TEAM AHEAD OF ODI SERIES – SCCC Site

Somerset will have three representatives in the England camp for the forth-coming ODI and T20 matches against Pakistan, because in addition to Jos Buttler and Craig Kieswetter, head coach Andy Hurry will be working alongside Andy Flower as one of his assistants.

Andy began his career as a physical training instructor in the Royal Marines, before starting off with Somerset on a consultancy basis working with some of the injured players back in 2001, so he has come a long way since then.

'I was originally asked to go out to work alongside the England coaching team for the one day series to gain some experience as part of my personal development,' Andy said.

'However Richard Halsall, who is one of the assistant coaches, is return-ing home because his wife is having a baby, so I will now be working in his place, helping Andy Flower, and making up the numbers in the support staff as well. I will be another pair of hands to help and someone else to bounce a few ideas off.'

Before he set off for Abu Dhabi, Andy said: 'I am very excited about the whole thing because it's an ambition of mine, and has been since I was a young schoolboy, to get involved with a full England team, so I am really made up about it.'

'I think that this is a reflection on what has been achieved by the Somerset team because as any coach will say, you are only as good as the team. I have been very fortunate to work with a highly successful and talented side.'

The Somerset head coach flew out to Abu Dhabi on Tuesday evening in prep-aration for the warm-up game between England and England Lions on Friday. The first ODI against Pakistan begins on Monday February 13th and he will remain with the England camp until the end of the tour on February 28th.

Andy will be linking up with Somerset players Jos Buttler and Craig Kieswetter, who have both been selected for the England ODI and T20 squads, in addition to which he has already had contact with several other members of the tour party.

'I have been quite fortunate in my time with the Club in that I have man-aged to build up good relationships with some of the international players. I met Andy Flower a couple of times and have been very impressed with him as a coach. I know some of the England management team as well so I won't be going into unknown waters.'

Andy is no stranger to that part of the world because he had a year work-ing in Abu Dhabi back in 2005 before returning to Somerset as head coach, a post he has held ever since.

Somerset captain Marcus Trescothick said: 'It's great experience for Andy to be involved and gain an insight into what the international arena is all about and work with Andy Flower and all of the players who will be out there.'

'I know that he is really excited about getting out there and it will be brilliant for him to see what it's all about.'

Marcus added: 'I think it is a well-earned reward for all of the hard work that he has put in back here. We have been on the up and up for the last four or five years, and Andy has been at the forefront of that, so to get that reward and go right to the top is what everybody aspires to and dreams of.'

In his absence Second XI coach and Academy Director Jason Kerr will be overseeing the winter training programme of the Somerset players at the County Ground.

FRIDAY, 24 FEBRUARY. COUNTY STORES TAUNTON. THE STRAGGLER ANNUAL DINNER

The Stragglers is one of the country's oldest cricket clubs, having been founded in 1900. They are a focal point for nomadic cricketers of Somerset and play a few fixtures in the season. They stage their annual meeting in Taunton on the last Friday in February and enjoy bonhomie, a carvery, a quiz and some kind of after-dinner entertainment. This evening around sixty club members and their guests assembled and I had the honour of speaking to them. They are a very warm and appreciative audience who clearly know their cricket and county club inside out.

SUNDAY, 26 FEBRUARY. TAUNTON

The Somerset Cricket Board is the governing body responsible for all 'recreational' i.e. amateur cricket in the county. It therefore organises, administers and manages the game from where we derive many of our young cricketers. They manage age group sides, from the boys' and girls' Under-11s to the slightly less sprightly Over-50s. Our club enjoys a very good relationship with the board and it is obviously vital that we do so.

Somerset Cricket Board has today announced the appointment of Andy Fairbairn as Cricket Development Manager. This is a key appointment for the SCB and he will start his role at the County Ground before the end of March.

MONDAY, 27 FEBRUARY. ABU DHABI

It's been many years since two Somerset players have played in the same England team, so the selection of Craig Kieswetter and Jos Buttler has created a lot of interest in the West Country. Both have made good impressions and we are beginning to consider contingency plans for wicketkeeping during parts of the forthcoming season.

SOMERSET DUO TASTE ENGLAND T20 SUCCESS OVER PAKISTAN – SCCC Site

Somerset duo Craig Kieswetter and Jos Buttler are celebrating tonight after England's dramatic five-run T20 win over Pakistan.

The pair were part of the England squad which clinched the series 2-1 in Abu Dhabi earlier today.

Kieswetter, who recently signed a new long-term deal with the Cidermen, hit 17 off 17 balls, before he was caught by Shoaib Malik off Saeed Ajmal's bowling.

Buttler, 21, came in to bat at sixth but only made 7 off 13 before being dismissed lbw, again by Ajmal.

But the Taunton-born youngster was to make an important impact in the field.

He ran out the impressive Asad Shafiq with some quick thinking and pin-point throwing into the hands of his Somerset team-mate Kieswetter, who stumped Pakistan's top scorer.

England scored 129-6, while the hosts only managed 124-6.

MARCH

FRIDAY, 2 MARCH. TAUNTON. MEETING WITH GUY LAVENDER, CEO OF SOMERSET CCC

The relationship between chairman and CEO is vital in any organisation. I enjoyed a strong and fruitful relationship with Richard Gould for over four years, and while we always planned that he would move on to further his career, it was with some trepidation that I had to accept the reality when it came in the spring of 2011. We had experienced some amazing highs and lows and had notched up some significant achievements at the club. We had earmarked Guy as a potential successor some years before when we met him during a visit by Lord Coe to the County Ground. Despite liking the cut of his jib, we proceeded with a formal process and had over eighty applications from the world of sport and business. It is worth mentioning that when we ran a similar process in 2005 on Peter Anderson's retirement, we attracted only a handful of applicants. The club's success and raised profile had clearly added steroids to the process. Guy Lavender performed with great aplomb through the process and won the short list by a healthy margin. He has shown himself to be an exceptional manager and like his predecessor has supreme interpersonal and leadership skills.

•••

We have had the confirmation we expected that both twins would be selected for England U19 duty this year. A very proud moment for their family and Instow Cricket Club in North Devon, where they first developed their love of the game and learnt to ply their trade.

OVERTONS BOTH SELECTED FOR ENGLAND UNDER 19s – SCCC Site

The Overton twins Craig and Jamie, who are both members of the Academy at the County Ground have been named in the England 15-man Under-19 squad for their tour of Australia, where they will take on the hosts, India and New Zealand in a quadrangular one-day series.

The 17-year-old North Devon based all-rounders have represented England Under 19s previously.

Jamie played in the series against South Africa, and the pair went on a training camp to South Africa just before Christmas.

Both were selected to play in the series in Bangaladesh, where Craig enjoyed considerable success. Sadly, however, Jamie had to withdraw from the party at the last minute after sustaining an injury in training, from which he has now fully recovered.

Jason Kerr the Academy Director said: 'It's great news that Craig and Jamie have been selected for the U19 quadrangular series in Australia.

'This is another fantastic opportunity to develop their skills and knowledge in unfamiliar conditions against strong opposition.'

Jason went on: 'Craig had a very productive trip to Bangladesh and will want to build on those performances. Unfortunately Jamie missed Bangladesh. However, I'm sure he's relishing the opportunity to get back in the fold and showcase his talent.'

England Development Programme head coach Tim Boon said: 'This tournament will be a fantastic opportunity for all the players to gain experience of Australian conditions and test themselves against quality opposition ahead of the ICC's Under-19 World Cup – which will also be held in Australia later this summer.'

The full England U19 squad: Adam Ball (captain, Kent), Mo Abid (Lancashire), Shozair Ali (Warwickshire), Daniel Bell-Drummond (Kent), Ben Foakes (Essex), Brett Hutton (Nottinghamshire), Aneesh Kapil (Worcestershire), Sam Kelsall (Nottinghamshire), Jack Leaning (Yorkshire), Craig Overton (Somerset), Jamie Overton (Somerset), Rammy Singh (Durham), Shiv Thakor (Leicestershire), Reece Topley (Essex) and Sam Wood (Nottinghamshire).

The itinerary for the tour is: Thursday, 29 March: Arrive in Australia. Monday, 2 April: Warm-up game. Thursday, 5 April: England v Australia, India v New Zealand. Saturday, 7 April: England v New Zealand, Australia v India. Monday, 9 April: England v India, Australia v New Zealand. Friday, 13 April: Semi-finals. Sunday, 15 April: Final.

SUNDAY, 4 MARCH. TAUNTON

The West Country is festooned with livestock farms, and in the rural communities there is growing excitement and a sense of optimism for the forthcoming summer when the cows are 'turned out' from their winter sheds – and one can't help but draw a comparison with the letting loose of our players onto the green baize of the County Ground from their own winter pastures!

SOMERSET PLAYERS ITCHING TO GET OUT ON COUNTY GROUND – SCCC Site

The County Ground was a hive of activity on Friday as head groundsman Simon Lee and his colleagues were carrying on with their preparations for the start of the new season.

Simon said: 'Things are looking good for the start of the season and I am very pleased with the way that everything has gone during the winter. The grass has grown well and the surface of the outfield is much more level than it was.'

He added: 'Hopefully when the players report back for pre-season on Monday week they will be able to get outside working in the nets.'

Certainly the players are relishing the prospect of reporting back for pre-season.

Before that they have a few days off and next weekend will take part in a team building exercise away from Taunton after which they are straight back into the start of pre-season – hopefully out on the grass.

To get a taster of how it felt to be back outside on the grass the players had a fielding session in the sunshine, to end the week, which made a welcome change from working in the Indoor School where most of them have been training during the winter.

Marcus Trescothick said: 'The preparations have gone really well for us and we are all ready to get going now and for the batters to start facing bowlers and for the bowlers to start coming in off their full run-ups.

'We are now excited at the prospect of the new season, especially when the sun is out like it is today and we can get out and have a run around. It was tough out on the grass to begin with because it was a bit damp, but to get the feel of being outdoors instead of indoors was great.'

The captain added: 'The ground looks just fantastic and the square is in good shape. The ground staff have done a lot of work on it this winter and with the sun out it looks great. Hopefully we will get this weather when we report back for pre-season on March 12th.'

James Hildreth was another who was pleased to get outside again. 'We have trained pretty hard over the winter and the last few weeks have gone well for us. We have been restricted to the Indoor School the whole time and it has been really useful working on the bowling machines and on our fielding skills, but the last couple of days have been nice so we have been able to get outside, which is brilliant.'

Hildy added: 'We did a fielding session which was great. We did some high catching drills and just to get that feeling of being outside in the sun and on the grass was brilliant. The County Ground looks so good at the moment that it is teasing us and we just want to get going now.'

Reflecting on the last few weeks Jason Kerr, the Second XI coach who has been in charge of the winter programme during the time that head coach Andy Hurry has been away with the England team, said: 'It has been a fantastic time from my point of view. The players have worked incredibly hard whether it has been physically or on their skills, but they get to the point where they are desperate to get outside and we have certainly reached that point now.'

Jason went on: 'They are all looking forward to having a few days off and a little bit of down time. Hopefully the weather holds and next week when they report back for pre-season we will be working outside.'

With the new season creeping ever nearer, tickets for all matches, including T20 and the match against South Africa, have just gone on sale on-line on this site, so don't miss out, order your tickets for the big matches now!

TUESDAY, 6 MARCH. TAUNTON AND FAREHAM

The familiar Electoral Reform Society envelope is in today's post. Just one candidate in the Chairman's election campaign. Strikes me as ironic in the week that Putin was elected as President for the third time! This will raise a smile with Giles – I must tweak his tail with an SMS. Giles Clarke has presided over a highly successful period at the helm of the ECB. It's not my job to be his cheerleader in this book, but even neutral observers must acknowledge the concrete achievements of Team England and increasing participation levels in the game generally. To the casual observer his abrasive, direct and sometimes aloof manner can cause friction, but when you work at close quarters with him you appreciate his other qualities. He is a loyal, highly intelligent and compassionate man of integrity and I'm proud to call him a friend. That's not to say we've not had our differences! I was on the end of his hair-dryer when I labelled the ECB's scheduling of the CB40 semis and final in 2010 as 'towering incompetence'. I returned his sentiments on that occasion at full wattage and we agreed to differ. We've had several robust discussions on other topics in recent years, as in our respective roles the standpoints of the ECB and Somerset do not always synchronise. At the end of the day, though, the relationship between the nineteen shareholders of the ECB (counties and the MCC) needs to be businesslike and productive. We are one and the same thing and the epitome of a symbiotic business model. Somerset is fortunate to have a former chairman at the top table of world cricket, and we all wish Giles well in upholding England's interests in the challenging and sometimes unpredictable environment of the ICC.

•••

I log on to the club's site with my iPhone and get a pleasant surprise – the mobile version of our site is up and it looks well organised and sharp. I email Guy and compliment him and the team on achieving it ... and ask him when we are going to get our own app!

WEDNESDAY, 7 MARCH. FAREHAM

It is Sir Isaac Vivian Alexander Richards' sixtieth birthday! A reminder to all fans of one of the game's greatest ever cricketers who played for Somerset between 1974 and 1986. How he came to play for our club is the stuff of legend! He was discovered by Bath bookmaker Len Creed, a Somerset committee man who saw him playing when on holiday in the Leeward Islands. Creed paid Viv's fare to England and persuaded him to qualify for Somerset in 1972 and 1973 by playing for Lansdown in Bath. He remains a great favourite of Somerset fans – only last week 'Somerset la la la', a knowledgeable and inveterate twitterer, reminded us all in less than 140 characters of Viv's 300, in a single day, on his way to 322 against Warwickshire on 1 June 1985!

The following quote from one Somerset great to another is worth retelling. During 1983, when India were in the West Indies, Sunny Gavaskar dropped down from his usual opening berth to number four. When he came out, Viv said, 'Man, it don't matter when you come out to bat, the score is still zero.'

I believe it's a matter of some regret that the new laws and regulations relating to overseas players mean that feats such as Viv's discovery for Somerset are now extremely unlikely. The game has accepted severe restrictions on the eligibility of non-English-qualified players to play in the UK and in so doing has effectively swapped talented overseas players for less talented Englishmen. I recall discussing this in 2006 with club skipper Justin Langer: we agreed that developing cricketing talent isn't a numbers game. If it was, India would dominate all forms of the game. The game has eschewed quality in favour of quantity. Proponents of the restrictions on overseas payers will point to the recent success of Team England in long and short formats of the game. I disagree; I believe the success stems from other factors such as central contracts, improved academies and the rise of T20. A significant but rarely mentioned benefit of T20 has been its ability to persuade some of the best athletes to opt for a career in professional cricket – previously many of our best potential cricketers were lost to football and rugby.

An example of an exceptional athlete opting for cricket when he could just as easily have chosen rugby is Jos Buttler, a prodigious cricketing talent in a very unassuming and unflappable character. He was at school with my son Ed at King's College, Taunton, for five years and they frequently opened the batting together. I lost count of the number of times they would put on 100 for the first wicket and Ed would still be in single figures! Five years pacing the boundary and touch line (rugby) meant Linda and I got to know Jos' folks very well. John and Pat are a very genuine couple whose unconditional love and support of their youngest son has played a big role in nurturing and developing his talent. Typically they always put the credit elsewhere, but they should be immensely proud of the contribution they have made to Somerset and English cricket. By the time Jos' career is in its twilight many years from now, I will wager all cricket lovers will be rather heavily in their debt! As Dave Egbeer, a local league umpire, put it, 'Some players are good, a few are very good and a handful are game-changers. From the age of 11 Jos has been a game-changer.'

FRIDAY, 9 MARCH. TAUNTON

Our club has eight Area Committees and each plays a role in representing SCCC in their region. Taunton Area has been very active over the winter, organising a variety of different events. The post below is a good example of just how well these can work – 130 people turning up to hear Marcus Trescothick talking about the forthcoming season!

TAUNTON AREA ROUND OFF THEIR WINTER PROGRAMME WITH ANOTHER SUCCESS – SCCC Site

The Taunton Area Committee of Somerset CCC rounded off their winter programme of events with a highly successful evening on Wednesday when Marcus Trescothick was their special guest.

Almost 130 were present to enjoy the hot buffet before taking part in a question and answer session with the Somerset captain that proved to be most interesting and provide a real flavour for the season ahead.

Mary Elworthy, the Taunton Area secretary, said: 'The evening was a fantastic success and Marcus was absolutely terrific in the question and answer part of the evening.'

Mary added: 'We are very grateful to Marcus for coming along and helping to make this another most enjoyable cricketing occasion. We would also like to thank everybody who has supported our events during the winter and now look forward to the new season.'

Profits from Wednesday evening will go towards extending the County Ground.

THURSDAY, 15 MARCH. TAUNTON

I've just returned from a long-haul overseas trip and am meeting Guy Lavender to chew the fat on several issues. Good to see a typically upbeat piece from Craig Kieswetter, who amazingly is now one of the squad's senior players. Guy arranged a 'character building' exercise for the squad last weekend, utilising his military background and network. I read the report last night and it has highlighted areas of strength and development.

CRAIG KIESWETTER PROUD TO BE PART OF SOMERSET CCC – SCCC Site

Craig Kieswetter is back at the County Ground training with his Somerset colleagues after spending much of the winter away involved with the Lions and on England one day duty.

'It's colder than what I have got used to over the winter but since I have returned we have been quite lucky to be able to get outside and run our planned pre-season programme so far according to plan.'

'Spirits are high with everyone and despite it being a little damp and misty outside we are playing cricket on the grass which after a winter when a lot of the guys have been in the gym is a real breath of fresh air.'

Talking about his own game Craig said: 'I'm feeling pretty good with where I am at with my cricket at the moment. I have done a lot of hard work during the winter, especially with being involved on England programmes, and things are starting to come together for me quite nicely.'

'This winter was good for England, with two series wins over Pakistan, and also good for me personally, but there are still a few areas that I need to work on and keep on tinkering with. All in all, though, I am feeling quietly confident with the progress that I am making in my game.'

With so many youngsters coming through the ranks at Somerset, even though he is only 24 years old, Craig is one of the more senior players in the squad, having been involved with Somerset since 2006.

'This will be my sixth season as part of the first team and it's nice to think that I have got some experience that can help some of the younger guys. We are getting all of the 'keepers together and doing some integrated sessions, and now I feel I have some responsibility as one of the senior players.'

He went on: 'James Regan is one of the young wicketkeepers coming through and he has been training with the squad this week, and he has certainly no lack of energy or enthusiasm and takes me back to when I was his age and just setting off. It's good that we are all working together and hopefully I can share some of my experience with him and help him to progress.'

Talking about the coming season Craig said: 'I suspect that we will be favourites for one or maybe both of the one-day competitions, purely on past form. However for us as a club and a group of players we try not to get ahead of ourselves.

'Obviously we want to win trophies and that is why we play the game, but it can be quite dangerous to look to far ahead.

'We are focusing massively on the first championship game against Middlesex on April 5th, which isn't too far away now, and hopefully we will get our campaign in that competition off to a good start. Over the last couple of years we have started slowly in the four-day format so we are putting a lot of emphasis on that first game and trying to get off to a good start.

'We want to win games, we want to win trophies, we want to be posting 400 plus on the board and we want individuals to be stepping up and taking responsibility at crucial times.'

Craig added: 'These are exciting times at Somerset. We have got some fantastic players on board, some great people on the coaching side of things and some great fans. I think that we are very different from where we were when I first played for Somerset. We are very professional and we are consistently looking to perform to our maximum potential and that's why it makes me feel really proud to be part of this Club.'

FRIDAY, 16 MARCH. TAUNTON
Email to Sally Donaghue, SCCC's Operations Manager

Sally,

Re Monday / Tuesday aboard HMS Somerset.

Can you let the Captain know I once did my RYA Power Boating course (Level 2) and if it's all right with him I'll take the helm as we dock in Devonport.

Thanks.
Nasher

PS In case I fluff the manoeuvre can you check the Club's 3rd party insurance will stretch to a Type 23 Duke class frigate.

MONDAY, 19 MARCH, 6.30 A.M. TAUNTON RAIL STATION WITH GUY LAVENDER
We are en route to collect the club's bell, which we presented to HMS *Somerset* to accompany them on their last tour of duty. When safely retrieved, it will be

used by umpires on the balcony of the Andy Caddick Pavilion to signal the start of a session's play.

Our club is an important part of the community it serves. We have always tried to cultivate relationships with other clubs and institutions in our locality. Andy Hurry our Head Coach is a former Royal Marine and this has helped foster a strong relationship with the corps, who have a Commando based in Norton Fitzwarren near Taunton. In 2009/2010 they served an arduous tour in Afghanistan and lost fourteen Royal Marines, and many others suffered life-changing injuries. Andy ('Sarge') Hurry arranged for cricket kit and other paraphernalia to be sent out to forty RMC to enliven their cricket matches while in theatre. We also flew their regimental colours at every home and away match for the duration of the tour. All bar one ground co-operated with our request – apparently the MCC's rules forbid the flying of flags at Lord's, no matter how good the cause. We were very proud to be asked to host the regiment's official homecoming in March last year, and after their march past in the town centre almost 3,000 serving Royal Marines and their families enjoyed our facilities in a secure and welcoming environment.

I wonder what lies in store for Guy and me aboard HMS *Somerset* in the next 36 hours! We are due to sail with the 'Duke' class frigate from Portsmouth to her home port Devonport. Meanwhile our First XI will be playing the first pre-season friendly at the County Ground as we entertain Glamorgan.

TUESDAY, 20 MARCH. PLYMOUTH

Guy Lavender and I have safely retrieved the club's bell together with a picture given to the club by HMS *Somerset* which contains a very tasteful photograph of said bell taken East of Suez. The ship's company were outstanding hosts and last night, while cruising off Portland, treated us to a simulated attack by two hostile aircraft. Happily from our point of view both were 'splashed' by sea wolf missiles and we were able to retire safely to the wardroom to recount various tales. We were both greatly impressed by the professionalism and morale of the ship, which was a compliment to Captain Bristow and his crew. We will continue to work at fostering future relations with the ship and her company and already there has been talk of a cricket match to come.

It looks as though the CEO and I had a better time than our First XI, who have initially stumbled against Glamorgan. We were rather glad that being at sea we were unable to keep up with the score yesterday. Captain Bristow clearly had a better day than Captain Trescothick!

In the pre-season friendly at The County Ground we managed a somewhat modest total of 137, having won the toss. Glamorgan in reply cantered past us to achieve 229 for five at the close. Interestingly, young Craig Meschede (Mesch) was the pick of our attack.

TAUNTON

Newspapers are reporting continuing discussions between Chris Gayle and the WICB. We expect Chris to honour his contract, as our plans include him, and some members have bought T20 tickets because of him being contracted to us. Let us hope common sense prevails!

CHRIS GAYLE'S WICB DECISION DELAYED – ESPN Cricinfo

Chris Gayle's expected return to the West Indies team has been delayed after no decision could be arrived at during Monday's high-level meeting, which was expected to resolve the year-long dispute between the player and the West Indies Cricket Board. Chaired by Prime Minister of St Vincent, Ralph Gonsalves, the meeting was also attended by WICB chief executive, Ernest Hilaire and officials from CARICOM.

A resolution would have seen the former captain available for West Indies team's ongoing series against Australia, which continues till April 27. Gayle, however, is contracted to represent Bangalore Royal Challengers in this year's IPL, from April 4 to May 27, and county side Somerset, in the English Twenty20 tournament. The clash of dates between the West Indies team's international commitments (the current series is followed by a tour of England between May 5 and June 24) and Gayle's contractual obligations could be a possible reason for the delay in the talks.

Before the meeting, the *Jamaica Gleaner* had reported that Gayle was likely to either submit an apology or retract his comments made against the board and the coach Ottis Gibson during a radio interview.

In February, the WICB chief executive Ernest Hilaire said he wanted Gayle to make his priorities clear, saying that Gayle could not ask for unconditional no-objection certificates (NOCs) to play domestic Twenty20 tournaments around the world and simultaneously make himself available for West Indies selection.

Gayle attended Runako Morton's funeral in St Kitts on Saturday and was spotted in the stands during West Indies' second ODI against Australia, in St Vincent. He last played for West Indies in the 2011 World Cup, and has since taken part in Twenty20 leagues around the world, including the IPL, the Big Bash League in Australia and the BPL in Bangladesh. He has turned out for Jamaica in the domestic one-day and four-day competitions. He was left out of the WICB's 30-man squad for a fitness and training camp ahead of the home series against Australia.

TUESDAY, 20 MARCH. TAUNTON

I receive a phone call from a well-known cricket journalist who asks me to confirm that we've signed Ricky Ponting as our overseas player from the end of May, when Vernon Philander returns to duty with the Proteas. We are due to discuss this issue on Friday this week, so I explain we've not yet made a decision, but because the caller was – as he invariably is – understanding and restrained in his approach, I undertook to call him when we have done so. I've learnt in business and sport that it is no use simply being a fair weather friend to the media, i.e. contacting them when you have something you wish to say. It works far better for both parties if an open and straightforward dialogue exists.

WEDNESDAY, 21 MARCH. TAUNTON

A typical 'up and down' two days in cricket. A portent of the season almost upon us, no doubt! The result didn't matter, but I was glad two batters hit their straps with Marcus Trescothick (Tres/Banger) and Nick Compton (Compo) both hitting imperious hundreds. However, this is offset by the news I had last night from Guy Lavender that both Steve Kirby (Tango/Kirbs) and Gemaal Hussain picked up injuries. If these are significant it will be crucial (to our early season's prospects at least) that CSA don't intervene at the eleventh hour and decide to rest Vernon Philander ahead of their tour here! A period on tenterhooks looms large.

FRIDAY, 23 MARCH. TAUNTON

I spoke to Craig Kieswetter (Bagel) yesterday as he's at Ed's 21st-birthday celebrations. I hadn't seen the scorecard and asked him how it had gone. He said 'Quite well – I got a few.' It appears he's learning the art of understatement!

Against Worcestershire in a two-day friendly we managed 287 for five at tea thanks to a robust 155 from Bagel, with Jos also chipping in with an unbeaten 71. James Hildreth (Hildy) also showed some early season form with a bright partnership with Bagel when needed. After tea our depleted pace attack set about the men from the Midlands and Adam Dibble (Officer/Dibbs) and Peter Trego (Tregs) led the attack respectably.

•••

Lewis Gregory is another excellent product from our age-group and Academy system. He hails from Devon, a county which has produced many fine cricketers for Somerset and England. In 2010 he captained the England U19 side with distinction and made his first-class debut shortly afterwards. He was frustrated by injury last season but prior to that was taking wickets with impressive regularity in limited-overs games. He's worked very hard to overcome injuries and regain full match fitness, and it's a just reward that he's been identified and selected to join the MCC squad, announced today, that will compete in the Emirates Airlines T20 and the traditional curtain raiser for the season against the reigning county champions.

•••

The Management Sub Committee met for a regular update. This committee operates as the de facto Board of the club and has derogated powers from the club's General Committee to take the necessary decisions to manage the organisation and its many moving parts. There's never any shortage of topics to discuss, but since most members are volunteers with full-time roles elsewhere, I keep the meetings to under two hours. Key issues today were progress and next steps on our application for Category B status, the hotel project, financial performance year to date and an update on cricketing matters by Brian Rose. We remain on tenterhooks over the arrival of Vernon Philander. He's playing rather too well in the recent Test series for the Proteas, and Rosey is concerned that Cricket South Africa may elect to rest him ahead of the tour here. Matters aren't helped by reports of alleged corruption and suspensions of senior officials at the top of CSA. We still don't have the NOC (no-objection certificate) which all home cricket boards need to issue to allow a cricketer to play overseas.

•••

The County Ground has been given the honour of hosting an evening event on 21 May with the Olympic Torch, and some 6,000 people are expected to enjoy festivities. Guy Lavender has been exercised by various officials sticking their oars in to advise and assist on what to do in the event of wet weather etc. Simon Lee, our groundsman, is rightly sensitive about thousands of souls trampling around the ground, as we host Durham the following day!

The club has a very active programme of community involvement all year round. Many supporters are aware of the more visible events, such as staging concerts and homecomings for the Royal Marines. People will be less aware of a lot of other good work put in by club players, staff and volunteers. A good example is the Chance to Shine (CTS) initiative, in which we support schools all over the South West region. The Cricket Foundation launched Chance to Shine in May 2005 and set out to bring competitive cricket, and its educational benefits, back to at least a third of the country's state schools over a ten-year period. Chance to Shine is delivered through individual projects, working with county cricket boards across England and Wales. Each project provides a structured coaching and competition programme for a group of up to eight primary and secondary state schools. The group of schools is supported by professional, qualified coaches engaged by one local cricket club.

The scheme also provides equipment, facility development (including playground markings and non-turf pitches) as well as training for state school teachers and coaches. Working with the Somerset Cricket Board and twenty-one cricket clubs in 2012, we sent coaches into 107 primary and secondary schools. So far we've coached over 4,000 schoolchildren on this programme and Banger, Compo and Kirbs have been directly involved. We also provide free tickets to schools for all LVCC games and Women's Internationals and host, at no cost, all CTS 'Reward and Recognition' events. We also run the payroll for all CTS coaches.

Withywood is a cricket 'centre of excellence' that has been set up in an economically deprived area of Bristol with assistance from The Merchant Venturers in the city. The initiative has received £20,000 of funding via the SCB and has also brought South Bristol back into the Somerset County Cricket Club fold.

Playing for Success is a scheme which aims to teach children aged ten to fourteen 'at risk of disaffection' through the medium of cricket. Somerset County Cricket Club was one of the first to adopt this scheme eight years ago, and since then 1,639 primary children and 1,124 secondary students have attended our programmes at The County Ground. Taunton Deane Council cut funding as part of their spending squeeze, but we have opted to continue the programme and cover the costs incurred.

Focus Clubs is another initiative where professional clubs support the recreational game. We have thirty-six such Focus Clubs in Somerset and we have funded the infamous Jimmy Cook and outreach coaches to every one of them. In addition we provide ten tickets to CB40 for the first fifty clubs who sign-up and compete in 'NatWest cricket force' and we also host 'Reward and Recognition' days at fixtures throughout the season.

Women's and girls' cricket is thriving and is another means by which we engage with our local communities. Somerset County Cricket Club was the home of women's cricket during the Women's T20 World Cup and this provided real momentum, which we have capitalised upon. We now have two teams in the ECB South West League, while our Senior Women's team competes in the National Premier League. In 2011 the SCB funded a Girls' Emerging Players Programme (EPP) for the first time and now we have age-groups established at U12, 13, 15 & 17, mirroring what has worked so well in the boys' game.

Disabled cricket has been a great success and Jon Tucker's side has won the National Championship in three of the last five years. The team proudly paraded their trophy at our CB40 fixture against Essex. We fully parallel the able-bodied game with excellent coaching, high quality kit and celebrating their success on every occasion.

In recent years we've nominated charities as beneficiaries and in 2011 a programme of events raised over £30,000 for Children's Hospice South West. In September 2011 Banger's Bike Ride (a mixed peloton of players, staff, celebrities and supporters) cycled the length of the South West peninsula over five days, visiting all three children's hospices in our region and raised a significant sum in the process. Last year the NSPCC were our chosen charity and members and supporters enthusiastically backed a number of events across the year.

We are proud of how we serve our community. We are in a position to do some good work and it is very gratifying to see how very effectively the club's players, staff, volunteers and supporters combine to do this.

•••

Speculation continues as to the intentions of both Somerset and one Ricky Ponting (Punter) for later in the season. Following inaccurate reports earlier in the week that we had signed him, his manager has tweeted the correct version of events and the media are beginning to pick this up. We haven't made any decisions yet in relation to overseas players for later in the season and Rosey will almost certainly wait and see what the requirements are nearer the time. If the front seven fill their boots early season and we lose a strike bowler to injury I doubt Punter would fit the bill!

A report in the *Hindustan Times* of all places stated that the former Australian captain has rejected the opportunity to play county cricket this year as he aims to play one last Ashes series in England in 2013. The report went on to state that 37-year-old Punter had been linked with English side Somerset but his manager James Henderson denied the reports via his Twitter account.

SATURDAY, 24 MARCH. TAUNTON, LONDON

At the station to catch the 8.25 a.m. to London. It is my son's 21st birthday tomorrow and we are celebrating by going to see Chelsea play Spurs followed by dinner. Ed's pals include Jos Buttler, his opening partner at King's College, and Craig Kieswetter, whom he has also known since school days. Both are joining in the celebrations and should be in good heart after some strong personal performances yesterday against Worcestershire. The game itself petered out into a draw.

MONDAY, 26 MARCH. WELLINGTON, NEW ZEALAND

Twitter reports that Vernon Philander is the fastest man to the 50-wicket milestone in Test history. Six for 81 for him against New Zealand today.

Just Proteas (@justproteas)
3/26/12 7:26 AM
Big Vern became the fastest man to 50 Test wickets in 116 years. It was his 6th five wicket haul.

TAUNTON

The Chris Gayle availability saga continues ... as does Vernon Philander's. Earlier emails today from Guy Lavender (who is supposed to be on holiday in Rome doing a gladiator's course, but that's another story) suggest CSA's latest is that a decision will be made tomorrow re his availability for us!

This from the *Deccan Herald* just now ...

GAYLE SIGNS AGREEMENT WITH WICB, BUT WITH THE IPL RIDER –
Deccan Herald

Explosive opening batsman Chris Gayle has signed an agreement with the West Indies Cricket Board (WICB) with a rider that he is honour-bound to play in the Indian Premier League (IPL) and the English Friends Life Twenty20 league this season, making it difficult for his return to international cricket.

It was revealed Sunday that Gayle had signed the agreement, brokered by Caribbean Community and Common Market (CARICOM), with the WICB a couple of weeks ago in a bid to resolve his long-drawn-out impasse with the regional body, reports Jamaican daily *The Gleaner.*

'The Board was advised that Mr Chris Gayle has signed the CARICOM-brokered agreement, but with a "side letter" from Mr Gayle,' the WICB said in a release yesterday. 'Prime Minister, the Honourable Dr Ralph Gonsalves, provided a copy of Mr Gayle's "side letter". The matter was discussed and the Board will respond to the Honourable Prime Minister shortly,' it added.

It now transpires that Gayle's return to the West Indies team to play in the series against Australia is hitched to his contractual obligation with the Indian Premier League (IPL) club Royal Challengers Bangalore and English county club Somerset.

After guiding Royal Challengers to the final of the IPL last season, the 32-year-old Jamaican signed a new deal to play in this year's edition. He has also inked a one-year deal with Somerset to play in the Friends Life League. The IPL will be April 4 – May 27 and the Friends Life Twenty20 June 12 – Aug 25.

THE COUNTY GROUND. PRE-SEASON ONE-DAY FRIENDLY V SURREY

A solid all-round performance, including five wickets for Craig Meschede, saw Somerset to victory by 50 runs with 16 balls to spare over Surrey in the one-day pre-season game at the County Ground.

Following on from the defeat at Lord's in last season's CB40, this is a 'monkey off the back' result. Apart from Treg's excellent 99 and another fine knock from Bagel (obviously well recovered from Ed's 21st celebrations at the weekend) the standout performance was from young Craig Meschede (Mesche). Dennis Breakwell spotted Craig while he was playing for a visiting South African school side at King's College in 2008. I happened to be walking the boundary during a match and Dennis summoned me. 'This kid's the best 16-year-old I've seen since Peter Willey,' he claimed. I immediately phoned Brian Rose, and as he was in the vicinity he came straight over. From there things happened quite quickly, and following a meeting with Mesche's parents and the school, Craig signed for Somerset. He has developed well since, and, but for his period to qualify as a domestic player, he would almost certainly have featured in England's junior sides. We will see much more from this talented young all-rounder.

TUESDAY, 27 MARCH. THE COUNTY GROUND. PRE-SEASON FRIENDLY V SURREY. DAY 1

The last pre-season game got under way today and there were some good signs on display. However, in the best season we've ever had (two one-day finals and County Championship runners-up in 2009) we lost every pre-season friendly.

It proved a batting day at Taunton as Hildy and Bagel reached centuries and Tregs fell just short in the nineties. By the close Surrey were 22 for one, with young all rounder Chris Jordan nicked out just before stumps. An interesting and hard-fought day is in prospect tomorrow.

WEDNESDAY, 28 MARCH. TAUNTON

The Vernon Philander availability issue continues, but the article from Cricinfo below will be welcomed by our cricketers, managers, and of course the supporters.

KIRSTEN CONCERNED OVER PHILANDER WORKLOAD – ESPN Cricinfo

Gary Kirsten admitted that it is a 'little bit concerning' that seamer Vernon Philander will head straight into two months of county cricket after a busy season. Philander played in seven of the eight Tests South Africa contested this season and turned out in all formats for his franchise, the Cobras. He will not have a break until the end of May, a month before South Africa's tour to England.

Kirsten said despite the packed schedule, Philander must honour his contract with Somerset because he agreed to it before he became a nationally contracted player. Kirsten was consulted about the decision and encouraged Philander to accept the Somerset offer because of the experience it would allow him to gain. 'That decision was made during the first Test against Australia in November,' Kirsten said. 'Philander asked me my opinion and I said I didn't think it would be a bad idea to get used to the bowling conditions there. I don't think anyone would have thought that he would play seven Tests and get 50 wickets and really play a major part and bowl a lot of overs for us.'

Philander stunned the international stage with his consistent wicket-taking and was awarded a CSA contract in January, which comes into effect on April 1. Philander's Somerset contract was subject to conditions relating to whether he was able to secure an IPL deal. When he went unsold in the February auction, Philander's agreement with Somerset kicked in. He will play eight matches starting on April 5, when they host Middlesex in their first Championship match.

Kirsten said it is vital Philander sees out his contract but hopes CSA can work with Somerset to ensure he is not overworked or burnt out. 'He wasn't under CSA contract when he signed the Somerset contract. He needs to honour his contract, that's important. But we would like to create a relationship with them and say these are our needs going forward in terms of the Test series,' Kirsten said. 'What's important for me is that he has a window period, a conditioning period. We would like to create that. We will chat to Somerset and see where they are on it and hopefully we can get a significant conditioning period. As it stands at the moment he is due to come back at the end of May.'

County seasons are known to be gruelling on most and South Africans have sometimes struggled to keep up. Dale Steyn was one of the bowlers who had a tough time adjusting during his 2005 stint at Essex, and Lonwabo Tsotsobe also battled in his time at the same county last season. Kirsten said Somerset have promised to be accommodating with Philander but even if they are not, he should have ample rest. 'They've been quite good about it already. They've said we are not going to over-use him but I know how the county circuit works. There's no such thing as over-use when you've got a game on the line,' Kirsten said. 'He has got a month off when he gets back and then we go to England, so it's a decent break.'

Philander's England experience is being eagerly anticipated after his explosive start in Test cricket. He is level as the second-fastest bowler to

50 Test wickets, achieving the feat in just seven matches. Although not expressly quick, Philander has shown the worth of being a crafty bowler and has gone from rookie to being the leader of the South African attack in a short space of time.

The secret to Philander's success seems to be nothing more complicated than rewards for discipline and skill, and it's a testament to the work he put in at domestic level. 'He is very consistent, he has got good control and gets subtle movement of the ball both ways.'

Phone call from Rod Bransgrove, Chairman of Hampshire CCC. He is seeking guidance on what we pay our young players. We have a natter about football too, as Rod is a Spurs fan, while my allegiance lies with a certain side doing rather better than his in West London.

A 'down the line' live contribution to the *Cricket Show* on BBC Radio 5 Live at 8 p.m. The phone is working itself into quite a frenzy on the forthcoming season's T20 and in particular The Cat (Phil Tuffnell) is bringing to life the spectacle of a front three for Somerset of Trescothick, Gayle, and Kieswetter. I'm pretty sure I too got carried away in the pre-season hype and failed to dampen any ardour, instead probably heaping more brushwood upon the fire.

•••

Finally today, Brian Rose texts me to say he has been given renewed assurances that Chris Gayle will honour his contract with us in the T20 this season. Fingers remain crossed – one less problem to contend with!

THURSDAY, 29 MARCH. THE COUNTY GROUND. PRE-SEASON FRIENDLY V SURREY. DAY 3

Our cricket management had targeted the matches against Surrey as *the* ones to win pre-season as on paper they are as tough an opposition as we are likely to face this season. I popped into the ground earlier and met up with Club President Roy Kerslake, and we chatted away in the glorious sunshine and watched Kirbs and young George Dockrell scythe through the Surrey middle order. With Murali Kartik having moved on, the first team spinner's role is up for grabs, so to see George bag six for 33 on his first run out for us this season is very interesting.

We ran out comfortable winners thanks to Dockrell and Kirbs taking nine between them. So, from next week it is for real.

FRIDAY, 30 MARCH. THE COLIN ATKINSON PAVILION. MEDIA DAY AND LONG ROOM LUNCH

The traditional gathering of the first-team squad and the club's senior officers for photographs in whites and also in the one-day kit. Interviews are also given to the media amid growing interest in the club's fortunes and challenges for the season. Last year we were labelled favourites in all three competitions – a yoke we managed to shake off before the first match against Warwickshire was even completed! This year we are far more comfortable with the more modest expectations.

At midday we were joined by Long Room members, club staff and sponsors for the season's opening lunch. We launched this event in 2010 and around fifty guests turned up. This year 268 were booked in and it proved to be a very enjoyable event – the highlight being a well-run Q & A session with three players who reminisced in turn about last season and revealed their hopes and aspirations for the new one. Brian Rose gave a masterful performance in his own Q&A. One member, who enquired as to the possibility of an awning on the Long Room balcony, was invited to wear a hat.

TAUNTON

James Regan is another product of our age groups and Academy, and tomorrow is a day he will never forget: he has been selected to play for the First XI against Cardiff University in the traditional UCCE fixture, and so he makes his first-class debut. All of Somerset will wish him well. Another proud distinction for King's College, too; James is the fourth present member of the first-team squad to have attended the school. A record, we think.

•••

It's time to pay tribute to our in-house commentary service, which has had an extraordinary journey. During the winter of 2008 it became clear that the local BBC Radio were not going to be able to cover Championship cricket in the way that they had previously, and the club was keen to provide some kind of service for its members. The timing of this fortunately coincided with an offer of equipment from the RNIB and some sponsorship from Blackacre Farm Eggs, the outcome of which, after some discussion, was the launch of the Somerset ball by ball commentary service for the 2009 season.

Guy Wolfenden, the club's Commercial Manager at the time, asked Richard Walsh to assemble a team of volunteers to attend a training session. The service was begun after this with just a small handful of volunteers, probably as few as ten at the start of the 2009 season. Initially they often broadcast from the balcony in front of the CEO's office in the Colin Atkinson Pavilion before being housed in the 'Potting Shed'. For those unfamiar with the Potting Shed, it is a radio commentary position atop the Old Pavilion which bears an uncanny resemblance to a wooden garden shed. In the early stages volunteers were working double shifts, but as time has gone on more have come forward and now we have as many as twenty-four on the list of voices that can be called upon. At the start of 2010 the service was granted a limited licence to broadcast, and it relocated from the Potting Shed to the base of the Botham Stand and then to the Sky TV commentary position in the Old Pavilion, where it has remained ever since. In addition to tuning in to the radio frequency, the commentary has been expanded through the Somerset County Cricket Club website. And hereby hangs a tale: having been provided with the data on the online service, I was staggered to see that by last summer listeners in no less than forty-six countries were regularly tuning in!

The beauty of the Somerset ball by ball service is that all of those who broadcast are Somerset supporters who care passionately about their county club. They all have a varying depth of cricketing knowledge, and hopefully the content of their commentary is not only informative but also entertaining.

The service's Director General is the omni-talented Richard Walsh, who organises and runs it on a day-to-day basis. Among those who have been involved from the outset are Roy Kerslake, Julian Cattenach, Richard Oliver and Paul Bird. Others who have been on board and dedicated a lot of their time and energy include Eric Cole, Paul Harper, Bill Luckett, Tom Doyle and Jane Hamlin.

On behalf of all of our listeners, wherever they may be, I'd like to take this opportunity to congratulate 'DG Walsh' and all his co-presenters on what they've built up and achieved, and to thank them warmly on behalf of all Somerset supporters.

•••

Late night SMS from Guy Lavender concerning Vernon Philander: 'Last minute hitch with CSA resolved. Only now left arguing about the flight. He will be here Monday'.

Phew!

APRIL

SUNDAY, I APRIL.

Another seasonal highlight is the first of the month, and the ECB and counties have combined with a rather innovative marketing ploy featuring British Bulldogs and the T20 competition.

ECB TURN BULLDOGS TO BALL-DOGS – ECB site

British Bulldogs will know no boundaries this summer.

The ECB today announced that British Bulldogs will be shrugging off their lazy reputation this summer, as they take up a fetching role in this season's Friends Life T20 competition.

This summer will see an army of the loveable dogs dotted around the boundaries of the nation's cricket grounds, with the sole purpose of returning balls that have been dispatched over the boundary.

The move comes after a players' consultation revealed that unnecessary chases over the boundary were increasing the risk of injury and sapping energy during the games.

The ECB have consulted a series of dog experts to ensure that the Bulldogs are fully prepared for their role, both from a physical and psychological perspective. Considerations have also had to be taken with regards to maintaining the condition of the ball.

Paul Taylor, in charge of training the Bulldogs, commented: 'Bulldogs are traditionally considered a lazier breed of dogs, but they've proven to be a great hit so far in training. Their low centre of gravity makes for a more efficient pick-up and their sturdy build means they are less risk adverse than say, a poodle.

'There have of course been some unforeseen difficulties, most notably the toilet habits of the average British Bulldog. However, the Bulldogs have now been trained to ensure that they do not relieve themselves on the playing surface and dog handlers will be on hand at all times as an extra precaution.'

An ECB spokesperson said: 'Cricket encapsulates all that is right about Britishness and we wanted to take this a step further with the introduction of the ultimate British dog.'

'Friends Life T20 is all about doing something different and we're proud to try something that will save the players exerting unnecessary energy and risking injury, while also providing added entertainment to the action on the pitch.'

MONDAY, 2 APRIL.

After the Mediterranean Spring as soon as the first first-class game gets underway the temperature halves to 11°C! The boundary at Taunton Vale, the adopted second home of our club, is festooned with brave souls draped in blankets and heavy duty clothing to stave off the cold. Still, it's not raining – that's forecast for later in the week during our match with Middlesex!

The match turns out to be a record breaker with the second-wicket pairing of Compo and Hildy putting on 450 in 94 overs – an all-time record for any Somerset pairing. The other notable feature of the game was wicketkeeper-batsman James Regan making his first-class debut.

•••

I tweeted: 'How many times have two batters on the same team in the same innings scored double hundreds?' Twitter at its best and I was obliged to @DavesSCCnews for the following information:

TWO DOUBLE HUNDREDS IN A TEST INNINGS: RARE RECORD

When V.V.S. Laxman completed his double century in the ongoing 3rd Test against Australia in Delhi, a little after Gambhir had completed his, the duo joined a rare club of 'twin double centurions in a single Test Innings'. Here is a compilation of the other instances of this record – I have manually compiled this list, and it is not yet complete. Should be a finished product in a day or two.

1. Pakistan vs West Indies, Venue: Jamaica, 26 Feb –4 Mar 1958 (six-day Test)

Chasing Pakistan's 1st innings total of 328, West Indies piled up a score of 790. Opener Conrad Hunte scored 260 and Gary Sobers scored his famous 365 not out.

2. Sri Lanka vs South Africa, Venue: Colombo, 27–31 July 2005

After dismissing the tourists for a sub 200 score, Sri Lanka went on to make 756/5 declared. This included a triple hundred from captain Mahela Jayawardene who fell 1 short of Lara's mark of 375. Kumar Sangakkara narrowly missed his triple hundred falling for 287, else a record of two triple hundreds in an innings would have been one massive one, and unlikely to be ever overtaken.

3. Sri Lanka vs Zimbabwe, Venue: Bulawayo, 14–17 May 2004

Sri Lanka's 1st Innings total of 713 for 3 included two double centuries, one each by Kumar Sangakkara and Marvan Attapattu. Both double hundreds came at good pace – Sangakkara's 270 came at a strike rate of 74 while Attapattu's knock of 249 was even better at 76.85.

4. Australia vs England, Venue: Kennington Oval, 18, 20, 21, 22 Aug 1934 (Timeless Test Match)

Australia lost a quick 1st wicket when opener Brown fell with the total at 21. His opening partner Ponsford was joined by the Don and by the time the second wicket fell, the score card read 472. Bradman got out for 244 – if Sangakkara and Attapattu were quick, this was a lightning knock. Comprising 32 boundaries and 1 six, Bradman's 244 came at a strike rate of over 90. Ponsford's 266 was more sedate at 63.33.

5. Australia vs England, 13–19 December 1946 (six-day test), Venue: Sydney Cricket Ground

Both Sid Barnes and Don Bradman compiled identical scores of 234 in the 1st Innings of this Ashes Test. What were not identical were the scoring rates - the Don himself scored a slow double by his standards, at a strike rate of 59.09 but it was Barnes' knock which was a specially laborious one. In his 649 minutes vigil at the crease, he faced no fewer than 667 balls – the innings was spread over 3 days!

6. England vs India, 13–18 January 1985, Venue: Chepauk, Chennai

Openers Fowler and Mike Gatting both got double centuries for England in the 1st Innings of the Test. While Fowler scored 201, Gatting got 207.

7. Australia vs West Indies, 5–11 May 1965 (six-day test), Venue: Bridgetown, Barbados

Both the Australian openers, Bill Lawry and Bob Simpson, scored double hundreds as Australia declared their 1st Innings at 650/6. Simpson's brave second innings declaration made it a very interesting Test but he was fortunate in being saved from the blushes as time ran out on West Indies when they were just 11 short of the target, with 5 wickets remaining.

Narrow Misses:
India vs Pakistan Multan Test: Rahul Dravid declared when Tendulkar was on 194. Sehwag had scored a triple hundred in the same innings.

In the 1984 Faisalabad Test against India, Qasim Umar got a double hundred in the 1st Innings but the record was missed by the narrowest margin when Mudassar Nazar was unlucky to be dismissed on 199.

In Independent India's 1st Test series against Australia in January 1948, Don Bradman scored a double hundred in the 1st Innings of the Adelaide Test. But this unique rare Test record of two hundreds in an innings was missed as Allan Hasset was left stranded on 194 when the last Aussie wicket fell.

During the 1st Test of the 1981 New Zealand - Sri Lanka series a most unique record was narrowly missed – 'twin double hundreds in the second innings of a Test match'. Andrew Jones missed his double hundred by 14 runs. The one who did go on to get his double hundred was more unfortunate though – Martin Crowe got out for 299.

Another chance to get this unique record came India's way in the famous Kolkata Test against Australia. That opportunity was lost in a very similar way as in the above Test – while one batsman (VVS Laxman) narrowly missed his triple hundred, his partner Dravid was unfortunately run out when his score was 180.

TUESDAY, 3 APRIL.
The County Championship previews are compulsive reading, and this one in the *Guardian* caught my eye.

COUNTY CHAMPIONSHIP PREVIEW: SOMERSET – Barnaby Read and Andy Bull

The shrewd signing of all-rounder Vernon Philander could turn the perennial challengers into champions this season.

Vernon Philander has taken 51 wickets in seven Tests for South Africa and how he performs in his two-month spell could determine Somerset's title hopes.

2011 in a nutshell: A case of never the bride once more for Somerset as the domestic game's nearly men fell short in the finals of both one-day competitions. At times excellent in the championship, a little more consistency and they would have been genuine title contenders

How they finished in 2011:
County Championship: 4th in Division One
CB40: Lost in final
Friends Life T20: Lost in final

What they'll be playing in this season:
LV County Championship Division One,
CB40 Group B (The Group of Death)
Friends Life T20 Midlands/Wales/West Group

Captain: Marcus Trescothick

Director of cricket/coach: Brian Rose/Andy Hurry

Ins: None

Outs: Charl Willoughby (released)

Overseas players: Vernon Philander (SA), Albie Morkel (SA) – T20, Chris Gayle (WI) – T20

Key player Philander is an excellent signing and should make a massive impact at Taunton, and a lot is expected of Morkel and Gayle in the T20. Without a doubt Trescothick is the main man and his volume of runs will help determine Somerset's success

How will they get on this season?

Philander looks like the shrewdest move of the season. Since the deal was agreed last November, Philander has played seven Tests for South Africa and taken 51 wickets at an average of 14.15 each. Somerset have him for two months, and eight matches, and that spell could determine whether they can finally win the Championship. Without him, their bowling attack may struggle, especially now that Charl Willoughby has left. The batting, from Trescothick down, should look after itself, but the side remains curiously prone to dramatic collapses.

WEDNESDAY, 4 APRIL. SEASON'S EVE

The media, terrestrial and social, are pregnant with speculation! Every narrative shimmers with hope. The consensus appears to be that there is no consensus. The County Championship is brimming with talent and that's only in the second division. The First Division has nine sides each with a chance of winning the most coveted prize in county cricket. The one thing I can guarantee at this time of the year is that the unexpected will puncture the season's aspirations and also its rhythm. Our team news is that young Craig Meschede is selected to play as an all-rounder at number eight tomorrow against Middlesex. Let's hope the weather doesn't spoil what looks like a great curtain raiser.

Our side is from: M. Trescothick (capt.), A. Suppiah, N. Compton, J. Hildreth, C. Kieswetter (wkt), J. Buttler, P. Trego, C. Meschede, V. Philander, S. Kirby, G. Dockrell, L. Gregory.

THURSDAY, 5 APRIL. THE COUNTY GROUND. LV=
COUNTY CHAMPIONSHIP, SOMERSET V MIDDLESEX. DAY 1

The County Championship's opening fixture was heavily curtailed by rain – a portent of the season to come perhaps? After all the waiting Vernon Philander opened his account in some style. Play only began at 2.45 p.m. and closed early at 5.35 p.m., but in that period Vernon bowled with zest and control taking three for 21 from 12 overs.

A satisfactory start to the season in the 35 overs available today.

•••

The Somerset Cricket Museum offers supporters a great experience at any time of the year, but it can be a particularly enjoyable way to spend time during stoppages of play. The museum is located in the 'Priory Barn' on the eastern boundary adjacent to the Indoor School and has had many alterations and additions throughout its long history.

The beautiful building is thought to have belonged to a nearby Priory and like the club has survived several existential crises, but perhaps none graver than the Dissolution in the reign of Henry VIII, after which most monastic buildings throughout the land were destroyed.

In 2010/11 the Somerset Cricket Museum was re-opened to the public after undergoing a major refurbishment thanks to funds bequeathed to the Trust which runs and maintains it so sensitively and efficiently.

The work that was undertaken at a cost in excess of £300k has seen a complete transformation of the interior of the building, including a new layout and design and new display cabinets and graphics. Visitors are invariably fascinated and impressed at the quality of the exhibits and curation. The Somerset Cricket Museum has built up a reputation for being one of the best of its kind in this country and it has very tastefully preserved the heritage of Somerset County Cricket Club.

FRIDAY, 6 APRIL. THE COUNTY GROUND. LVCCI, SOMERSET V MIDDLESEX. DAY 2

I am in Switzerland skiing with my family on an Easter holiday. Having encouraged my daughters to turn off their data roaming because of the exorbitant costs of European roaming with all UK service providers, I'm ashamed to say that without the slightest pang of guilt for my hypocrisy I turned mine on so that I can stay updated and follow the game. This involves several surreptitious glances while in transit.

However, the gremlins strike and the ECB app, which is a lifeline while overseas, begins to play up and only the England score is kept up to date. I failed to see the irony in the delayed score actually slowing down our mini batting collapse and emailed Gordon Hollins, the ECB's Managing Director of County Cricket, and shared my problem. He couldn't do anything about our late middle-order collapse but did manage to get a techie to fix the bug on the app. Almost as it was fixed, the tail steadied itself and we managed to achieve the fourth batting point.

•••

Nick Compton finished unbeaten on 58 as we closed in on a Middlesex first-innings total of 246 on the second day of the County Championship match at Taunton. Philander was the pick of our bowlers, claiming five for 43 from 20 overs.

We closed on 202 for three, with Craig Kieswetter 50 not out, having added 99 for the fourth wicket with Compton against some determined and accurate bowling.

Being only 44 adrift, we will hope to bat on tomorrow and establish a first-innings lead.

•••

The speculation about 'will he, won't he' starts up again with more reports about deals and rows between the WICB and Chris Gayle. Guy Lavender emails me with the latest confirmation of the ambiguity in the player's position. We don't have a legal leg to stand on – it seems the national cricket boards hold all the cards and a board can override a legal contract between club and player if it so desires!

CHRIS GAYLE AND THE WICB HAVE REACHED AN UNDERSTANDING – ESPN staff report

Chris Gayle and the WICB have reached an understanding that paves the way for the former West Indies captain to return to the national team as early as the upcoming tour of England, Caribbean Media Corporation (CMC) has reported. However, the deal's success will be tested by an ongoing lawsuit – to which Gayle is a party – between the West Indies Players' Association (WIPA) and the board. Gayle hasn't played for West Indies since the 2011 World Cup.

The agreement between Gayle and the WICB was brokered by CARICOM (the Caribbean Community) and had the involvement of St Vincent Prime Minister Ralph Gonsalves. According to the report, a meeting will be convened between the two parties to 'tidy up residual matters' after both parties expressed regret for their actions. 'In the light of all of this, the WICB and Mr Gayle agree that the way is now clear for his active return to West Indies cricket, subject to all necessary fitness considerations,' the report quoted from the agreement. 'A date is to be set for this meeting, convenient to all parties, including Mr Gayle who is currently in India,' Baldwin Spencer, the Prime Minister of Antigua and Barbuda, and the chairman of the Prime Ministerial sub-committee of cricket, was quoted as saying.

Gayle has reportedly said he will be unavailable for West Indies duty for the entire duration of the IPL, which ends on May 27. West Indies are due to tour England for a full series between May 5 and June 24 and Gayle's participation in the IPL means he will miss the Test series. However, he was prepared to forego his contract with Somerset and play for West Indies in the one-day and Twenty20 games on that tour. He also said he was available for the World Twenty20 this year and that he was not seeking to 'cherry pick' the series he played.

In a statement dated March 29, the board said it was 'disappointed' over Gayle's unavailability during the IPL but in the 'spirit of compromise and subject to agreement being reached on all outstanding residual matters' it would convey Gayle's unavailability to the selectors.

The board hoped Gayle would drop the lawsuit concerning No-Objection Certificates filed by the WIPA against it, though Gayle, in a statement last week, said he could not 'possibly contemplate withdrawing unilaterally from proceedings', especially when such a move would affect all West Indies players. The board, though, has since written to Prime Minister Gonsalves, arguing that Gayle's participation in the lawsuit was not consistent with the agreement reached with the board.

It also questioned why Gayle could not withdraw from the lawsuit unilaterally. 'As the lawsuit was started by WIPA without him, and his claims are set out separately, we do not understand why Mr Gayle says he cannot contemplate withdrawing from the lawsuit without WIPA.'

'Our efforts must surely be focussed on bringing about the resolution of all outstanding matters between the board and Mr Gayle.'

SATURDAY, 7 APRIL. THE COUNTY GROUND. LVCCI, SOMERSET V MIDDLESEX. DAY 3

After the near collapse on day two the guys have battled really well and by the close of the innings have built a very useful lead of 105. The team have worked hard with our support staff on mental toughness over the close season, and it was encouraging to see Compo referring to how they had consciously pulled up the ladder to survive a period of excellent bowling from determined adversaries. It was clear that everyone with a heart had felt for Compo as he went on 99 – he had richly deserved his ton.

SUNDAY, 8 APRIL. THE COUNTY GROUND. LVCCI, SOMERSET V MIDDLESEX. DAY 4

I'm travelling back home from Crans Montana in the Valais region today, and I know I face a day of anxiety trying to retrieve the latest score as we travel by train and plane. As we leave the hotel, the score is a highly discouraging 93 for one as the Middlesex top order have added to their overnight total without further loss. As we travel by rail along the shores of Lake Geneva the news gradually improves as the Middlesex batting begins to crumble. By the time we reach Geneva airport George Dockrell, aided and abetted by pressure from the quicks, has scythed through the middle and lower order with a magnificent six for 27.

My spirits have lifted considerably. I then start to fret about whether the wicket is breaking up and the other travails that frequently befall a side chasing a modest total in the fourth innings. While we wait in the satellite terminal at Geneva, tea is taken in Taunton and I try to distract myself on my iPad. Only 72 runs required. Easy – just like a blue piste!

We are called to board the flight to Bristol just as Tres and Arul walk out to the middle. SMSs and tweets are now flying about as optimism and dread simultaneously take hold of the Somerset diaspora in equal measure. John Gannon, Director of eCar and one of our major sponsors, is texting me, and just as I board the plane he informs me that Tres is out third ball! Oh Christ! On the plane I am told by a steward, who clearly isn't a cricket fan, to turn my phone off. Just before I do, another SMS from Gannon – Arul's perished and we are 13 for two!

I endure a flight thinking about countless permutations of how we can easily get the 72 required, or, alternatively, how easily we can fall short.

After 90 minutes in what feels like solitary confinement on EJ 6026 we land at Bristol. I immediately ignore all the futile requests from the aircrew and turn on my iPhone. Inexplicably I can't get a damn signal. We are in the concourse before I get one and my phone is blitzed by SMSs and emails with … thank God … the news that we won by six wickets.

The day's hero was 19-year-old Spin King from Dublin, George Dockrell, with his six-wicket spell.

After the most abysmal start to the last two seasons, 22 points from the first game is uplifting stuff.

SIDMOUTH, DEVON

The Somerset Second XI notched up a victory in their opening match of the 2012 season when they beat Devon by six wickets at Sidmouth on Easter Sunday.

Tom Abell (watch out for this young man next season), Dibbs and James Regan (Ronnie) also made solid contributions.

TOWNSVILLE, QUEENSLAND, AUSTRALIA

Meanwhile on the other side of the world Craig Overton (Coverton) was making his mark with the England U19 side.

CRAIG OVERTON BLASTS ENGLAND UNDER 19s TO VICTORY – SCCC Site

Somerset's Craig Overton was very much to the fore as he blasted an unbeaten 68 at slightly better than a run a ball to see England Under 19s maintain their unbeaten record in the quadrangular series out in Australia, involving the hosts, India and New Zealand.

Batting first at Townsville, India were restricted to 268 for nine from their 50 overs, Jamie Overton, who opened the bowling, sending down six overs for 23 runs, while Craig bowled two overs for 11.

In reply England Under 19s were 124 for three when the 17-year-old all-rounder from North Devon came to the wicket and proceeded to score 68 which included eight 4s and a 6 to see his team to victory with just two balls to spare.

England Under 19s top the table and now face India again in the semi-final, also in Townsville, on 13th April.

WEDNESDAY, 11 APRIL. TAUNTON

Meeting with the ECB's Major Match Group's technical inspection team. We have applied for Category B status, which would give us the right to host England ODIs and International T20s. Much work has already gone into our application, on capacity, facilities and various other plans, so this is a very important step for Somerset County Cricket Club. We gave a very comprehensive presentation, Q&A and a tour of the County Ground's much improved facilities.

Following the meeting a flurry of emails and phone calls happen as Guy and myself seek to elicit feedback and prepare to advance our application to the next stages.

I have a humorous exchange with Giles Clarke, who is seemingly on a beach somewhere in Asia and disturbed by a tsunami warning following two substantial earthquakes. He has wisely moved to what he described as a 'grandstand position'. Two hours later, his nerves calmed by a drink or two, the tsunami alert is thankfully cancelled.

GENERAL COMMITTEE MEETING, THE LONG ROOM, TAUNTON

Quite a long meeting as the full complement of assembled members are brought up to date on several areas and various issues are debated. The Management Sub Committee has derogated powers to manage the club, and this meets every month as a normal board might. The General Committee is next due to meet in June, by which time the County Championship will be at the half-way stage and we shall be amidst the excitement, fun and fury of the T20.

One interesting issue was whether Chris Gayle would be likely to appear for us in the T20. Brian Rose responded honestly that although he had signed a contract, and the WICB had issued the necessary NOC, probably the tea lady at the Kensington Oval had as good an idea as to the likelihood of his turning up as anyone directly involved in the matter! Realising we have done everything correctly and to the letter of the various laws and regulations, and that our legal advisers tell us we can now do no more, a sense of humour is the best refuge as we are held in abeyance.

Another issue, which has caused a flutter of enquiries to the CEO, are reports of shootings in the corporate area of Somerset Cricket Club! Unsurprisingly, those who heard only the headline have been sufficiently concerned to enquire with us as to the details. It transpires the shootings have in fact taken place; but, mercifully for us, at Somerset Cricket Club in Barbados! Luckily no one there was seriously injured either.

POLICE REISSUE APPEAL FOR WITNESSES TO GOOD FRIDAY SHOOTING
– Caribdaily online

A 39-year-old man has been arrested and bailed in connection with a gun incident at Somerset Cricket Club in the early hours of Good Friday. Police are now stating two men, aged 18 and 41, were lightly injured during the 2.45am incident.

THURSDAY, 12 APRIL.

It's early morning and I bump into Roy and Lynn Kerslake at traffic lights near the station. They are off to Edgbaston for our second County Championship match against Warwickshire and I'm off to London on business for two days. Guess who has the better deal!

I sit on the platform waiting for the 8.19 a.m. and start belting out emails to Guy Lavender, following up on yesterday's meetings. There are, as ever, many loose ends and issues to consider.

I've made the fatal mistake of checking the score on the ECB app, hoping to see Wawks under the cosh with Philander and Kirby tearing their top order apart. Instead I am almost poleaxed with the news that we are three down for 13! I'm reminded of one of Vic Marks' pearls of wisdom – 'You can't win a first-class game in the first session; but you can lose it.'

There's better news on the commercial front – the Cidermen, as we're known, have signed Thatchers Cider as a sponsor. They are a very welcome and highly relevant addition to our commercial partners, and not only because their products are great favourites with the players and supporters.

•••

The 2012 *Wisden* has been launched this week, and new editor Lawrence Booth has weighed in with some outspoken and pointed observations about India, T20 and the IPL, which is presently underway. This has drawn some immediate retaliatory fire from that well-known wallflower

KP with an article in *The Times of India*. Cricket has been described as a fragile ecosystem, and invariably strong opinions tend to be rebutted with equal violence as social media and 24-hour news disseminate opinions at the speed of light around the globe.

The article below may well have been the one match that started a massive bush fire which raged unchecked for most of the summer.

ENGLAND JEALOUS OF IPL: KEVIN PIETERSEN – *The Times of India*

Jealousy could be the reason for negative attitudes in England towards the cash-rich Indian Premier League (IPL), Delhi Daredevils batting star Kevin Pietersen said.

The Twenty20 IPL was an instant hit when it began in 2008 as a mix of glamour, entertainment and international stars playing short-form cricket, but it has attracted little interest in England.

'It (the IPL) is very much struggling to find acceptance back home,' the South Africa-born England batsman, who is playing for Delhi Daredevils in the ongoing tournament, was quoted as saying on Thursday.

'It saddens me because I have had an amazing time at the IPL, and it's down to a lot of jealousy I think which is sad. It saddens me all the negative publicity the IPL gets in the (British) media, I don't know why.'

His comments came as the *Wisden Cricketers' Almanack*, in its latest issue, blamed the influence of T20 games for India's recent dismal run in Test cricket which saw them lose eight successive matches in England and Australia.

'The disintegration of India's feted batting line-up has coincided with the rise of a Twenty20-based nationalism, the growth of private marketeers and high-level conflicts of interest,' wrote *Wisden* editor Lawrence Booth.

'It is a perfect storm. And the global game sits unsteadily in the eye. India, your sport needs you.'

Pietersen, the only big England star taking part in this year's IPL, said experience gained in the tournament will be useful when England tour India for a Test and one-day series later this year.

'It will benefit the team (England), especially because we will be touring India later in the year,' he said.

'Playing another month in the subcontinent honing my skills, training with the spinners and practising, I consider myself so very fortunate.'

England fast bowler Stuart Broad was forced to miss this year's IPL due to injury, while pace spearhead James Anderson and leading spinner Graeme Swann went unsold at the auction in February.

England failed to cope with spin on their recent Asia tour when they lost four of their five Tests, three against Pakistan in the United Arab Emirates and one in Sri Lanka.

EDGBASTON. LVCCI, WARWICKSHIRE V SOMERSET. DAY I

Any schadenfreude I felt in the wake of our batting display against Middlesex was dispelled quickly today. We collapsed to 95 for eight after winning the toss. Philander came to a rescue of sorts with a stubborn 38 and, with Dockers, put on 47 for the ninth wicket. We limped to 147.

Dibbs nicked two out by the close but Varun Chopra, a double centurion against us last season, was ominously still there at the close. We need wickets early tomorrow to stay in the game.

FRIDAY, 13 APRIL. EDGBASTON. LVCCI, SOMERSET V WARWICKSHIRE. DAY 2

This was what Rosey calls a good day's attritional cricket with us managing to contain Wawks to a lead of under 100 and then scrapping hard to claw our way back into the contest. The stand-out contribution for me was another very adhesive innings by Compo, who stayed in the middle and helped us to achieve a modest lead of 31 by stumps. We have six wickets remaining to build a lead tomorrow – hopefully one large enough to give the bowlers a chance of gaining victory on day four.

Talking to Roy Kerslake, it sounds as if a key unknown factor is going to be the weather, which has been changing by the hour apparently.

•••

It has become common currency to suggest that media coverage of county cricket is declining. I disagree with this. The space given over in traditional newsprint might be less than it once was, but the online coverage is substantial and varied. In addition to the online version of the newspapers (*The Times* coverage of cricket in their app is excellent), social media and blogs provide a rich and varied diet of analysis and comment. A good example of a new and distinctive source is the Middle Stump site. It has gained awareness and traction with a point of difference as an 'edgier' social media site following the game. They very politely approached me for an interview by email which I was happy to do for them.

ONLINE INTERVIEW WITH THE MIDDLE STUMP

Q. It must be a huge privilege doing a Q and A with The Middle Stump. Are you enjoying our blog so far?

A. It's a pleasure. And so is your blog.

Q. Things seem to be going down well in the West Country? Who likes their cider the best out of the Somerset players? And is Thatchers still the best stuff? Comes from Sandford, near where I have relatives.

A. We are known as the Cidermen of course. The players are very fond of Thatchers and when in India for the CL T20 we suffered withdrawal symptoms and requested supplies to be shipped out. I've little doubt this wonderful cider and its proven beneficial effects (an apple a day ...) lay behind our phenomenal run to the semi-final!

Q. How was the Champions League T20 trophy last year? Semis, wasn't it?

A. It was a terrific experience and reminded us all of how unpredictable cricket can be. We arrived knackered from a Lord's final, minus our captain, without a regular wicketkeeper, and proceeded to dispatch all comers until we met the eventual winners Mumbai Indians in the semi-final – and we would have won that if Buttler hadn't poleaxed Kieswetter with a vicious on drive! The Indians love their cricket; but received our very loud renditions of the Blackbird song after each victory with a mixture of bemusement and terror.

Q. Do you think T20 will take over from the four-day game?

A. No I don't believe that any more than I believe rock music will kill off classical music. There's room for both and we should celebrate the fact we've discovered a new format which so many fans enjoy.

Q. What is your view on players playing it ahead of playing for their country such as certain West Indians at present?

A. I think that's entirely a matter for the individual players. One volunteer is better than 10 pressed men!

Q. Is it ruining the domestic game?

A. T20 is now widely accredited as having improved key cricketing skills, fielding and slow bouncers being just two examples. Also teams will now set about chasing 200 or more in the last session to win a CC match. Unheard of before T20.

Q. Somerset showed a profit of £408k last year. What is the secret to your success?

A. Obviously it's a secret and I can't tell you! We are a members club and we own our ground so we have no shareholders to pay nor ground rent to find. Also, with our new catering, events and retail assets we have built a substantial income outside of cricket. The County Ground used to be busy for 40 days a year – now it's busy for 340 days.

Q. Do you miss the halcyon days of Somerset in the 70s and 80s when Garner, Richards and Botham ruled the roost?

A. Of course – who wouldn't. But we are in another golden period and have the most terrifically talented young squad who will help keep us at the top of the game in England ... and win trophies eventually.

Q. How long have you got Vernon Philander?

A. He leaves us in the second half of May.

Q. And what is your view of people saying that offering him an opportunity to get used to English conditions will hurt the England side later in the year?

A. I am a cricket fan first and foremost, and cricketers of the calibre of Vernon Philander would grace any cricket pitch and richly entertain all supporters lucky enough to see him play. Players of his calibre should be welcome anywhere and anytime. It's true he will learn about bowling in English conditions but also England batters will get to know more about him. Lastly, Team England will want to play and beat the best team SA can muster – not one that has been unfairly deprived of the best possible preparation.

Q. At the Middle Stump, we have always been told by the ladies that it is best to come second. Are you tired of Somerset coming second all the time, and will that change this year?

A. I'd suggest it's better to come second than to miss out on the experience completely. I think everyone will be delighted should we come first now and again.

Q. When are you going to get the Giles Clarke job? Is the Somerset chairman role the predecessor for the ECB role? A bit like a Yorkshire fast bowler in the thirties!

A. It is a great privilege to chair a famous club like Somerset and my priority is to continue to lead the club towards better things. Since 2004 we have completed three of the four phases of the redevelopment of the County Ground – we now need to complete the final phase. We are also been working towards gaining Category B status for the County Ground which if granted will bring ODI's and International T20s to the West Country. There can be no greater prize than that! Once we've achieved that, and we will, it would be for others to decide whether I can serve the game at a higher level.

Q. Who are your best three young cricketers in the country?

A. Craig Kieswetter, Jos Buttler and Marcus Trescothick.

Q. Best bar at a cricket ground in the country?

A. The Taunton Long Room.

Q. Favourite ground other than Taunton?

A. West Bagborough CC.

Q. What are your plans for the next year?

A. To win silverware, achieve Category B, make further progress towards the final phase of development of the County Ground, and to lead the Somerset Chairman's XI to victory over John Gannon's eCar side.

SATURDAY, 14 APRIL. EDGBASTON. LVCCI, WARWICKSHIRE V SOMERSET. DAY 3

I wake and recall that today is the centenary of the *Titanic*'s sinking – I'm following the tweets from #realtimetitanic. It occurs that one sinking may follow another and we may be due a batting collapse at Edgbaston after closing on 127 for four, having deployed new night-watchman Dockrell.

There's only one thing for it. Linda and my daughters are off to Bath, so I decide to head to Edgbaston to witness events first hand.

Courtesy of Cross Country trains and a cricket-mad British Asian taxi driver I make Edgbaston just past 11 a.m. – in time in fact to see young Dockers perish before I've even reached the Wawks Committee Room. The omens aren't good. The sky also looks like a grey duvet.

Before lunch I sat with Rosey and caught up with the latest twists and turns. We've had an unintelligible one-liner from the WICB adding nothing to man's knowledge of whether we might see Chris Gayle for the T20. Plan B is in train, and one du Plessis is an attractive potential replacement.

Vernon won't be playing against Notts because of wear and tear considerations, but in return Gary Kirsten has agreed that his stay can be extended to allow an extra match – against Middlesex at Lord's. There is more bad news that young Dockrell will be going to the U19 World Cup with Ireland after all, so will leave us mid August. The hunt for a high-class spinner is thus already underway, with some gentlemen from the subcontinent in the frame.

I join the Warwickshire Committee in their new and exalted surroundings – it's amazing what £35m of capital expenditure can do for a cricket ground! I don't think it would be irreverent of me to suggest that our hosts were probably looking forward to the match finishing sometime today; but as so often cricket proves a thoroughly unreliable mistress and our middle order find form and bat quite brilliantly to sail well beyond expectations and end up posting a more than respectable total of 354 – a lead of almost 260. Compo and Buttler were imperious, with the former effortlessly achieving yet another 100 (now at almost 500 first-class runs for the season) while Jos frustratingly succumbed in the nineties. Better still, as our tail wobbled at one stage, two of the three wicket-taking deliveries shot through at little above shin height! Roy Kerslake and I nodded to each other in the knowledge that our seamers would have very happily taken note of the wicket's misbehaviour. With the left-handed Dockrell eyeing the rough in equal anticipation, the tables might be turning before our very eyes!

Or so we thought. By the close, under two hours later, Warwickshire's top order had progressed almost without incident half-way to our supposedly stretching total for the loss of just the openers. Sir Alex Ferguson once said, 'Bloody football eh!' He should try bloody cricket.

With our account ending on 354, Warks need a chunky 254 for victory. At the close they have reached 123 for two. Tomorrow promises to be interesting, to put it mildly.

SUNDAY, 15 APRIL. EDGBASTON. LVCCI, WARWICKSHIRE V SOMERSET. DAY 4

I've been dispatched to collect our youngest daughter from the depths of rural Somerset. She has been on what 15-year-olds call a sleepover party. There's some kind of mix-up on the arrangements as the RVP is empty, but still I have my iPhone and there's just about enough signal for me to enjoy the hopefully imminent Wawks batting collapse! Here we are after half an hour's play and the score seems stuck on 132 for two. Can it be the weak signal, or have we pinned them down with spin out of the rough, fast accurate seam bowling, or perhaps both. Frustrated, I switch from the ECB app to the Sky Sports one. It makes no difference! I decide to write a little more for this book in the hope this will take my mind off it and somehow might help a wicket or three to fall.

I get an update – the score was stuck in cyberspace. Wawks have moved on to 145 for two now and with the sun out here I'm thinking perhaps the wicket may have flattened out at Edgbaston.

Still, we've a world-class seamer leading our attack. Wickets must start to fall. Get one, get two as they say.

Wicket! 145 for three now. Big Vernon has his man. Maddy gone. We could do with nipping out Porterfield, who has played rather well so far.

On the drive home naturally I don't peek at the score! Had I have done so, my mood would have darkened as they have climbed towards 200 for the loss of only one wicket this morning.

I make a phone call to a mate who is off to see Chelsea v Spurs at Wembley this afternoon, and we discuss arrangements for our flight to Geneva tomorrow morning. Having finished the chat with him and attended to a WhatsApp from my son, I check the ECB app. Christ – 'golden arm' is doing the business. Wawks have lost three wickets to Tregs for very few. Game on.

The game continued to see-saw until eventually, after a collapse from 190 for three to 211 for eight, the Wawks tailenders resist quite brilliantly to see them over the line with two wickets on hand. A brilliant finish to four days of tough, attritional cricket. It suggests to me that the CC1 is going to be a very hard-fought affair once again this season.

Whoever said county cricket was boring?

MONDAY, 16 APRIL. BRIANÇON

I described Dick Edmonds, Somerset member, Jos Buttler's schoolmaster and a friend from university in an earlier chapter. Today, with two other pals from the same university group, we are travelling to Briançon in France to visit another mate who hasn't seen Dick since his diagnosis.

Dick has continued to face his ordeal with oesophageal cancer with great courage and stoicism and all those who know him are so moved and impressed by his fortitude. We began, as only men on tour can, with a couple of drinks at Bristol airport for breakfast!

At least there's no cricket to concern ourselves with today, but we've already had an extensive debrief on the Wawks match en route to the airport earlier.

TUESDAY, 17 APRIL. HOVE

Our 'Twos' are a very young side – one of the youngest in recent years. They lose out to Sussex at Hove in a limited-overs game. The fixture list for the Second XI is much improved on what it was seven or eight years ago. The ECB arrange both league cricket and a one-day Trophy through the season.

WEDNESDAY, 18 APRIL.

Adam Dibble has been struck with the fast bowler's curse, the intercostal muscle injury. This is particularly frustrating for 'Dibbs' as he played very well at Edgbaston last week with ball *and* bat. He will be in the good hands of Brewsey and Dazz, our dynamic duo who manage the team's physio, injury prevention and strength and conditioning work, which has been instrumental in our extraordinarily low attrition rate due to injury. More on them later. For now, though, with Gemaal also injured, and Alfonso Thomas in the IPL our fast bowling attack is three players light!

THURSDAY, 19 APRIL. VALMOREL, SAVOIE, FRANCE

Today is the fifth anniversary of Somerset's highest ever innings score in first-class cricket, made appropriately enough at the County Ground. We amassed 850 for seven declared in reply to our guests' rather paltry 600 for four declared.

I awake to rain outside, which prompts me to check the latest UK weather. I wish I hadn't! Hard on the heels of drought warnings and hosepipe bans, the Met Office begin issuing severe weather warnings of storms and hail-stones the size of golf balls!

I thought VP was being rested for this match, but the team news seems to include him alongside Lewis Gregory. With three fast bowlers missing at present we may have had no alternative!

TRENT BRIDGE. LVCCI, NOTTINGHAMSHIRE V SOMERSET. DAY I

Trent Bridge is renowned as a result wicket, and over the years Notts have developed several formidable fast bowlers. Perhaps the most formidable being the England pairing of Harold Larwood and Bill Voce, both of mining stock. G. Hunt, appearing for Somerset in 1930, was so troubled by Voce's vicious in-swingers he played left-handed to him and right-handed to the rest of the attack.

We won the toss and inserted Notts on a green top and were rewarded by them subsiding to 93 for six. We were on and off in showers all day long apparently, but in the periods of play Tregs is coming to the fore, as he tends to do when our backs are to the wall, taking three for 24.

Brian Rose makes a good point in his article on the club's site re the Category A ground's drainage systems. The sand-based system can disperse up to 200mm of rain an hour – a monsoon. Whilst this is to be welcomed, it rather works against the argument that the present County Championship is a paragon of fairness. Grounds with conventional drainage like Taunton will lose many more days with rain-soaked outfields over the season. The solution of course is for the ECB to fund the upgrade of all the remaining first-class grounds to the same standard. The issue is made more acute when the number of T20 fixtures has been reduced from eight to just five home matches. Rained-off T20 fixtures cost a county an inordinate amount of money – probably as much lost revenue as two entire CC matches!

FRIDAY, 20 APRIL. TRENT BRIDGE. LVCCI, NOTTINGHAMSHIRE V SOMERSET. DAY 2

The weather remains highly unpredictable. Mike Atherton has written a thought-provoking piece in *The Times*, querying the quality of cricket achievable when playing so early in the spring. As if to prove his point, wickets were falling like ninepins in both divisions of the County Championship yesterday. We are walking part of the South West Coast Path over the next few days, and with temperatures forecasted to be in low single figures I'm not sure who I feel sorrier for, me or the cricketers.

I caught up with Guy Lavender after close of play, and the news that Tres had left the field with what looked like a serious foot injury took the shine off things at Trent Bridge, where Notts had made 162 (thanks to a typically belligerent innings of 104 from Chris Read) and we posted 78 for one in response in a day truncated by more rain. The other item of note was Tregs's first Michelle (five for).

Going into day three we are just 84 runs behind with nine wickets in hand, although there has to be considerable doubt about Tres taking any further part in the match.

Guy Lavender had more news from off the pitch – the electrical sub-station adjacent to the Caddy Shack (Andy Caddick Pavilion) caught fire and has plunged half of Taunton town centre into darkness! The CEO now isn't sure which is the trickier issue: the skipper's scan, or dealing with the bride's mother, as we've a wedding in the Colin Atkinson Pavilion tomorrow!

SATURDAY, 21 APRIL. TRENT BRIDGE. LVCCI, NOTTINGHAMSHIRE V SOMERSET. DAY 3

Today our trek around the South West Coast Path gets under way and I'm somewhat anxious, as last year on a different part of the same coastal walk things went badly – on the pitch, that is. It was our opening game of the season at Taunton and we were playing Warwickshire. Naturally there had been a discussion at home about where my loyalties lay. On the one hand I could have supported my dear wife in her quest to walk the entirety of the coast path (all 630 miles of it from Minehead to Poole Harbour!) in a three-year period, or on the other I could indulge my passion for Somerset cricket by spending four days 'on my arse' at the County Ground.

Anyway, the natural order of things prevailed and we set off on the walk on the Friday and I'd sort of made a promise to myself that I wouldn't check the score during the day, as there was a 50 per cent chance despair would be the result and there was much to enjoy on the coast with our friends.

Unbeknown to me as we set off along the beautiful North Devon coast the gods had conspired to puncture our pre-season confidence by inflicting on Somerset the sixth largest Championship defeat in history. Warwickshire lost the toss and we put them in on a 'bottle green' surface. They batted entirely untroubled throughout the first day, with Varun Chopra making a career-best 174, and proceeded to amass a total well beyond 600 before deciding enough was enough and letting us enjoy the wicket. Clearly it held no demons, as even one of the world's best spinners Ajantha Mendis had gone for the worst figures in his five-year career (four for 183 in just 24.3 overs).

When eventually the Somerset innings got under way, I was savouring the spectacular views of seals, remote coves of custard-coloured sand and an azure Atlantic, totally unaware that absolute carnage was under way in Taunton. I remember stopping to tie a bootlace at a style and, as Linda and our pals were a little ahead, and I had a signal on my iPhone, I thought I'd sneak a quick look at the score. I think I must have emitted an audible groan as our party asked if I was OK. What greeted me was something in the region of 38 for seven. In an instant my walk along one of the planet's most stunning coastlines, festooned with magnificent natural sights and sounds, had been transformed into a weary trudge along a windswept muddy path by the sea.

Warwickshire dismissed us sometime during the third day for the princely total of 210, some 432 runs in arrears and a mere 282 runs shy of avoiding the follow-on. We were duly invited to bat again, and this time we *really* made a hash of it, only detaining fans for long enough to watch another 50 runs to be amassed for the loss of all ten wickets. By this time my walk had descended into sheer hell, the only positive being that the other two husbands on the expedition were Scottish and so knew about as much about cricket as I knew about tossing the caber. 'How's it going at the cricket, Nasher?' Joe or Bruce would ask out of politeness now and again. 'Actually it's finished early,' I may have muttered. 'Bad weather, eh?' asked Joe. 'Yup, but not bad enough,' I said.

Somerset were crushed by an innings and 382 runs. In a chat I had shortly after the game with Brian Rose and Vic Marks we agreed the only positive we could take from the experience was that we had convincingly cast off the yoke of being firm pre-season favourites for the County Championship title!

Cricket devotees everywhere will empathise with the game's unique ability to expunge all hope from a seemingly invincible position and then quite para-doxically raise one's spirits when everything has seemed utterly hopeless.

Perhaps this is why the game has sometimes been described as a metaphor for life.

•••

Back to the present, and on day three Compto, Arul and Hildy all made centuries. It meant that, on a pitch where only one Nottinghamshire batsman could score more than ten, their bowlers were unable to claim even a single bowling point. We lost just two wickets in gaining all five batting points and declared with a lead of 283. It also meant that with more than a week to go to the start of May, Compo has already accumulated 685 first-class runs at an average of 137 and is easily the leading run-scorer in first-class cricket this season, with Hildreth – who now has 411 – the second highest.

Finally this is the birthday of Somerset's first-ever captain, Stephen Cox Newton. He spent nine seasons playing for the county, and captained the side for the last five of them, including 1890, the year when we lost our first-class status.

SUNDAY, 22 APRIL. TRENT BRIDGE. LVCCI, NOTTINGHAMSHIRE V SOMERSET. DAY 4

Yesterday was an extraordinary day at Trent Bridge. We were the first side this season to achieve eight bonus points, and Compo and Hildy now lead the CC batting aggregates. A terrific way to compensate for the loss of our beloved skipper.

I spoke with Guy Lavender and Roy Kerslake and the news on Tres isn't good. He may be out for two months, but we shall be keeping our counsel until we have a formal prognosis on Monday. We are fortunate to have an experienced captain in Hildy who seems to bat well under the additional pressure.

On the other hand there is good news from England – both Overton twins are to be made available to us for a fortnight. Also Gemaal is back sprinting, so badly needed reinforcements for our depleted fast bowling department are in sight.

The good news ended here today. The weather came to the rescue of Notts, but not before Kirbs broke down with a 'hammy', which rarely means anything other than a lengthy spell on the sidelines. Notts made their way to 169 for four during an on-and-off day for showers, with Tregs again having to carry the attack, which he did with some style.

MONDAY, 23 APRIL.

The very sad news reaches me that Dan Hodges has died. He has been a loyal and caring devotee of our club and has touched the lives of many cricketers across our region. He was greatly respected and loved by many players. We owe him a great deal and we shall celebrate and properly acknowledge his huge contribution to Somerset County Cricket Club. An obituary to Dan appeared on our site today.

SOMERSET MOURNING THE LOSS OF DAN HODGES – SCCC site

The Somerset cricketing community is mourning the loss of Dan Hodges who has sadly passed away at the age of 75.

Over the past three decades Dan carried out many coaching roles in Somerset including County Under 11 Coach, District Coach, Organiser of Kwik Cricket and several Youth Cup Competitions, Chairman of Taunton Youth League, and coaching the Somerset Disability XI.

Dan Hodges' influence has touched the playing career of literally thousands of youth players, several of whom have progressed through to the professional ranks, not least for his gently delivered words of wisdom.

Over the years Dan picked up a number of national and regional coaching awards including being voted South West Coach of the Year in 1994 as well as proudly receiving a Sky Outstanding Coaching Achievement Award from local legend Sir Ian Botham in 2007.

Andy Curtis the Chairman of the Somerset Cricket Board said: 'We have lost not only a legendary contributor to Somerset recreational cricket, but a personal friend of the many volunteers who worked alongside him.

'Despite his failing health in the past two or three years, Dan continued to play a leading role in running Taunton Youth League activities, as well as coaching and leading the highly successful County Disability team to two national titles. His competitive spirit was as strong as ever.'

The SCB Chairman added: 'He was a true ambassador for the game of cricket – not only because of his enthusiasm and technical knowledge, but also the manner in which he expected the youngsters to play the game. He will be greatly missed by his colleagues at the Cricket Board, and more importantly by the many young players that he nurtured over the years.'

•••

As I was given to understand over the weekend, the news on Tres is that he will be out for around six weeks. It's a big blow, but setbacks like this are part of the game and it is an opportunity for others to step up to the mark as they did in the Champions League last year.

•••

Having returned from another punishing walk on the South West Coast Path I email Compo and SMS Tregs with personal messages congratulating them on their recent achievements. I believe in a club like ours it matters that the Chairman takes the trouble to acknowledge significant achievements and in other circumstances to lend a sympathetic ear or a helping hand when a colleague needs it. I think a club's culture is founded on the small things that people fortunate enough to be in senior positions actually find time to do.

TUESDAY, 24 APRIL.

Guy Lavender and I spoke last night following a phone message left by Nick Hoult of the *Daily Telegraph*. Nick was asking whether, since Gloucestershire had handed back the ODI against New Zealand, Somerset would be bidding for it. We agreed it would be best if Guy called him back, as I'm still in deep Cornwall with erratic signal strength!

SOMERSET HOPING THAT TAUNTON GETS ITS DAY IN THE SUN AS RIVALS GLOUCESTERSHIRE LOSE SPOT ON INTERNATIONAL ROTA –
Nick Hoult, *Daily Telegraph*

Bristol has lost the rights to host a one-day match between England and New Zealand next summer, which could pave the way for Taunton to join the international ground circuit. Somerset are considering bidding for the match which the England and Wales Cricket Board put back out to tender yesterday.

The ECB's Major Match Group is halfway through assessing an application from Somerset for their Taunton headquarters to be promoted from a county ground to one capable of hosting one-day internationals.

Gloucestershire were granted next year's 50-over match against New Zealand on condition they obtained planning permission for a £10 million overhaul of facilities at their Nevil Road ground. That application was rejected by Bristol city councillors earlier this year, forcing the ECB to look for an alternative venue. They emailed the counties yesterday, inviting bids for the match.

'We are midway though the technical assessment process by the Major Match Group on behalf of the ECB and that process will continue for a couple of months,' said Guy Lavender, the Somerset chief executive. 'It depends on the outcome of that but in principle we would love to bid.'

'Our stated ambition and aim is to bring international cricket to Taunton. There is an appetite in this area for international cricket.'

Somerset are an ambitious county whose recent success on the field is reflected off it with record profits last year of £408,000. Their Taunton ground has hosted matches during World Cups but needs to increase capacity from its current level of 8,000 and improve media facilities to meet the ECB's requirements.

Bristol is due to host one-day internationals against India in 2014 and Sri Lanka in 2016, but those matches are also conditional on improving the ground.

Gloucestershire have resubmitted their planning application, which will be heard next month. The decision of the council will be crucial to the club's immediate future.

'We are disappointed but it is not something we were surprised about,' said Tom Richardson, Gloucestershire's chief executive. 'We have had to resubmit our planning application. We are behind schedule and would not be ready in time to host the match.'

•••

I knew this was coming, but it is disappointing to receive the final confirmation that George Dockrell will play for Ireland in the U19 World Cup later this summer. He will be sorely missed through the middle and late part of the season as a result. Players are falling like flies at the moment. This particular departure will have a bearing on Rosey's choice of an overseas player for the second half of the season: spinners are match winners as the season progresses and conditions favour them.

WEDNESDAY, 25 APRIL.

The volume and pitch of comments about how weather conditions are unduly interfering with the quality of cricket is distinctly rising. Mark Ramprakash has weighed in from the player's perspective, while Lawrence Booth has highlighted some extraordinary statistics based on analysis of the first three games. His perceptive article appears below. This will provide the ECB with yet more quandaries as decisions on the season's structure remain filed in the 'too difficult basket' at HQ.

TOP SPIN NEWSLETTER – Lawrence Booth, *Guardian*

T.S. Eliot is never more regularly quoted in county cricket circles than he is in April, his now almost clichéd 'cruellest month'. Yet what other literary reference does a better job of encapsulating the current state of mind of our domestic batsmen?

After three rounds of championship matches, a dizzying set of possibilities presents itself: either county batsmen aren't very good; or the bowlers are outstanding; or the art of building an innings is vanishing fast; or conditions are unplayable; or batsmen, wrongly assuming conditions to be unplayable, are trying to make hay while the sun doesn't shine.

You may be able to add to the list.

But, wow, the numbers! In 22 so-called four-day matches thus far, there have been 15 all-out totals of 150 or fewer (not including Glamorgan's brave but doomed declaration on 103 for nine against Hampshire), and a further 15 scores of under 200.

That's right: in a mere three rounds of games, 30 innings have closed before a single bonus point has even been plucked from the lowest-hanging of county cricket's branches.

Only a few have breathed rarefied air: Kent made 537 for nine against Yorkshire; Nottinghamshire compiled 403 in the second innings against Worcestershire; and Somerset – for whom Nick Compton (685 first-class runs at 137) and James Hildreth (411 at 102) are this month's black swans – declared on 445 for two against Nottinghamshire.

There have been ten scores above 300 but below 400, and a decent handful of totals between 200 and 300.

But, overall, the chances are you'll be struggling for those first-innings bonus points – especially if you're Nottinghamshire (118, 161 and 162 in their three first innings, despite that second-innings 403), or Worcestershire (130 and 119), or Glamorgan (124, 95 and 103 for nine declared). Northamptonshire haven't got past 134 in three attempts out of four.

Now, unless you believe that what we are witnessing is the thin end of a wedge marked 'Twenty20' – the inevitable consequence of a world in which speed is of the essence – then it's probably fair to say that conditions, both real and imagined, are playing their part.

In other words: yes, the ball is swinging more than usual under damp skies and, yes, it's doing a bit more off the seam – but it isn't swinging and seaming so much that batsmen need to forgo the fundamentals and aim in a blind panic across the line.

Those who witnessed, for example, Surrey's second-innings collapse at Lord's, where they were skittled for 137 in pursuit of 141 to beat Middlesex, attest to the latter.

And yet it would be counterintuitive to ascribe everything to scrambled minds. Good bowlers, after all, are doing what good bowlers do, and taking wickets in helpful conditions: Graham Onions has 16 at 10 for Durham; Steven Finn seven at 14 for Middlesex; Andre Adams 13 at 17 for Nottinghamshire; and Alan Richardson 17 at 14 for Worcestershire.

The question that matters more is whether this is good for the game. And here the critics might point to other analyses: Darren Maddy five wickets at 11; Steve Magoffin nine at six; Rikki Clarke five at 18. Old members of the seam-bowling union might legitimately argue that the brand is being cheapened.

Isn't it the case, though, that cricket throughout the whole of April is now a fact of life? Even with a shorter Twenty20 tournament this year, the need to cram everything in before the Champions League in September means ambitious batsmen can set themselves a new target: 500 runs before the end of April.

Anyway, batsmen generally get their moment in the sun during the warmer summer months. Not for nothing was Neville Cardus able to rejoice in the myth that the scoreboard at Trent Bridge always read 360 for two. (One hundred and sixty for nine doesn't have quite the same ring ...)

Perhaps if we looked at the county season as an elongated four-day match, these discrepancies would be easier to accept: help for the seamers early on (April), flattening out on the first evening and second morning (May and June), at its best for batting on the second afternoon until tea on day three (July), some help for the spinners (August), and perhaps a bit of uneven bounce for the quicks (September).

It's one reason why county batsmen might be better off putting T.S. Eliot out of their minds, and turning instead to Hal Borland. 'April,' he wrote, 'is a promise that May is bound to keep.' We shall see ...

•••

In the meantime, the Seconds are also losing games to the weather. Their fixture against Middlesex is badly disrupted at Taunton Vale Cricket Club today.

•••

The announcement today of Greg Kennis' appointment as Head Coach of the Somerset Cricket Board is a significant one and has been long in the making. The club and SCB have jointly run an extensive process to find the best candidate and we were unanimous in our final choice. You can't buy a cricket squad as Manchester City have done, as ECB rules and regulations, together with economic reality, make this impossible – you have to patiently build a professional squad. This takes countless hours on the cricket pitches and gymnasiums of the West Country. Greg will now play a leading role in shaping the age-group teams and subsequently the Somerset first team squad of the future.

Somerset Cricket Board will announce the boys' 2012 county squads on the club website on 1 May.

Greg and new appointee Andy Fairbairn are now exploring the possibility of a similar position being introduced within women's and girls' cricket in the not too distant future.

•••

I'm travelling back to Somerset from Cornwall and the weather forecast looks grim for the CC1 match against reigning champions Lancashire. I'm greeted by yet more injury news: Steve Kirby has torn a quad and will be out of action for four weeks! Thankfully the Overton twins have been released from England U19 duty and are available for squad selection.

•••_

I'm struck, given that there's been no first-team cricket since Sunday, just how much is still going on at the County Ground! The last, but by no means least, item today is the announcement that Guy Wolfenden (Wolfy) is moving on to Edgbaston as their Head of Commercial next month. As the club's article notes, he's been a great contributor to Somerset's develop-ment for a long while. We will miss him but he goes with our gold-plated endorsement to Warwickshire and our best wishes for his future. I think it's the mark of a quality organisation or company when its people can grow, improve and then move on to develop their careers. We will be recruiting on the front foot, as this is an exciting role for the right individual. Guy Lavender and I are of the same opinion – every vacancy we have is an opportunity to recruit an outstanding person, and good people are the difference between great organisations and average ones.

THURSDAY, 26 APRIL. THE COUNTY GROUND. LVCCI, SOMERSET V LANCASHIRE. DAY I

I was away at a board meeting of The History Press today and perhaps it was just as well! As I've always said to my children, 'Some days you're the puppy and some days you're the lamppost.' Today, our pace bowling drastically weakened by injury, Somerset were the lamppost. 'Tomorrow is a new day,' as a wise man once said. Below is George Dobell's account of the first day.

After the board meeting I'm introduced to Michelle Tilling, who is to be the commissioning editor of this book and I'm immediately impressed by the fact she's a fellow cricket fan and was in fact a scorer for nine years. Then, remembering we are in Stroud, I ask the inevitable question of her: 'Are you a Gloucestershire member?' and nervously anticipate her reply. 'No', she says, 'Essex. It's a Graham Gooch thing!' We chatted about the book, my thinking, rough timings and various other things. Michelle is going to be a delight to work with, I decided; the signs were good when I checked the score from the County Ground (200-odd for two), and seeing my countenance at this she empathised as only a genuine cricket fan could.

ROSE LOOKS TO LOAN MARKET TO BOOST EXPOSED SOMERSET

ESPN – George Dobell at Taunton

Starting this game bottom of the table and having failed to pass 250 in any innings, Lancashire are already on the brink of maximum batting bonus points after taking a heavy toll on an attack as green as the emerald outfield. Steven Croft, with the fourth first-class century of his career and the first by any Lancashire batsman this season, added 208 for the fourth wicket with Ashwell Prince in just 49 overs. The pitch is unusually true for this time of year, but to concede over four an over in April says as much about the bowling as it does the batting.

This was an oddly uncompetitive day's cricket. Much of the time it resembled a fixture between a county and a university side as an injury-depleted Somerset team was exposed for its inexperience. As a result, Somerset will send for reinforcements in the coming days.

'We will look into the loan market very quickly at the end of this game,' Brian Rose, Somerset's director of cricket told ESPN Cricinfo. 'I only have one more bowler in reserve - James Overton - so we have already started to look at some names that aren't playing. There don't seem to be many options, but it is an area we are going to explore.'

Perhaps, had James Hildreth at slip, held on to a low chance offered by Prince off Peter Trego when the batsman had just seven, things might have been different. As it was, though, Prince and in particular Croft were content to put away the poor ball on a decent pitch offering little margin for error. They rarely had to wait for long. Somerset struggled with their line and length throughout, with a tendency to pitch too short punished in such easy-paced conditions.

'Our back-up bowlers let us down a bit,' Hildreth, Somerset's stand-in captain, admitted afterwards. 'We had simple game plans but we didn't execute them properly. It's a bit disappointing, but we have to remember that some of these bowlers are young.'

If it is the hope that hurts, then Somerset supporters can take some comfort from the day's play. While the final weeks of recent seasons have been characterised by agony as the team threaten to win their maiden championship title only to fall away at the last, this year there will be no such pain. It is highly unlikely that Somerset will win the championship this year.

They do not have the depth in their bowling attack to mount a sustainable challenge. With Alfonso Thomas absent on IPL duty and Steve Kirby, Geemal Hussain and Adam Dibble injured, they have been obliged to rely too heavily on a band of talented but inexperienced bowlers. Craig Overton is barely 18, George Dockrell and Lewis Gregory are both teenagers and Craig Meschede is, aged 20, the oldest of the four. They have played just

27 first-class games between them. Indeed, Glen Chapple, the Lancashire captain, has played more first-class cricket than all six members of the Somerset attack combined. While Somerset could claim, with some justification, they have suffered some ill-fortune, they might also reflect on the wisdom of allowing Charl Willoughby to depart for Essex. Their squad is too thin.

It would be unreasonable to expect too much of their callow recruits. Overton, tall but red raw, has just a hint of Stuart Broad about him and may well develop into a fine cricketer. He also claimed his maiden first-class wicket when Prince punched one to mid-wicket. Gregory bowled horribly most of the time, but also ended Karl Brown's delightfully fluent innings with a good, full ball and has, just occasionally, a turn of pace that suggests there is plenty of untapped talent lurking within. Neither they nor Meschede are yet ready for this level, but all are worth perseverance. Somerset have simply asked a bit much of them a bit soon.

More disappointing was the performance of Vernon Philander. The South African removed Paul Horton early, leaving a straight one, but generally failed to utilise the new ball by making the batsmen play in that crucial first hour and conceded four an over throughout the day. Six no-balls underlined his lack of rhythm. Somerset, it should be noted, would have bowled had they won they toss.

This is a decent pitch, though. Croft, who scored the winning runs here when Lancashire clinched the championship, rated it the best he has seen this season. 'There's nowhere better to bat,' he said. 'Hopefully this will kick start our season.'

The way in which one delivery from left-arm spinner George Dockrell took off and leapt over the shoulder of batsman and keeper for four byes suggests that Simon Kerrigan may yet find a little more joy in the surface.

Somerset also expect to hear confirmation of Chris Gayle's availability within the next couple of days. The West Indian, signed for this season's FL T20 is believed to be on the brink of resuming national team duties and may well, as a consequence, become unavailable for Somerset as a result.

PHONE CALL WITH IAN LOVETT, CHAIRMAN OF MIDDLESEX CCC

While waiting to collect my youngest daughter from college I'm listening to the BBC Radio 5 Sports Extra live commentary of the match when my opposite number from Middlesex rings. I like Ian, he's a shrewd fellow, excellent company and has a keen sense of humour which always brightens any chat with him. I share with him the fact that our scoreboard has packed up much to the consternation of the crowd and commentators at the County Ground.

Quick as a flash he retorts that having just checked the score (310 for four) it might be an idea if we didn't fix it!

Ian is one of four ECB Directors drawn from the small gene pool that is the eighteen counties' chairmen, so has a role to play in deciphering and explaining ICC/ECB policies and protocols and passing pearls, or pineapples, to the rest of us. Today he's calling me to explain how the ECB policy in respect of the new drainage system will work. In keeping with several ECB policies in respect of money it is somewhat less than straightforward.

FRIDAY, 27 APRIL. THE COUNTY GROUND. LVCCI, SOMERSET V LANCASHIRE. DAY 2

I wake at 3.18 a.m. for some reason, still thinking about drainage systems! Fortunately Linda is away so she's not disturbed. I once read that Richard Branson always sleeps with a pencil and paper by his bedside to capture ideas which came to him in the small hours. Well, I keep an iPad by mine, which is far more dangerous, as I wake, make notes like this and worse, then start browsing Facebook, Cricinfo, Twitter, etc ... Next thing I know it's 5.20 a.m!

I'm off to the County Ground today which is always a great treat. There will be old friends and new challenges which always greet the club's officers, often to do with what's going on out in the middle, or more likely the off-field repercussions of it. I hope the men in cardigans with pipes have got the scoreboard working, otherwise I will be in for another ear-bashing!

As I sip my morning tea and gaze westwards I would be less than honest if I said I wasn't contemplating the chances of rain. My conscience is reproaching me as I find myself on willitraintoday.co.uk with thoughts about some reinforcements for our depleted attack to even up the contest. In the absence of rain or a world-class spell of bowling from one of our lads, I can see us batting after tea probably 600 in arrears. Not the best backdrop to tonight's function.

INTERVIEW ON RADIO 5 LIVE SPORTS EXTRA WITH KEVIN HOWELLS

The morning has been a fine example of cricket's ability to totally confound all of us as Philander and Tregs ripped through the middle order and tail to leave Lancs at 395 for nine at lunch.

As an early lunch is taken I'm recruited as filler for the BBC live commentary team and I join them in the Potting Shed for a fireside chat about the domestic structure, the Lions selection, our development plans and our ambition to achieve Category B status.

I'm also asked about this book, and the Beeb unashamedly plug it along with my twitter account! I'm duly grateful.

Vic Marks too is on duty today in the Potting Shed and lends a certain *TMS*-like quality in contrast to my own amateurish efforts.

•••

The club is delighted at the news of Nick Compton being selected for the England Lions squad against the West Indies in May. Compo has worked hard on his technique, strength and conditioning and his mental approach since joining us three years ago. He richly deserves his opportunity and those who know him well wouldn't be remotely surprised if he grasps this opportunity and presses for full England honours in due course. More learned observers have already commented that he has a two-speed game and can score very quickly when conditions are appropriate and the situation calls for it. What he has learnt is the value to the team of not selling his wicket cheaply. Inevitably comparisons are drawn between Nick and his illustrious grandfather – I do love some of the quotes about Denis. Here's one by Basil Easterbrook, the brilliant sporting journalist from Torquay: 'He could do all the right things superbly, but when he broke all the rules the ball still ended up at the fence.'

THE 'OLD PLAYERS' DINNER' – THE COUNTY ROOM

The thing about non-PC labels is they do tell you what's in the tin! This annual dinner is always on the last Friday in April when there's a home CC match and starts at 7.30 p.m. sharp. Being West Country based, the event is usually lite on 'in my day' type content, but there's no shortage of anecdotes, reminiscences and a few groans about the old-style pension scheme. Well, scheme is putting it rather grandly – it seemed to have consisted of a whip round amongst members in the Old Pavilion and a few hearty back slaps.

Tonight's dinner lived up to expectations in the Long Room and there was a good turn out from the former players. I sat next to one of the very few Somerset players to have been born in California! Dennis Silk played for our club between 1952 and 1960 while pursuing a distinguished career in education which culminated in him becoming Warden of Radley. He and his wife are charming dinner companions. One good tale was of a game against Derbyshire at Chesterfield. Derby had two very useful seamers in Les Jackson and Cliff Gladwin who were also pretty tough, spiky characters. Dennis was batting with club captain Maurice Tremlett, who had given him a significant additional incentive with the promise of his club cap if he got his maiden fifty in this innings. Spurred on by such an illustrious prize, he dug in against the fierce but frustrated attack. It took him 49 balls, during which he played and missed several times, to get the single he needed to achieve his landmark half-century. During this period of play, after a particularly fruitless and unlucky spell, Les Jackson decided to have a bit of a word with young Dennis. 'You bloody f**king f**ker' left his lips in the wake of another play and miss by our doughty opener. The captain decided to lend his partner some support, so he ambled down the wicket in the bowler's direction and while doing a spot of gardening looked up at Jackson and said, 'Well bowled, Jackson. Oh, and well f**ked too.'

SATURDAY, 28 APRIL. THE COUNTY GROUND. LVCCI, SOMERSET V LANCASHIRE. DAY 3

No play today yet as I write and the weather forecast for tomorrow could hardly be worse! The Met Office has issued an amber weather warning and we are to expect uprooted trees and small dogs along with around two inches of rain in old money. Today might be the last chance of any valuable CC points so let's hope we take the last wicket quickly. No play, no wicket and no points. It all rests upon tomorrow!

SUNDAY, 29 APRIL. THE COUNTY GROUND. LVCCI, SOMERSET V LANCASHIRE. DAY 4

There was no day four! The threatened monsoon arrived and by 10 a.m. the umpires declared play abandoned for the day. It was the same virtually everywhere else, with Surrey v Durham achieving the rare distinction of having all four days abandoned despite having the Category A drainage at The Kia Oval. 'Nil points' for both – a UK Eurovision Song Contest score!

MONDAY, 30 APRIL. TAUNTON

There's no County Championship fixture for us this week, so a well-earned break and time to take stock. Rosey is quoted in the media as saying we would have taken third at the end of April after four matches, especially since we're several men down with injuries and another away on IPL duty.

This week will feature our first CB40 match at Surrey under lights on Friday which should be a good contest – weather permitting. We find ourselves in the delightfully entitled 'Group of Death', so this is going to be a stern test of our depleted squad's character.

I've texted Richard Gould, Surrey's CEO and Guy Lavender's predecessor, and forearmed him with the warning that I shall be taking up the standing invitation which exists to all club's senior officers at away fixtures.

I also texted Banger to arrange a visit to see how he's coping with being cooped up at home in recovery mode from the operation he had last week on his foot. He had tweeted the X-ray, and four rather grim-looking pins were very visible! I should have known better – 'I'm at the ground mate' is the reply! Unsurprisingly he's very keen to get back ASAP.

I hear back from two other county chairmen and one CEO of whom we've made discreet enquiries about whether they might be prepared to lend us any seam bowlers for a while. Probably unthinkable in some major sports, but in cricket the loan system is still used to good effect, in particular from another division as young cricketers can gain invaluable experience. No dice, however, as surprisingly all have their own mounting injury problems and in two cases a professional staff reduced to only sixteen full-time players! A sign of the times.

Lastly I receive a call from a player who needs help finding a car for the summer. I know a local Premier League umpire who doubles up as service manager at a local dealership, and I'm sure he would try to help. Predictably he offers to see what they can do and a meeting is set up.

MAY

TUESDAY, I MAY. TAUNTON

I pop into the club to have a catch-up with Guy Lavender. We were going to meet in Olio & Farino's, the Italian restaurant underneath the Somerset stand; however, it has received extensive flood damage in the recent downpours. We revert to the Caddy Shack. No shortage of topics, ranging from the latest on the injury front (a series of disasters) to the WICB's latest proclamation over Chris Gayle, which leaves none of us any the wiser, an update on the Category B application, the hotel and Old Pavilion, March accounts, personnel, Elton John, Guy Wolfendon's replacement, the Olympic Torch evening, the latest on the Barnicotts building trials and tribulations, sponsorship developments, ECB CEOs meeting, goings on with the youth development set-up, disciplinary issues and arrangements and team news for the Surrey CB40 on Friday.

We receive a great variety of letters over the course of a year. Most are written in good spirit, and mercifully only a few tend to be 'inappropriate', rude or angry. We recently received one very interesting letter from a supporter which the Chief Executive and I found certainly worthy of mention. The author of it likes to sit in the Old Pavilion amidst the old comfy seats. The view is behind the bowler's arm, so it's always been a popular spot. The spectator had written seeking our help. He told us how, on arriving home after a recent day's play, he noticed, or rather it was pointed out to him, that his teeth were missing. The letter didn't make clear whether it was a complete set of false teeth that had gone AWOL or just a top or bottom set. Either way he was asking if an item matching this description had been found and handed in to the club. Failing that, he asked if we would be good enough to organise a search of the general area. No such item had been handed in, and as we considered it unlikely that another supporter had taken them home, a search was duly arranged. Unfortunately the missing teeth were never recovered and we don't know to this day whether the letter was in jest or whether an opportunist is now making do with an ill-fitting set of a fellow member's teeth. It is a long shot, but should a reader have any information pertaining to the false teeth, the club's office would be keen to hear of it or even take delivery of the teeth should they be found. Thank you.

Other than all the above it's all quiet.

WEDNESDAY, 2 MAY. LONDON

I'm away in London for three days on other business. No sooner have I made the station than SMS and twitters are alive with Yorkshire's falling-out with Ajmal Shazad, their England capped seamer. Obviously our ears prick up, as we're four fast bowlers light at the moment and high quality English-qualified bowlers are like hen's teeth. Our cricket management triumvirate are in session and Guy Lavender and I are awaiting smoke from their chimney. We rehearse the possible consequences.

THURSDAY, 3 MAY. INDIA

Chris Gayle has made his decision to return to the West Indies fold, which naturally we find very disappointing as a contract is in place and the necessary NOC has been issued by the WICB. We've acted honourably and professionally throughout this episode and will now move to our back-up plan, which is to sign du Plessis, who is a very fine cricketer and T20 specialist.

CHRIS GAYLE SET FOR RETURN TO WEST INDIES FOLD AS OPENER TURNS DOWN SOMERSET DEAL – *Daily Telegraph*

Chris Gayle's stand-off with the West Indies Cricket Board could be over after he turned his back on a deal with Somerset in the hope of returning to international cricket.

The big-hitting Jamaican left-hander has not played for his country for more than a year following a spat with the WICB.

But following talks with the WICB, the 32-year-old has reneged on his Twenty20 contract with Somerset in a bid to free up his availability for the West Indies' tour of England starting this month.

'I wish to advise that as of today, I have written to Somerset CC and advised them that I will not be honouring the commitment I made to them when I signed a contract with them for the 2012 (Friends Life T20),' Gayle said in a statement.

'I made it clear to them that my decision was made because of my commitment to West Indies cricket and to West Indies cricket fans, and because I believe that it is time for the WICB to make a decision which will provide a clearer view of my own future.'

'I understand that by making this decision, it may place me in a position of considerable risk, since I am foregoing a signed contract, without any guarantees whatsoever, with only the hope that I will be selected to play for the West Indies again.'

'I have now satisfied all of the requests of the WICB and their selection panel, with whom I met via teleconference yesterday, and to whom I reiterated previous assurances given to the board regarding my availability.'

'So that there is no doubt, I confirmed to the selectors that I was available for West Indies duty in all forms of cricket, immediately following the conclusion of my contractual obligations to my IPL franchise, Royal Challengers Bangalore.'

Gayle has not played for West Indies since the 2011 World Cup, but he has been in outstanding form in the IPL.

He is third on the tournament's run tally and has scored 81, 87, 4, 86 and 71 from his past five innings.

The West Indies tour of England will begin on May 17 with the first of three Tests.

The team is also slated to play three one-day internationals starting June 16 and a solitary Twenty20 international on June 24.

BIRMINGHAM

Brian Rose and Marcus Trescothick are meeting with Ajmal Shazad to discuss his future plans and a potential move to us.

He would be a very fine acquisition to our squad, and it's moments like this that remind me of the importance of the club's fourth objective: financial strength. A few years ago there would have been no point in us meeting him; we simply couldn't have afforded him. So, cricket isn't about making money – but it sure is easier sometimes if you do!

•••

The social media are alive with comments re Chris Gayle's change of heart and, hard on the heels of that, reaction to the announcement of the alternative overseas player. Yet again the Somerset members and supporters impress by taking the line that there's no point crying over spilt milk – what's gone is gone. The best reaction to adversity isn't to fight it but to get over it. We had a reserve plan and we are able to activate it.

FRANCOIS DU PLESSIS NAMED AS CHRIS GAYLE TWENTY20 REPLACEMENT– *Bridgwater Mercury*

Somerset have bounced back from the disappointment of Chris Gayle with an 'exciting' signing in South African Francois du Plessis.

The 27-year-old is a top order batsman who bowls leg spin and Director of Cricket Brian Rose said it is a fantastic signing for the club.

He added: 'He is a three-dimensional player and it is very exciting.'

'You are never going to be able to replace Chris Gayle, but what we have now is two South Africans in Taunton that will be in the World Cup squad.'

'He is a world class player and has proved himself as one of the best around.'

Du Plessis has scored 1160 runs from 61 Twenty20 matches at 24.68 with a top score of 78 not out.

With the ball, he has claimed 49 wickets with a career best of 5-19.

Rose said he hopes du Plessis will be available for the majority of the Twenty20 fixtures pending his commitments with the national team.

But he said that the all rounder will be available for the first match on June 13 against Warwickshire.

FRIDAY, 4 MAY. THE KIA OVAL. SURREY V SOMERSET. CB40 UNDER FLOODLIGHTS

After a busy day yesterday, even by cricket standards, with the withdrawal of Chris Gayle, subsequent media and supporters' interest, and then the same on the announcement of his replacement Francois du Plessis, today we hope to be able to get to the business of playing the game after what is, by modern standards, an extended break!

Today sees a mouth-watering opener as the finalists in last season's competition meet to get the 2012 version under way at The Oval. We are both in the 'Group of death' along with Scotland, Durham, Hampshire, Glamorgan and Nottinghamshire, so a very tight group is in prospect with some fierce contests. Players will also be mindful of the forthcoming limited-overs series this summer, and several have points to prove to the omnipresent England selectors.

Richard Thompson and Richard Gould have been typically gracious hosts and have warmly extended invitations to several of us. I'm really pleased that the long-suffering Mrs Nash and my son Ed are able to come along, as well as some business guests, although we will be making a sharp exit around 6.30 p.m. We will have a train to catch back to Taunton, as one of our daughters is off to China and the Far East early in the morning, and we want a 'last supper' of sorts before she disappears. Another frustrating train journey in prospect, then, as the intermittent signal on First Great Western will only fleetingly reveal details of the match before plunging us back into darkness and ignorance.

I also have a lunchtime meeting before the match with Gordon Hollins, the MD of professional cricket in England and Wales. We will be having a detailed catch-up, and in particular I want to update him with regard to our Category B application. It contains several subtleties and options and we need him to fully grasp the nuances. Between business meetings today I've also penned a similar note to Giles Clarke reinforcing a few points we discussed on the phone yesterday.

The news earlier today from Guy Lavender on the meeting in Birmingham between Rosey, Tres and Shazad is that the prospects are put at 50:50.

During the game I hear from Guy Lavender that there's now a potential problem with Faf du Plessis, and Rosey bounces in later, asks for a quiet word, and rounds off what is by now turning into a ghastly evening. Apparently catching player and agent completely unawares, CSA have informed Faf today that he is to play on an 'A' team tour which will now make him unavailable for our T20 competition. Player, agent and Somerset are all somewhere between furious and perplexed!

I leave The Oval as planned to get the train back to Taunton as the Surrey innings draws towards its close. I leave Damien Lane, a colleague from the City and a major Surrey fan, in the tender care of Roy Kerslake and Guy Lavender. He promises to keep me abreast of the score as I know internet access on the London–Penzance line is somewhat hit and miss. It felt like it was going to be one of those matches and, sure enough, a drip, drip of falling wickets punctuates the packed train journey home. We are in trouble by the time we reach Reading and, before Castle Cary, my friend, Nic Pothas, who is in the PCA's box at the game, SMSs me the reassuring words 'You're dead tonight buddy' – we were seven down and still well over 100 in arrears.

•••

Our Seconds also lost out by a big margin to their Surrey opponents in the Championship match at Reigate Priory on Friday. We are forced to play a scratch side as the Twos have been raided to shore up the First XI.

SATURDAY, 5 MAY. TAUNTON

As readers will have seen, the discussions between the club and Chris Gayle have been very constructive in a difficult and challenging set of circumstances. I always try (without always succeeding) to see through difficulties and issues by identifying what an acceptable end point, or points, would be. Identifying and accepting those can help you to choose a course to follow through what might be a maze, a moral one or otherwise. Once we were fully apprised of Chris' difficulties it became apparent that wrestling on the floor with him and his advisers wasn't going to achieve anything useful. Instead we opted for an amicable agreement, with the prospect of him playing for Somerset County Cricket Club at some future date. This was an outcome worth pursuing, and as the correspondence below shows, our positive suggestion was not only readily accepted but repaid with interest.

SOMERSET END GAYLE ROW – *Sporting Life*

Somerset will not be taking legal action against Chris Gayle following his decision to play for the West Indies rather than them this summer.

Gayle was contracted to Somerset in the Friends Life T20, following his stint with Royal Challengers Bangalore in the Indian Premier League.

But the destructive opening batsman announced on Thursday, in an attempt to heal his rift with the West Indies and end a year-long international exile, that he instead intends to be available for his country's limited-overs matches against England.

Somerset acted quickly to sign South Africa batsman Faf du Plessis in place of the West Indies master-blaster – and after toying with the possibility of suing Gayle, they have had a rethink.

Chief executive Guy Lavender issued a statement on the club website, which read: 'Having taken legal advice and reflected on the situation over the last 24 hours, we have concluded that it is not in the best interests of Somerset County Cricket Club, Chris Gayle, or cricket more generally to pursue this matter any further.'

'We wish Chris well and hope to see him back playing for the West Indies this summer.'

•••

Exchange of letters with Chris Gayle:

Dear Chris,

Thank you very much for your email. I do sympathise with the position you have found yourself in and understand how difficult a decision it must have been. I am sure you appreciate that your decision not to honour your commitment to Somerset constitutes a renunciation of a binding legal contract. However, in the circumstances, I do not feel it is in the Club's best interests, or yours, to pursue this matter any further.

However, recognising the circumstances, I wonder whether you would agree to allow us the first opportunity to contract you, should you become available over the next few years to play Club cricket in England?

You are a magnificent player and we will be very sorry not to see you representing Somerset this summer. Best of luck and I hope that matters resolve themselves with the West Indies Cricket Board.

Mr A. Nash
Chairman Somerset County Cricket Club

And Chris' reply:

Dear Mr Nash,

I wish to first and foremost express my heartfelt thanks to you and the other members of Somerset CC for your decision not to pursue any action against me. As you would appreciate this has been an extremely difficult decision for me. I must admit that receiving your letter this morning was comforting, and I appreciate this support more than you will ever know.

I would like to say up front that I am happy to agree to your request that I allow Somerset the first opportunity to contract me should I become available to play county cricket in England in the near future. Indeed, I also wish to advise that given the history of this matter, if for some reason I am not selected for the West Indies and an opportunity arises to rejoin the team for the 2012 season, I would certainly avail myself to the Club. I do understand it may not be possible, but one never knows.

Should I be picked for the West Indies and be a part of this summer's tour and the opportunity arises and subject to the team's commitments, I would also be more than happy to consider making a visit to Taunton at a mutually convenient time to meet you personally, as well as other members of the club and the players should they be home at that time.

Once again I am sincerely grateful for the club's magnanimous gesture, and wish for Somerset every success this season. I look forward to being part of the Somerset family in the very near future.

Yours sincerely,
Chris Gayle

LUCY SHUKER FUNDRAISING BALL – THE COUNTY ROOM, COLIN ATKINSON PAVILION

Lucy Shuker is a phenomenon. She lost both legs in a motorcycle accident and rebuilt her life by taking up wheelchair tennis. She has achieved considerable success and is one of the world's leading players. My mixed doubles partner Diana Hakin (a tennis coach) knows Lucy well and was responsible for inviting Linda and me, John and Julie Gannon (our mixed doubles opponents and club sponsors) to join her table at a fundraising dinner in the County Room. We gladly accepted, and a very enjoyable evening ensued, culminating in an auction of lots where we ended up buying a doubles match against Lucy and her coach. At the time of writing, because of her many commitments competing in the UK and overseas, we haven't yet managed to play the fixture, but it's something other than the season to look forward to in the New Year!

SUNDAY, 6 MAY. TAUNTON

We wake to a 'Push alert' on Flight+ that the plane carrying my daughter Virginia has landed in Beijing. Hopefully there's public wi-fi there, so she can get onto WhatsApp and let us know she has met her boyfriend 'Sharpy' there as planned! He was arriving from New Zealand, so the potential for things to go awry is colossal!

MONDAY, 7 MAY. TAUNTON

A WhatsApp message appears from Sharpy's smartphone – he and Virginia did meet yesterday as planned at Beijing airport and are off to see the Great Wall. I'm relieved, but I do wonder why they are going to meet Rahul Dravid.

TUESDAY, 8 MAY. TAUNTON

A lull in our season is in full flow! Looking in the press my eye is caught by a Top Spin piece by Lawrence Booth, who has been keeping tabs on one of Somerset's greatest ever captains, Brian Close. You can't keep a good man down, it seems.

TOP SPIN NEWSLETTER – Lawrence Booth, *Guardian*

Tales of Brian Close's toughness long ago crossed the line between legend and cliché. (The best bit about the footage of the bombardment he received at Old Trafford in 1976 is the way he refuses to punch gloves during his mid-pitch meetings with John Edrich.)

But news has reached the Top Spin from the always reliable Leeds-fitness-centre grapevine that, even at the age of 81, he's still at it. On a clear day in the sauna, Close can apparently be spotted shadow-boxing. Suggestions that he is imagining Michael Holding on the end of his left jabs remain unconfirmed.

Our quest to sign Ajmal Shahzad has proved unsuccessful. Understandable in many ways, not least because of the distance of Taunton from his home and family in Yorkshire. Our search will continue, but barring another county fall-out I suspect it's highly unlikely we shall find someone soon enough. Let's hope Vernon Philander has a blinder at Durham this week. With Middlesex dispatching Worcester convincingly over the weekend with a contrived result, it underlines just how competitive CC1 is going to be this season. Unless we can bring our strike bowlers back quickly we are going to find the going very hard indeed. As ever in first-class cricket the batters can prevent a defeat, but it's the bowlers that usually provide victory.

•••

Crisis is an overused and overblown word, but the latest news from our physios does prompt me to use this C word. Jos Buttler and Jamie Overton are added to the injury list. We are literally down to our last eleven senior players for the CC1 match against Durham. Jason Kerr will fulfil the twelfth man duties. Next in line for drinks duties could be Guy Lavender or me.

LAST ELEVEN MEN STANDING FACE DURHAM – SCCC site

James Hildreth will lead a team made up from Somerset's only 11 available senior players in the LV= County Championship match against Durham at Chester-le-Street, starting on Wednesday.

The county suffered yet another injury blow today when Jos Buttler split the webbing on a hand during fielding practice.

His absence means than no fewer that six first team players are ruled out of the Durham game by injury, while Nick Compton will also be missing on England Lions duty.

As well as Compton, Marcus Trescothick, Steve Kirby, Gemaal Hussain, Adam Dibble, Jamie Overton and Buttler are unavailable.

Overton is awaiting the results of a scan on an elbow problem and if they are positive will be flown up for the Clydesdale Bank 40 match against Durham on Sunday.

His twin brother Craig will play in the Championship fixture. Alex Barrow makes his first appearance of the season and is likely to open the batting with Arul Suppiah.

Such is the extent of Somerset's injury list that Academy Director Jason Kerr is set to fulfil the 12th man duties. Spinners George Dockrell and Max Waller will both play.

Director of Cricket Brian Rose said: 'In all my time with Somerset, including as a player and captain, I have never known so many key players to be ruled out at the same time.'

'We must have run over a black tiger, rather than a black cat, to cause such a crisis in personnel. I'm beginning to wonder what will happen next.'

'I don't think I'll be taking my glasses to Durham. Otherwise I might be next in line for selection!'

'Sometimes adversity brings out the best in a team and we have to hope that is the case over the next few days.'

Somerset: A. Suppiah, A. Barrow, J. Hildreth (capt), C. Kieswetter (wkt), P. Trego, L. Gregory, C. Meschede, V. Philander, C. Overton, M. Waller, G. Dockrell.

WEDNESDAY, 9 MAY. CHESTER-LE-STREET. LVCCI, DURHAM V SOMERSET. DAY 1

An eye-catching all-round performance from one of our rising young stars, about whom I've written earlier in this book, dominates match reports. Mesche not only starred with the ball as we skittled Durham for 125, he also played well with the bat, hitting a fiery 60 out of a total of 220 for eight to leave us well placed at the end of the first day. Not for the first time Bagel also weighed in with a valuable contribution, being undefeated on 60 at the close with two wickets standing. A lead of 100 tomorrow and a second batting point would be good from here.

THURSDAY, 10 MAY. CHESTER-LE-STREET. LVCCI, DURHAM V SOMERSET. DAY 2

Well, we never made our second batting point *and* Bagel is still in – there was no play against Durham due to rain. Meanwhile in Taunton the annual Early Season Dinner for our age-groups takes place. Organised by the Somerset Cricket Board, it is a veritable frenzy of enthusiasm and expectation. I am due to address the serried ranks of young players, parents, coaches, friends and club personnel, so I turn up very early hoping for a word with Guy Lavender. Pulling into the car park at 6 p.m. the place is a hive of activity. Some of our young players have tasked their parents to bring them straight from school, so have already been here for a while! Talking to the parents it's clear that some of those aged 10–12 are so excited they have already lost a night's sleep.

The SCB invented this occasion last season, and so this is the second dinner. Guy Lavender, Marcus Trescothick, Darren Venness and I are there to represent the professional game, and it becomes absolutely plain to us quite early on in proceedings that this is a runaway success. You could literally feel the atmosphere. The County Room was stuffed with people, trophies, kit and palpable fun and bonhomie. It was a real triumph to behold. One of the evening's highlights was Banger (indefatigable despite his serious injury and plaster cast) presenting trophies to all the players who achieved hundreds or five-fors last season. What a credit he is to the club and his profession.

As Mark Twain said, 'A good impromptu speech takes three weeks to prepare,' and I'd been thinking for some time of the right tone and message. Here's the speech I delivered:

In football a sheikh or oligarch can *buy* success ... you can't with a cricket club ... thank God for that! We have salary caps and no transfer market. You have to *build* success in a cricket club. This is why age groups and our player's pathway is so important and why this annual dinner – this being the second – has been set up. It is to recognise the importance of developing young cricketers for Somerset County Cricket Club and to thank the many people for the part they play in this.

Sixteen members of our current first team squad of twenty-one were born in the West Country or went to school here! In this room ... is most of our first-team squad for the next twenty years or so! I can also guarantee you that ... based on history ... in this room too are some future England players!

So, some thank-you's: through you, Chairman Andy Curtis, to the *SCB*, our partner cricket *clubs and schools*, all the many *coaches* ... and of course last, and by no means least, to all the *parents* of our young players. Without your efforts the players wouldn't be here!!!!!! You all do so much fetching and carrying, laundry, packed lunches, first aid etc, encouragement ... You do as much as anyone to develop our players and we value that greatly. *Players, please show your appreciation for all those who support you ...*

•••

To the *players* I say this. Wear your badge with *pride* as you have *earned* your place as a Somerset player. *A round of applause for all of you ...*

Carlsberg don't do cricket clubs ... but if they did!!!!!! Your club isn't any old cricket club ... it is a *very* special club. If you were an age-group player for say Norwich City – a good premier league club – you should also be proud. *But* if you travel as a Norwich player to ... Cape Town ... Chennai in India or ... Christchurch in NZ, I doubt whether the football clubs there will have heard of your club. I've been very fortunate to have travelled the world with business and cricket and I can tell you, if you visit any cricket club, anywhere in the world, they will know Somerset and you'll receive a warm welcome and be treated with respect.

Why is this?

1. In an age when the average lifespan of a company in the UK is just eight years Somerset CCC is *137* years old this year. We've played cricket here since 1881. And we are still getting better.

2. We have developed players for England since the 1880s, when Arthur Fothergill toured South Africa. Since then no fewer than twenty-three Somerset cricketers have played Test cricket for England ... one even played rugby for England too ... Our first team squad *now* has six players who have played for senior England teams in recent years and another six who have played for the Under-19s.

3. The world's greatest ever cricketers have all played here at The County Ground ... Don Bradman, Garry Sobers, Jack Hobbs, Brian Lara, Sachin Tendulkar, Shane Warne, Murali, Glenn McGrath, Roberts and Marshall, Larwood and Voce, Richard Hadlee ... the list goes on ...

4. Some of the world's greatest cricketers have also played for Somerset and are part of the family that is SCCC ... Steve Waugh, Viv Richards, Graeme Smith, Greg Chappell, Ian Botham, Ricky Ponting, Joel Garner, Sunny Gavaskar, Justin Langer, Sanath Jayasuriah ... and of course Marcus Trescothick and Andy Caddick ...

Boys, you are part of one of the world's greatest cricket clubs and I promise you everyone here, the CEO, our chefs, physios, security staff, will all work to help you achieve your dreams as a Somerset player ...

•••

Lastly, I'd like to leave you with a thought. Cricket is a very tough game. You need to be physically fit and strong to excel. Our coaches, nutritional experts and medical staff will help you to achieve this ...

But *mentally* cricket is even tougher. It's like life. One day you are flying high; the next you are shot down in flames. I've four children, now mostly grown-up. But I've always reminded them that some days you are the *puppy* and some days you are the *lamppost*. We will help you to develop strengths to deal with these challenges too.

And look at how our first team – five players aged 20 or less – faced their mental challenges this week at Durham! The average age of the Durham side was 34!

Harold Gimblett is our club's leading run-scorer. Let me tell you about how he became the puppy instead of the lamppost ...

Young Harold from Bicknoller had a two-week trial with Somerset in May 1935. He was 20 years of age. There wasn't an Academy in those days!!!!!!!

During the second week of his trial it was decided he wasn't going to make it. He was told by former club captain and club secretary John Daniell the bad news, he simply wasn't good enough. He was given 35 shillings for his efforts (under two pounds) and his bus fare home.

However, on Friday *Laurie* Hawkins reported sick. Harold was told to get himself to Frome for the match the following day against Essex. Wickie Wally Luckes was going to take him from Taunton. But Harold missed the bus from Bicknoller and his lift to Frome. So ... he hitched a lift in a *lorry* there instead! He arrived, somewhat dishevelled, in the nick of time. We won the toss and batted. We were 35 for three within an hour and 105 for five at lunch. Dickie Burroughs fell soon afterwards and young Harold came to the crease - with a bat borrowed from club legend Arthur Wellard. *We were 107 for six.*

Harold's first run came off his third ball. Shortly afterwards he was tonking Essex leggie Peter Smith for 15 an over. He reached his fifty with a six over midwicket *in just 28 minutes from 35 balls.* Wellard fell, then Luckes. Bill Andrews joined Harold at the crease. We were eight down. Harold pressed on and notched up his maiden first-class hundred in just 63 minutes. This became the fastest century of the 1935 season and it was made out of 130 runs while he had been at the wicket. *He finished with 123 of the innings total of 175 with three sixes and seventeen fours.* Somerset won the match by an innings. Harold went on to score 23,007 runs at 36 for Somerset, and to play Test cricket for England, in a career lasting nineteen years. Boys, he was the lamppost on Friday and a day later he was the happiest puppy in town ... He took his opportunity. And that story reminds us of the importance of mental toughness.

So boys, when you face your next moment of doubt, and you will because cricket is like that, the next time you feel like the lamppost, you just remember young Harold, what he overcame, and remind yourself of what you can do if you take your opportunities when they come along ...

A toast ... to Somerset County Cricket Club.

Enjoy tonight and go well this season.

SOMERSET AGE GROUP PRESENTATION NIGHT HAILED A GREAT SUCCESS – SCCC Site

The Somerset Age Group Presentation Evening that took place in the County Room on Thursday evening has been deemed a great success by all who attended.

This was the second year that the event has taken place, and was once again generously sponsored by Season's Holidays, and master-minded and brilliantly compered by Piers McBride.

Around 250 people were present at the event – comprising players from all eight age group squads, Under 11s through to Under 17s, parents, Coaches and Team Managers – as well as Andy Nash the Chairman of Somerset CCC, Chief Executive Guy Lavender and Somerset Captain Marcus Trescothick.

After team photographs and a most enjoyable meal, Andy Nash spoke eloquently and passionately of the importance of Somerset producing their own home grown talent, and that statistically and historically it was perfectly reasonable to assume that sitting in the room were members of Somerset's First XI – or even the England team – in 2025.

The Chairman related the fairy tale debut of Somerset legend Harold Gimblett – initially discharged after a trial for the professional playing staff but suddenly recalled because of a spate of injuries to score a century in his debut match at Frome.

Skipper Marcus Trescothick presented County Caps and team kit to all boys new to the squads this season, as well as awards to each player who had registered either a century with the bat or five wickets with the ball in 2011.

A very well-supported auction followed, with several Somerset players pledging an hour's one to one coaching.

This and the accompanying raffle realised the magnificent sum of around £6,000, all of which will be ploughed back into the Clowance Trust fund for the betterment of youth cricket within the county.

SCB Chairman Andy Curtis said afterwards: 'What particularly impressed me, given the enjoyment and marvellous atmosphere around the room, was the very evident impression that Team Somerset was represented here in all its aspects – a strong partnership of all the stakeholders in what has become a very strong and well organised youth system – players, parents, Coaches and Managers, but equally importantly the presence and support of leading representatives from the professional side of the club.'

The SCB Chairman added: 'After only two years since its introduction, this fantastic event is quickly assuming a very prominent place in the cricketing calendar for the County Club and the youth system alike.'

FRIDAY, 11 MAY. CHESTER-LE-STREET. LVCCI, DURHAM V SOMERSET. DAY 3

No play due to rain. Tangible disappointment as we've got Durham on the ropes. Only a day left so the odds move towards a draw.

I have a board meeting near Gatwick, so am on the very familiar platform five at Taunton station – and who should be there, hobbling but wearing his trademark smile? Banger! We reprise last night and agree it was a great occasion. Marcus is off to summarise and comment for ITV on the IPL matches today. We discussed last night and the age-groups dinner and then how Marcus thinks the 16/3 points for a win/draw has had the unintended consequence of producing 'results wickets' in the CC. This has tilted the game too far in favour of the bowlers, the skipper thinks, and I'm sure he's right. Perhaps this is why England batsmen returning to county cricket are now struggling for runs? Similarly, the bowlers who look devastating on the county tracks may find the Test grounds' shirt fronts a different proposition. I'm reminded of Athers' view that cricket is a complicated game and even minor changes can trigger significant unintended consequences – maybe here's another!

I phone 'Wrighty', the Notts Chairman who in turn is Chairman of the ECB's cricket committee, and pass on Banger's observation. He takes the point. I also ask him if he would hand over their work on Cricket in the Community which has been lauded in the ECB corridors of power as an exemplar. We can learn from this on our own Category B application.

I then talk with Kevin Howells of the BBC on some queries he has relating to our interview on BBC 5 Live recently. He wants to clarify that it is ECB policy to reduce the amount of cricket played, which I'd stated and, he reminded me, I also told our AGM. He had been given to understand from another source that this was not in fact ECB policy! I managed to retrieve on my iPad the briefing notes following the Ettingham Park seminar, and also the Schofield report conclusions, and to my relief there it is in black and white: 'The ECB wish to reduce the days played by between 8–12 in a season'. It follows that this can only be done by effectively wiping out a limited overs competition or reorganising the CC.

SATURDAY, 12 MAY. CHESTER-LE-STREET. LVCCI, DURHAM V SOMERSET. DAY 4

The general opinion is that we are likely to run out of time today in pressing for victory. I'm travelling to the US on business for a week, so frustratingly spend seven hours or so in radio silence above the Atlantic. On landing my frustration increases as we clearly came very close to what would have been a tremendous victory for our young and inexperienced side. Rain delayed the start yet again and a couple of spilled catches put paid to our chances. Despite our young lions taking wickets at regular intervals the senior Durham pros – skilfully corralled by ex-Somerset player Mark 'Blackie' Blackwell – hung on well for the draw.

SUNDAY, 13 MAY. CHESTER-LE-STREET. CB40, DURHAM V SOMERSET

The Overton twins look set to make their first joint appearance for us today. What a proud moment for Mum and Dad. Let's hope the guys take confidence from the 'winning draw' with the red ball into this game.

As it turns out, fine individual contributions from Jamie Overton and Alex Barrow are not quite enough to save Somerset from a 14-run Clydesdale Bank 40 defeat. However, we all draw considerable heart from our young side's performance, which is a testimony to our age-group and Academy system and bodes well for our future.

TUESDAY, 15 MAY. CHARLESTON, SOUTH CAROLINA

On checking emails and social media before heading off to today's meetings in Charleston SC, I'm alerted to a very nice witty piece on Somerset County Cricket Club by Steve James in the *Daily Telegraph*. Richard Gould should be credited with dropping the Sabres suffix to our limited-overs branding. I agreed with his proposal back in 2009 that we should focus on 'Somerset' as the brand. It seems that the proliferation of monikers has got under Mr James' collar, exacerbated I suspect by the fact that his home county have even dropped the word Glamorgan! Since then we've upped the ante a bit with our We Are Somerset campaign, which is intended to capture the culture and ethos we strive so hard to nurture.

County cricket isn't immune from the macroeconomic environment, and the news from the EU is dire. It appears the Greeks are going to continue to face both ways simultaneously, rejecting austerity but wanting to hang on to the bailout monies. The only consensus amongst those who are supposed to know what the consequences will be is that no one knows what is likely to happen! To those of us entrusted to be the stewards of companies and clubs the uncertainty is of major concern.

SIMPLY SOMERSET STAND OUT IN THE COUNTY JUNGLE WHERE THERE ARE LIONS, SHARKS, BEARS, PANTHERS AND FOXES – Steve James, *The Daily Telegraph*

I love Somerset. I love watching the bucolic majesty of Marcus Trescothick. I love the youthful brilliance of Jos Buttler, the chattering chutzpah of Craig Kieswetter, the studied leave of Nick Compton, the fast-handed strokeplay of James Hildreth, the tattoos of Peter Trego, the devotion to weight training of the trainer Daz Veness, even the goatee of chairman Andy Nash. As for that lovely potting shed that acts as a commentary box, in which I was once showered with broken glass, well ...

OK, maybe this is getting a little silly. Nash may not even have a goatee any more. I haven't seen him for a while. Some of the above is indeed true, but there is a much more important reason why I love Somerset. It's because they are Somerset. Pure and simple. No nickname. Just Somerset.

Among the counties they stand alone in that respect. Once they were the Sabres, but they have since deemed the moniker superfluous. If only the others would follow suit.

Even worse, my old county Glamorgan no longer exist in one-day cricket. They are now the 'Welsh Dragons'. Cardiff City's Malaysian owners wanted something similar for their football club. The idea lasted about a day before it was binned. I wish Glamorgan would do the same. But they won't. Not yet anyway.

High levels of farce will be reached in the Friends Life T20 when the South African Martin van Jaarsveld and the Australian Shaun Marsh arrive to swell further the foreign enclave at the club. There will only be a handful of 'Welsh Dragons' in the side.

I'm with Matthew Engel on this subject. When in 1999 the England and Wales Cricket Board first announced the list of nicknames for county teams in that season's Sunday League competition, the then editor of *Wisden* wrote: 'The people running cricket have become desperately obsessed with gimmickry. It's rather sad because nicknames are something that evolve. This is like a pub being renamed. When imposed by a marketing department it tends not to work. It's harmless but rather sad.'

Hear, hear. The initiative was the idea of the ECB's marketing department. 'This season the idea is to reinforce the new aspects of the new league and introduce nicknames that will be relevant to young supporters,' a spokesman said back then. 'It's good from a marketing and PR point of view.'

Really? They are still a gimmick. Can you name them all without resorting to Google? You've only got 16 to go anyway. Just be careful with Derbyshire, Hampshire, Middlesex and Yorkshire. They now have different nicknames from those first adopted in 1999. And please remember that Surrey, after being the Brown Caps for a while, have reverted to their original nickname.

Here are the answers. We have the Derbyshire Falcons (formerly Scorpions), Durham Dynamos, Essex Eagles, Gloucestershire Gladiators, Hampshire Royals (formerly Hawks), Kent Spitfires, Lancashire Lightning, Leicestershire Foxes, Middlesex Panthers (formerly Crusaders), Northamptonshire Steelbacks, Nottinghamshire Outlaws, Surrey Lions, Sussex Sharks, Warwickshire Bears, Worcestershire Royals and Yorkshire Carnegie (formerly Phoenix).

Get them all? You really need to get out more. I may have missed the odd change along the way. I didn't miss the April Fools' joke one year, though, when Kent announced that they were changing their name from the

Spitfires to the Stallions. For a brief while that story was even posted on the ECB website.

In fairness, however, the ECB did come up with a decent joke this past April, claiming that they were going to use British Bulldogs as fetchers of fours and sixes on the boundary edges during Twenty20 matches this season. It fooled a few, including a couple of eminent writers.

Mind you, at least the counties' traditional names are still used in front of the nickname. There was a time when, like Glamorgan this year, there was a move to using just the nicknames, a bit like in South Africa where they have the Lions, Titans, Knights, Dolphins, Warriors and Impi. I can guess where the Cape Cobras are from, but the others?

In the Australian Big Bash League we now have the likes of the Perth Scorchers, Hobart Hurricanes, Brisbane Heat and Adelaide Strikers. Sydney and Melbourne have two teams each – the Sixers and Thunder in the former and the Stars and Renegades in the latter. But I can forgive that. These are new identities, city-based franchises that differ from those playing in the other forms of the game.

Now there's a thought ...

WEDNESDAY, 16 MAY. THE OVAL. LVCCI, SURREY V SOMERSET. DAY 1

Business over with at The History Press Inc., I'm travelling north from the beautiful city of Charleston SC (voted regularly by the readers of Condé Nast as the USA's top city) towards Boston via Washington DC for the Tristar board meeting. At the airport, courtesy of the ECB app, I was cheered considerably to see that openers Arul Suppiah and young Alex Barrow had seen off the initial assault by Surrey's seamers at 63 for none.

Alex Barrow is another home-grown talent of King's College (along with Jos Buttler and Craig Meschede) and was a key member of the side which won the college the 'Wisden School of the Year' award in 2009. Some achievement for a school with only 400 pupils. He progressed along our Player's Pathway and hails from Frome near Bath – strangely enough, where my mother was brought up!

Amongst the morning's flurry of emails and messages, an SMS arrives from Brian Rose letting me know we've got first refusal on Saeed Ajmal for three months from July to September. More good news, but Guy Lavender will be very conscious of the financial implications.

I board my flight and enter radio silence for about ninety minutes. US Eastern time is five hours behind the UK, so by the time I'm in Washington Dulles we will be well into the afternoon session.

I land at Dulles and immediately turn on the iPhone to await a signal and the news it will bring.

•••

Oh joy! 150 for one. And while I'm waiting to board a flight to Boston we achieve the first batting point and Arul gets his eighth first-class hundred. We press on and have reached 243 for two as I re-enter radio silence. Looks like two batting points before tea!

•••

Landed at Boston and the news is outstanding at 350 for three. Centuries from Arul and Hildy, together with another fine score from Compo, have put us in a decent position.

THURSDAY, 17 MAY. THE OVAL. LVCCI, SURREY V SOMERSET. DAY 2

I wake in Boston MA and the news is mixed from the first hour! We've lost four wickets to the Surrey seamers which may indicate that, as the Church would put it – 'it's a bowler's day!'. However, I also see that 'Joverton and Coverton' are wagging furiously for the last wicket, which hints again at their potential. We clinch the fifth batting point, throw the bat some more to bat Surrey out of the game, declare and put them under the pump. At stumps they are still well shy of avoiding the follow-on.

We are also hoping to clinch the services of Richard Levi to boost our T20 squad and that news has now broken. Our members and supporters have been very understanding about the run of bad luck we've had trying to cement the position of our overseas players. If Levi can be confirmed he'll receive our fans' customary warm welcome. We are told he's another fine cricketer.

•••

Somerset County Cricket Club has always supported the armed forces. 40 Royal Marine Commando are based just outside Taunton at Norton Fitzwarren and we've a long history of association. We sent cricket equipment to them in Afghanistan during their 2010/11 tour and hosted the Commando's homecoming at the County Ground. We locked the ground down, having gained contributions of food and drink from many sponsors and local firms, and around 3,000 Royal Marines and their families celebrated their return after a very arduous tour. The Tickets for Troops is a good initiative and we support it enthusiastically.

SOMERSET SUPPORT TICKETS FOR TROOPS AGAIN IN 2012 – SCCC Site
Somerset County Cricket Club have announced today that this summer
they will be supporting the Armed Forces charity, Tickets For Troops, by
providing 50 free tickets for the following CB40 fixtures at the County
Ground, plus the game at Bath on July 22nd – Sunday 27th May v
Hampshire, Sunday 15th July v Scotland, Sunday 22nd July v Durham
at Bath RFC, Saturday 28th July v Welsh Dragons, Sunday 12th August v
Nottinghamshire, Monday 27th August v Surrey. Somerset CCC has been
a long supporter of Tickets For Troops, donating tickets to servicemen and
women since the charity's inception in 2009.

   The tickets they provide, as a mark of appreciation for the hard work
and sacrifices troops make on our behalf, offers a fantastic opportunity for
members of the Armed Forces to escape, with their families, the stresses
and strains of everyday military life.

FRIDAY, 18 MAY. THE OVAL. LVCCI, SURREY V SOMERSET. DAY 3

Surrey (286 for six) trail Somerset (512 for nine declared) by 226 runs. Roy
Kerslake and I exchanged lengthy SMSs last night and concluded that we
needed to get Surrey out before lunch to keep a win in sight. They are a dangerous and aggressive batting side, and Hildy will be conscious of what can
be chased by a side on a shirt-front!

   Surrey were dismissed soon enough and we resumed, but wickets kept falling, leaving us 278 ahead with three wickets standing. I'd imagine we will
hope to score briskly and ask Surrey to chase 300-plus. In my view it's worth
showing them something to try and force the win – another draw for three
points isn't Championship form!

   I've also returned to the UK today and more normal service can be resumed
on following the current games. Being several hours out of sync with BST
and only skittish access to WIFI is not to be recommended.

•••

An SMS from Rosey confirms we've signed and obtained from CSA the NOC
for Richard Levi. A sense of *déjà vu* strikes!

•••

This day in 1935 saw the debut of Harold Gimblett. As the celebrated journalist David Foot wrote: 'Harold Gimblett is the greatest batsman Somerset
has ever produced.' Gimblett scored at a fast rate throughout his career, and

hit 265 sixes – 'surely a record for a regular opening batsman', according to Eric Hill, his post-war opening partner and since then a long-time journalist watcher of Somerset. However, Harold appeared in only three Tests, none of them against Australia, and he left first-class cricket abruptly, suffering from mental health problems that would remain with him to the end of his life.

As I mentioned in my speech at the age-groups dinner earlier in the month, Gimblett's arrival in the first-class game was the stuff of legend. Indeed, *Wisden*, in its obituary of him in 1979, wrote: 'The start of his career was so sensational that any novelist attributing it to his hero would have discredited the book.'

SATURDAY, 19 MAY. THE OVAL. LVCCI, SURREY V SOMERSET. DAY 4

Somerset resumed the second innings of their Championship match against Surrey at The Oval this morning on 154 for seven, a lead of 278 runs.

This has been a terrific contest, with the advantage seesawing between the sides. The first hour was likely to be crucial, and so it proved, but there were even more twists and turns to come in a pulsating day's cricket.

Surrey, chasing just over 300, made a strong start and appeared at one point to be cruising. Then cricket did what cricket does and a spell of high-class spin bowling from George Dockrell turned the game back in our favour. Surrey collapsed from 96 for one to 148 for six, but then Rory Hamilton-Brown played a true captain's innings of 70 and shepherded the tail through to the close and the draw.

Again our makeshift and very young side had dominated the opposition for much of this contest and come very close to achieving an excellent victory.

•••

I am a Chelsea fan and tonight we are, against the odds, appearing in the final of the European Champions League against Bayern Munich. We are the underdogs for several reasons; four key players are unavailable through suspension, including skipper John Terry; Bayern had a smoother progression to the finals, implying they are the better side; our centre-backs are both just back from extended absence through injury, and finally Bayern are playing on their home ground – the inspiring Allianz Arena – in front of a crowd of 69,000, dominated by passionate Bavarians. But as Gary Neville put it while summarising, '... sometimes it's written in the stars!' And so it proved as the Blues 'parked the bus' to clinch the draw and then won the most dramatic of penalty shoot-outs against the Germans, with Didier Drogba scoring the winning penalty with his last kick of a ball for Chelsea.

The lessons and parallels for SCCC are clearly evident. Apart from the basic principle that you never give up, it's the importance of an indomitable team spirit forged under duress. I also recall the T20 final at Edgbaston in 2011 when Leicestershire, bottom of CC2, won against all the odds. It was probably written in the stars above Grace Road.

SUNDAY, 20 MAY. TAUNTON

No cricket today – a relatively rare lull in the season! Meanwhile preparations for the County Ground hosting the Olympic Torch are in full swing.

Marcus Trescothick will be playing his part in the history-making 2012 Torch Relay and, despite being still in his plaster cast, is expected to be 'running his leg' early evening.

We are very aware of how fortunate Somerset County Cricket Club is to be involved in such an iconic event. On the evening itself some 6,000 people thronged into the County Ground to witness the torch and attend a related concert.

MONDAY, 21 MAY. TAUNTON

Today is a regular monthly meeting of the MSC (Management Sub-Committee) which has powers delegated to it to run the club as a board might run a company. We are meeting at Milsted Langdon, a local firm of accountants, as our facilities have been given over to LOCOG for the Torch Relay and procession.

As always, the meeting begins with cricket, and Brian Rose reports on several areas: performance, injuries, contracts, overseas players, likely England call-ups, the Academy and the Twos (the Second XI). We've had to cancel some Seconds' fixtures as the side has been raided to support the Firsts!

The discussion on finance is a fairly ordinary voyage through the ups and downs of the profit and loss account and cash flow. We are broadly on course, and the latest estimate for the fiscal year sees us making between £300k and £400k operating profit and about £100k higher at the EBITDA (Earnings Before Interest, Taxation, Depreciation and Amortisation) level.

Guy Lavender briefs the meeting that we've been awarded a four-day first-class fixture against the touring Australians next June. Gasps around the table! This is the equivalent of being a student whose financial position is transformed, out of the blue and for a considerable while, by a windfall from a distant aunt! This news remains embargoed but will be extremely well received by supporters and the region generally.

We then discuss the latest on the ground redevelopment plans. Two main strands to this: first, Phase IV of the project to improve the facilities and increase capacity; second, our application for Category B status and the associated ability to bid for and host England ODIs and T20s. Phase IV also breaks down into separate parts, namely the building to replace the aged and decaying Old Pavilion, and a hotel. We've progress on the former as it seems the new ECB Media deal and associated MOU will include a grant of circa £1m capital towards strategic projects. This allied to some Local Government (Providential) funding at circa 4 per cent over fifteen years and some members' scheme brings the £3m estimated build cost into reach. We decide to progress towards architect's drawings.

The hotel meanwhile appears frozen in aspic, and the worsening economic climate is sending developers and hoteliers scurrying away as fast as the attendees of a WI meeting on seeing a mouse. The important issue now is for any new pavilion replacing the Old Pavilion to be able to accommodate a hotel being attached/integrated at a later date. It's at times like this that we must remember that the club has prospered at the County Ground since 1881, so there's no need for an unseemly rush. Our job as mere stewards of this club is to hand it on in better nick than we found it when our watch began – we won't be betting the club in order to rush a project through.

Lastly we discuss the huge success we had with our age-groups dinner. We resolve to do our bit to include the girls and young women next year and continue to build on the excellent initiative of the Somerset Cricket Board.

•••

I email Giles Clarke – our Elton John tickets and badges have arrived. Elton is performing at the County Ground on Jubilee Sunday. He proclaims he's bringing his own cider, as any self-respecting West Countryman would. It should be a great occasion. Ticket sales are down on expectations owing to poor economic conditions, but we opted not to promote the event, so it's the promoter who takes the financial strain. We can sleep easy and look forward to what will be a superb evening.

TUESDAY, 22 MAY. THE COUNTY GROUND. LVCCI, SOMERSET V DURHAM. DAY I

I'm at my familiar early morning position on Taunton's rail station awaiting a train to London en route to Middlesbrough. A company I chair has its manufacturing facility there, and I'm visiting it before the company's board meeting tomorrow in Harrogate. What is relatively unusual today is the earlier time – I'm catching the 7.18 a.m., and the platform is seething with well over a hundred people. What then strikes me is how many are standing transfixed, staring at their smartphones. A few are stabbing at the screen, either to bring it to life or perhaps playing a game involving some kind of digitised pins and effigies of the boss. Gone are the days when people on the platform would engage in gentle repartee, about cricket or the like. Now, these poor folk are clutching these devices as though they are receiving an infusion of the very elixir of life.

I refuse the urge to do likewise – anyway I just had my own transfusion while sitting in my car ten minutes ago, where amongst other things there was an email from Nick Compton thanking me for a recent introduction to the local BMW dealer, as a result of which he is now the proud recipient of a Beemer on seemingly attractive terms. He has kindly invited me to meet his folks, who are over at the moment from SA. I wish him well and remind him that the entire cricket world want to see him emulate Graeme Hick's 1,000 first-class runs by the end of May. Good luck, Compo.

Another email is from John Stern of *Wisden/Cricketer* magazine fame. I penned an article for him last season and we got on as well as you can do on email! He explains he's at Taunton for the Durham game for *The Times* and would like to meet. I let him know I'm around all day Friday and will seek him out.

A chat with Roy Kerslake reveals that only one Durham Committee member is visiting. Without wishing to sound too sepia about things, there's a noticeable trend of declining numbers of visitors. Somerset is well known for its warm welcome, with generous helpings of food on an almost continuous basis that are legendary. If we're noticing fewer guests it's probably a general trend.

•••

This is a good time to mention the only Committee Room steward in the official ECB county handbook ... our own Frank Betts. Frank came into the world in Birmingham on 21 May 1921 and retired after a long and satisfying career as a publican and hotelier, the sunset of which came at the Cranford Hotel in Exmouth, Devon, in 1983. After just three days at home with his wife, or 'under Deb's feet', and frustrated at not having enough to do, he brought his retirement to an abrupt halt almost as soon as it started. His accountant made a few enquiries and this resulted in a meeting at the County Ground with the then club secretary Des Hunt. Sensing quality, Des moved immediately to take Frank on to run the famous Stragglers Bar on match days. A year later, having played himself in, Frank stepped up to occupy the crease as the County Ground's licensee, taking over from Mrs Webb who had occupied the position for some time. Twenty-eight years later there's no sign of a return to the 'temporarily postponed' retirement and he continues to serve the club, staff and all guests in the club's Committee Room area with great efficiency, courtesy, and a very dry sense of humour.

Frank lost his devoted wife Deb in 2008 after a long battle with cancer, during which Frank also served as her carer. Despite the protestations of many members that he should forgo his Committee Room duties while Deb was ill, he stoically carried on, never once complaining nor showing any signs of duress. The club hosted Deb's wake and a great many club officials and members attended to show their support for him. Now 92 years young, he drives himself to and from Chard every match day – and on quite a few in between – and last season rather proudly notched up not one but two speeding tickets in the process. In the winter he still insists on 'reporting for duty' and he's become a dab hand at decorating. Our St James boxes are now resplendent following titivation by him over the winter. In Essex, blokes like Frank would be called 'diamond geezers'. To us he's just Frank, and he is one of the treasures that are the fabric of Somerset County Cricket Club.

•••

We welcomed back Alfonso Thomas (Fons) today in what turned out to be a tough gig.

Summer had belatedly arrived, and in high temperatures the visitors tucked in. At tea we were looking down the barrels with Durham at 264 for two, but the team kept at their tasks and were rewarded in the final session with a clatter of wickets. As skipper Alfonso said: 'I would certainly have settled for a close of 353 for eight at lunchtime.'

WEDNESDAY, 23 MAY. THE COUNTY GROUND. LVCCI, SOMERSET V DURHAM. DAY 2

I wake in Harrogate where I've a board meeting today and scan *The Times*. Somehow John Stern has the Saeed Ajmal story, which he mentions in his write-up on the day's play. I drop a quick email to Guy Lavender and Brian Rose. My understanding is that Rosey has secured first option to sign him, but we considered this so sensitive that we didn't even mention his name to the MSC on Monday!

There were Twitter stories last night querying whether Marcus' injury has in fact ended his playing career. I decided to nip that in the bud and tweeted the following: 'We don't know when he'll be back: all we know for certain is he will be back. You can't rush a legend. #somersetccc'.

Looks like another hot day in Taunton, so let's hope we can mop up the Durham tail quickly and turn the tables by posting a big total. This is a good opportunity for Compo to clinch the talismanic 1,000 runs. He moved 64 runs closer in what were reported as supreme batting conditions, but he still needs another 67 to make the historic landmark.

We had an up-and-down day, dismissing Durham fairly early on and then moving briskly to 199 for three. Then followed a mini collapse to put the visitors in the driving seat as we lost another three wickets for only ten runs.

•••

The three spires are one of the iconic views in county cricket, and the nearest spire belongs to St Mary's church, which lends us divine inspiration now and again. There has been an annual service for as long as anyone can remember, and this coming Sunday the church will host the 2012 gathering. Fortunately our club chaplain, the Archdeacon of Taunton and even the Bishop of Bath and Wells diocese are all cricket mad, so we shall be in good hands. In 2010 the Bishop's XI played my XI as part of the Diocese's bicentennial celebrations, and a very enthusiastic ecclesiastical crowd turned out to watch a keen contest. Appropriately enough, the more religious side won on the day as my XI ran out of talent at key movements in the game.

ANNUAL CHURCH SERVICE TO TAKE PLACE ON SUNDAY MAY 27TH – SCCC Site

The 2012 Annual Somerset Church Service will be taking place on Sunday May 27th ahead of the CB 40 game against Hampshire on Gimbletts Hill at 12pm.

The guest speaker at the service will be John Reed, the Archdeacon of Taunton, who has been playing clergy cricket for nearly 40 years and is a regular at the County Ground.

Ahead of the service Rob Waldron the SCCC Chaplain who will be in charge of the proceedings on Sunday said: 'I always enjoy the Somerset Church Service which over the years has always been well attended.'

Rob added: 'Due to the current spate of injuries we will be including prayers for healing!'

All are welcome to attend and if the weather is inclement the Church Service will be transferred to the Long Room.

THURSDAY, 24 MAY. THE COUNTY GROUND. LVCCI, SOMERSET V DURHAM. DAY 3

Before leaving for the ECB AGM and the first-class counties chairmen's meeting I popped in for breakfast in the Player's Restaurant. Guy Lavender, Brian Rose and several others joined in with the players. An excellent chance to catch up generally and also to plan a media briefing we are carrying out tomorrow over lunch.

Below is a nice piece by Paul Bolton of the *Daily Telegraph*, which eloquently describes how our young guns put Durham to the sword and also encapsulates how the wickets at Taunton have improved by bringing the bowlers back into the game towards the end of day three.

SOMERSET v DURHAM: TEENAGER GEORGE DOCKRELL LEADS THE YOUNG GUNS TO SWEEPING THREE-DAY VICTORY – Paul Bolton, *Daily Telegraph*

Taunton: Somerset (400-9 dec & 152-5) bt Durham (384 & 167) by 5 wkts

The future of Somerset cricket is in good hands according to their director of cricket, Brian Rose. On day three of this highly entertaining game on a supposedly lifeless Taunton wicket, teenagers George Dockrell and twins Craig and Jamie Overton set up an unlikely but hugely gratifying victory over Durham.

At 18, the twins are the latest in a long line of prodigious youngsters to have been discovered, developed and subsequently exposed to the first-class game by Rose and academy director Jason Kerr. The production line is in good order with Rose confirming that others will follow in the coming seasons.

'We have brought through some seriously good players over the past few years and that's a process I would like to continue,' said Rose.

In this game alone, there were three teenagers on the field and as many more under the age of 25. Twelfth man Lewis Gregory celebrated his 20th birthday yesterday and Craig Meschede and Andrew Dibble, also 20, have already performed with aplomb in the County Championship this summer. However, the pick on this occasion was the 19-year-old Dubliner, Dockrell.

Having played a minor role in guiding Somerset to 400 for nine declared in their first innings, he joined forces with the Overton twins to send Durham cart-wheeling towards a third championship defeat of the season.

Former Somerset all-rounder Ian Blackwell was his first victim at 131 for five, followed in quick succession by Phil Mustard, Liam Plunkett and Callum Thorp. At one stage, the young Irishman had taken four wickets for no runs off 10 balls.

Durham, despite a valiant 32 from Paul Collingwood, were bowled out for 167 with Dockrell finishing with six for 29.

Somerset lost five wickets in chasing 152, but 73 from Arul Suppiah saw them safely home and temporarily to the top of Division One.

THE KIA OVAL. ECB AGM FOLLOWED BY ECB FIRST CLASS COUNTIES CHAIRMEN'S MEETING

I've attended ECB meetings for five years now and they've improved significantly. Meanwhile the fortunes of English cricket have improved immeasurably as a good management team has got to work on key aspects of the game.

Relations with Government are comfortably the best of any of the major sports, and concrete evidence of this was the excellent co-operation over the Pakistan betting scandal which broke during their tour in 2010; similarly the decision by Government to allow the Edgbaston Test to proceed during the social unrest in the 2011 summer, and finally the decision to preserve the present broadcasting status of international cricket in the UK. None of these events received widespread coverage, but without doubt if any of these decisions had gone 'the wrong way' the repercussions for cricket would have been serious. Big financial hits cause significant collateral damage as the law of unintended consequences gets to work.

The ECB now has financial reserves destined to settle at around £30m, and this provides the game with the ability to withstand a severe shock such as a sudden cancellation of a Test match. The investment in recreational (amateur) cricket has also been increased with concomitant results in the middle. Participation levels are up across the board as well-funded and well-organised initiatives like 'Chance to Shine' have preached the gospel of cricket in deprived urban areas. Girls' and women's cricket are booming and of course England's women's team is the world's leader. It's the same positive story in disabled cricket, where our own county, captained by Jon Tucker, are the dominant team, having won the national title several times in recent years.

England's men's team is the best in the world at present, which we've never been able to say before. The victory in the T20 World Cup presaged a golden era for our national side which subsequently went on to clinch the number one position in Test cricket as well. These things just don't happen by accident.

Both of today's meetings, compared to some volcanic ones I've attended previously, proceed without incident and we chairmen are briefed at our meeting by the ECB executives on the prospects and likely outcomes of the new media deals from 2014. These will form the basis of the MOUs (Memoranda of Understanding) between the ECB and each of the eighteen counties. This revenue forms an important part of any county's income and is usually received with simultaneous feelings of relief and disappointment. What is plain is that the ECB are going to be increasingly demanding on setting standards for counties to achieve and each of us will be incentivised and encouraged (stick and carrot) to do better against a set of objectives.

Relations between fellow county chairmen are very cordial. We are all unpaid volunteers and consequently we supposedly retain some sanity and perspective in our honorary roles. We would all gladly kill each other on the pitch, but off it there's a very good level of sharing of lessons learned and best practice. An excellent example has been the ECB's initiative of using the mystery shopper technique to compare and contrast how well each county deals with enquiries for ticket purchases. All the results are way below American service standards in the NFL for example (no surprise there), but even at our uniformly lower level the mystery shoppers had quite a voyage of discovery. Gordon Hollins, to whom it fell to break the findings to us, quite wisely preserved the dignity of those with truly Jurassic service levels, drawing a veil of anonymity over their findings. Our CEOs had been given the very same results recently and it was plain that those in disgrace had possibly not yet got around to sharing the feedback with their chairmen! We at Somerset got a pretty good end of term report, with a few 'could do betters' which we are working on. The meeting petered out rather than finished due to a dearth of complaints or lectures around the table so we adjourned to sample some delightful Surrey hospitality at the 'People's Oval'. It had been described as such earlier in the day as a mischievous counterpoint to the recent reports – accurate or otherwise – that the Lord's redevelopment is to be rather asymmetrically progressed in favour of the members' facilities.

A very fine BBQ was enjoyed by all present. The Chairman of Durham, Clive Leach, whom I've known for over twenty years, had to leave early – much to my chagrin – as back in Taunton our young guns were giving his elder statesmen a real hammering.

There's no doubt in my mind that one of the most attractive and endearing features of the domestic game is the great variety amongst the counties. We all prosper and suffer in almost equal measure over the long term, and rarely in the field of human endeavour are Kipling's impostors of triumph and disaster met so often. The agonies of the counties as we take it in turns to navigate periods of failure, duress and member insurrection, are the salt which gives this great game of ours its flavour.

The day's results from the various contests our teams have been engaged in begin to filter through, but we are all far too diplomatic to allow either schadenfreude or despair to be openly displayed. Surreptitious glances at smartphones are an art form at such occasions, and even though I'm well tooled up with my iPhone, Giles Clarke on his antediluvian Blackberry is somehow ahead of me on the score from Taunton. The meeting, now well infused with Pimms, wine and bonhomie, has morphed into a social gathering and after supper the guests begin to drift away in ones and twos as the evening draws to a close. Mutual invitations are strewn like confetti, and the good thing is that many will be heartily taken up as the season progresses. Richard Gould walks with me to the Hobbs Gates and we bid farewell. I reflect, on my journey back to the Docklands, how lucky I've been to work with CEOs of the calibre of him and Guy Lavender. Both are truly exceptional operators and outstanding colleagues.

FRIDAY, 25 MAY. TAUNTON

Returning from meetings yesterday I've enjoyed reading on the train, courtesy of my iPad, the many positive comments and write-ups in professional and social media of our 'young guns'.

On arrival at Taunton I drop in at the ground, where my car is parked, to see Guy Lavender and discuss the ECB meetings and various issues arising therefrom. I finally locate him with Dazz in the indoor school. Dazz is looking on with an expression mingling confusion and anxiety as our CEO is busy packing his own parachute for a jump later this afternoon! Lavender is an ex-Para. Neither of us wants to put him off for fear he might pack it incorrectly! We make a tactical withdrawal and leave him to it. I'm reminded of an ad in our local paper: 'Parachute for sale. One owner. Never opened. Small stain.'

•••

I wander over to the outdoor nets and watch our lads going through a pretty strenuous session in the tropical heat. There's a really great buzz as the senior pros are putting the younger guys through their paces.

•••

Elton John has withdrawn from three concerts in the USA this week following a respiratory illness which put him in hospital! The promoter, Marshall Arts, has made reassuring noises. He probably hasn't heard of our curse on foreign arrivals this season. Perhaps one of our young bucks could stand in – they've done pretty well so far!

SATURDAY, 26 MAY. TAUNTON

The team enjoy a few days off, having earned an extra one by winning in three days against Durham, and gear themselves up for the CB40 on Sunday. The weather is Mediterranean and a very large crowd is expected. Having lost our two opening games in the 'Group of Death' we badly need a win tomorrow to be in the mix for the final stages.

SUNDAY, 27 MAY. THE COUNTY GROUND. CB40, SOMERSET V HAMPSHIRE

The day breaks hot and still, and various phone calls make today's arrangements. As the County Room is fully booked for Sunday lunches, we and the Lavenders are sharing the Sammy Woods box with several guests. The only snag is that this box is a glass cage and has no balcony, so we've made plans to escape what will be the most suffocatingly hot room as soon as we can after lunch.

A good crowd in excess of 4,000 bask in the glorious Somerset sunshine, but not alas in the result. We are thrashed by Hampshire who sail past our well-constructed total with consummate ease as openers Adams and Carberry put on almost half the required amount in just 15 overs. We've now lost our opening three CB40 fixtures and dreams of a third successive Lord's final are receding. Other than a convivial lunch it was a day to forget.

TUESDAY, 29 MAY.

The Seconds are back in action, having had to cancel some fixtures because we couldn't raise eleven fit men. Their ranks had also been depleted by several being selected for first-team duty.

I note from newsnow.co.uk that Gloucester's appeal is due to be heard by the Planning Committee on Wednesday. It looks very challenging for them whether they win or lose, frankly – I expect them to win, but as we know only too well, winning planning consent is the easy bit of redevelopment. You then have to turn plans into funded reality, which in this climate is going to be extremely challenging.

Fast bowler Steve Kirby, who is returning to fitness after a period of injury, played club cricket on Saturday and will play in the second of the two Seconds games today. We need him back to lead the attack. Tregs and the youngsters are doing brilliantly well to hold it together, but the strain on them is considerable. Gemaal, although featuring against Durham in the CB40, is also being nursed back to fitness after a serious injury.

WEDNESDAY, 30 MAY. WORCESTER. LVCCI, WORCESTERSHIRE V SOMERSET. DAY 1

A piece I come across on Cricinfo reminds me of the sheer brilliance of Viv Richards in his prime. According to everyone who witnessed it, on this day in 1984 he played what has been acclaimed as the greatest innings in one-day international history, smashing England all round Old Trafford in the first Texaco Trophy match. His score of 189 came off only 170 balls, with twenty-one fours and five sixes. What made the innings so great was its context: West Indies were 102 for seven at one point, then 166 for nine. Thanks to Viv they ended up making 272 for nine, and went on to win by 104 runs. Of the last-wicket partnership of 106, Michael Holding made 12. Eldine Baptiste was the only other West Indian even to reach double figures.

Now Nick Compton is on the threshold of achieving another landmark in cricket history if he can score another 59 runs to add to the 941 he already has. He has potentially six sessions and two innings – weather permitting! He would become the first batter for twenty-four years to reach the target.

•••

It doesn't go to plan. We lose the toss and Worcester decide to bat. They do so all day and close on 270 for three.

•••

No comment has yet been made on the fact that Alfonso Thomas is skippering the side. This will be picked up in due course. Guy Lavender and I discussed this on Monday when Hildy asked Rosey to be relieved of the captaincy for personal reasons. We respected that but saw no advantage in a proactive announcement at that stage.

THURSDAY, 31 MAY. WORCESTER. LVCCI, WORCESTERSHIRE V SOMERSET. DAY 2

How typical of this game! Compo has been held up not only by the pure chance of us losing the toss but also by the first century opening partner-ship Worcester have managed all season! I spoke to Roy Kerslake, who put it succinctly – he said we would bowl a whole lot worse than we did and take a stack of wickets!

After some typically spirited bowling from Tregs, who achieved a five-for, we opened our account. After thirty minutes Alex 'Bazz' Barrow was removed and Compo came in to try and make history. He didn't fail, but he didn't succeed either, the bloody weather denying him his chance. Play was abandoned after three hours of rainfall, leaving Compo stranded not out but still a few runs short.

JUNE

June is well known for being a record-breaking month for cricket in Somerset. Over four days in June 1899 (or four afternoons to be more exact) at a junior house match at Clifton College between Clarke's and North Town, Arthur Edward Jeune 'James' Collins recorded the highest ever score in cricket of 628, batting for a total of six hours fifty minutes. He was somewhat 'ahead of the clock'. Not content dominating with the bat, in the best tradition of Somerset all-rounders, he went on to take seven for 33 in North Town's first innings and four for 30 in the second. Unsurprisingly, his side came out on top and nicked the match by an innings and 688 runs.

Collins was commissioned into the Royal Engineers and, sadly, he was killed in action along with several of his pals in the First Battle of Ypres in 1914. Who knows what might have become of him on the cricket field? A plaque commemorating his historic innings was installed at Clifton College in 1962.

FRIDAY, I JUNE. WORCESTER. LVCCI, WORCESTERSHIRE V SOMERSET. DAY 3

You know even before play resumes that cricket being cricket will see Compo make his required runs ... but a day late! He did leapfrog Kent's Rob Key, who got there on 2 June in 2004, and thus became the earliest to reach this milestone in twenty-four years since Worcestershire's Graeme Hick posted 1,000 on 28 May 1988. Chasing 340 we made our way to 277 for seven by the time play was halted for bad light – with Compo sailing on towards 1,100 runs with a combative and well-constructed hundred.

•••

I speak to my commissioning editor at The History Press today, and she tells me they are publishing Paul Nixon's autobiography and that some of Nico's content is going to be pretty sensational. No pressure on me, then! I rack my brain for more salacious stuff ... and then I remember I'm the club's Chairman, so discretion must form the greater part of valour!

I popped into the club earlier and saw the preparations for the Elton John concert on Sunday evening. Something which looks as though it came from the set of *Close Encounters of the Third Kind* is now squatting in front of the Old Pavilion, and our effervescent groundsman Simon Lee is stalking the contractors, ensuring his beloved square is well protected. Two other items of note occur: first, Lisa in accounts manages to overcharge me on my account by a couple of grand owing to some ghastly accounting error; second, the ECB Chairman, who is attending with Judy, has let it be known he's bringing his own drink – rumoured to be a local cider! Despite a chat with Guy Lavender, Giles is unimpressed that the promoters are in charge of the venue and have a strict no-BYO policy. So, I can predict that the immovable object will meet the irresistible force at the Prior Bridge Road gate sometime early on Sunday evening. I know who my money is on!

•••

The media still haven't picked up that we've switched captain – our third in as many months. Hopefully this will now be a minor item as and when it's reported.

SATURDAY, 2 JUNE. WORCESTER. LVCCI, WORCESTERSHIRE V SOMERSET. DAY 4

The match looks dead as a contest without a deal between the captains: too much time has been lost to rain and bad light. However, there are some things to savour. Bagel removed his pads and then took two wickets for three runs with his off spin. He now leads our bowling averages for the season. The other highlights were Bazz's first-class debut as a wickie and of course Tregs' and Compo's individual efforts with bat and ball.

However, two pieces of news lift the wintry gloom! First, I receive a text from Brian Rose explaining that we've agreed terms with the mighty Irishman Kevin O'Brien, who will be strengthening our squad for the T20. This comes with a health warning that our neighbours and old adversaries Gloucester are likely to be 'surprised and disappointed' that he's moving south.

The second positive bit of news is our own public announcement that we are to be the first county to host Australia on the 2013 Ashes tour. This is a great honour for the club and one we shall rise to make the very most of. It will be a big boon for supporters, who will come in their hoards to see Somerset's finest attempt to puncture the Aussies' confidence and unsettle their build-up for the Test series by inflicting a defeat, as we've proudly done to several touring sides in the past. It will also be a boost for us financially, and the local community commercially, as the first three days will sell out and – weather permitting – we'll set new attendance records at the County Ground.

I met up with Guy Lavender at Olio and Farina's and we had one of our regular catch-ups where we discuss the club's many affairs. As always our topics ranged from the stratospheric (hosting the opening first-class game against Australia next season before the Ashes series begins) to the more mundane (ice-cream parlour sales). One item of major significance is the confirmation that the ECB are to change the basis on which the annual payments to the counties are distributed. Instead of flat payments to all eighteen over a five-year period, an increasing element of 'performance related' measures will feature. We applaud this as it gives us the opportunity to press for more improvements and success, both in terms of the development of more excellent young players for England and further ground improvements in capacity and facilities. Specifically we can make the case for up to £1m in grant monies to part fund the new pavilion which is needed to replace the ageing Old Pavilion and St James Stand. This has the potential to facilitate the next phase (Phase IV) of the redevelopment of the County Ground. We need to ensure we seize the potential offered by this policy.

SUNDAY, 3 JUNE. THE COUNTY GROUND. THE ELTON JOHN CONCERT

Sir Elton first came to our club in 2006, when a crowd of 20,000 turned out to enjoy a terrific evening. The problem with staging concerts is that there are more venues than concerts, so supply and demand are out of kilter. This year we've been successful in again persuading Marshall Arts, the promoters, to select the County Ground to host another spectacular. It is the Queen's Diamond Jubilee weekend too, so the stage was set for a great occasion and we weren't to be disappointed.

Numbers attending were down, probably as a result of competing Jubilee events, and also economic hardship caused by successive years of recession.

The set and ground looked terrific and we arrived to find queues stretching back almost to the station! The weather was reminiscent of last season's T20 campaign when we had four home games completely washed out. It started raining at breakfast and it continued intermittently throughout the day. Just before the support act, 2cellos, began, the heavens really opened – it was almost as if the cricketing gods were sending us a message about a rock concert being staged upon one of the games most hallowed squares.

The revellers' and the band's enthusiasm remained undimmed. In the same way Somerset crowds of old stoically withstood a procession of abject defeats, this crowd were determined to party and we witnessed several surreal sights. Chairman of the ECB, Giles Clarke, clearly enjoyed himself and at one stage began rhythmically gyrating to the music, although judging by his movements he appeared to be listening to a different song to the rest of us. Appropriately enough someone arrived as the Queen in all her finery, while it was hard to sort some of the others in fancy dress from those simply trying to keep dry.

I couldn't help but notice with Guy Lavender that the dreadful weather did have one beneficial effect – our bars and catering outlets were besieged as people either sought refuge from the rain or simply decided to drink their cares away. It looked as though we were going to have a bumper evening on the commercial front.

The evening looked to be a huge success, and a well-sated and ecstatic crowd finally dispersed around 9.30 p.m. after an encore of 'Your Song' rounded off a set lasting almost two and a half hours by the master entertainer. The County Ground has hosted some amazing events and sights since 1881, but this one will have been right up there and will have generated some fine and enduring memories for all those present.

MONDAY, 4 JUNE. TRENT BRIDGE. CB40, NOTTINGHAMSHIRE V SOMERSET

I went past the ground this morning on my early morning bike ride (my nod to a healthy lifestyle!) and saw that the dismantlement of the set was progressing surprisingly fast. This spurs me to drop an email to our CEO, to congratulate him on another job very well done and also to 'compliment' him on his dancing. He emailed back and said that he hadn't been fitting, as I'd suggested, but moving involuntarily and broadly in time with the beat thanks to some lubrication from Thatchers' finest!

GROCKLES

As an antidote to more Jubilee stuff I have a casual look at the latest from the Grockles. They are passionate Somerset fans and cricket enthusiasts who exchange their views on a site called grockles.com

Sites such as this have their detractors because, protected by a veil of anonymity, posts can be inappropriate, sometimes rude and on occasions downright libellous. It is a fact of life that people in public roles and positions get abused, and some people must surprise even themselves at just how much bile they can muster.

Grockles, I'm very glad to say, is an exception to the rule and I think they are an exemplar of how such sites could and, frankly, should be run. The site is characterised by banter and interesting comments and some very perceptive and thought-provoking points. The analysis can also be very well-researched and would make professionals like The Analyst doff his cap. The site is well moderated – not an easy role – and as a result it is a force for good in Somerset cricket, and I'm relieved that the club doesn't find itself in a hostile stand-off as a great many professional sports clubs do. I respect their views and as a ginger group in our midst they have a real role and contribution to make. It's very plain to any reader that they are first and foremost genuine Somerset fans and their emotions ebb and flow along with our fortunes.

They have made some interesting comments about Notts under an article entitled 'The bridge of sighs' and, like me, have a feeling in their bones that we will win today and finally get our CB40 campaign on track.

It wasn't to be, and 'bridge of sighs' turned out to be right. Our total of 209 never looked like enough and so it proved. Our fourth consecutive defeat has all but extinguished our CB40 campaign, as only the three divisions' leaders and the best second-placed county compete in the semi-finals. I've always maintained there is a strong argument for quarter-finals, as once counties are effectively beyond hope of a semi-final slot, cricket managers, coaches and captains almost inevitably decide it is better to rest key players and focus on the competitions where the opportunity of a trophy remains. Once this happens, the quality of the cricket and the intensity of competition begin to fade and the supporters can be left feeling a little short-changed.

TUESDAY, 5 JUNE. LORD'S. LVCCI, MIDDLESEX V SOMERSET. DAY 1

A welcome relief from our poor start with the white ball is now in prospect as newly promoted Middlesex entertain us. This promises to be a stiff contest as on paper the visitors' squad looks strong in all departments, but especially perhaps in the seam bowling department.

However, rain once again had the final say at Lord's where, despite the fact it is only the first week in June, this will be Middlesex's penultimate first-class match of the season at home. By the time the heavens opened at 3 p.m., only 48 overs had been completed. The players retreated into the pavilion and that was it for the day. Our hosts had the best of the day's play, reducing us to 130 for four, with each of the four bowlers on show taking a wicket.

WEDNESDAY, 6 JUNE. LORD'S. LVCCI, MIDDLESEX V SOMERSET. DAY 2

With Guy Wolfenden having moved onwards and upwards to Edgbaston, we have been running a process to recruit our new Head of Marketing and Sales. The search and recruitment specialist Peter Tucker of Novo Executive produced Guy Lavender for us, so we are hoping his purple patch will continue on this assignment. Guy, Steve Elworthy the ECB Marketing Director, Charles Clark and myself form the interviewing panel. Our CEO, to his great credit, has organised the process with military precision and has even prepared questions for us to use, allocating them to each of us. I catch a mischievous glint in Charles Clark's eye as we spot the opportunity to sow confusion amongst the panel by either asking someone else's questions or by going completely off-piste with some new ones. We stuck to the plan for the first candidate, but by the time we got to the fourth a somewhat more freewheeling approach was under way. The candidates were a very capable cross-section from rugby, football, horse racing and, interestingly, Butlins! All four gave a very good account of themselves throughout the day, and the presentations we asked them to prepare produced some very original and pragmatic suggestions for how the club could do better in marketing and selling itself.

We graded the candidates on several criteria and staggeringly we were unanimous in our rating and prioritising of them! Guy was left to ruminate overnight and we said we would talk in the morning.

Meantime, at Lord's, things could hardly be going any worse! The Middlesex top order was filling its boots and each and every checking of the score in between candidates' interviews produced audible groans.

A magnificent stand of 245 between Chris Rogers and Joe Denly ensured that Middlesex are now well on top in this game. Earlier, Tim Murtagh, Toby Roland-Jones and Gareth Berg had claimed three scalps each as we succumbed for 173 – losing our last five wickets for just 43 runs.

This looks to be nowhere near enough after Middlesex skipper Rogers made 173 at almost a run a ball and Kent import Denly contributed an unbeaten 105 as the hosts closed on 321 for two – a lead of 148.

THURSDAY, 7 JUNE. LORD'S. LVCCI, MIDDLESEX V SOMERSET. DAY 3

I am travelling to Spain today for business and pleasure and am delighted to be escaping from probably the wettest early summer in living memory. The weather forecasts are uniformly terrible, which is exactly what I wanted to hear. Our only chance of saving this game, and thus hopefully maintaining our position of third in the table through the break for T20, is for several sessions to be lost to rain. The weather gods duly oblige and most of the day is a wash-out. Conversely, on arrival in Barcelona I'm reminded of why my family and I love this country so much – something to do with over 300 days of sunshine a year.

The first day of the Third Test against the West Indies is also a total wash-out, which will be very expensive for Warwickshire and the ECB as all tickets are to be refunded and the expected windfall from catering and bar sales will be decimated. I was at Wawks earlier in the season and their Treasurer very kindly gave me a tour of their magnificent new facilities. These didn't come cheap, of course, and the club's balance sheet is currently freighted with over £30m of debt – an eye-watering sum for a cricket club.

FRIDAY, 8 JUNE. LORD'S. LVCCI, MIDDLESEX V SOMERSET. DAY 4

While I awoke to utterly magnificent Mediterranean conditions, things at home were going from bad to worse. Flash floods had engulfed parts of mid Wales and the cricket schedule was being decimated.

For the first time in decades a second successive day at a Test match was abandoned without a ball being bowled. My friends at Edgbaston will be cursing their bad luck as losses against expectation will be substantial and, unlike in most businesses, there's no prospect of recovering them.

Bizarrely, a micro system of dry weather took hold over Lord's and almost a full day's play was possible. Middlesex immediately declared, forsaking the certainty of a fifth batting point to press for victory. It was a torrid day for Somerset, as it was for me, following the score. Wickets fell with grim regularity and, but for stubborn resistance by Compo, skipper and Tregs, we would have lost.

I exchanged SMS messages with my opposite number at Middlesex, Ian Lovett, and let him know how lucky he had been! But for the rain I was confident we would have been 100 ahead at stumps last night and would have given them a torrid session and a bit to withstand today! He rightly wasn't having any of it and enquired if I had thought about working for Sky as a pundit.

SATURDAY, 9 JUNE.

For players, coaches and managers a welcome mid-season mini-break now takes place, with the Championship suspended while the T20 block is played. The competition has become the fulcrum upon which many counties' finances now pivot. But it is the weather which is the main concern for the counties. Charles Hartwell, the Finance Director at Yorkshire, says: 'We have a home T20 fixture against Lancashire at the end of June. We are hoping for a crowd of 13,000. That match alone should earn us more than all our Championship games put together, so it's very important to us that it goes ahead. Financially, T20 cricket is very, very important to us. The format captures a different audience and brings in bigger crowds.' For a county who worship the long format – having won it more times than any other county – their Treasurer's public love affair with T20 will probably have several Yorkshire members on smelling salts!

The tournament has been reduced to ten fixtures this season, so we are left praying that the weather doesn't wreck as many matches as it did last season when we had four home games washed out. At Somerset each T20 fixture generates on average as much revenue as two whole Championship matches – eight days of cricket – and the equivalent of four home CB40 games. It follows that they are financially very significant to our club too. Consequently we insure against bad weather which, while not fully compensating us, does help cushion the blow in the event of abandonment. Our premiums, however, have risen markedly due to our four claims in 2011. The bottom line, as the accountants and treasurers would remind us, is that with fewer fixtures this season the weather has the potential to smash counties' financial compasses to bits. I shall keep my fingers tightly crossed.

The signing of Kevin O'Brien is also publicly confirmed today – we've done well to attract him as he is a very effective exponent of the short game with bat and ball. I'm sure he will also add some energy to the dressing room as sometimes only someone from the Emerald Isle can. There are no problems with his registration, thankfully, as being Irish he doesn't fall into the morass of difficulties which affect 'overseas' players.

SUNDAY, 10 JUNE.

Returning from Spain and I am following the Test match en route and I'm reminded of cricket's ability to confound everyone and overturn expectations. Before play began yesterday the overwhelming view in the *TMS* box was that, given the wicket had been sweating under covers for two days, this was not a toss to lose as the seamers would be making it go around corners. The reality was far from it. Schadenfreude was most definitely evident amongst the commentators as England captain Strauss won the toss and invited Darren Sammy to bat.

A day later, as I board my flight home, the West Indies have just gone through 400 and there are contributions right the way down the order. Now, far from expecting the West Indies to be rolled over in the three remaining days of this Test, you would have to say the odds are moving in their favour, as runs on the board exert pressure, and pressure means mistakes by the side who are chasing.

As I disembark at Bristol the early collapse confirms my fears – the front three are back in the hutch for a little over 60! But what a cameo played by Tino Best, the greatest ever Test innings by a number eleven coming in at eleven. Yet again, this game's ability to produce the unexpected is what keeps all of us fans hooked.

MONDAY, 11 JUNE. THE COUNTY GROUND

On Monday morning another of my regular catch-up sessions with Guy Lavender, who continues to remain unrelentingly positive despite no shortage of challenges! We discuss, *inter alia*, financial results for April, latest player arrivals for the T20, the appointment of our new Head of Marketing and Sales, the leaking roof in Olio & Farina's, a forthcoming schoolteachers versus dads match, Phase IV of the ground redevelopment, overseas players' accommodation, Kent's renewed financial challenges following the wash-out of their festival at Tunbridge Wells, logistics for the forthcoming T20 fixtures, the Elton John concert debrief, student labour over the holidays, England's selection of Somerset players for the ODI and T20 squads which will be announced tomorrow, progress on this book, and the forthcoming ECB Major Match Group visit in July and our planning in advance of it. Oh yes, and we discussed the bloody weather forecast: rain is forecast *every* day in Taunton for the next week! Our insurance underwriters will be getting twitchy once again, as will we because advance ticket sales have been very strong indeed; we can look forward to a bonanza in takings in our food outlets and bars – provided the sun shines!

Reflecting on our meeting as I write this, I'm struck again by the sheer breadth and diversity of the work involved in the running of a cricket club. The club's full-time executives really do need the ability to manage 'up and down' and to be extraordinarily flexible, as the topics they face range from the very challenging to the more urbane and repetitive. Routine certainly isn't the word to describe what they do.

•••

With the T20 fast approaching, this is perhaps a good time to reflect on this format's present position. The format was 'introduced' to the professional game in England back in 2003, so it is now in its tenth season. It was conceived and launched as an antidote to the decline of audiences (live and TV) for the first-class game, which was causing a great deal of angst in cricket generally.

The 'new' format rapidly took hold from 2003 and very quickly the newborn baby was off the teat and on to solids. By 2005 – when Somerset won the competition – it was a muscular and adolescent youth well on its way to becoming a mainstream format of the game. There have been a few wrong turns along the way, most notably the game's ill-conceived and short-lived partnership with a con man based in the Caribbean; but with the benefit of hindsight they will probably be described by cricket historians as growing pains of a sort. As part of the 'review' into what went wrong, including how we ever got into bed with Stanford, we came across some very amusing anecdotes. One which appealed to me was the story to emerge from a helicopter charter company. Naturally the ECB took Stanford at his word when he landed his 'company' chopper on the hallowed turf at Lord's as the Stanford T20 competition was launched. Rich, successful corporations often show a penchant for things which fly and float, so there was no reason to be particularly suspicious at the time. After the event, however, it transpired that his company didn't own the chopper at all! Apparently his entourage arrived at the helicopter charter company with various stickers bearing Stanford corporation logos and slogans; the manager at the charter company did raise his eyebrows on seeing Stanford's flunkeys plastering the airframe with the tacky golden stickers, but kept his own counsel at the time!

The two huge advantages T20 has are the length of the contest, which at about two and a half hours' playing time reflects what most sports fans can give to a contest (and I'm referring here to those who regularly follow football and rugby in winter and cricket in summer – their numbers dwarf those who will spend days on end at a county's ground watching Championship cricket) and the fact that, perhaps uniquely, the spectators are spellbound as something happens literally with every ball. Dot balls are the least exciting to watch for the 'lite' cricket fan; but even they will be cheered and appreciated by the fielding side's supporters.

There are still some members on smelling salts over the introduction of T20, but they are now in a shrinking minority. Top coaches and players all testify to the technical improvements in batting, bowling and fielding brought about by the new format. It has attracted many new supporters into the game, as attendances at most grounds are the highest of any format in the domestic game. Another benefit seldom highlighted is that it has provided the game with a new recruiting sergeant: prior to T20 many of cricket's brightest young talents were lost to the 'bigger' sports of football and rugby. T20 has allowed the game to retain some of the best athletes as the attractions of playing to far greater crowds, in more vibrant atmospheres, not to mention the greater sums now on offer for playing the game, have combined to improve a young cricketer's view of his career prospects.

The ECB (and I refer here to the ECB as its widest community) is still playing the hokey-cokey with this format as we struggle to find the optimal schedule for the competition. It has expanded and contracted in recent years like a pair of bellows as the game's policy makers have been confused by the way some counties have had astonishing success, with record crowds, while others have only managed to attract a few hundred fans. I'm convinced the format is here to stay and wouldn't be surprised to see the 50/40 format giving way in the long term. I say this because over time the supporter will govern which formats succeed – large attendances create an atmosphere fans enjoy and like to experience regularly. Any format playing to mainly empty grounds is in a vulnerable place, because if the seats are empty in the ground then so are the sofas at home. The media deals and all that they pay for are the difference between cricket being a major sport or a minority's pastime. The ECB had an annual income of £146m in 2011, and a significant part of that came from media deals. ESPN, Channel 9 and Sky will all play a key role in shaping the future game, because they are the conduit through which many of the fan's demands will be routed.

At the end of the day we should celebrate the fact that this great game of ours now has three mainstream formats which all work at present. Using an analogy with music, first-class cricket, much like classical music, can hold its admirers spellbound for considerable periods of time in one sitting. T20 is to cricket perhaps what rock bands are to music: a riot of noise and colour (for some lovers of classical music an unseemly din enjoyed by young layabouts), and all done and dusted relatively quickly. The 50/40 might be the Easy Listening or 'Radio 2' of the cricket world – definitely with a role to play and with a distinctive following, sandwiched between 'Radio 1' and 'Radio 3'.

The Morgan Review is, of course, directly caught in the flight path of the debate about the season's optimal fixture list, and later in the year some decisions will be made in respect of the 2014 season. T20 will be at the heart of this, and I expect this element of the game to be expanded once again, although the debate over whether to play it in a block – which allows the recruitment of the world's finest talent to add quality and lustre – or spread out over a longer period to provide ATV (appointment to view) with games following the tried and tested routes in football and rugby of a home game every other week, will be robust and colourful enough to almost be a spectator sport in its own right.

There will still be some people hankering after the urban franchise model. This was a stillborn concept in 2009, and as it came to light there followed a period of quite rancorous recriminations, the culmination of which was the litigation between ECB Chairman Giles Clark and plaintiffs IMG and Lalit Modi.

Commenting on this, let alone recommending the optimal format for the English domestic season, has almost become a contact sport, so I will simply make a forecast. I have an inkling that the following, or something pretty close to it, will be settled upon:

County Championship. No change. The benefits of the two divisions of nine have produced cricket of high quality and great intensity, and it is achieving its principle *raison d'être*, i.e. producing Test cricketers for Team England. First-class cricket will be played at the start of the week.

T20. Two divisions, with games played at home every other week on Fridays/Saturdays through the season. The block will be dropped.

CB40. This will take the brunt of the reduction in days sought by the ECB.

I anticipate a structure similar to that of the old C&G Trophy which ran successfully between 2000 and 2006. A bit like the FA Cup, it featured in the first two rounds only the Minor Counties and some of the eighteen first-class County Cricket Boards. From Round Three the rest of the professional counties joined in the knock-out competition. I'd expect the 40-over format to be retained (and sincerely hope it will be) because of the very strong preference for it by supporters who like the 1:45 p.m. start at weekends.

Beyond 2014 we must wait for the ICC's decision in respect of the balance of the limited-overs formats. In considering this, one should remember that the ICC's prime objective is to increase the number of countries playing cricket – it is not to maximise participation or audience levels in countries where the game is already mature and well-established. Based on falling attendances for the 50 ODIs almost everywhere save in England, it is quite possible that after the 2015 World Cup they will decide that the 50 will be jettisoned entirely in favour of the T20. Two countries where the ICC are resolved to establish cricket as a mainstream sport are the USA and China. The nascent T20 league in the USA and the increasing popularity of T20 in China (20,000 players and 2,000 coaches targeted by 2015) are pretty significant clues as to which way the wind is blowing! Were this to happen, as I think it will over the next five or ten years, unfortunately the rationale for the 40 will be gravely undermined. Its demise could come with the introduction of a second domestic T20 competition played in a block alongside the established season long Friday/Saturday league.

While I know for certain that I'll be wrong in forecasting the above, I'm not sure exactly how wrong I'll be – as with most forecasts made about cricket, I could well be very wide of the mark!

Some very interesting points made by England Team Director Andy Flower, interviewed on Sky by Mike Atherton at the conclusion of the series against the West Indies. The interview predictably focused on the recent and newsworthy retirement of KP from all limited-overs cricket for England. During the interview Andy Flower stated that ECB policy is at least in part designed to protect the 50-over game – he also admitted that KP wouldn't be alone in retiring from the traditional ODI format if the option were available.

The stage is now very well set, with England leading South Africa by just one point in the ICC Test rankings going into the three-match series next month. Somerset have a two-day fixture against the Saffies starting on 9 July, when we shall attempt to emulate the rigorous work-outs we have provided other tourists in the past. Our defeat of the Australians in a 50-over match prior to the 2005 series springs to mind, as does the very tough match we gave India last year where we ground them down to clearly 'win' the draw. Both sides' shortcomings were brutally exposed by

Somerset and neither truly recovered their composure in the remainder of their tours; both of which were convincingly won by England.

TUESDAY, 12 JUNE. THE COUNTY GROUND

We have been continuing to work behind the scenes on Phase IV of the redevelopment of the County Ground. The way ahead is becoming clearer, and Guy Lavender, Nick Engert and I are now aligned on the best way to proceed. Nick is one of the region's leading real estate and planning lawyers, who has been co-opted onto the club's MSC and General Committee.

I would summarise the current position as follows: redevelopment of the County Ground (improved facilities and increased capacity) began in 2004, and since then Phases I, II and III have been achieved to a very high standard and have incurred only a prudent level of debt – which is being paid to schedule. Despite severe economic headwinds we are now clear on how Phase IV could be realised. We need to complete this phase, as the Old Pavilion and St James Stand on the southern boundary are at the end of their useful working lives. Last year a structural survey confirmed their deficiencies and ruled out refurbishment as a viable economic option. A new pavilion-type building in this position will provide additional seating capacity, improved facilities for members and supporters and also additional year-round revenue-generating assets. When this is completed we will be able to achieve the outstanding conditions for the County Ground to be granted Category B status at a relatively modest incremental cost.

The hotel will be treated as a separate Phase V and can literally be 'bolted on' to the new pavilion as a future self-financing project – probably when economic conditions are more benign.

After a great deal of thought and consideration, and many moving parts, the way ahead for the next phase of the the County Ground's development now seems clear. Over the next twelve months we will work up the proposals, costings and aim to secure the support of the club's General Committee, ECB and other stakeholders. The importance of achieving Phase IV to Somerset's long-term future prosperity and wellbeing cannot be overstated. The County Ground will be one of the finest grounds in cricket, with outstanding facilities for players, staff and supporters, and with the means of generating solid year-round turnover and a healthy ongoing surplus. This will be boosted as and when we are selected to stage England ODIs and T20s.

•••

Meanwhile back to our core business of playing cricket. The hype and practice are under way in earnest as hard preparations take place, with some Seconds matches and also squad training at the County Ground. Every narrative coming out of the club on T20 shimmers with hope, as it must on the eve of this vital competition.

LEVI AND MORKEL HONING THEIR SIX HITTING SKILLS AT COUNTY GROUND – SCCC Site

Somerset's two T20 overseas signings Albie Morkel and Richard Levi were honing their six hitting skills at the County Ground on Monday morning ahead of the first home fixture against Warwickshire which gets underway at 5.30pm on Wednesday.

The South African pair have both got impressive records in T20 and are hoping that they will bring that little bit extra that Somerset need to see them across the winning line in 2012, after three seasons as runners up.

Right handed batsman Levi said: 'It's great to be here at Taunton, although I was greeted by a bit of rain. However that seems to be clearing up and hopefully we will get some good cricket in during the T20s.'

'I have been to England before but never to Taunton so I am really looking forward to it.'

'The guys tell me that it's a good wicket to bat on so hopefully I can hit a few balls out of the park. I have been told that Somerset get some good support so I am really looking forward to it.'

Richard Levi added: 'The boys here have been playing some good cricket and hopefully they can continue with that and this year top it off.'

All rounder Morkel said: 'I landed on Friday and got here early to try to get used to the country and the conditions at the ground. Sadly it has been a bit wet for the last couple of days, but today it's been good to get outside to stretch my legs and prepare for the game, and meet up with all the guys.'

Morkel is no stranger to Somerset's acting captain Alfonso Thomas because they have both played for the same team in South Africa.

'I think that Alfonso and me have played together back in South Africa for the last five or six years. We know each other well and each other's games pretty well also, so it will be nice to play under someone who knows what it takes to get you ticking and I'm really looking forward to the challenge.'

'You always want to play with a team that is successful and be in an environment that's nice to work and play in, so this year hopefully we can carry on with that success and take it one step further.'

Albie Morkel added: 'One of the main reasons for me signing for Somerset was that it is renowned to have a great batting wicket so looking at the side we have a strong batting line up. T20 cricket is exciting stuff and I can just see that after a few rounds of four day cricket there is plenty of excitement among the guys looking ahead to Wednesday.'

Even without skipper Marcus Trescothick and Chris Gayle we have a formidable T20 side and the batting in particular has been commented upon by many parties. What hasn't really been widely appreciated is Compo's 'second gear'! While he has gained recognition this season with his ability to stay at the crease and his dogged determination – often as the third opener – to accumulate runs, little has been said of his ability to accelerate. He demonstrated this amply yesterday in a practice T20 at Glamorgan where he bludgeoned his runs at a strike rate of *circa* 200. The selectors will have taken note and if he sustains this in the upcoming T20 competition he will almost certainly achieve greater recognition and get the call from on high.

COMPO BLASTS HIS WAY INTO CONTENTION – SCCC Site

Nick Compton blasted his way into the Somerset team selectors minds when he hit 213 in two T20 games for the Seconds against Glamorgan in Cardiff on Monday.

In the first of the two games the leading run scorer smashed 118 off 47 balls including 10 fours and nine 6s to help Somerset reach 207 for 4 in 18 overs.

Compton contributed 73 out of a opening partnership of 85 with Alex Barrow (9) in seven overs and 45 out of a second wicket stand of 65 with James Hildreth (30) before being out with the total on 150 in the 13th over.

Arul Suppiah batting at number four remained unbeaten on 35.

In reply Glamorgan were bowled out for 122 in 15.2 overs, Steve Kirby taking three for 8 from 14 balls, Glen Querl 3 for 26 off 4, while Gemaal Hussain took 2 for 18 off 2.

In the second game Somerset won the toss and opted to bat first again, as Compton hit 95 runs from 56 balls, including 11 fours and three 6s before being run out.

During his innings Compton added 73 for the first wicket with Barrow, who made 35, and 72 for the third wicket with Suppiah, who remained unbeaten on 57 when the innings closed on 216 for 3 off 20 overs.

Glamorgan in reply reached 194 for 5, Hussain taking 2 for 28 from 3 overs and Suppiah 2 for 31 off 4.

•••

As expected both Bagel and Jos have been selected for England white-ball duties. Jos will be disappointed not to have been retained in the ODI squad, but he has been extremely unlucky with injuries, splitting the webbing on his hand twice, which has cost him time in the middle and therefore the chance to press his case. He will be back and will be keen to take his opportunity to make his mark through our T20 campaign with bat and gloves.

•••

Had a further chat with Guy Lavender re ground redevelopment during the T20 practice match at Taunton Vale Sports Club (now well-established as our second ground), where our batters were smiting it to all parts. Nick Engert has also had a prolific afternoon on notes to us on the next steps of Phase IV.

•••

Twitter is very active tonight as the tenth T20 competition gets under way at Grace Road, where the competition's most successful side Leics CCC (three times winners) entertain a strong Notts CCC side. One tweet is from Steffan Jones, who was a very popular member of our side following two stints at the club, from 1997 to 2003 and from 2007 to 2009. Having retired last season, he's now teaching and coaching at Wellington School in Somerset, for which his background as a Cambridge rugby and cricket blue will equip him well. His Under-11 side have made it to the County Cup final, where they will meet Millfield. I tweet him my congratulations and responding he asks if the final might be played at the County Ground. We will see if we can help, as both schools are important pools of talent for the county and the boys would never forget the experience. A good example of how social media are now lubricating the wheels of cricket.

WEDNESDAY, 13 JUNE. THE COUNTY GROUND.
T20, SOMERSET V WARWICKSHIRE
Today The History Press Ltd – a company I'm privileged to chair – is having a board meeting at the County Ground. This is a very successful recipe and is popular with the company's management. We convene at midday, finish our meeting before 4 p.m., and then relax and enjoy the game. Our meeting last month was in Charleston, South Carolina, so this particular meeting is a pretty formidable contrast!

•••

Club President Roy Kerslake and I met early morning for coffee and spent about an hour chewing the cud over various matters. I've commented elsewhere in this book about Roy's many virtues, and to have him as a sounding board and wise counsel is invaluable to me. Having played the game at first-class level for Somerset and while at Cambridge, he has a level of understanding of this highly complex game that isn't conferred on those of us who have only played recreationally.

POTTING SHED INTERVIEW WITH KEVIN HOWELLS BBC 5 LIVE / RADIO BRISTOL

My phone rings and it is Kevin Howells from the Beeb, who says he would like 'a bit of a chat' about Muralitharan's recent *Points West* interview in which the Sri Lankan recommended that the English T20 competition would benefit from being played by a lesser number of city-based teams. This was seen as being only a short hop, skip and a jump from Gloucestershire CCC merging with Somerset CCC. He invited me to the Potting Shed atop the Old Pavilion to put a counter-argument, which I was more than happy to do.

I said that any merger would be a matter for Somerset members, all 6,500 of them, but I rather thought such an idea involving Gloucester would be about as popular as it would be on The Kop if they were invited to merge with Everton or, using a West Country example, if Bristol RFC were asked to merge with Bath RFC.

Having set the scene, I warmed to my theme and pointed out that Somerset CCC had been around since 1875, was still improving, and why on earth would we want to dilute our priceless brand values and heritage by merging with someone? Moreover, tonight's crowd of over 5,000 (on a cold, wet summer's evening, with the game starting while many people were still at work!) showed yet again that there was nothing wrong with T20 in Somerset. The fact that some other clubs couldn't sell it wasn't a reason to merge those who could.

There is of course another key difference. Major sport in the UK is tribal: always has been and always will be. Fans follow their teams for life, and success and failure are largely regarded as the impostors we all know them to be. In stark contrast the IPL and Australian Big Bash competitions were manufactured for TV. Media owners in the UK love our major sports and, judging by how much they are prepared to pay, cricket, rugby and football are extremely important to them. It's abundantly clear that British fans don't want ersatz sports teams: they want the genuine article.

I ended my sermon by pointing out that Richard Gould, Surrey's CEO, had just told me they have sold 12,000 tickets for a Thursday T20 and another 15,000 for the following day. Wouldn't it be nice if they could all come at once! We need to respect what the supporters can afford and spread the fixtures out accordingly. This is surely a more sensible route to take, rather than modelling the counties' golden goose on ghastly dumbed-down, made-for-TV game shows. I signed off with a West Country flourish on this topic – 'Mr Murali can stick that in his pipe and smoke it.'

The twittersphere was alive in the evening and the unanimous view, expressed in quite vivid Anglo-Saxon, was that Somerset fans would not exactly take kindly to a merger with any other club, at any time, under any circumstances! And to be fair to Gloucester fans I'm absolutely certain they would feel equally strongly.

LEVI AND MORKEL PROVE A BIG HIT ON THEIR DEBUTS FOR SOMERSET
— *Bristol Evening Post*

Somerset ended up with Richard Levi and Albie Morkel as their overseas players for this summer's Friends Life T20 more by accident than design after a frustrating winter in the transfer market.

But the South African duo proved their worth as top-class signings on debut last night as their flamboyant batting led Somerset to a 63-run opening-night Midland/Wales/West Group victory over Warwickshire at Taunton.

Levi, who opened the Somerset innings, scored a thunderous 69 off 34 balls – including four sixes and six fours – as his partnership of 67 in 5.2 overs with Morkel proved the cornerstone of the hosts' 191-6.

Morkel also impressed in his 30-ball 38 – which included one enormous six over the top of the Colin Atkinson pavilion – before being run out in a calamitous mix-up with Nick Compton.

But, even if Somerset did not realise it at that point, with the score 173-5 in the penultimate over, they already had more than enough runs in the bank.

In Warwickshire's reply, Somerset bowled superbly, with Max Waller taking a Twenty20 career-best 4-16 from his four overs as the visitors were reduced to 80-7 in the 14th over, before eventually being all out for 128 in 18.5 overs.

'It was good fun,' said Levi. 'It was nice to open with someone like Craig (Kieswetter) – the last time I batted with him was in a school game about seven or eight years ago!

'I think, regardless of where you play, once you get the run-rate above nine, it's always going to be hard for the opposition. The guys were looking at 160, but we batted well in the middle and at the end to get us over 190 – and the pressure built from there.

'Max Waller was unbelievable. He bowled the right pace, he hit his lengths – and he's been working hard the last couple of days on his T20 skills. His hard work paid off today and the rewards showed.'

Somerset, for one reason or another, had been unable to secure Kieron Pollard, Roelof van der Merwe, Chris Gayle and Faf du Plessis for Twenty20 action – and are also without their injured captain, Marcus Trescothick.

But they were still able to leave out James Hildreth – who missed only his fifth Twenty20 match for Somerset since making his debut in the format in 2004 – and Arul Suppiah and still enjoy an emphatic victory.

That was chiefly down to the stand between Levi and Morkel – so often rivals in domestic cricket in South Africa – although Kieswetter (20) and Jos Buttler (15) also chipped in, while acting skipper Alfonso Thomas finished with 3-17.

Stand-in Warwickshire skipper Varun Chopra, who took over the captaincy when Jim Troughton suffered back spasms in the warm-up, won the toss, and, with the threat of rain looming large, opted to put Somerset in.

But the rain did not arrive – and Somerset tore into the visiting attack, with Kieswetter hitting two sixes before trying to paddle-sweep Chris Woakes and being caught at short fine leg by Chris Wright.

Pete Trego pulled Woakes to Darren Maddy in the deep for three, before Buttler was held by Woakes at short third man off Jeetan Patel. But even as they slipped to 77-3, Somerset still seemed relatively comfortable with the combination of conditions and opponents.

Levi, who had initially been slow to score, and Morkel supplied the fireworks in a stunning stand, taking Somerset to 144-4 when the former attempted a further maximum and was caught at long-on off Maddy.

Morkel and Compton added 29 until their mix-up led to Morkel being run out, before Compton tried to paddle-sweep Keith Barker and was caught by Wright for 12.

But eight not out from Thomas and a single from Kevin O'Brien carried Somerset past 190, setting Warwickshire an asking rate of 9.6 per over to win.

They started brightly enough, with Chopra and Laurie Evans putting on 40 for the first wicket inside six overs, before the latter was bowled by a Thomas yorker for 17.

Will Porterfield, caught by Trego at extra cover, and Maddy, who was lbw, fell to successive Waller deliveries to leave the spinner on a hat-trick and Warwickshire 48-3.

Chopra was stumped by Kieswetter off George Dockrell for 37 – and, from there, Warwickshire, already on the slide, fell apart.

Rikki Clarke was bowled by Waller, Keith Barker by Kirby, and Woakes became Waller's fourth victim, held by Thomas for seven as it became 80-7.

From there, it was only a matter of time before Somerset wrapped up an opening-night victory, and although Steffan Piolet (26 not out) and Richard Johnson (14) briefly rallied, the hosts were comfortable victors.

Somerset now head to Bristol for tonight's Twenty20 derby against Gloucestershire. Kieswetter will not be available after joining up with the England one-day squad ahead of their first ODI against West Indies, which takes place at Southampton on Saturday.

THURSDAY, 14 JUNE. BRISTOL. T20, GLOUCESTERSHIRE V SOMERSET

I'm away on business in London this evening so unfortunately can't attend this fixture, which is sure to be very hard fought. Gloucester have had well-publicised difficulties and challenges of late, but all counties are used to wrestling with problems now and again – they will raise their game tonight against their old enemy. While we fight like cat and dog on the pitch, we've excellent relations with them off it, and we are always assured of a very warm welcome by their Committee.

As it turned out the only winner was the weather, as the game was abandoned without a ball being bowled!

SUNDAY, 17 JUNE. THE COUNTY GROUND. T20, SOMERSET V NORTHAMPTONSHIRE

Linda and I are entertaining friends in the Sammy Woods box for this game, and as they've travelled from afar I hope the weather will be a little more seasonal! The forecast has improved after an incredibly wet spell which finally put paid to the various hosepipe bans around the country.

The side has necessarily had several changes, as our 'new' Saffies Morkel and Levi have returned to SA for a T20 fixture. They will be back, but we will also have to do without Dockerell and O'Brien, who are likewise on international duty next week as Ireland entertain Australia.

We welcome back Cameron White who is playing for the Steelbacks today. He was a very popular character when he played for us back in 2006 and 2007. In the first match of the 2006 T20 competition he scored his first-ever T20 century against Gloucestershire, and two weeks later he smashed 141 against Worcestershire in just 70 balls – which survived as the highest score in T20 for two years. He also scored freely in the first-class game and so will return with fond memories of batting on our famous square. Let's hope he doesn't settle in too well today! He attempted to play for us in 2010 and got as far as The Castle Hotel in the middle of Taunton but sadly no further: he fell foul of a combination of the ECB's rather thorough registration process and some slipshod administration by us. He returned home without setting foot on the County Ground!

Although we fielded a side without Marcus Trescothick, Craig Kieswetter, Richard Levi and Albie Morkel, we notched up a five-wicket victory, a margin which conveys a clear message in a first-class game but often a rather misleading one in T20.

Northamptonshire's total of 137 (Cameron White top-scoring with 47 not out) appeared to be a somewhat below-par score. However, it was almost to prove too much, as Jos and Arul required 29 off the final three overs to win – they got there with just one ball to spare! The large crowd was also kept on tenterhooks by the prospect of a DL result as showers were a permanent threat during our chase.

With almost half our first choice team unavailable this was a confidence-building result.

MONDAY, 18 JUNE: THE TRAGIC DEATH OF TOM MAYNARD

I woke today thinking no cricket for us until Wednesday and so a couple of days away from the manuscript for this book. I couldn't have been more wrong. Mid-morning I was working online and up popped a headline from the *Daily Telegraph* which I simply couldn't believe. So incredible was it that I went to other sites to check what I was reading. I phoned Guy Lavender for confirmation and ended up breaking the tragic news to him.

I sat down, composed my thoughts and wrote to Richard Thompson, the Surrey Chairman, and my ex-colleague and friend Richard Gould, the Surrey CEO, expressing my shock and sadness at the tragic loss of one so young and passed on condolences on behalf of Somerset CCC.

We are due at The Kia Oval tomorrow as guests of Surrey for the England v West Indies ODI. We phoned Richard Gould to cancel, but he was insistent that we should continue with our plans, saying that to have a few grey hairs around would be a support rather than a hindrance. It will be a very sombre occasion.

TOM MAYNARD DIES: SURREY TEAM-MATES GRIEVE OVER 'FLAMBOYANT TALENT AND LOVELY LAD' – *Daily Telegraph*

Members of the England squad past and present have led tributes to Surrey batsman Tom Maynard, who died this morning after he was hit by a train in London.

Maynard, 23, was struck by a London Underground train at just after 5am in Wimbledon and was pronounced dead at the scene. It is thought that the Cardiff-born player may have been trying to avoid police when he died.

Maynard, son of former England and Glamorgan batsman Matthew Maynard, was hit by a District Line train that was travelling between Wimbledon Park and Southfields.

Maynard came through the ranks at Glamorgan, before moving to Surrey last summer, and was considered a rising star in the game having earned himself a place on the England Lions tour to Bangladesh and Sri Lanka at the start of this year.

His death has sparked an outpouring of grief on Twitter from leading figures within the game.

Stuart Broad, who is preparing to take on West Indies tomorrow in the second one-day international of this summer's ODI series, said: 'Absolutely gutted this morning to hear the news about Tom Maynard. A lovely guy and a great talent.'

Former England captain Michael Vaughan added: 'My thoughts are with Matt Maynard and family. Words cannot describe the terrible sad news.'

Flintoff echoed Vaughan's sentiments. Flintoff tweeted: 'Tragic news that a great lad, Tom Maynard, is no longer with us. All my thoughts are with his family at this awful time.'

As a mark of respect, Surrey's Friends Life Twenty20 game against the Hampshire Royals at the Kia Oval, that was scheduled for this Wednesday, has been postponed.

Maynard's death is the second time a tragedy has hit the London-based club in just over 10 years. In March 2002, promising England all-rounder Ben Hollioake was killed in a car crash in Australia.

Surrey chairman Richard Thompson said in a statement: 'Our thoughts at this awful time are with Tom's family and friends and all those that were close to him.'

'Tom Maynard was a prodigiously talented young batsman who had made an incredible start to his career and was clearly destined for far greater things. The impact Tom made in such a short period of time for Surrey CCC spoke for itself.'

'There is a profound sense of loss at the passing of Tom. To lose anybody at such a young age is an utterly senseless tragedy.'

Surrey team-mate Kevin Pietersen added his condolences on Twitter, writing: 'So unbelievably sad!! The Maynard family is so special!! Thoughts are with this special family!! Loads of love guys!! KP xxx #RIPTom'

Australia coach Mickey Arthur knew Maynard, and spoke of his shock at his death.

'It's a tragedy,' he said. 'The cricket family is so small you always tend to know everybody in it.

'I know his dad quite well – he was coach of the year in South Africa this year. Our thoughts go out to his family. It's a tragedy to lose such a talented player.'

Arthur was speaking alongside Australia captain Michael Clarke in Leicester, where their team will play the first warm-up match on their one-day international tour on Thursday.

'He was certainly flamboyant, had a lot of potential and a lot of talent,' the South African added of Maynard. 'Who knows where he would have ended up? But our thoughts are with the family, and I hope they get to the bottom of it.'

Clarke never met Maynard, but did know his father. 'I played against his father when I was at Hampshire a few years back,' he said. 'As the coach said, our thoughts certainly go out to his family.'

TUESDAY, 19 JUNE. THE KIA OVAL. ODI, ENGLAND V WEST INDIES

I attended the ODI with Guy Lavender and Dick Edmonds as guests of Surrey CCC. The mood was indeed sombre, but the quiet dignity and professionalism with which the Surrey staff continued to go about their business was as moving as it was impressive. The minute's silence observed by both teams before the game as a mark of respect to young Tom was a very profound tribute.

WEDNESDAY, 20 JUNE. LONDON

I'm on business in London today, and during the quieter periods my mind is wandering to the forthcoming visit to Taunton of the ECB's Major Match Group (MMG), who are assessing our bid for Category B status. On the train journey home I spend some time working on the content, as Guy Lavender is under the pump without a Head of Sales and Marketing until early August.

I popped into the ground on the way home to compare notes with him about tomorrow's festivities, the MMG planning and preparation and also to hear that owing to strong demand we are bringing in temporary seating for the Gloucester derby next Friday. We shall be hosting a crowd of between eight and nine thousand.

THURSDAY, 21 JUNE. EDGBASTON. T20, WARWICKSHIRE V SOMERSET

Before setting off to this fixture there's a Royal Ascot-themed Ladies' Day to attend at the County Ground. Taunton Area Committee have developed this alternative to flogging all the way up to Ascot and it takes place in the equally hallowed portals of The County Room. It has become a very popular event in our calendar, and given the considerable effort the ladies go to in dressing up for the occasion, pressure is beginning to mount on the gentlemen to up their game and don morning suits!

I went to the real thing a few years ago and must admit found it a ghastly experience. Despite being in the Royal enclosure thanks to some well-connected pals it was as far removed from my ideal day out as it's possible to be. We queued for about two hours in traffic to get into the course, parked somewhere in rural Berkshire miles from the stand, trudged in sub-tropical heat in what I regard as fancy dress to finally enter an enclosure packed with a lot of very drunk and loud people. As the day wore on, periods of complete inactivity were interspersed with bouts of screaming and shouting as the increasingly demonstrative guests implored their nags to victory. A plastic lunch, consumed standing up, was followed by more bouts of hollering and thundering hooves and then we all trudged back – still in tropical heat – into deepest Berkshire to try and relocate our cars. This journey was enlivened by a lot of guests being spectacularly unsteady on their feet, either because their heels had come off in the general melee or their gyroscopes had failed owing to interference by industrial quantities of Pimms or champagne. A lot of mascara had also run (ladies 'glowing' in the heat, tears at victory or defeat?) causing the appearance of some ladies' faces to bring to mind the White Cliffs of Dover with two seagulls crashed into them. Another monster queue ensued as we crawled back towards the M4. I haven't been since!

I had a similar experience when my long-suffering wife Linda – who was a professional baroque soprano – took me along to the ballet somewhere in Coventry Garden. To be fair I didn't attend in the most positive frame of mind and had already convinced myself it was going to be dreadful. My fears were realised as the show got under way at 7.30 p.m. and three hours later I looked at my watch and it was only 7.50 p.m.! For me Royal Ascot and the ballet are no match for a day at Lord's, Trent Bridge or the County Ground.

•••

We are back to the bare bones of a squad for today's game. In addition to continuing injuries, our two new Saffies remain in Zimbabwe, Bagel is on England ODI duty, the two Irishmen, Dockerell and O'Brien, are playing the Aussies at Stormont, while the Overton twins are sitting A-level exams at college in Instow. As a precaution Steve Snell, who did so brilliantly for us in the CL T20 last season, has been called up, and it looks as though he'll play as a batter this evening.

As it turned out, the weather-related curse which has afflicted Edgbaston returned and after a respectable start (59 for one in 7.1 overs) play was finally abandoned at around 8.45 p.m.

Some costs lie within a club's control, but unfortunately one of the largest doesn't, and Warwickshire will be counting the cost of play lost to the weather this month as last week's 25,000 sell-out against rivals Worcestershire was also washed out (without a ball being bowled) while three days of the Test match two weeks ago were also lost to rain.

FRIDAY, 22 JUNE. THE COUNTY GROUND. T20, SOMERSET V WELSH DRAGONS

Dawn breaks to yet another wet and windy day in a paltry summer here in the West Country. The sky looks like dirty washing-up water. It almost saps you of the will to live, as we've an important T20 against the rebranded Welsh Dragons this evening and already two of our four games have been washed out.

I have plenty of other work to get done today, so hopefully that will lift my spirits before the scheduled start at 5.30 p.m.

An evening of Wessex legend to match any from history unfolded this evening. Somehow the rain stopped just before the scheduled start of play and the crowds appeared almost like liquefaction from the stands. By the first over there were very few gaps, prompting our guests from Glamorgan to enquire if this was usual for attendance at the County Ground. I was able to reply that but for the appalling weather, which would have put off the long-distance commuters from North Somerset and Cornwall, we would have been rammed. Our visitors scratched their heads, as apparently their 13,500 free ticket giveaway for their first home fixture had only drawn a crowd of about five thousand. I'll leave Richard Walsh's write-up below to do justice to the game, which was one of the best domestic T20s ever. Somehow, with seven of our squad unavailable, having been 2 for two, we chased down 178 with a ball to spare and Hildy produced a world-class innings which enthralled the big crowd. Yet again cricket confounded all expectations as the game progressed. Hildy has some truly exquisite shots in his armoury, not least his late cut, which brings to mind John Arlott's 'He played a late cut so late as to be positively posthumous.'

HILDY BREATHES FIRE TO SINK DRAGONS – SCCC Site

James Hildreth produced the best match-winning one-day innings of his career to guide Somerset to a thrilling four-wicket victory over Welsh Dragons in an absorbing Friends Life T20 match at Taunton.

That is how the batsman himself described his first Twenty20 century, a magnificent 107 not out that brought victory with just one ball to spare in front of a packed County Ground crowd.

Hildreth reached his century off just 53 balls, with 15 fours and a six, as almost a one-man batting show enabled Somerset to overtake the Dragons total of 178-5, Lewis Gregory hitting a six in the final over from Jim Allenby to clinch the result.

Shaun Marsh had given the visitors hope with a sparkling 85 off 52 balls after they had won the toss. The Australian left-hander blossomed from a watchful start to hit 9 fours and 4 sixes.

But in the end even he was eclipsed by Hildreth's brilliance. Making liberal use of the sweep and reverse sweep, the Somerset player made a mockery of the fact that he was omitted from the team for the opening Friends Life T20 game with Warwickshire.

'That shook me up. I think it was the first time I had been dropped,' Hildy told this website.

'When I walked out to bat tonight we were in trouble and in a sense there was nothing to lose. But I definitely saw it as an opportunity to show what I was capable of in T20 cricket.'

'I would say it was my best one-day innings because it won the game. That was more important to me than making my first T20 century.'

'Hopefully, I have earned a place in the team for the next game. But, with Richard Levi, Albie Morkel, Kevin O'Brien and George Dockrell all due to return none of the players can take anything for granted.'

'We have a really strong squad this season, which was demonstrated tonight. I see no reason why we cannot go on to reach another final – and win it this time.'

Somerset team-mates were lost in admiration for Hildreth's innings. Nick Compton described it as 'outstanding', while skipper Alfonso Thomas said: 'James showed that, while form can be temporary, class is permanent.'

The hosts had plunged to 24-3 when Hildreth walked out to join Jos Buttler, who contributed 22 to a stand of 66. When Buttler was trapped lbw sweeping a quicker ball from the wily Robert Croft, Somerset needed a further 89 from just over eight overs.

Arul Suppiah and Steve Snell featured in useful partnerships dominated by Hildreth, who hit five of his boundaries in a single over from James Harris, before Gregory showed a maturity beyond his years to make a key contribution, his big moment coming when he lofted Allenby just over the head of Marsh at long-off for six.

Had Marsh not been a few yards in from the fence he might well have taken to catch and the outcome might have been different.

Earlier, Marsh had taken his time to size up the home attack, scoring only seven from the first 14 balls he faced. From then on he showed majestic form to lead his side to a challenging total.

The cautious start meant that the Dragons had only 31 on the board after the first six power play overs and 56 by the end of the tenth.

Allenby survived a stumping chance to Snell off Max Waller on 12 and went on to support Marsh with a fluent 33 before being well caught by Peter Trego over his shoulder at mid-wicket off the left-arm spin of Suppiah.

After Allenby departed, Martin van Jaarsveld took up the attack, scoring his 36 runs off just 22 balls, with 4 fours and a six. He was eventually caught at long-off to give Steve Kirby a well-deserved wicket.

The experienced paceman was the pick of the Somerset attack, conceding only 19 runs from his four overs. Even so the Dragons scored 122 from the last ten overs of their innings.

Somerset were without five first choice players – Richard Levi, Albie Morkel, Kevin O'Brien, George Dockrell and Craig Kieswetter – because of international duty. All bar Kieswetter will be back for their next T20 game away to Northants on Tuesday.

SATURDAY, 23 JUNE. QUEEN'S COLLEGE, TAUNTON

Women's cricket representing Somerset began in 1961 and since then it has developed well. No fewer than eight of our players have represented England and one the Netherlands. They have won the Second Division Championship twice, in 2004 and 2005. Under long-term skipper Steph Davies the side have continued to prosper, and when the First Division was expanded in 2009 Somerset were duly installed in it, having finished the previous season as runners-up.

The Somerset Cricket Board are working hard in our region to spread the gospel of women's cricket, and so it was very encouraging to see Queen's College organise an excellent competition for eight school sides from Somerset and Devon today.

CRICKET: QUEEN'S HOST GIRLS' TOURNAMENT – *Somerset Gazette*

Cricketers from Queen's College took part in the first girl's cricket tournament at their own college with seven Somerset and Devon schools attending this innovative and successful day.

In the group stages Queen's A team excelled, winning all of their eight over matches.

Haygrove School looked sharp throughout the tournament with some superb batting and bowling performances from their captain Cassie Coombs who later went on to win batswoman of the tournament.

In the afternoon, Queen's beat Uffculme. The Devon school fielded exceptionally well to restrict Queen's to 45 from their 10 overs, but in a nail biting finish Georgie Longbottom, who was later crowned bowler of the tournament, bowled a maiden over to help win the game by one run.

The final between Queen's A and Haygrove did not disappoint, with the result coming in the last over, a narrow three run victory for the Bridgwater-based school.

The competition was organised by ex-Somerset and Hampshire cricketer Flo Broderick to bring other girls in the area together for competitive cricket, and England and Somerset player Fran Wilson presented the trophies.

SUNDAY, 24 JUNE. TRENT BRIDGE. T20, ENGLAND V WEST INDIES

Another opportunity for the young guns from Somerset County Cricket Club to shine. I shall be following intently today, as no doubt will every cricket fan in the West Country.

TUESDAY, 26 JUNE. NORTHAMPTON. T20, NORTHANTS V SOMERSET

I was on business in London and travelled up to Northampton by train to watch a pivotal T20 contest. In many ways Northants are a club with a similar deck of cards to Somerset, and it was going to be interesting to compare notes on their current fortunes and future plans. I met up with Chief Executive David Smith, Chairman Martin Lawrence and Vice Chairman Gavin Warren. Their common theme was how their T20 was being rent asunder by the rain. As we consoled each other on this topic, a gospel choir were belting out some numbers on the far side of the ground in conditions more reminiscent of a monsoon in Asia than middle England in mid-summer. It was a decent initiative by our hosts to help draw the fans in and make some atmosphere, but in competition with the elements it was a tough task indeed.

Eventually the rain gave way to a sky which looked like pale lead, and following Herculean efforts by the ground staff the players began to emerge into the gloom and run through their warm-up routine. The inclement weather seemed to transmit itself into the Northants side, who simply had a shocker on the day and a rather one-sided contest did little to lift the spirits of the home contingent. For the fifth time this season the Steelbacks finished up on the losing side as we romped home by seven wickets with more than six overs to spare.

I joined the team bus for the long trek back home. Our first stop was about 100m from the ground as we invaded a service station for sustenance on the way home. Ah well, I thought, a can or two of cider will make for a sociable journey. I was to be disappointed, as the players amassed an incredibly dull assortment of rabbit food and low-calorie drinks. The journey back was replete with movies on iPads, iPods and banter. I had 'deep meaningful chats', or DMCs as my children call them, with Kirbs, Hildy and Arul as we hurtled across the motorway network of central and western England. We arrived in the small hours at the County Ground, whereupon I offered to drop Arul off at his house. This presented a challenge akin to the passing of a camel through the eye of a needle, namely how to get Arul's coffin into the boot of my Z4! We gave up and left it in the Caddy Shack.

WEDNESDAY, 27 JUNE. THE COUNTY GROUND. MANAGEMENT SUB COMMITTEE MEETING

This routine but important monthly meeting was scheduled for 9 a.m., and it was bleary-eyed start for me as I'd only managed a few hours' sleep. The usual assortment of issues abounded and, inevitably – and quite rightly mid-season – cricketing matters tended to dominate discussions.

THURSDAY, 28 JUNE. 8.19 A.M. TRAIN TO LONDON

I have business meetings in London today and tomorrow and in between dealing with emails and various company reports my mind wanders to the return to action of skipper Trescothick. He is our talisman and is missed by teammates, the opposition, commentators, members and fans everywhere. Banger has been out of the side since undergoing surgery on his ankle in mid-April, but now could be in the frame for the latter stages of this season's Friends Life T20.

News comes to me from colleagues that the fixture against our 'auld enemy' has sold out. The atmosphere generated at the County Ground on these sell-out occasions – now happily increasing in frequency – is terrific. Coach and players regularly refer to the Taunton crowd being our thirteenth man and they love playing to the packed galleries. When we eventually hold ODIs and England T20s here, this will become a very popular facet for England management, players and media who will grow to relish the positive effect of the 'West Country's Bull Ring' on England's prospects.

ANALYSIS BY SPIN CRICKET

The link below takes you to a very well-researched and analysed article on the state of county cricket. It's a thumping good read and will add considerably to readers' knowledge of the game at present around England and Wales.

http://www.spinoffcricket.com/wp-content/uploads/2012/06/48-59-State-of-the-nation-NEW.pdf

The table overleaf shows the total attendances at each county by format last season and, as 'Somerset la la la' has already tweeted, it shows our lowest T20 attendance is higher than the biggest at some Test match grounds! Lovers of the LVCC will note we had the highest aggregate attendance across the season of any first-class county – a statistic and achievement we can be justly proud of.

The financial analysis (p.145) is also revealing and shows Somerset in a good light. While County Cricket as a whole continues to rack up significant losses, we are the second most profitable club over the past two years.

FRIDAY, 29 JUNE. THE COUNTY GROUND. T20, SOMERSET V GLOUCESTERSHIRE

A sell-out crowd. Sunny spells between the showers. Bars and restaurants overflowing. Team on a high from thrashing Northants. Albie Morkel fit. Gloucester down in the dumps after a challenging season in the Second Division and very short on funds. What could possibly go wrong?

2011 Country Cricket Attendances (Source: *Wisden Cricketers' Almanack*)			
	CC	T20	CB40	Total
Surrey	35,325	83,843	26,765	145,933
Somerset***	55,645	31,589	24,665	111,899
Middlesex	30,545	59,862	15,301	105,708
Nottinghamshire	35,964	50,699	16,426	103,089
Sussex*	41,892	36,189	15,442	93,523
Yorkshire***	40,022	37,574	15,923	93,519
Essex*	34,087	36,815	17,737	88,639
Warwickshire	26,597	40,725	18,277	85,599
Lancashire	39,958	33,009	9,313	82,280
Hampshire	24,536	39,740	14,896	79,172
Kent	29,366	25,543	11,956	66,865
Durham	33,265	23,228	9,924	66,417
Gloucestershire*	23,562	16,366	17,084	57,012
Worcestershire***	29,833	12,418	9,491	51,742
Derbyshire	12,498	18,728	10,408	41,634
Glamorgan	18,495	15,108	7,070	40,637
Leicestershire**	11,620	14,091	4,429	30,140
Northants*	7,399	10,315	4,204	21,918
Total	530,609	585,842	249,311	1,365,762

* No of T20 matches abandoned.
For T20 and CB40, the figures are for Group games only.

Virtually everything on the night was the answer. We made a fairly feeble 140 and our visitors chased it down with 5.2 overs to spare, their skipper Hamish Marshall leading the way with 66, and we had 'chosen' the worst possible moment and fixture to notch up our first defeat in this season's Friends Life T20 competition. We looked a pale shadow of the side who had performed so well previously in the competition, and the large crowd went home very disappointed.

I watched an excellent programme called *The Four Year Plan* this week. It is a fly-on-the-wall documentary on QPR in the wake of its takeover by several billionaires. The palpable sense of optimism in the wake of their takeover proved pretty short-lived as a Grand Canyon of managerial failures undermined the team and led to a sequence of managers and despair for their faithful fans. The same film unit would have had fun at Somerset today. Our wheels well and truly came off and we were comprehensively outplayed in every department.

	2011	2010	Movement
Comparison of County Profits and Losses between 2011 and 2010 (all figures in £000's) (Source: *Wisden Cricketers' Almanack*)			
Derbyshire	20	-187	207
Essex	333	-23	356
Glamorgan	-1700	-366	-1334
Gloucestershire	2	-216	218
Kent	188	-595	783
Lancashire	-2966	-2114	-1852
Leicestershire	294	-405	699
Middlesex	9	-237	246
Northants	25	-27	52
Nottinghamshire	542	189	353
Somerset	481	69	412
Surrey	805	-502	1307
Sussex	-31	-156	125
Warwickshire	327	-2103	2430
Worcestershire	212	104	108
Yorkshire	-460	-1859	1399
Total	-2919	-8428	5509

Durham and Hampshire not yet declared.
Note: as counties highlight different aspects of profits in their announcements, the figures above will not always compare like with like between counties. For each individual county, however, like has been compared directly with like for the purposes of this article.

Our three remaining games now assume even greater importance if we are to make the quarter-finals, and it starts when we entertain Worcester on Sunday. Another sell-out crowd beckons and I know the team will be hurting after tonight's debacle and will want to make amends.

I had a chat after the game with Vic Marks, who was trying to formulate his piece for the *Guardian/Observer* this weekend. Together with Roy Kerslake we knocked about thoughts on the limited-overs game and the waxing and waning fortunes of the T20 in England. It will be interesting to see what he writes as his intellect and perspective always makes for interesting and stimulating copy.

JULY

Another first for Somerset County Cricket Club was in July 2003 at Cardiff when Glamorgan were entertaining us and the cricket was stopped for several minutes when around 200 seagulls invaded the pitch. We had a similar drama at the County Ground during a T20 fixture in 2009, when play was briefly held up with the memorable announcement 'Would the owner of the dolphin (the inflatable variety) please remove it from the pitch. Thank-you.'

SUNDAY, 1 JULY. THE COUNTY GROUND. T20, SOMERSET V WORCESTERSHIRE

In the wake of the hammering by our old foes Gloucestershire on Friday we need to bounce back for several reasons. First, we need to win two out of three remaining fixtures to achieve a home quarter final; second, confidence is always a brittle commodity and crunching defeats can turn into losing streaks; finally, we are all but sold out again and to lose at home in front of a capacity crowd deflates everyone at the club.

It's going to be a busy day because Giles Clarke is paying us a visit, as he does to all counties a couple of times during the season. Guy Lavender and I have some substantive issues to discuss with him re our Category B application, future strategy, England players, domestic structure and future ECB pool payments, to name but a few.

I met with Guy early on Sunday morning to review our presentation and also the emerging Business Plan covering Phase IV of the County Ground's redevelopment. We tried to concentrate amid the usual plethora of distractions – e.g. our food concessionaires were unhappy about damage to one of their food trailers allegedly caused by one of our groundsman's tractors! We managed to find the hour's peace and quiet we needed in a box, although in setting up our computer and projector we somehow managed to disable the entire ground's Sky satellite TV system, so we had a procession of anxious members of staff from various parts of the ground visiting us to enquire what we had done!

The meeting with Giles went well, lunch was scrumptious, the ground was packed and looked a picture, the showers went west of us – and there the good news ended for the day! We were hammered again, this time by 54 runs. To rub salt into the wound we also suffered a 6-run penalty for a slow over rate. Sloppy captaincy – pure and simple. Batting wise we collapsed from a promising 51 for one in 6 overs to a paltry 119 all out.

Just two games ago we appeared to have a grip on the Midlands/Wales/West Group; now suddenly we are under significant pressure to qualify for Finals Day.

At the end of play we held the regular fixture of the President's Tea, where all players, partners and children enjoy some pizza wedges, sandwiches, cakes (some made by Lynn Kerslake – Mrs President – who has a mean reputation for baking some of the finest in Somerset) and scones. The children lightened the mood, and the quality and deftness of some of their strokeplay in a game of Quick Cricket on the outfield might have been noted by some of their parents!

With the aftermath over, Linda and I trudged home. There was only one thing for it – switch sport for the evening and enjoy the European Cup final between Spain and Italy. What a match! Prior to the game many were talking up Italy's chances and many of exalted status within the game (Arsène Wenger for one) were denigrating Spain's negative play and line-up. By ten o'clock it was evident that football, like cricket, was eminently capable of confounding the experts. Spain had made an absolute mockery of their critics by playing something on a plane above what we've come to know as football. For long periods of the game the hapless Italians were reduced to a role of spectating as the ball whizzed around them mesmerically. There were periods when the only time they could regain possession was when retrieving the ball from the back of their net. Even without any recognised strikers starting the game, Spain ran out 4–0 winners, which is the equivalent of losing by an innings and 200 runs. Or perhaps a T20 by 54 runs!

MONDAY, 2 JULY. TAUNTON

It was a few minutes before 8 a.m. I'd been up a while attending to my emails and business diary, but I knew a far sterner test awaited me in a matter of minutes. At eight on the dot our gates swung open and through came our very own 'Barmy Army' of Harold and Marina. Since they retired back in the 90s they've worked for us on a casual basis as occasional housekeeper and gardener, and both are avid Somerset supporters and Taunton Town FC stalwarts. Marina swept in gracefully, full of smiles, as she always does, and met my cheery 'Morning Marina' with a clipped 'Ee wants a word with you' – 'ee' being Harold Needs, gardener supreme, a father of Taunton Football

Club, doyen of West Country cricket and searing critic. Rather than delay my scolding I went out to meet him. I could already see that he had an expression like a bulldog with a bee in its mouth.

It was a typical Somerset summer's day of 2012. The sky was like a grey duvet and the rain was slow and steady. A bit like Worcester's measured slow bowling yesterday. Steady, slow, and hard to get away.

As I joined Harold under the tailgate of his ageing Renault Megane his face cracked and he chuckled. My debrief then started. He put his finger right on some key issues. Sloppy captaincy (time penalty of 6 runs); overseas players who had under-performed in the stead of our youngsters who had done so well recently, and you can't see the scoreboard from the Somerset stand. All bullseyes to his credit. I exacted revenge by telling him straight – the car port was a bloody mess and it needed cleaning out ASAP. He got to it and I went to make him tea!

I came inside and Linda, still fresh from giving me her own stinging assessment of yesterday, joined in the chorus with Marina. Hell hath no fury like a woman scorned – well, here were two of them. There was no point keeping all this to myself, so I emailed Guy Lavender and arranged to see him for 'a brew'.

MEETING WITH GUY LAVENDER AT OLIO & FARINO'S, TAUNTON

I met with Guy to run thorough his personal performance over his first year with the club. I wouldn't say we have (thank God) a 'robustly performing management system' – that's something I always think is more appropriate for describing how a car engine is working. Human performance at any level is a combination of the rational, the emotional and the unexplainable. Guy Lavender has gone down exceptionally well with colleagues, members and peer group at the ECB and has achieved a great deal in a short space of time.

We moved on to discuss the two recent very poor performances on the pitch and found ourselves on the same page. I should explain that our policy is *not* to interfere in the day-to-day management of team affairs. We may have some experience of running complex organisations, but that does not equip us to manage cricketers, especially in relation to their individual or team performance in games. That is what the director of cricket, professional coaches and captains are for. As general managers we will support them and ask questions when it seems appropriate, but their already difficult roles would be vastly more complicated if they were to be 'helped' by folk who have never played the game at professional level. The price of this freedom, however, is accountability, and we do carry out reviews after the season has closed; and these are all the more searching and rigorous if performance is considered poor in the light of the investment the club has made and against, one hopes, sensible levels of expectation.

I hope that our cricket management and First XI can rediscover previous form and confidence to compete more effectively in the two remaining T20 away games. One thing we know for certain is that the return of Banger in two weeks or so will give the entire playing staff a boost.

•••

Lastly for today we announce that the Pakistani left-armer Abdur Rehman is joining us as our overseas player for the second half of the Championship. On a day when I see that because of intractable visa problems Worcestershire have finally given up on trying to land Tanvir as their overseas player, I hope this latest acquisition of ours proceeds smoothly. You never know: with George Dockrell off for a month captaining the Ireland Under-19 side at the World Cup, he might just provide us with a real tonic and boost on the run-in to the season's end.

I'm reminded of a nice quote from the 'off spinners union' – 'When you're an off spinner there's not much point glaring at a batsman. If I glared at Viv Richards he'd just hit me even further,' said David Ackfield.

REHMAN SET FOR SOMERSET MOVE – ESPN Cricinfo staff

Abdur Rehman, the Pakistan left-arm spinner, is set to join Somerset for the latter part of the season subject to being granted a visa. If the move is confirmed he will provide cover for George Dockrell who is due to be on international duty with Ireland.

Rehman has become a key part of Pakistan's Test attack, forming a spin partnership with Saeed Ajmal, and took 19 wickets in the whitewash against England earlier this year. The current Test against Sri Lanka in Colombo is his seventeenth, but he is not part of Pakistan's Twenty20 set-up, which should make him available for the remainder of the English season.

'Contracts have been signed with Rehman and a no objection certificate has been sent to us by the Pakistan Cricket Board,' director of cricket Brian Rose told Somerset's website. 'It just remains for Abdur to sort out a visa and, once that is done, we hope he will be with us in time for our champion-ship game with Warwickshire at Taunton, starting on July 18.'

'We looked at other possible targets, but he was always high on the list,' he added. 'He has an excellent first-class record, with a bowling average not dissimilar to Murali Kartik's. Rehman also bats reasonably well, going in around number eight, so that was also a plus point when it came to signing him.'

'The other positive is that he is not currently in Pakistan's T20 side, so once he joins us he should be available for the remainder of our season.'

Somerset have tried and failed to secure the services of a host of overseas players this season including Chris Gayle, Kieron Pollard, Roelof van der Merwe and Faf du Plessis. They currently have the South Africa pair of Richard Levi and Albie Morkel for the Friends Life T20. Somerset will be crossing their fingers about Rehman as a number of players have struggled to obtain visas this season.

TUESDAY, 3 JULY. BATH

Cricket enjoys several famous and very long-established cricket festivals: notably Cheltenham, Canterbury, Tunbridge Wells, Scarborough, Whitgift, Colchester and Bath. Somerset's festival in the world-renowned Roman city of Bath is one of the oldest in English cricket and we are committed to staging a game there every season. It is a significant challenge to sustain these festivals in the teeth of the increasing demands of our beloved Heath and Safety regulations and funding which is withering under the pressure of Local Government and Council cutbacks. The Bath and Wiltshire Area Committee have done a truly magnificent job in recent years of facing up to these challenges head-on and making the festival a greater attraction, which in turn has made the case for sustaining it even stronger. Last year a record gate of almost 8,000 supporters attended the T20 fixture against Essex because it was able to be played at The Rec (the home of Bath RFC), utilising three sides of the ground's stands for spectators. It made for a very special atmosphere and also notched up a significant surplus following years of losses for this event. Crucially, by using the rugby club's permanent facilities for seating and catering, instead of erecting temporary ones, huge one-off costs of erecting temporary facilities were avoided and the spectators were afforded far better facilities.

The key weakness, unsurprisingly, is the vulnerability created by using what is partly a rugby pitch as a cricket pitch. Ground staff at both clubs and volunteers worked extremely hard to produce a satisfactory wicket, which was quietly growing adjacent to the temporary stand at The Rec while Bath RFC were busy playing only metres away.

Sadly the weather, for the umpteenth time this season, intervened to wreck our plans and we had to relocate the festival CB40 game against Durham back to Taunton. We will try again next year.

THURSDAY, 5 JULY. THE COUNTY GROUND. WOMEN'S ODI, ENGLAND V INDIA

Our guests today for the Women's ODI were Giles Clarke and Clare Connor. We lost no opportunity to remind the ECB Chairman of the more appealing features of Somerset County Cricket Club and the County Ground, and he was subjected to an hour's sit-down briefing on the snakes and ladders of life in a shire county. Clare Connor was treated somewhat more deftly and we spared her trial by PowerPoint, instead having a very convivial lunch while an entertaining contest played out in the middle. Our main course was spiced up considerably when England captain Charlotte Edwards was adjudged lbw – which even from our limited vantage point looked like a poor decision. Not only was she several strides down the wicket, but the delivery also appeared to have pitched well outside leg. Clare was suitably restrained, but not so Giles, who began to overheat at such a harsh verdict on one of England's finest servants.

It turned out well enough. Mithali Raj's unbeaten 92 for India proved in vain as England prevented India from clinching their five-match ODI series. Eventually, it was quite a comfortable win for England, with the target overhauled with almost 3 overs and three wickets remaining.

•••

Our injuries are mounting, and another blow was confirmed today when Steve 'Tango' Kirby (incidentally one of the most erudite, courteous and well-mannered fast bowlers you're ever likely to meet) was laid low with a 'hammy' suffered during the Friends Life T20 defeat by Worcestershire on Sunday. Tango is expected to be out for at least three weeks, possibly longer, which means he will miss the remainder of Somerset's T20 group campaign, plus some Championship and Clydesdale Bank 40 games. We will miss him, because even if he's not taking wickets at his end, his hostile pace and nagging accuracy can help produce them at the other.

Problems rarely come in single file in a County Cricket club, and we also learn that Adam Dibble will miss the rest of the season as a result of knee surgery, having already been under treatment for a side strain. With the Overton twins soon to be required by the England Under-19s for World Cup duty, our squad will again be stretched to the limit.

FRIDAY, 6 JULY. CARDIFF. T20, WELSH DRAGONS V SOMERSET

I'm on business in London today and have plans to travel to the SWALEC to watch tonight's T20 but, once again, the weather is intervening.

Having whipped us on Sunday, Worcestershire, with a game in hand, are in the box seat. They took a point from another No Result mid-week and went top on a superior net run rate.

The forecasts are for biblical weather conditions across the country and over 100 flood warnings are in force. As I leave London I speak with Guy Lavender and I decide to keep my options open by heading from Paddington to Bristol Parkway instead of Taunton. Depending upon conditions there, I can either carry on to Cardiff or head south-west for home.

As we head west the rain increases in severity and Twitter is the harbinger of unremitting gloom from cricket grounds all over the country. Matches are queuing up to be abandoned and the penultimate round of T20s gradually fall like dominoes. From Bristol I check in with Guy and it looks hopeless. I take the next cross-country train to Taunton and the inevitable is confirmed shortly afterwards.

This sets up a sort of Super Sunday, with all three potential quarter-finalists in our group in action, and the results will determine who goes through and who enjoys the considerable advantage of the home tie.

The other noteworthy news released today is that, as expected, Jamie and Craig Overton are both confirmed in the final U19 World Cup squad. A great honour for them and for Somerset as two more graduates of our youth system and Academy win honours of real note.

SUNDAY, 8 JULY. WORCESTER. T20, WORCESTERSHIRE V SOMERSET

The Met Office figures tell us that we've had the wettest quarter since records began and it has taken quite a toll on the summer's schedule, with County Cricket and international fixtures badly affected. Today two of three sides in the Wales, West and Midlands group can qualify for the quarter-finals, with our hosts Worcestershire, Warwickshire and us all on eleven points with one to play. Let's hope that both games can enjoy 40 overs and the fans get their money's worth today.

I passed the County Ground earlier this morning while out for some exercise on my bike and saw a lush and verdant pitch full of the Proteas' green and yellow kit. We've many guests and supporters due to arrive in the next two days for our game against the tourists, and we shall hope for a good – albeit probably contrived – contest in the two days available to us.

Before then we need a win today to secure a home T20 quarter-final and the income which will go with it. We don't budget to reach the knock-out stages of any competition, nor to achieve any prize money in the LVCC, so the financial windfall is always welcome, not to mention the bonus it brings for supporters.

Meanwhile at Wimbledon the hand of history is on Andy Murray's shoulders as he attempts to be the first Brit to win the tournament since the 1930s. Watching several matches on TV one has to acknowledge that tennis, like cricket, does pressure rather well!

We played extremely well, with some fine individual performances from several players, and chased down a modest target with a well-paced reply. It was one of those T20s where success in reaching an inadequate target rarely looked in doubt.

SOMERSET CLINCH HOME QUARTER-FINAL v ESSEX – SCCC Site

Somerset's South Africa-born players took leading roles as the club clinched a home tie against Essex in the Friends Life T20 quarter-finals with a seven-wicket win over Worcestershire at New Road.

First Albie Morkel (3-30) and Alfonso Thomas (2-21) shared five wickets to help restrict the home side to 119-7 after Thomas had won the toss.

Then Richard Levi (19) and Nick Compton (42 not out) shared an opening stand of 33 in 3.4 overs to put their team well on the way to a victory that secured top spot in the Midlands/Wales/West Division.

That ensured them of home advantage in the last eight and when the draw was made live on Sky TV it paired Somerset with Essex on either Tuesday July 24 or Wednesday July 25.

Director of Cricket Brian Rose told this website: 'It promises to be another cracking cup tie atmosphere at Taunton with a sell-out crowd.

'Essex may have finished only third in their group, but they have some very talented one-day players and we will give them full respect.'

With Somerset 43-1, the match at Worcester was delayed by rain. But it proved only a brief interlude and James Hildreth's unbeaten 35 helped Compton see Somerset to their target with seven balls to spare.

An excellent bowling performance had seen George Dockrell concede only 18 from his four overs, while Lewis Gregory took 1-21 from four and Max Waller gave away only 15 runs from three.

Kevin O'Brien took three catches as only Phil Hughes (45 not out) of the home batsmen could make much impression.

Brian Rose added: 'It was a very professional performance from start to finish. We bowled well and some of the catching was outstanding.

'That meant we limited Worcestershire to a reasonable total on a slow pitch. Then we batted sensibly and paced our innings very well in the conditions.

'It is satisfying to have won the group, having dominated it for so long, and we cannot ask for more than home advantage in the quarter-finals.'

The full quarter-final draw is: Somerset v Essex, Notts v Hampshire, Sussex v Gloucestershire, Yorkshire v Worcestershire.

•••

Our Committee Room steward Frank Betts, about whom I wrote earlier in this book, has been 'off games' with bronchial problems and has had to endure a spell in hospital – we've all been concerned about him. I rang him this evening and had a chat. He's worsened his plight by slipping in his bathroom and cracking a rib, poor chap. He had been following our progress at Worcester today and is aiming to come back to the role he enjoys so much in time for the quarter-final later this month. He sounded upbeat and his sense of humour was still evident, but having been that poorly at 91 years of age, and now with a cracked rib, it must be very debilitating for him.

MONDAY, 9 JULY. THE COUNTY GROUND. TOURIST MATCH, SOMERSET V SOUTH AFRICA. DAY I

England and South Africa will play for the honour of being the world's number one Test cricket nation when they meet later this summer in a disappointingly thin three-match series. We have been allocated the Proteas' first competitive game on this tour and traditionally we enjoy large attendances for games against touring sides. In recent years we've entertained Australia, India and Pakistan and have provided each with more than meaningful practice and acclimatisation. While the two-day game doesn't qualify for first-class status, it will be everyone's first look at the tourists and they will want to make a strong start to the tour. Crushing defeats or losing draws can unsettle a touring side and hand an early psychological advantage to England. Supporters remember only too well the mauling we gave the Australians in June 2005 which ended up wrong-footing their tour at its outset. Chasing a sturdy 342, a strong start by our overseas players Graeme Smith and Sanath Jayasuriya set the tone, and two young bucks Hildreth and Gazard hit the winning runs with four wickets and three overs to spare.

With several Saffies presently in our squad, there will be some old friendships to be rekindled and probably some old scores still waiting to be settled too. I expect the game to be a no-holds-barred contest and our enthusiastic and knowledgeable crowd will create an excellent atmosphere.

We had numerous committee guests join us today which made for a very enjoyable day. Lord Archer is a passionate Somerset supporter and always enlivens proceedings, and with support from some private equity men, Mike Gatting and Dusty Miller and two accountants, the stage was set! It didn't disappoint, and after a disastrous start featuring two run-outs and with the score at one point a paltry 32 for four the mood sank as guests began to wonder if we would make it to lunch. They hadn't reckoned on the steel in our middle order, and Tregs and Hildy set about making one of the world's finest attacks look ordinary. A swashbuckling display followed and the good crowd (over 3,000 on a grey Monday) reacted to create a fine atmosphere. We came in off our long run for lunch – which means we had all three courses.

At tea I did an interview with the BBC up in the Potting Shed, and the subject of the T20 came up again as it was topical. Michael Vaughan is the latest to punt the idea of nine city cricket franchises, and again I warmed to my task of defending the counties. Replacing 100-year-old brands with synthetic city teams simply isn't what Somerset fans and members want, and they wouldn't support it. We achieved two sell-outs and three big gates for our five home T20s, and several other counties achieved far bigger gates than us. Surrey, despite being asked to play a crazed schedule of four home games in a week (caused principally by the Olympic effect), had a total gate in excess of 25,000 attend the two games on Thursday and Friday. Imagine how well we would do with T20 if we arranged the schedule to suit the fans!?!

The day took a considerable turn for the worse, however, when Mark Boucher was struck in the eye by either ball or bail while keeping to Imran Tahir. The freak incident looked serious by his immediate reaction. We rang contacts at the Musgrove Park Hospital, Brian Rose went with the South Africans to A&E, and two eye surgeons made themselves immediately available. Mark was operated on straight away and I don't think it is an exaggeration to say that the entire cricketing world had their fingers crossed tonight that he will not have suffered any lasting damage to his vision.

TUESDAY, 10 JULY. THE COUNTY GROUND. TOURIST MATCH, SOMERSET V SOUTH AFRICA. DAY 2

Thoughts today begin with Mark Boucher. I went to see the Proteas in their dressing-room and spoke with Gary Kirsten and skipper Graeme Smith. A press conference was planned for 1 p.m., when a statement from Boucher would be read by Smith. It was poignant – the injury was severe, and investigative surgery at the MPH had produced a negative and challenging prognosis. With great composure and bravery Boucher decided retirement from international cricket was the best course of action, and so the following very dignified statement was read by his close friend and captain:

> It is with sadness and in some pain that I make this announcement, but due to the severity of my eye injury I will not be able to play international cricket again.
>
> I prepared for this UK tour as well, if not better, than I have prepared for any tour in my career. I had never anticipated announcing my retirement now but circumstances have dictated differently.

I have a number of thank-yous to make to people who have made significant contributions during my international career, which I will do in due course.

For now, I would like to thank the huge number of people, many of whom are strangers, for their heartfelt support during the last 24 hours.

I am deeply touched by all the well wishes, and I wish the team well in the UK as I head home on to a road of uncertain recovery.

And so a great South African warrior and player reached the end of the road. All at Somerset wish him well, and on behalf of our club we've offered to arrange a fundraising event in the future for a wicketkeeper of the rarest talent.

CRAIG HITS PURPLE PATCH AS TOUR GAME ENDS IN DRAW – SCCC Site

Craig Overton had an afternoon to remember as Somerset's dramatic two-day tour match against the South Africans drifted towards an inevitable draw at Taunton.

The young seamer took three wickets for one run in the space of seven balls as the visitors replied to Somerset's 312-8 declared with 282-9 declared, Hashim Amla top-scoring with 64.

By the close Somerset had made 50-1 in their second innings and, while the match will always be remembered for Mark Boucher's horrific eye injury, several young players in the home ranks will be left with happier memories.

Alex Barrow was unbeaten on 31 in Somerset's second innings, left-arm spinner Jack Leach had the satisfaction of bowling Amla with the last ball before lunch, and Academy wicketkeeper James Regan took over from Barrow behind the stumps after the interval, taking a catch off Overton to dismiss Dale Steyn for a first ball duck.

That put Overton on a hat-trick as he had bowled former Somerset player Vernon Philander with his previous delivery. Robin Petersen survived the next ball, but in his following over Overton pinned J.P. Duminy lbw for 53.

Just for good measure Craig later took a catch in the deep to dismiss Morne Morkel for 38 off the bowling of twin brother Jamie.

At the close Craig told this website: 'It felt good to be on a hat-trick against a Test nation. I was happy with the ball I bowled next, but it didn't quite happen.'

'I was more worried about the catch. I was circling under the ball and certainly had time to think about who the bowler was. Jamie told me later I would have been in trouble if I had dropped it.'

'Getting Vernon out gave me particular pleasure. The ball came back at him a bit to bowl him.'

'I tried to treat it as a normal game. You know you are up against better players and you have to be more precise in all you do.'

Craig and Jamie will be shortly leaving to represent England in the Under-19 World Cup in Australia.

'We are away next week playing against Ireland and then come back for a week before leaving for Australia,' said Craig. 'It's going to be great experience for both of us.'

After the start of day two had been delayed an hour by rain, Jacques Kallis, affected by the traumas of close friend Boucher, retired not out on his overnight score of 45.

From 96-2 at the start, the tourists progressed sedately to 134 before AB de Villers, who had replaced Kallis, was bowled off a thin inside edge by Peter Trego for 23, having faced 39 balls and hit 5 fours.

Amla dropped anchor and reached a solid half-century off 105 balls, with 5 fours. But Duminy briefly livened up proceedings, launching a big six over mid-wicket off Leach, making his Somerset debut.

After all the first day drama it was almost as if the South Africans had set their stall out for a quiet morning. Amla had faced 135 balls and hit just five fours when bowled by Leach to make it 187-4.

Overton's three wicket burst stunned the tourists after the interval. Duminy had hit 4 fours and 3 sixes in facing 100 balls when becoming his third victim.

On his departure, Morkel produced some extravagant blows, striking 5 fours and a six. With Kallis electing not to continue his innings, the South Africans declared when Imran Tahir fell leg before to George Dockrell for a duck, Robin Petersen ending unbeaten on 33 off 60 balls.

When Somerset batted again Arul Suppiah bagged a pair, trapped lbw by Philander. But Barrow produced some attractive strokes as he and Nick Compton saw things through until the team shook hands at just before 5pm.

WEDNESDAY, 11 JULY. THE COUNTY GROUND. GENERAL COMMITTEE MEETING

Today we focused upon the New Pavilion project and its related Category B application. The cricket review was soured somewhat by another piece of bad luck on the overseas player front – Albie Morkel was being called up as cover in the Proteas' Test squad.

THURSDAY, 12 JULY. THE AGEAS BOWL. LVCC2, HAMPSHIRE V YORKSHIRE

A company of which I'm a director had a strategy meeting at the Ageas Bowl today, and the southern skies looked highly promising with large tracts of blue stretching away to the horizon. Our business session began and before long was accompanied, not by the unmistakeable sound of willow on leather, but the equally familiar splash of rain on roof! Shortly after midday the chances of further play looked slim as a torrential downpour took hold. Our meeting finished, and with all hope of a resumption of play having evaporated, we adjourned to the rather comfortable surroundings of the Executive Club and began to cast around for friends from Hampshire CCC. Soon Chairman Rod Bransgrove hove into view and it didn't take us long to lead him astray. He joined us for an hour or so and between us we put all kinds of matters to rest. The multi-faceted deal between the cricket club and Eastleigh Borough Council had still to complete, Rod explained, in the sort of quietly resigned way that people use when talking about a process where the speed matches that of a slug climbing stairs.

•••

In the evening we attempted to play a game of cricket in the CB40 competition at the SWALEC for the second time in as many weeks. Once again the weather gods were against us and the match was abandoned without a ball being bowled.

This was Glamorgan's thirteenth entire day of cricket this season to be lost without a ball bowled. Little consolation that we took a point each from the NR.

Among those hoping to see the game was former Somerset captain Justin Langer, who earlier had popped back into the County Ground and had some interesting points to make in an interview with the *WDP*.

JUSTIN LANGER: SOMERSET WON'T HAVE TO WAIT LONG FOR TROPHY SUCCESS – *Western Daily Press*

Justin Langer believes the culture and standards in place at Somerset mean it is inevitable the county will end their wait for a trophy before long.

The former Australia opener and Somerset skipper was back with the squad yesterday, making the fruitless trip to Cardiff for last night's scheduled CB40 game against Welsh Dragons, which was abandoned without a ball being bowled.

He, his wife and children also visited Taunton and Hampton Beauchamp, the village they made their home during Langer's four-year stint at Somerset.

After spending some time in the nets with the Somerset squad as they waited for the umpires to call the match off last night, Langer spoke of his admiration for the approach of the county.

Somerset have reached the last three domestic Twenty20 finals, losing all three, as well as losing back-to-back CB40 finals. They face Essex in the Friends Life T20 quarter-finals at Taunton on July 24 – and Langer is confident Somerset will soon find themselves among the honours again, having last won a trophy in 2005.

'Essex are a good side on paper, but Somerset have shown for all these years that they keep scrapping, they keep making the finals,' said Langer, who is now the batting coach and assistant coach for Australia.'

'A lot of people say they haven't won any silverware, but I tell you what, they will be the envy of many counties. They are such a powerhouse county in the first division and have been for five or six years now, so they should be very proud of their achievements.'

'I'm sure there are lots of counties out there who would wish they had made one final in the last few years – Somerset have made lots of finals.'

'They have got to take that one next step – but if they keep doing what they're doing, keep working hard and keep building that great culture they've got, the silverware will follow.'

'Culture is sustainable – performance isn't. Even Sir Donald Bradman had fluctuations in performance, but you can sustain your culture. I went back to Somerset today and the place was buzzing – and that's about the culture.'

'I came back last summer and it was inspiring walking back into the Somerset changing room – the place was buzzing. I'd never seen that in a county cricket club and the leaders of the club should be very proud of that.'

Last night's call-off gave Somerset their first point in this season's CB40 – after four straight losses. However, they remain in contention in both the LV= County Championship and Twenty20 despite a raft of injuries and problems relating to the availability of their overseas players.

'What I really admire about Somerset is that they keep fighting,' said Langer. 'I know they've had some injuries and they've had some lack of availability of players – but they keep fighting, they keep scrapping and they're still in the competitions.'

'That's a great credit to the coach Andy Hurry and his staff – and it's a great credit to the philosophy and culture they've developed at Somerset that they keep fighting and working so hard.'

'Often, the harder you work, the harder it is to surrender – and you see that with these guys. They don't surrender too often.'

Langer also suggested he would recommend a stint with Somerset to any aspiring young Australian cricketer.

He said: 'It's a great place and I'm a huge fan of Andy Hurry – I think he's done a great job. I would without any hesitation, recommend to any young Australian to come and play at Somerset.'

SUNDAY, 15 JULY. THE COUNTY GROUND. CB40, SOMERSET V SCOTTISH SALTIRES

Today began with sun streaming in through the bedroom windows and my hopes were immediately raised that we might see some play at Taunton. I dragged myself out onto my bike for a circuit round Taunton's periphery and along the canal which skirts the County Ground. The prospects for play looked good as the ground staff were busily going about their tasks before the game.

Our guests today included the surgeons who attended to Mark Boucher last week following his severe eye injury. They were very grateful for the club's hospitality and we in turn made clear our appreciation for all they had done for our patient. The latest news was that there was hope Mark would recover vision in his eye and it now remained to see how much; but Cape Town's finest ophthalmics were on the case.

The Scots had travelled in force and our hospitality ramparts were almost in danger of being overrun, but we coped and a very enjoyable occasion was boosted by our first victory in this season's CB40. Interestingly there was a scintilla of hope amongst our guests as we managed to post 206, which at one time would have been considered well short of a competitive score at Taunton. However, the wily amongst our supporters now know that work over recent seasons to provide a better balance between bat and ball has consigned many of The County Ground's shirt-fronts into the history books. And so it proved, on a worn wicket the Saltires laboured from the very first over and never once caught up with the DL target, being dismissed in the 32nd over for 146. Young Craig Meschede was the pick of our attack returning, four for 27 in his eight-over spell.

MONDAY, 16 JULY. TAUNTON

Tomorrow sees the long-awaited visit of the ECB's Major Match Group, who are assessing our application for elevation to Category B status. We have prepared long and hard for this, and today Guy Lavender was briefing all the departmental heads on the visit and their roles in it. It was done with commendable military precision and our troops retired to their own rehearsals and preparations. We ran through our presentation for the nth time, and once again the Chairman and CEO could only get a postage-stamp-sized image on the screen. Sarah Trunks, our long-suffering in-house IT guru, rode to the rescue and with a few lightning-fast keystrokes made the image fill the screen.

On the eve of the visit Guy and I were invited to join the MMG members at Brazz (a local restaurant in the centre of Taunton) for a pre-match supper, which we happily did. The MMG is comprised of a number of folk from varied backgrounds. The breadth of experience has served the group well in its nigh

A Jaffa!

LBW bowled by young Craig Meschede.

Plumb!

Above: The Somerset stand and the Pegasus development which kickstarted the transformation of the County Ground.

Fetch that Colly.

Left: Bagel in the runs.

Below: Gregory accounts for Masters.

That's some catch!

Bagel and Jos in party mood.

Above: Another catch for Bagel.

Left: The infamous 'Wedmore shovel'.

The refurbished Colin Atkinson Pavilion.

A record for Compo and Hildy at Taunton Vale.

Big Vern.

Pre-season Media Day shows the club's vision.

Left: Brian Rose – the legend retires.

Below: The celebrated 50 for Treggs.

The southern boundary and Potting Shed atop the Old Pavilion.

Sharp keeping.

Above: Friday night is T20 night.

Below: Lewis Gregory meets 'the growler' ... and he's pushing the contraption round the gym.

Above: Attack!

Left overleaf: Four more.
Left: Jos the all-rounder.

Above: Jos gets airborne as another wicket is taken.
Below: Buttler looks like his hero, former Blackburn keeper Brad Friedel.

Above: Great stop Bagel.
Below: A word from the master.

Skipper motivates a young spinner.

Another ton for Tres.

That foot injury.

Banger in more familiar guise.

Above: Max the leggie does it again.

Compo takes another plaudit.

Compo hits another boundary in his record-breaking summer.

Below: Another victim for Tregs.

A hundred for Tregs.

Below: Bagel is as keen as mustard!

Tregs' 50th led to great scenes of jubilation on the pitch, and recognition off it.

Another wet day in the summer of 2012.

Above: 'Manny' gets his man ... again.

The man from Thwaites is 'castled'.

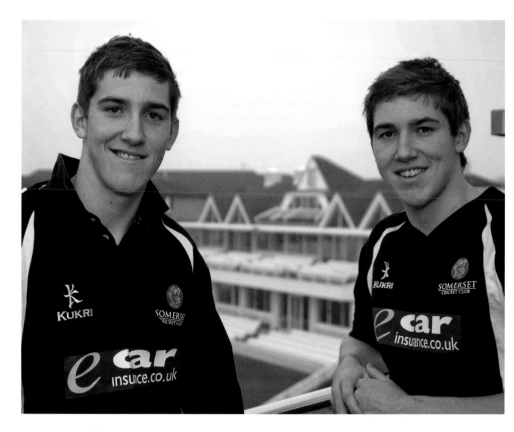

Above: The pride of Instow. Jamie and Craig Overton.

Another victim for Vernon Philander.

The Marcus Trescothick stand bulging at the seams.

Stumpy: the Somerset CCC mascot having a well-deserved rest. Occasionally the odd player has been known to assume the persona while Somerset are batting!

A typically colourful crowd for the T20 at Taunton.

Captain Marcus
Trescothick. Also a
brilliant slip fielder.

on impossible task of feeding the five thousand with the cricketing equivalent of a few loaves and fishes. Somehow the professional game has ended up with more Test grounds (Category A) than there are fixtures to feed them. Their dietary requirements have also been increased by the debts incurred as they have upgraded facilities and greatly increased capacity. It's akin to there being nine superstores trying to eke out a living on Taunton's High Street. Readers may well ask, 'So they must need another international ground like a hole in the head, then?' Our answer is the County Ground is seeking to host smaller ODIs and T20s against the likes of Sri Lanka, New Zealand, Bangladesh etc, where our lower-cost footprint means we can do this not only more attractively (a packed County Ground will look a good deal more appealing on TV than a half-empty Edgbaston) but also far more profitably.

TUESDAY, 17 JULY. THE COUNTY GROUND

The big day has arrived and Guy and I completed our pre-match warm-up sitting on his balcony awaiting the call to the meeting in the Taunton Long Room. The call came, the miniscule image was avoided, and we blazed away. The tour of the facilities passed without a hitch and by 3.30 p.m. the main meeting was over. We stayed on with Gordon Hollins (interestingly I just misspelt 'Hollins' with only one 'l' and Apple's Pages Autocorrect renamed him Holiness, which for the MD of professional cricket in England and Wales seems entirely appropriate) and Brian Havill (the ECB's FD). They proceeded to debrief us on today's meeting and moved on politely but forensically to interrogate our Business Plan. We had prepared thoroughly and the rest of the working day proceeded as smoothly as Trescothick on his way to another first-class century.

The business over, Guy, myself and our financial wizards, Alex Tetley and Malcolm Derry, retired to the nearby Rising Sun for much-needed refreshments.

WEDNESDAY, 18 JULY. THE COUNTY GROUND. LVCCI, SOMERSET V WARWICKSHIRE. DAY 1

This clash between first and third at the turn of the season is unlikely to be without influence on the destination of the season's silverware, and both sides are behaving accordingly. The Warwickshire committee have sent eleven men and women down, which speaks volumes in itself.

We put Warwickshire in, and with memories still fresh of last season's experience, when we did likewise and lost by over an innings, their openers set about our make-do attack (four fast bowlers and one spin bowler either injured or unavailable because of international duty) before rain brings proceedings to a shuddering halt. About half an hour later we are back out

– only briefly, but it is a session we dominate with one wicket falling for the addition of 2 runs in 2 overs. Championship form!

And then the heavens truly opened and play was washed out for the remainder of the day. We did what one should always do when off for rain, which is to come in off one's long run-up for lunch … which means starters and some red with the cheeseboard. This had the desired effect of eliciting some magnificent stories from our guests. John Bridgeman told how he listened to the England v Australia Test on the radio in 1938 as Len Hutton slowly inched towards the Don's record total of 334 and then surpassed it when he amassed 364 during England's first-innings effort of 903 for seven declared. He still displays some emotion today as he recalls it.

We had Somerset's own 'mobile *Wisden*' in for lunch in the form of Nigel Preston Esq. Nigel, or Prezzer as he's known locally, has a mind stuffed full of cricketing facts and stories, a mental filing cabinet capable of content retrieval which would put google in the shade. Prompted by some eager questions, he and his counterpart from Wawks competed impressively without a glitch. John Bridgeman admitted to being caught out only once with the question 'Who were the only two cricketers to open the batting *and* bowling in the same Test match?' The answer apparently is Cyril Washbrook and Reg Simpson, playing for England against New Zealand.

John was reminded of Viv's 322 in a day against his county – he had been here for that too. Warwickshire's Chairman Norman Gascoigne was also there with his delightful wife Carolyn. We found time to be serious, and peering over his glasses, as only an ex-banker can, he told me that Giles Clarke was hoping to put a paper before the ECB board this month addressing the financial problems caused by the unprecedented weather conditions. This is an ECB Chairman's code for 'we might get more money from the central pot'. We shall see – our meeting with ECB magnates only yesterday did nothing to encourage any optimism in this direction.

The stories and repartee gradually abated but the rain didn't. Play was abandoned around 4 p.m. and everyone drifted away, hoping for better things tomorrow. Wawks closed on 27 for one.

The other news of note today was that both Jos Buttler and Craig Kieswetter have been named in the England thirty-man squad to take part in the T20 World Cup in Sri Lanka later this year. For Somerset County Cricket Club to have both these young men is a significant achievement and many in the SCB and our Academy will toast this news later today. The squad of thirty will be reduced to fifteen on 18 August, with England scheduled to play their opening game against Afghanistan on 21 September.

An article on our site later features Banger talking up next week's T20 quarter-final against Essex, which achieves its objective of whetting the supporters' appetites and no doubt hastening some to buy their tickets.

England are making the centrally contracted players available, so Essex's batting will be stiffened with the inclusion of Cook and Bopara. Rosey has also been busy working on Cricket South Africa and this is rewarded with the release of Albie Morkel to us.

THURSDAY, 19 JULY. THE COUNTY GROUND. LVCCI, SOMERSET V WARWICKSHIRE. DAY 2

On this day in 2006 Justin Langer achieved the highest-ever score by a Somerset batsman when he notched up 342 at the Guildford festival against Surrey. He went on to be a highly successful captain of Somerset, and he, Sue and his four daughters became firm favourites in the club and the local community.

I'm away on business in London today, and a feast of cricket is in store with the first day of the Test at The Oval against South Africa – and for me, as a 'one-eyed' county chairman, the rather more weighty matter of day two of Somerset v Warwickshire at the County Ground.

Staggeringly, the weather forecasters are predicting we may see a glimpse of summer this week! Now that would be something.

Literally as I'm typing this on the train to Paddington I see an ESPN alert flash up on my iPhone: 'Start delayed – England v South Africa'.

Meanwhile play at the County Ground see-sawed throughout the day, with the Championship leaders in trouble at 162 for six at one stage and Alfonso looking the pick of our still depleted bowling attack. But then Warwickshire skipper Jim Troughton was joined by Chris Woakes in a seventh-wicket stand of 204, which spanned 50 overs and saw both reach centuries. Woakes eventually fell for 107, but Troughton was unbeaten on 132 at the close, having helped the visitors to 387 for seven. The visitors will aim for maximum batting points in the morning and then tear into us.

FRIDAY, 20 JULY. THE COUNTY GROUND. LVCCI, SOMERSET V WARWICKSHIRE. DAY 3

Today I'm a guest of the Surrey Chairman Richard Thompson at The Oval for day two of the First Test against South Africa. As usual their Committee Room is packed with a very interesting bunch of people from the world of cricket and beyond.

Linda and I sat with Mickey and Shelagh Stewart and amongst other things were able to swap notes on Chelsea, as the Stewarts are also avid Blues fans. Mickey recalled something very interesting about Banger; when serving as a panellist for the *Cricketer Magazine* Mickey had adjudged him to be one of the finest young players he had ever seen.

The Stewarts are keen musicians and delighted Linda with a story about the famous band leader Vic Lewis, who after his war service in the RAF became very popular leading his swing jazz band around the country. Apparently, he would never commit to any bookings around the UK until he had time to digest Surrey CCC's fixture list. He planned his itinerary of concerts around it! Mickey is a great raconteur and had some wonderful stories.

John Major was there at his beloved Oval, and for those who haven't had the pleasure of meeting him I can confirm that he is another whose love of the game includes a phenomenal recall of cricketing facts, figures and history. However, John Bridgemen's teaser question 'Who were the only two cricketers to open the batting *and* bowling in the same Test match?' stumped even the ex-PM!

It rained of course and play was interrupted. This gave rise to an incident which says much about the game, past and present. One Surrey institution is the collective known as 'Past Presidents' – an august body of men who have served the club in this exalted capacity seemingly since time immemorial. One hove into view (meandered might be putting it too strongly) while the ground staff were doing their stuff after a rain break and let the present Chairman know that in his day the Committee would be lending a hand mopping up. Richard Thompson swiftly realised this wasn't so much being aired as an historical recollection but more as a suggestion, and moved swiftly and diplomatically to defuse the situation.

The Leicestershire Chairman, Paul Haywood, was a fellow guest with his charming wife. Paul has a commendably straightforward and no-nonsense approach to the game, probably born of his background as a professional player. He took over at a very tough time at Leics CCC, which had been destabilised by management changes and financial pressures. With some good folk around him, he has restored some pride and financial stability. We've met several times and most notably when they deservedly beat us to win the T20 last year at Edgbaston. He related a true story about how a Leicester player once caused quite a brouhaha with *Wisden*. Readers may know that each year every county has its formal photographs taken in both first-class and limited-overs kit. These photos feature the whole first-team squad, together with support staff and the club's senior elected officers, and appear in various publications including the hallowed *Wisden*. Like all group photographs the occasion can be lacking in enjoyment given the repetitive nature of the tasks in hand. One year Leicester's Matthew Brimson took it upon himself to enliven proceedings by partially exposing himself. Such was the photographer's devotion to duty that he failed to notice the indiscretion, as did several layers of production staff, and the offending photograph duly took its place in the season's publications. The 2000 edition of the game's bible was duly published a whole week before the 'oversight' came to light.

•••

Meanwhile at the County Ground, resuming on 387 for seven, Warwickshire lost their last three wickets in the space of 17 balls for the addition of 13 runs and so clinched their fifth bonus point. Similarly, Fons ensured we achieved maximum points by two wickets with consecutive balls in the 110th over, ending with six for 60, equalling his best return for Somerset.

Our batting performance was mediocre in comparison, as several players got a start then fell for one reason or another. We managed to save the follow-on, but only thanks to Wawks dropping our last man when we were 152 behind! Who knows what might have been had we been asked to bat again? Patel of New Zealand was the pick of the attack, achieving his career-best figures of seven for 75, while the ever dependable Compo remained unbeaten on 73, bringing his Championship total to 935.

In the 22 overs of play that remained we captured three key wickets. Westwood, leg before to Gemaal Hussain, with the total on 32; Evans caught by Jos; and the dangerous skipper Troughton run out by the same man. The visitors ended on 66 for three, with Chopra not out 27, to set up an interesting final day with all three results still possible.

SATURDAY, 21 JULY. THE COUNTY GROUND. LVCCI, SOMERSET V WARWICKSHIRE. DAY 4

Summer has arrived! Another gripping day of cricket beckons, with a fascinating end to our LVCC game as well as day three of the Test.

Ex-Somerset skipper Graeme Smith bats beautifully and becomes only the seventh player to score 100 in his 100th Test.

I go into the County Ground and witness an extraordinary passage of play. We have dragged ourselves back into contention by skittling Wawks for just 124 in their second innings. We need 271 for victory.

Our start could have been scripted by the cricketing gods. We lose both openers for next to nothing in 2 overs. Bagel and Compo then show why they are international class players by putting on 166 for the fourth wicket. At this point we *only* require 90 from almost a full session's play. But Keith Barker had other ideas, and Guy Lavender and I watched from the balcony of the Caddy Shack as he took five wickets for 19 runs in the space of 26 balls – Bagel was among them, although he amassed a quite magnificent 152 before perishing. In the end Tregs and Gemaal Hussain guided Somerset nervously home, and Somerset County Cricket Club's Chairman and CEO danced a sort of jig of celebration. We had thrust ourselves into title contention by taking 21 points and going third in the Championship with a quite brilliant victory. It was to be the only first-class match Wawks lost all season.

SUNDAY, 22 JULY. THE COUNTY GROUND. CB40, SOMERSET V DURHAM

Virginia, my middle daughter, is doing her bit for the county today by joining the serried ranks of casual staff who comprise our excellent catering operation. As I drop her off at the County Ground before 11 a.m. queues are already forming at both the Priory Bridge Road and St James' gates. With the sun 'cracking the flags' the portents feel good for today's game against Durham.

Tres is back, having come through the Seconds game at Essex without being troubled, and there will be a big welcome for him. Perhaps not quite on a par with that afforded Drake in Plymouth after the Armada; but it will be up there as West Country receptions go.

Sure enough, at just before 1.43 p.m., Marcus led his team out for the first time in three months, and the ground erupted. Yet again the magnificent Somerset supporters turned out in their droves and very noisily greeted their talisman.

I had the chance of a quick catch-up with the physios, Brewsy, Dazz and Andy, who were all running through their own early morning routines. Watching in a mixture of awe and bewilderment was Jason Kerr, the Head of our Academy and Players Pathway, and whenever I get the chance I ask him about the talent factory he runs for us. There are some more fine products destined to appear on the verges of the professional squad next season, including two prodigiously gifted batters.

For once the script wasn't ruined and we ran out comfortable winners and lifted ourselves off the bottom of our CB40 table. Bagel followed up his century against Wawks with another today of fine quality and some power.

MONDAY, 23 JULY. THE COUNTY GROUND. EVE OF T20 QUARTER-FINAL

England have not enjoyed as good a weekend as Somerset. Yesterday Amla became the first Protea to score 300 and SA declared, having lost only two wickets. Only four times in history has a team won a Test match having only lost two wickets! Another record was also set, Hashim Amla's innings was the longest in the entire history of Test cricket – it has been suggested by some eagle-eyed observers that he was clean shaven as he went in to bat! I'm not sure anyone has got Amla out since Somerset debutant Jack Leach did at Taunton!

In between various emails and phone conversations, the *TMS* sweepstake suggests SA will triumph sometime between lunch and tea today – which is precisely what unfolded later in the day!

While in the town centre I bumped into Compo and Richard Levi in one of the coffee shops which are now festooned along Taunton's High Street. Levi confirmed he had brought his railway sleeper of a bat with him and that

Albie had been released by the Proteas' Test squad for the game tomorrow. We shall bat down to about number thirteen by my reckoning. A mouth-watering contest in Mediterranean conditions beckons, and I hear from the club that we are all but sold out for the match which, bearing in mind that it starts at 4.15 p.m., is some achievement.

TUESDAY, 24 JULY. THE COUNTY GROUND. T20 QF, SOMERSET V ESSEX EAGLES

I have a board meeting to attend in the Cotswolds at 10 a.m. and en route my thoughts of The History Press are punctured by Guy Lavender's dulcet tones on BBC Somerset Sound as he's interviewed about the game later today and our prospects. He was suitably statesmanlike and neutral in describing the significance of the game and what might follow. We are of course just two victories away from a third appearance in the Champions League T20, which this year is being hosted in South Africa in October. The players will be acutely focused on this as they relish pitting themselves against the world's best players.

I arrived at the ground around 3 p.m. and it was, in the modern vernacular, rocking! Somerset's thirteenth man was all too evident in a riot of colour and noise which would have done a passable impression of Rio's carnival.

Giles Clarke was our guest, along with a dozen Essex Boys who frankly weren't sure whether Cook and Bopara should play. As it turned out their misgivings were probably right!

We ran out comfortable winners, thanks to a solid team performance, and I shall leave Graham Clutton's article below to describe the game.

Immediately following the end of the game we convened in the home dressing-room and sang and boinged (bounced up and down while in a circular huddle) to our battle hymn 'Blackbird'. Albie Morkel joined in spirit but clearly didn't know the words, which is hardly surprising as I doubt Afrikaans can do Wurzel Tree or Gurt.

At the station after the game the Tractor Army (Somerset's peloton), not the steadiest on its feet it must be said, snaked its way onto trains heading to all points of the compass. I bumped into Compo, who was on the London train, and we had a natter about the game and various other items.

Later I caught up with Guy Lavender and it struck us that, given membership does not include the knock-out phases of the limited overs competitions, the crowd and their thirst will have produced a very significant and unbudgeted windfall. In fact, we will have made more profit in one evening game than from the entire three-week CL T20 campaign in India last season! Now that is food for thought.

JAMES HILDRETH'S HALF-CENTURY HELPS SOMERSET DEFEAT ESSEX TO REACH FRIENDS LIFE TWENTY20 FINALS DAY – Graham Clutton, *Daily Telegraph*

Somerset are hoping to make it fourth time lucky in twenty-over cricket after booking their place at this summer's finals' day in Cardiff, courtesy of a 27-run victory over Essex.

Champions in 2005, at the Oval, Somerset have lost in the last three 20-over finals to claim the unwanted tag of English cricket's perennial one-day bridesmaids.

Still, they will get another chance to at least reach the final of this season's competition, thanks to 58 from James Hildreth and a bowling of fielding performance of real quality.

Having won the toss, Essex were celebrating as early as the first ball when Craig Kieswetter, on the back of successive centuries at the weekend, holed out to Alastair Cook at long off. Marcus Trescothick helped a leg side delivery into the grateful hands of Graham Napier, at 39 for two, before Richard Levi and Joss Buttler provided an even keel.

Buttler, having struck 33, picked out Cook, at long off, in the 11th, and thereafter, it was left to the outstanding James Hildreth to give Somerset a fighting chance. The 27-year-old struck nine boundaries in passing 50 off 33 balls and was the one batsman to conquer an Essex attack that was disciplined throughout.

Reece Topley was the pick of the Essex bowlers, with three for 27 from four overs, although Napier and left-arm spinner Tim Phillips both had their moments as Somerset were constantly kept in check. It was left to Hildreth and an unbeaten 17 from Lewis Gregory to help Somerset post a total that, in the end, was good enough.

Like their hosts, Essex found themselves in early trouble as Mark Pettini departed in the second over and Ravi Bopara, two balls later, off the bowling of Peter Trego, without scoring. Owais Shah plundered successive boundaries off Gregory, in the fourth over, but when he top-edged Albie Morkel to George Dockrell at third man, Essex were suddenly 23 for three.

Cook showed few signs of anxiety, despite the loss of James Franklin, who was run out from third man by Gregory. However, his departure at 53 for five left Essex in deep trouble and though Ryan ten Doeschate struck 47 from 24 balls, and provided the visitors with hope, it is Somerset who are Cardiff bound.

WEDNESDAY, 25 JULY. LONDON AND LEEDS

I'm aboard the 5.50 a.m. from London Kings Cross to Leeds to attend my eldest daughter's graduation. A very proud day for any parent. She WhatsApped me last night and 'encouraged' me not to be late for said ceremony and also 'suggested' I don't bring my iPhone with its emails and cricket scores! Hence the 5.50 a.m. We had a truly great day and celebrated her achievement with her friends and their families.

Arriving in London later this evening I settled down to enjoy an intensely competitive T20 quarter-final without the additional pain or pleasure of seeing Somerset play. The Notts v Hants game was a belter, which see-sawed throughout the second innings as run accumulation was frequently stalled by the clatter of poles or a catch. It went to the penultimate ball and was an outstanding advertisement for both teams and the T20 format at county level. It seems all four QFs were excellent contests and each had an attendance that frankly we could only dream of in county cricket just a few seasons ago.

Finals day takes place at Glamorgan's SWALEC Stadium on Saturday, 25 August, with the order of the semi-finals to be determined in the coming days.

THURSDAY, 26 JULY.

On this day in 1934 Jack MacBryan, who had a distinguished career with Somerset, made his debut for England against South Africa at Old Trafford. He was to become one of ninety players who only appeared in one solitary Test match for England. Unfortunately, although he took the field as the 221st Englishman to represent his country, in a rain-affected game he neither batted nor bowled. Because he was never selected again, he has the most modest figures of the 655 players to have appeared for England. (653 players are bracketed by two Yorkshiremen – No. 1 Tom Armitage, 15 March 1877 in Melbourne, Australia; No. 655 Joe Root, 13 December 2012 in Nagpur, India.) His figures are as follows:

Name: Jack MacBryan. First Test: 25 July 1934. Last Test:28 July 1934.
M: 1 Inns: 0NO: 0 Runs: 0 High: 0 Avg: 0 Balls: 0 Wkts: 0 BB: 0 Avg: 0

I'm at a board meeting in London today and follow that up with a long train journey to the North for another one tomorrow. My journey is cheered by news filtering through of incredible goings-on in an age-group side as well as some great feats by two of our young players appearing for Dorset as they defeated a strong Shropshire side in the Minor Counties competition – opener Chris Jones and slow left-armer Jack Leach. Jones hit 175 in the first innings and 188 in the second, while Leach took eight wickets in the match.

Meanwhile, young Harry Rous, who is scoring hundreds for fun this season, compiles another very adroit 155 for Taunton school. However, even these impressive feats are eclipsed by an extraordinary stand of 200 for the last wicket by our U17s. The future looks bright today, and the article below describes the extraordinary achievements of two U17 Somerset cricketers.

SOMERSET UNDER 17 DUO SET NEW BATTING RECORD – SCCC Site

Two Somerset Under 17 cricketers Will Godmon and Harry Veal rewrote the record books when they shared a remarkable tenth wicket partnership in the two day ECB County Championship Group 4A game against Devon at Taunton Cricket Club.

After opting to bat first the Somerset innings was in tatters at 101 for nine just after lunch on the opening day and it was odds on they would be bowled for not many more.

However not out batsman Godmon, whose score was into the 40s at the time, and last man Veal had other ideas and set about compiling a record breaking last wicket partnership of 231.

Godmon had played well in all the p.   but it was Veal who was the revelation, playing with maturity and confidence right from the start.

The Devon side along with the crowd expected a quick end but these two had different ideas.

Godmon did most of the scoring early in the partnership but Veal looked solid as Somerset reached tea on 165 for 9.

After the break the pair blossomed and no matter what Devon offered, they resisted and batted with skill and stubbornness.

Godmon reached a richly deserved hundred and the last wicket pair survived for a further two hours until the close by which time they had moved Somerset on to 282, Godmon unbeaten on 161 while Veal was not out 38.

Somerset continued on day two and it was Veal who took most of the strike and looked the senior partner as he pulled a big six off the opening bowler. On 73 however Veal was leg before to the Devon spinner leaving Godmon unbeaten on 173, a fantastic knock.

The partnership was worth 231, which is certainly a 10 wicket record for Somerset and most likely also in the ECB Under 17 competition, and helped the hosts reach 332 all out.

In reply Devon started slowly but soon opener Josh Malling was into his stride and looking good. However after lunch, having scored 35, he was caught behind by Godmon off the bowling of James Arney.

Devon's following batters did well without taking the game away from Somerset and several got into the 40s but didn't make the big score to seriously threaten a win.

At the close 314 for 8 reflected a tight game in which the Somerset
bowlers had worked hard and shared the wickets, but the stars of the
show were Godmon and Veal.

FRIDAY, 27 JULY.

The carousel which has been our overseas players experience continued to
twirl today. No sooner had Morkel has been called up for Test duty, than he
and Levi are confirmed as being available for T20 Finals Day. On the other
hand the whereabouts and likely appearance of Abdur 'Manny' Rehman
remains a mystery wrapped in an enigma.

A lovely quote by Rosey picked up by various media puts it well ... 'As with
a lot of things this season, I have a Plan 15b in place, so I have potential
options if he [Rehman] doesn't come. But I'm not going to let it go – I'm going
to pursue it right down the line – because he is the bloke we want.'

We are next in action tomorrow facing Glamorgan CCC at Taunton in the
CB40. Fresh from three straight wins in three different competitions, our side
are full of confidence and are not giving up on reaching the semi-finals in the
CB40 despite losing our opening four games.

•••

The *County Gazette* carries a story about Banger and HMS *Somerset*'s famous
bell being in action again, this time to mark the opening of the Olympics on
Friday morning. The Royal Navy is supporting the event by letting the bells of
all available ships ring for three minutes at 8.12 a.m., twelve hours before the
Opening Ceremony begins.

Somerset, and a famous school in our vicinity, have an extraordinary and
unique Olympic record. There aren't many schools who can claim to have
four Olympic gold medallists in one year! Blundell's of Tiverton can make this
boast, however, as they provided four players (Corner, Cuming, Montagu-
Taylor and Birkett) to the Great Britain team which won gold at the only
Olympic Games ever to feature cricket. In 1900 the Games were in Paris,
where four countries were due to compete in a cricket tournament. Team GB
was represented by The Devon and Somerset Wanderers, while the French
team was principally comprised of yet more Englishmen who happened to
work at the British Embassy in the city. The Dutch and Belgians were meant
to make up the four semi-finalists, but they withdrew before a ball was
bowled in anger, and so the two remaining teams received a bye to the final.
The 'Wanderers' arrived in Paris the day before the final, which took place on
Saturday, 19 August. We were dismissed for 117, but the French side were
ripped apart by Fred Christian, who ended up with seven wickets as France

limped to the inadequate total of 78. Team GB built on their first-innings lead and declared at 145 for five, leaving the French to chase 194. In their second dig France collapsed and were all out for 26. And so we won by 158 runs – but with only five minutes left to play!

The crowd was disappointing, and brings to mind a Sheffield Shield game in Australia, as apparently the 20,000-capacity Vélodrome de Vincennes was populated by just twelve gendarmes.

On the account of receiving byes to the final, Team GB was awarded only silver for our victory and France bronze. In 1912, however, the IOC saw the error of their ways and in a meeting to define what events would feature in the modern Olympiad the conversation somehow segued back twelve years and our silver medal was upgraded to gold. Each member of the successful Team GB side also received a miniature model of the Eiffel Tower. To commemorate this feat the game is to be restaged this summer by the Old Blundellian Cricket Club (OBCC), of which I'm very proud to have been appointed an Honorary Member.

SATURDAY, 28 JULY. THE COUNTY GROUND. CB40, SOMERSET V WELSH DRAGONS

We had Colin Sexstone in today as our guest. He's well known to us from his Bristol City and Gloucestershire CCC positions. I hadn't met him before and was greatly taken with his open and warm manner, knowledge of the game and his abilities as a raconteur!

He shared a great tale from the Cheltenham cricket festival when he was CEO of GCCC. During a particularly popular one-day fixture they were overrun by too many fans trying to get in, so having little choice in the matter and being fresh out of options, Colin gave the order to lock the gates. Unsurprisingly, this did little to calm the fervour of those held up outside, some of whom had travelled from far and wide for a day's cricket in the beautiful setting of Cheltenham College. Meetings were hastily convened and the original decision was overturned – it was now in order to admit a further thousand or so of those thronging outside the gates. Here the story takes a humorous turn at Colin's expense. In those days the 'management suite' at the festival took the form of a small and only partly stable caravan, and this was well known to GCCC members, it appears. Shortly after the gates were opened Gloucestershire's angry peloton picked up pace, and through the small window in said caravan Colin's assistant could see it heading in their direction. Colin took the only course of action open to him and decided to hide in the van's single windowless bedroom! When the marauding hordes arrived they didn't for one minute buy the 'he's just popped out' line of defence and they began hammering on the sides of the frail establishment, baying, 'We know you're in there, Sexstone.' He was rescued by the start of play!

Finally, in respect of our lunch, Guy achieved a new height in sartorial
elegance today by appearing in a white jacket, no doubt brought on by the
unusual appearance of sun and blue skies. He had been mercilessly ribbed in
the player's pavilion and quite rightly had little respite in the Colin Atkinson
Pavilion. This triggered another story from Colin, who once arrived at Ashton
Gate in a white suit – presumably around the time that the Del Monte TV ads
led to an outbreak of them. He was greeted by his then chairman at Bristol
City, who asked if there was going to be community singing at Ashton Gate at
half-time. The suit hasn't been seen in public since.

Tregs excelled with the bat today, blasting 81 off just 43 balls to propel us
towards a three-wicket victory over Glamorgan. We chased down a target of
251 with 13 balls to spare, Tregs dominating an opening stand of 92 with
Banger, who contributed only 14. Nick Compton hit 53, while Dean Cosker
took two for 37.

Chris Cooke's superb 137 not out, including four sixes and eleven fours,
had inspired the Welsh side to a creditable total of 250, but the South African
lacked support, with only Walters contributing to a significant partnership.

Unfortunately our victory was marred by injuries, as Craig Meschede dam-
aged a finger and Alex Barrow was briefly knocked out when crashing head
first into an advertising board when trying to prevent a boundary. Thankfully
he recovered in the treatment room.

SUNDAY, 29 JULY.

No cricket for Somerset today, but plenty happening around the country as
usual. I'm also very conscious today of the 1,200 tickets Somerset CCC have
been offered for the Finals in Cardiff (all the other finalists have the same
amount), with demand from a membership of 6,500 and countless other
supporters certain to be a heavy multiple of that. We don't even have enough
for the club's own staff! I emailed Gordon Hollins, the MD of county cricket
at the ECB, and voiced my concerns. I also spelt out the unintended consequences of holding the Finals at such a small ground, e.g. a deliberate virus
attack on the club's website which had caused it to crash! Gordon is a good
man and understands the game from a county's perspective and he emailed
me back within the hour – this being a Sunday – and pointed out that from
2013 through to 2016 the Finals Day would be at Edgbaston, which of
course has a capacity some 8,000 greater than the SWALEC. Little comfort
to our many members and supporters, but the points have been noted, albeit
not in time for 25 August this year.

Since I've been out at Sunday lunch with family I see a flurry of additional
emails have arrived, including a masterpiece from Gordon Hollins attempting
to placate a member (Somerset, as it happens) who clearly isn't in the mood to

be placated. It's also apparent from Gordon's pleadings that complaints have been piling up at Yorks, Sussex and Hampshire. Cardiff must have been chosen as the location for Finals Day before demand rose for the domestic T20, but we are clearly going to take a major shoeing from media and fans alike for (whatever the reason was) choosing a venue that is way beneath the capacity that is now required.

An additional problem is also coming to light (I've learnt that in professional sport problems never come in single file) in the lack of accommodation in Cardiff on 25 August. With 70,000 speedway fans at the Millennium Stadium for their World Cup, there's literally not a hotel bed left in the city. I do my own check on laterooms.com and bookings.com and I can see that the complainants are not exaggerating. For Sussex and Yorkshire fans, one set of whom is guaranteed a berth in the final – which will finish between 10.00 and 10.30 p.m. – it won't be possible to return home by public transport or to find any hotel accommodation in the city. They are going to be incandescent about our perceived lack of planning.

MONDAY, 30 JULY. TAUNTON

The article below caught my eye on Cricinfo today as it was a topic I discussed with Charl Willoughby last year when we spent time together attending a meeting with one of Somerset CCC's major sponsors. The question at issue was why South Africa is producing so many cricketers of such high calibre? Charl had obviously already considered it and said it was because for two terms a year most schools in the country would play cricket every day of the week. He also told of how his schoolmate, Jacques Kallis, not only played every day, but also stayed on when the game had finished for extra practice with his father. Readers of Matthew Syed's brilliant book *Bounce* will recognise the 'purposeful practice' characteristic here, which he argues convincingly is a better explanation for superior performance than the oft-quoted 'natural talent'. There are numerous examples buttressing his argument, notably Jonny Wilkinson and David Beckham's endless practice sessions with rugby and football balls; Desmond Douglas in his garage playing table tennis with his brother; and Mark Cavendish, 'the Manx Missile', training on his bike on the Isle of Man, where the devotion to the sport of Dot Tilbury MBE, in organising regular practice and competition produced a disproportionate amount of cycling champions. For me there's an example closer to home in Justin Langer, who, on his rare days off while skipper at Somerset ,could often be found 'shadow batting' at the wicket for lengthy periods. Young aspiring cricketers should take note! In sport, practice really does make perfect.

SCHOOLS GIVE SOUTH AFRICA THE EDGE – Will Hawkes, ESPN Cricinfo

Higher standards in grassroots cricket and warmer weather are two vital advantages South Africa has over England

Not all South Africans resent every run Kevin Pietersen scores against their side. 'I'm very proud [of him] – every time he hits 100 I feel bloody happy for the bloke,' says Mike Bechet, who taught Pietersen cricket at school. 'He's gone beyond the idea of being a traitor. I just see him as a professional, the same as an accountant going to work in London. I've got no hang-ups about anyone playing for England. We'd rather they played for South Africa, but there you go.'

Bechet and his fellow South Africans can afford to be magnanimous. It is no exaggeration to say that over the past half-dozen or so years, South Africans – or, to be more exact, Southern Africans – have done much to reshape and improve the English game.

That's most obvious in the role that Pietersen (for all his risible uncertainty about whether he wants to play one-day internationals) and Jonathan Trott have played in establishing England as the world's foremost Test side. And then there's Andy Flower; Bechet is probably not alone in his country in regarding England's tough-nut coach as a South African, philosophically at least. 'For Andy Flower, read Southern African,' he says.

This advance in Test cricket has been matched by a similar revolution in county cricket, where an influx of tough, hard-working South Africans, be they Kolpak, overseas or English-qualified, has undoubtedly raised standards. 'English cricket has come a long way in the last ten or 15 years,' says Surrey all-rounder Zander de Bruyn, who has played extensively in both countries. 'The cricket here is just as hard now as it is back home.'

Among those who have done particularly well are Martin van Jaarsveld (who played for Kent under Graham Ford, when the club was jokingly referred to as Kent Free State) and Jacques Rudolph (once of Yorkshire, most recently of Surrey), both of whom were among the heaviest run scorers in the first decade of this century.

Until the Kolpak regulations were tightened, it was not unusual to find five or six South Africans in a single county team: when Leicestershire faced Northamptonshire in a 50-over game in May 2008, there were 11 South Africans on the field.

Few counties have felt short-changed. 'I would think the majority of South Africans that have come to this country have given great service to county cricket,' says Brian Rose, director of cricket at Somerset. 'There aren't many examples of people that have gone home early, for example, or done badly. I can't think of very many at all.'

A look at the England top order demonstrates how crucial schooling is, particularly for batsmen: those who didn't grow up in South Africa (Andrew Strauss, Alastair Cook, Ian Bell) went to private school. They benefited from the sort of facilities that most cricket-loving youngsters can only dream of.

Even now, in the post-Kolpak era, the three highest run scorers in the County Championship First Division (at the time of writing) were born in South Africa: Nick Compton, Ashwell Prince and Michael Lumb. And be in no doubt that there are still plenty of South Africans about. When Compton's club Somerset hosted Middlesex in a Championship match in April this year, seven of the 22 players had been born in South Africa. Among them was Craig Kieswetter, the South Africa Under-19-turned-England one-day-international wicketkeeper. He is the brightest star in a gaggle of young England hopefuls with links to the land of Nelson Mandela.

Anyone expecting the South African influx to end any time soon is likely to be disappointed. This also means that there have been fewer opportunities for cricketers raised in the UK. Some would say they have been hard done by, others that the standard of young cricketers in the UK is still not as high as it is in South Africa.

That's certainly the view of Rose. 'Young South African cricketers seem to be two or three years advanced in both maturity and physical strength compared to people in the UK,' he says. It's clear that while England has taken plenty from the Rainbow Nation, there are still lessons to be learnt about player development.

Few people have a better insight into why this might be than Bechet, the first XI coach at Maritzburg College in KwaZulu-Natal since 1993. Bechet is also a selector for the South African Schools and Under-19 sides. He knows South African youth cricket inside out – and having presided over six schools' tours of England since 1993, he understands the English game pretty well too.

It is his view that England's school cricketers still aren't as tough as their South African counterparts, for all the apparent advances made in the professional game. For him, South African schools' cricket is more competitive, more disciplined and – perhaps most controversially – more democratic than England's system.

'We've got a hell of a competitive school set-up here and guys go hard at each other,' he says. 'We've got regular inter-school competition – there's a lot at stake, there's history behind it and people keep a close eye on who's beating who. With no disrespect, because I think English cricket is in a great situation at the moment, the schools there don't seem to be as competitive.'

Some might question the significance of schools' cricket. Does it matter that so many English schools appear to have forgotten cricket exists, for all the good work done by Chance to Shine? Don't the clubs pick up the slack?

To describe South African school cricket as democratic would be a stretch, perhaps, but it might be in a better state than England's private-school dominated scene. In South Africa, a number of state schools (Maritzburg is somewhere in between: it is part of the government system but charges some fees) can compete on a level playing field with the private schools, even given the dismal legacy of apartheid.

The English school that Bechet describes as 'the yardstick of English school cricket' is, inevitably, a private one – Millfield in Somerset, where Kieswetter completed his education after he moved to England at the age of 17. Here, as in the professional game, a South African approach has reaped rewards, says Bechet.

'They're tough,' says Bechet. 'I think [Millfield cricket coach and former England seamer] Richard Ellison has brought a toughness to that school because he's worked in South Africa. He came out and played here a bit. I remember the first time we played them, he said, "My boys can learn a lot from you guys. Little things, like discipline, how we all dress the same on the field."'

Some may dismiss Bechet's words as those of a proud South African, but the results of his school's last tour to England, in 2010, bear him out: played 15, won 15. Eton were beaten by 102 runs, Wellington College by eight wickets, Millfield by 72 runs. These are scorelines that suggest Martizburg, at least, are significantly tougher than their English counterparts.

Not everyone believes the superiority of South African youngsters is all down to a culture of high-intensity competition, though. The weather plays a key role too. South Africa's warmer weather makes for better, more reliable wickets – crucial in a batsman's development. 'You get a sharp eye at an early age,' says Rose. 'If you compare that to playing on some low wet wickets, dull wickets in England – it takes longer to develop. People are leaving school at the age of 18 in England who are still very young in nature.'

Seen in this light – or lack of it, in England's case – it might be that South African-raised youngsters will always be a step ahead of their England counterparts because they've played more cricket, thanks to the weather. It's a factor that de Bruyn noticed when his son was over last summer. 'He always wants to be outside and playing, but when it's raining you can't really go outside,' he says. 'They play more in South Africa because of the weather. People get outside more.'

For all that English cricket is engaged in a constant losing battle with the weather, though, it's undoubtedly true that the game at the top level has toughened up of late. Few can have failed to notice that the England players are fitter than ever and that they seem more focused than ever. The fact that it has become worthy of comment now when England field badly demonstrates the advances in professionalism that have been made.

Bechet is not alone in thinking that this toughness has come from South Africa. One player, for him, demonstrates how England has cleaned up its act. Trott has drawn frequent criticism from English observers for his ponderous, sometimes ugly approach, but even his biggest critic must admit he has an enviable desire to win.

It's a desire to win that was honed on the fields of South Africa, Bechet says. 'He is a bit of a nutter. When he was at school here at Rondebosch [a boys' school in Cape Town], he was an aggressive bugger. I know that, I saw him. My teams have competed with him. He is tough, tough. I don't want to say horrible little bastard, but you know what I'm saying? He fights you to the death.'

The current series will undoubtedly be defined by a similar intensity, not least because both teams are cut from the same cloth. The English, though, face another battle away from the Test arena if they are ever to be able to thrive without a helping hand from the South African school system.

TUESDAY, 31 JULY.

I'm tempting fate by saying things are quiet at the moment, but I'll make the most of it by focusing instead on what happened on this day in 1956! It was the Laker Test and fifty-six years later there's no sign of it being repeated.

LAKER'S MATCH – AUSTRALIA v THE UNSTOPPABLE FORCE – *The Cricketer*

History was made at Old Trafford when Jim Laker took his 19th wicket in the fourth Test against Australia, including all 10 wickets in the second innings. Laker had warmed up for his day of reckoning by taking 9 for 37 in Australia's first outing, the best-ever return by an England bowler in Ashes cricket. In the second innings he was unstoppable, and when the last man, Len Maddocks, was trapped lbw, Laker had taken all 10 wickets for 53 runs. No less astonishing was Tony Lock's match return of 1 for 106 in 71.4 overs. The Australians were said to be fuming about an Old Trafford pitch that had been deliberately underprepared to suit the spinners, but as their captain, Ian Johnson, said afterwards: 'When the controversy and side issues of the match are forgotten, Laker's wonderful bowling will remain.' No one else has taken more than 17 in a first-class match.

Our injury jinx has re-emerged with Alex Barrow (concussion) and Craig Meschede (tendon on finger) unavailable for a period following incidents in the last game against the Welsh Dragons. With the Overton twins and George Dockrell all away in Australia for the U19 World Cup, and still no sign of Abdur Rehman (how we could do with him at Aigburth!) because of visa problems, we are once again facing significant challenges in getting a well-balanced team of eleven fit men on the pitch.

AUGUST

WEDNESDAY, 1 AUGUST. AIGBURTH, LIVERPOOL. LVCC1, LANCASHIRE V SOMERSET. DAY 1

In the same way that Laker's record was said to have been helped by pitch conditions at Old Trafford, it has also been said that Lancashire's triumph in the LVCC last year was assisted by the square at Aigburth, which has a reputation for producing result wickets – as well as some of the best teas on the circuit! This takes nothing away from their well-deserved triumph as the toss ensures fairness on tracks conducive to exciting cricket. Both counties need a result in this match, although this season we're battling at opposite ends of the table.

Owing to the non appearance of Rehman's visa, Jack Leach has been selected to play and thus makes his first-class debut for Somerset CCC. He's played for Cardiff University, so has some experience of the long game. Tweets are flying, wishing him the best for his big day, and I join in. Another proud moment for Somerset CCC as Jack is yet another product of the West Country as he hails from Taunton and graduated through our age-groups and Academy.

While Banger marked his welcome return to the first-class game today, it was Tregs who got the accolades as Somerset took the game by the scruff of the neck. Tregs finished with figures of four for 34 from 18.2 overs as Lancashire struggled to 129 for five. On yet another rain-affected day Lancashire were indebted to Ashwell Prince for holding their innings together after Trego had claimed the wickets of both Stephen Moore and Paul Horton in a ten-over opening spell that cost just 12 runs. However, the former Weston-super-Mare goalkeeper returned in the evening session to put an end to Lancashire's recovery.

Agathangelou – a debutant for Lancashire – and Gareth Cross will resume their innings tomorrow, with Lancashire hoping that their last pair of recognised batsmen can build a respectable total on a wicket where runs have proved hard to come by.

THURSDAY, 2 AUGUST. AIGBURTH, LIVERPOOL. LVCCI, LANCASHIRE V SOMERSET. DAY 2

Today is the anniversary of our lowest innings score in first-class cricket, which was achieved at Bristol in 1947, when we subsided to the somewhat inadequate total of 25, with six players failing to trouble the scorers. Gloucester won the match at Ashley Down by 316 runs.

I receive a call from David Morgan about T20 Finals Day, as he is President of Glamorgan CCC and will be our host for the day. David is a very highly experienced cricket administrator, having not only chaired the ECB but also having served as President of the ICC. He is great company and a mine of knowledge about the game and its various goings-on. He visited us last summer as part of the Morgan Review process and you couldn't help but be impressed by his immense knowledge coupled to a warm engaging personality. He asked how our application for Category B was proceeding, and I told him that, having made a strong case, and also being able to comply with the all-important technical specifications, I had to be optimistic. We chatted about the cost of achieving every single specification, and very perceptively he said I might find it useful to know that Cricket Australia applied for international registration for the Olympic stadium in Sydney, but when they did so they discovered they couldn't meet the minimum boundary length behind the bowler's arm! Nevertheless the stadium did achieve its registration and David told me he had subsequently attended both an ODI and a T20 there. He added that Somerset might find the precedent useful. A remarkably perceptive comment or a very well-informed one. I suspect probably both.

Meanwhile at Aigburth, after Lancs were dismissed for a modest 185, we responded with a skinny 149. It looks like the sort of game where any first-innings lead might prove highly significant.

FRIDAY, 3 AUGUST. AIGBURTH, LIVERPOOL. LVCCI, LANCASHIRE V SOMERSET. DAY 3

Typical day of see-sawing cricket. I snatched the score now and again through the morning session and was pleasantly surprised to see Lancs wickets tumbling with great regularity. I phoned Roy Kerslake, half expecting to hear the wicket inspectors had been called, but not a chance of it. He said two run-outs, an lbw from failure to play a stroke, and two caught at deep extra showed there was nothing amiss with the wicket. He then rather ominously told me Prince was still in and how we needed him out to press home our advantage. The afternoon session wore on, and so did the evening one, and sure enough Prince clung on limpet-like and found admirable support from the Lancs lower order. As I write this at just past 6 p.m. Tregs has just accounted for the South African for 129 invaluable runs. So, a day to go, we are to chase around 280, and all three results remain possible. The only con-solation is that Roy – as usual – was right, there's no evidence of too many demons in the wicket. Tomorrow could be a vital day in our LVCC campaign. Win, and we go top with six to play, and four of them at home. Lose, and the gap ominously continues to widen between us and Wawks.

In the 11 overs of play that remained after the Lancs innings closed, we lost Arul for 3 with the total on 13, before Compo and Banger batted through to close, by which time the score had moved on to 22. Another 258 needed tomorrow.

SATURDAY, 4 AUGUST. AIGBURTH, LIVERPOOL. LVCC1, LANCASHIRE V SOMERSET. DAY 4

Overnight Sussex have thrashed Worcs by an innings to go third. Meanwhile the Olympics are getting into their stride with gold at last for Katherine Grainger – her heart's desire. The 'never say die' PhD law student went into her race as rowing's eternal bridesmaid, having won silver at Sydney, Athens and Beijing. She triumphed, and showed the sporting world that bridesmaids can become brides. All Somerset fans will know where I'm going with this!

However, for the umpteenth time this season a fascinating finale was denied all parties by more rain. The day's play was abandoned as a draw without a ball being bowled.

SUNDAY, 5 AUGUST. LEAMINGTON SPA. SEMI-FINAL OF ECB NATIONAL (SOFTBALL) COMPETITION

Our disabled team have a superb track record in competitions and have made it through to yet another final. Unlike our First XI, since 2005 they have managed to cross the line in finals with regularity.

SOMERSET DISABLED CC THROUGH TO NATIONAL FINAL – SCCC Site

Somerset Disabled CC won their way through to the final of the ECB National (softball) Competition when they beat Derbyshire at Leamington on Sunday. Batting first Somerset had reached 60 for two off 19 overs when the game was abandoned because of a torrential downpour. There was no further play so the game was decided by a bowl out, which Somerset won 2-0 thanks to England International Kieron Cosens and skipper Jon Tucker both hitting the stumps. The final against Lancashire will be held at the home of Derbyshire CCC on September 17th.

MONDAY, 6 AUGUST. TAUNTON

Abdur 'Manny' Rehman has arrived and will make his Somerset debut tomorrow against Notts. He has taken 81 Test wickets, with a best of six for 25 against England last January, and 436 in first-class cricket at an average of 26. He has a top Test score of 60 and has scored more than 2,500 first-class runs.

We are twenty points behind Warwickshire and we need to string at least a couple of four-day wins together to stand a realistic chance of overhauling the First Division leaders.

TUESDAY, 7 AUGUST. THE COUNTY GROUND. LVCCI, SOMERSET V NOTTINGHAMSHIRE. DAY I

Tregs took his first-class wicket tally for the season to 41 as only 8 overs were possible on the opening day of the match. *Another* day lost to the elements.

Meanwhile, 12,000 miles away, three of Somerset's brightest young stars are gearing up for the U19 World Cup. Craig and Jamie Overton are continuing their fine run of form, while George Dockrell is preparing to captain the young Irish side. The tournament begins later this week.

WEDNESDAY, 8 AUGUST. THE COUNTY GROUND. LVCCI, SOMERSET V NOTTINGHAMSHIRE. DAY 2

Only 15.4 overs were possible, following just 8.1 on the first day, as our visitors progressed from 18 for one to 48 for three, losing Michael Lumb for 16 and Alex Hales for 12.

THURSDAY, 9 AUGUST. THE COUNTY GROUND. LVCCI, SOMERSET V NOTTINGHAMSHIRE. DAY 3

I'm on a family holiday in Spain, where temperatures are reaching 100 degrees in old money. We are all praying for better weather at home as the business end of the season approaches and the quest for points intensifies. With four of our five remaining games at home, and the arrival of Abdur Rehman, we are hopeful of mounting a title challenge, especially as Wawks are showing some signs of fallibility for the first time this season.

Banger set another Somerset record by taking five catches in an innings as the visitors were skittled for 156 in a little over 54 overs in another rain-affected day. Gemaal bowled 3 warm-up overs from the river end, but on switching to the Old Pavilion end he had figures of 6-4-6-4, which as one observer put it 'might have been good enough for even Roger Federer'. We then barrelled past their meagre total with Hildy and Jos in prime form. However, our lead at stumps was only 31 and it is very hard to see anything other than a draw emerging from the contest.

FRIDAY, 10 AUGUST. THE COUNTY GROUND. LVCCI, SOMERSET V NOTTINGHAMSHIRE. DAY 4

My current holiday reading is *The Last Flannelled Fool* by Michael Simkins. Simmo and I became pals after being introduced by a mutual friend, business colleague and fellow cricket nut Tony Morris. In fact Tony helped Simmo produce *Fatty Batter* (still by a country mile the funniest cricket book I've read) which has now been superseded by his latest tome. I commend both books highly.

Announced today is the mother of all pieces of research, to be conducted by the ECB, in which 'hundreds of thousands of County Cricket fans' will be offered the opportunity to air their views on the structure, schedule and promotion of County Cricket. The results will be reviewed by the ECB Board this winter and incorporated into planning for the 2014 county season and beyond. The results will be considered by the ECB Board alongside findings from the Morgan Review, which in 2011 consulted a wide range of the sport's stakeholders, including commentators, officials, current and former players, counties, supporters and other sporting bodies. David Collier, Chief Executive of ECB, has said: 'ECB has taken significant steps to improve our county game and is committed to improving the match-day experience for county cricket's loyal and valued supporters.'

'Approximately 1.5 million fans attend county cricket every season, and we are intent on getting more people through the gates into our county grounds. Along with the Morgan Review, this piece of research is essential to our planning for the future of county cricket, and we are committed to listening to the opinions of fans.'

Mary Elworthy and her partner Mike Coggins are two of the county's most loyal and ardent supporters. Mary has been secretary of the Taunton Area Committee for many years and has hosted a BBQ every season at her homestead. This year's gathering was labelled probably the best yet and was attended by 130 fans and many players and staff. Caddy has honed his skills as Head Chef and the club's sponsors generously support the event. It is an excellent example of what makes a members' club tick, and the £2,500+ raised this year will be reinvested into the club's facilities.

SATURDAY, 11 AUGUST.

My phone rings and it is George Dobell, one of the doyens of cricket reporting on the county circuit. He asks if it is true that Banger is likely to leave to join Surrey. I'm happy to confirm I know of no such plan, nor even susurrations in that direction, and I think it highly unlikely.

An email from Guy Lavender contains the unwelcome news that Fons has sustained a Grade 1 tear of a hamstring and so will be out for a period.

Another phone call from Paul Haywood, Chairman of Leicestershire CCC, to discuss a generic point in relation to players' contracts.

An article is posted on the club site which points to Somerset's ongoing support for our disabled team and also continuing tributes to the great work carried out by Dan Hodges for cricket in the county.

CHARITY CRICKET DAY FOR DAN HODGES – SCCC Site

A Twenty20 Charity Cricket Day in memory of the Somerset Disabled CC former coach Dan Hodges who sadly passed away earlier this year, will be taking place at Taunton Deane CC on Sunday September 2nd.

During the day, which is sponsored by Somerset County Sports, there will be two matches, the first of which, between Somerset Dragons and Huish and Langport Youth XI, begins at 11am, and that will be followed by a game between Somerset Disabled CC and Somerset All Stars.

In addition to being the coach for the highly successful SDCC, Dan was heavily involved with coaching many thousands of young cricketers across the County including several who are currently in the Somerset First XI.

Entry to this special day is free and throughout the event there will be a barbeque and bar, in addition to which there will be a raffle, with all funds raised going to the Somerset Disabled CC.

SUNDAY, 12 AUGUST. THE COUNTY GROUND. CB40, SOMERSET V NOTTINGHAMSHIRE

Today is the closing ceremony of London 2012, and along with all sports fans I've been hugely impressed by the organisation and flair of the Games' organisation, along with the faster, stronger, higher feats of the athletes. At the other end of the spectrum it is disappointing to see that KP is dropped by England, no doubt for 'behind the scenes' reasons of which we are unaware.

Later in the day 'Manny' Rehman wreaks havoc with Notts in the CB40 clash, setting a new record for Somerset in the competition with six for 16 and leading us to a five-wicket win.

We needed only 29.2 overs to reach their target, Craig Kieswetter leading the way with a brutal 44. His whirlwind start featured four fours and a six off the first 5 balls of the third over, sent down by Patel. Banger returned to form with a well-constructed 87 at better than a run a ball, containing ten fours and a six.

The spell by Manny, who took wickets at both ends, bettered the previous best 40-over bowling spell by a Somerset player, set by the one and only Sir Viv, whose six for 24 against Lancashire at Old Trafford in 1983 had proudly stood for almost thirty years!

•••

Meanwhile in Townsville the U19 World Cup gets under way and the Overton twins (Joverton and Coverton) are in the thick of the action. England eventually went down by six wickets. Batting first, England were bowled out for 143 in 38.3 overs, Craig Overton going in at number five and making 35 off 81 balls, while twin brother Jamie chipped in with 14 off 13 balls lower in the order. Australia slipped to 9 for two but recovered to reach 147 for four off 35 overs, with Jamie claiming two for 34 off his 8 overs – both caught by his brother Craig!

MONDAY, 13 AUGUST.

Guy Lavender calls me in Spain at 9 a.m. sharp BST and we have our prearranged catch-up, going through the list of items we agreed by email over the weekend. There's no shortage of topics we need to discuss!

The agenda is:

- Cricket management
- Players and potential movements/new signings
- Cat B application
- Finance
- New Pavilion project
- Progress
- Sub Committee composition
- Timescales
- Ground development – scoreboard etc
- C&B
- Commercial
- AOB

We plough through the list, making some decisions, slating others for discussion and for the MSC and/or General Committee, and inevitably a couple go into the 'too difficult' basket, to await greater clarity or perhaps divine intervention to show the way ahead.

TUESDAY, 14 AUGUST. THE AGEAS BOWL. CB40, HAMPSHIRE V SOMERSET

Annoyingly Abdur Rehman has been recalled by Pakistan as ODIs are added at the last minute to their tour of Australia. No sooner has Manny settled in than he's being recalled to international duty simply because some T20s are replacing 50-over ODIs. He isn't in the 50 squad but he's a mainstay of Pakistan's T20 squad. This leaves us very badly depleted once again. As a wise man once said, 'If this were a script for a novel it would be rejected as being too far-fetched.'

I note the ECB will be having their own mental capacities exercised by the ongoing KP saga. He is a brilliant batter, a once in a generation talent, so one hopes a solution can be found.

Later in the day we produce arguably our most impressive performance of the season, beating Hampshire by 50 runs to keep our once-improbable bid for a CB40 semi-final place alive. Although missing no fewer than nine injured or unavailable players, we not only won a fifth successive CB40 game – having lost our first four – but also struck an early psychological blow ahead of our Friends Life T20 semi-final against Hampshire a week on Saturday.

This evening we are just two points behind leaders Hampshire with two games to play. Pete Trego's brutal 61 at a strike rate of just under 200 and a brisk 51 from Jos enabled us to post 228 for eight on a typically challenging Rose Bowl track. Baz chipped in with a useful 29, and Gemaal smashed two big sixes and a four from the last over which added 23 invaluable runs. We then made the all-important start with the ball, claiming early wickets, and soon the hosts had slipped to 15 for three. Our batters' performance today bought to mind a lovely saying of WG: 'I don't like defensive shots, you can only get threes.'

Jos' contemporary James Vince kept Hampshire in contention with a sub-lime innings as he and Liam Dawson put on 73 for the fifth wicket. Tango and Gemaal then weighed in and Hampshire slumped to 168 for eight in the 34th over. Kirby and his old Gloucester partner struck again, soon cleaning up Briggs and Vincent to wrap up a very handsome victory.

•••

I receive a very humorous congratulatory SMS from Hampshire Chairman Rod Bransgrove. I reciprocate and the stress and anticipation of our semi-final against this very effective and dangerous limited-overs side goes up another notch or three.

WEDNESDAY, 15 AUGUST.

Our Category B application and the New Pavilion project come to life. Guy Lavender sends me the draft Terms of Reference we discussed yesterday, and I have to think about them inbetween cooling down in the pool (this has been one of Spain's hottest summers of recent years, with temperatures regularly in the late thirties) and reading! If only some of this weather could have adorned this English summer. Instead we are headed for the wettest summer in a century!

THURSDAY, 16 AUGUST. LORD'S. THIRD TEST, ENGLAND V SOUTH AFRICA. DAY 1

The first day of the Third Test is preceded by a report in the *Daily Telegraph* by Nick Hoult that West Indian pace men Yohan Blake and Usain Bolt are making noises about appearing in Australia's Twenty20 Big Bash League as the Sydney Sixers registered interest in the pair. Yohan Blake, the world's second fastest man, was at Lord's today to ring the five-minute bell before play and promptly declared himself to be a better cricketer than he is a runner. During an interview with one of his cricketing heroes, Michael Holding, he claimed he could match the speed of Jamaica's most famous fast bowler. He also said he hoped to play in the Australian Big Bash Twenty20 league, a publicity stunt that could also include Usain Bolt, another cricket nut. The Sydney Sixers have expressed an interest in signing Blake.

Far more significantly, Blake also revealed that he would most like to play for Somerset or Sussex in England, and that he has a bowling machine in his garden at home 'turned up to 90mph'. Well, there wouldn't be any need for boundaries, and one wonders how many partners he might run out in an innings, or indeed whether a batter has ever been 'lapped' between the wickets!

FRIDAY, 17 AUGUST.

On this day in 1891 at Cheltenham, Somerset County Cricket Club recorded one of their greatest ever victories over local rivals Gloucestershire, whose line-up included not only WG but his brother EM. Having won the toss we decided to bat, and reliable Somerset, Oxford and England opener Lionel Charles Hamilton Palairet (in his obituary in *The Times* his batting style led to him being labelled as 'the most beautiful batsman of all time') compiled 100 out of our first innings total of 255. Woof of Gloucester, whose bite was clearly worse than his bark, took eight for 125.

Gloucester opened with WG and Radcliffe and in just 14.2 overs were dismissed for a modest 25, with Sammy Woods taking five for 14 and slow left-armer E.J. 'Ted' Tyler recording career-best figures in first-class cricket of 7-2-10-5. The extras' score of 1 was the sixth best return on the hosts' scorecard.

The second innings was a little better for Gloucester as they managed triple figures, but only just, achieving 100. Ted Tyler – who went on to be one of the ninety cricketers who played just one Test for England – took another 'Michelle' in this innings, giving him ten wickets in the match as Somerset ran out winners by an innings and 130 runs.

Unusually all is quiet on the Western Front (Somerset), but there's no let-up elsewhere. *TMS*'s broadcast is enlivened considerably by an encounter between Geoff Boycott and rock star Alice Cooper. Aggers had ushered Alice and his wife into the *TMS* box for the lunchtime interview and cordially introduced one legend to the other. On hearing 'Alice', Yorkshire's President wheeled around and shook the surprised lady by the hand saying, 'Nice to meet you, Mrs Cooper.' Only in cricket …

Meanwhile, at Edgbaston, Bagel leads an England Lions fightback with a brilliant ton against Australia 'A'. Our wicketkeeper-batsman was reportedly timing the ball superbly in his unbeaten 112, his second first-class century of the season and the tenth in his career, in helping the Lions recover from 53 for four to 240 for five before bad light brought proceedings to an early close.

SATURDAY, 18 AUGUST.

We are unbeaten in any competition since 1 July, which is a remarkable run of form. Now the side is preparing for what could be a decisive CB40 in Edinburgh. After a ghastly start, the spectre of semi-final qualification is beginning to materialise.

Injuries remain a key concern, in particular in the seam bowling department. An email from Rosey informs me we are considering ex-England paceman Saj Mahmood on loan before the season's window closes tomorrow.

•••

The article by Richard Walsh below is included because it speaks to a vital ingredient of Somerset's prospects and future, namely the emergence of a number of young players from our age-groups and Academy.

BRIAN ROSE: SOMERSET'S YOUNGER PLAYERS HAVE RISEN TO CHALLENGES – Richard Walsh, *This is Somerset*

Brian Rose could be forgiven for thinking the world and the cricketing gods were against him this summer – but Somerset's director of cricket is choosing instead to see the positives in his club's plight.

Somerset have been beset by injury problems, issues over the availability of their overseas signings, and age-group international call-ups this season, not to mention Craig Kieswetter and Nick Compton's involvement with England at various levels.

They travel to Scotland for tomorrow's win-or-bust CB40 group game with their last ten fit senior players, plus left-arm seamer Robert Mutch, who has been taking wickets regularly for their second XI. Alfonso Thomas, Compton, Craig Meschede, Max Waller and Adam Dibble remain injured, Marcus Trescothick is rested after feeling soreness in his foot at Southampton on Tuesday, Gemaal Hussain has a hip problem, Jamie Overton, Craig Overton and George Dockrell are on international under-19 duty, while Kieswetter is with England.

What remains is a core of experienced players – Pete Trego, Arul Suppiah, James Hildreth, Jos Buttler, Abdur Rehman and Steve Kirby – plus a host of eager youngsters.

And Rose, rather than bemoaning his team's misfortune, can instead see the beginnings of something very special indeed.

'I think it has actually been good for the club in one way,' he said. 'Yes, we have had a whole battery of really serious problems to deal with, but what it has done is open up the field to the rest of the squad.'

'Some young players have had opportunities in the first team they wouldn't have expected – and, the fact they have performed has not only increased the senior players' confidence in them, but increased their own confidence in their ability.'

'We saw that against Hampshire in the week [Somerset won by 50 runs in the CB40], where, yes a couple of senior players picked up the tab in terms of taking responsibility – Trego, Hussain and Kirby, for example – but, around them, younger guys like Alex Barrow and Jack Leach played with confidence.'

'And when you think that we have got Kieswetter, Buttler, Lewis Gregory, Dockrell, the Overton twins, Meschede, Barrow, Chris Jones, Leach, Waller – all guys aged between 18 and 24 – then it's clear that the next seven or eight years are going to be very exciting for Somerset.'

'I am often being asked about us coming second five times in the last few years – but, in one way, it may be a precursor to something a lot greater.'

Rose believes a combination of academy-reared talent and carefully selected overseas stars can help Somerset enjoy a continued period of success over the coming years.

'These young lads have a lot of talent – and, if we can keep promoting the best overseas players, then it bodes really well for us,' he said.

'You look at the impact Rehman has had on the team – he has come in and, in two or three games, had a really profound input and built a great rapport with the side. And Somerset now have the ability to attract the best overseas players.'

SATURDAY, 18 AUGUST.

Negative news today from Cricket Ireland about our young spin king George Dockrell. Cricket Ireland won't be releasing him for Finals Day, which seems a poor decision – never mind the perspective of Somerset County Cricket Club or Ireland, this seems a poor decision from the player's perspective. Many professionals will never feature in a final, and most perhaps may only have one opportunity in a career. Looked at through that lens, it's a decision that seems to me to have relegated the player's tangible best interests in favour of a theoretical advantage to his national team.

On a brighter note, an SMS from Rosey confirms we've agreed terms with Saj Mahmmod to join us on loan until the end of the season.

SUNDAY, 19 AUGUST.

I exchange emails with Roy Kerslake. We are both positive about our improving prospects for the CB40 competition and speculate as to the team we will field for the vital fixture today against Scotland at Bothwell Castle.

The hosts began poorly and collapsed to 75 for six, but then salvaged some pride by reaching 163. However, we had more than enough firepower and were 53 runs ahead of the required rate when the elements brought a premature end to proceedings and Messrs Duckworth and Lewis administered the last rites.

MONDAY, 20 AUGUST.

I'm lying by the pool mid-morning when my phone comes shrilly to life. It's Gordon Hollins from the ECB. Rather clumsily a wet hand dabs at the right part of the screen, and Gordon's dulcet Scottish tones stir me from my slumber. He's calling with an update on our application to the ECB's Major Match Group for Category B status and thus the right to bid for ODIs and T20s featuring England. Earlier in this book I describe why this is important for Somerset County Cricket Club and our future at the top table of cricket in England and Wales. The update is upbeat and we cover the detailed next steps. Guy Lavender has skipped off to France for a quick break with his family, so I leave him a message.

The tension and excitement are now building before Saturday's Finals Day, and I see that, in the wake of the Olympics, the club site is featuring the story that club mascot Stumpy is 'going for gold' in the annual highlight of the mascots' race. He has not shown his best form in several previous attempts, which I think has more to do with the poor aerodynamic qualities of the Wyvern's suit he is forced to wear rather than any physiological failings of his. The piece below by Ralph Ellis sets the scene rather well.

TWENTY20 FINALS BETTING: CAN SOMERSET BURY GHOST OF NEAR MISSES? – Ralph Ellis, Betfair

The men from the west country are certainly up for this Saturday's Twenty20 finals day and bettors reckon they're the team to beat too. Ralph Ellis explains why he isn't convinced ...

They are the hottest tickets in town. They sold out in a day. Hundreds have queued to go on a waiting list in case some more were made available. The website has crashed several times under the weight of demand.

No, we're not talking the Olympics here, or even the Paralympics. This is Somerset's share of the 16,000 places at Saturday's Twenty20 finals day in Cardiff. 'We thought selling two per member was reasonable – but we were wrong,' admitted chief executive Guy Lavender. 'We're very disappointed we can't meet the demand.'

Clearly down in Cider country they think this could be the year that all the disappointments come to an end. Every year since 2009 they have set off to finals day full of optimism, watched their side reach the last two, and then suffered defeat. Last year was the worst when they looked like winners against Leicestershire but then the middle order collapsed.

This time, however, it seems the older members who recall the great days of Botham, Richards and Garner think they are in for a winning day out. And Betfair's market seems to support them – Somerset are heavy odds on at 1.65 to win their semi-final over Hampshire and then 3.3 favourites to lift the Twenty20 trophy. But it might not be so simple.

True, canny director of cricket Brian Rose (he was captain back in those Botham and Richards glory days), has made sure he will have their South African stars Richard Levi and Albie Morkel available. The touring team's management were impressed with how professionally Somerset handled things when Mark Boucher injured his eye so severely at Taunton, and have bent over backwards to help out the county in return. The presence of Levi, who holds the world record top score for T20 after making 117 not out against New Zealand in February, will be a big plus.

But the rest of Somerset's squad is currently ravaged by such a horrific injury crisis that Rose will be, in the sort of terms beloved by some football managers, 'down to the bare bones'. The current list under treatment includes skipper Marcus Trescothick, plus Alfonso Thomas, Nick Compton, Gemaal Hussain, Adam Dibble, Craig Meschede and Alex Gregory.

Then there's the psychological effect of all those near misses in the last few seasons. Somehow they seem to have found a way to snatch defeat from the jaws of victory in a succession of finals, and not just in T20. They have lost the last two CB40 finals as well. To get over the line and win one will take a massive collective will, and with so many players missing it won't be easy.

Finally, there's the very nature of the game. The shortest format of cricket is literally hit or miss, which means when you put four county teams together on one day you can't consider any one of them to be the favourite. It's too much of a lottery, decided by one brilliant catch or daft run-out.

All those people queuing for tickets in Taunton might not like it, but even the ones who got lucky and are on their way to Cardiff might be in for as much disappointment as those who missed out.

TUESDAY, 21 AUGUST. THE COUNTY GROUND. LVCCI, SOMERSET V SUSSEX. DAY 1

The fourth from last LVCC game starts today, with the race for honours and avoidance of relegation hotting up considerably. Durham have undergone a renaissance, winning their last three – win another and they'll be in contention for the Championship itself! Surrey too won a real cliffhanger against their ancient foe Middlesex last week, but this week take a break as other counties shape their fortunes.

We are in the midst of a chronic injury crisis which has plagued us all season. That said, it has provided an opportunity for younger squad members to stand up and be counted, and this they have done impressively. It augurs well for the club's future.

Meanwhile, down under, England U19s have not made the cut for the semi-finals despite the best efforts of the Overton twins and are now consigned to the play-off stages.

Today's game is nicely poised. Sussex have risen from mid-table to second place on the back of some very impressive recent performances, and we may well vie with them for Championship honours, especially as we meet again at Hove next month. The highlight of yet another rain-shortened day is skipper Marcus Trescothick's majestic 89 not out before the players trudged off at 2.50 p.m., never to return. Another 11 runs and it will be his fiftieth first-class century, a prodigious record. Banger has struggled for form following a long injury lay-off and is playing only his eighth innings of the season. He had made only 8 runs in three Championship innings before this game, but today, against a strong Sussex seam attack, he was soon driving the ball with his trademark timing and power.

WEDNESDAY, 22 AUGUST. THE COUNTY GROUND. LVCCI, SOMERSET V SUSSEX. DAY 2

Another day breaks hot and blue in Spain, and I can only hope it is doing likewise back in Taunton. Moreover the forecast for the weekend is looking decidedly dodgy for Cardiff, and having lived in Swansea for three years I know only too well that when it rains in South Wales it does it in some style. Linda and I are returning from our family holiday for Saturday's Finals but are booked to return on Sunday to rejoin our children here in Levante. Which means that if the reserve day is needed we won't be there. That said, the forecast for Sunday looks equally poor at present.

Being positive, along with his many fans and admirers, I'm hoping Marcus will notch up his fiftieth first-class hundred today and lay the foundations for a big first-innings lead. Realistically we need a win this week to sustain our challenge in the LVCC.

Unbeaten on 89 overnight, Banger went on to make 123 off 230 balls, with twenty fours, before being dismissed shortly before lunch. We then undid his work on the foundations by losing our last five wickets for six runs, with Monty Panesar claiming career-best figures of seven for 60. We were bowled out for a disappointing 247, thus bagging only one bonus point.

By the close Sussex had replied with 161 for six, Gemaal Hussain and Abdur Rehman taking two wickets each and leaving the game delicately balanced for the last two days.

During the day the ECB announced that Craig Kieswetter would not be available for Somerset's last three Championship games and Jos Buttler would miss the last two. Both players will be available for T20 Finals Day on Saturday. The Championship run-in just got a whole lot tougher for us – an excellent example though of how cricket keeps a level playing field between the counties; just as you scent success your side is weakened by one or more of your star players being snaffled up for international duty.

THURSDAY, 23 AUGUST. THE COUNTY GROUND. LVCCI, SOMERSET V SUSSEX. DAY 3

Sussex resumed in a somewhat sickly position at 161 for six, still 86 runs behind our first-innings total. However, an unbeaten 57 from Amjad Khan and a tenth-wicket partnership of 32 between him and Monty gave the visitors a modest 32-run advantage as we set about our second dig. We began brightly enough with Banger and Arul adding 84 for the first wicket – over 50 to the good with ten wickets standing. What could possibly go wrong from here?

Skipper feathered an arm-ball from Monty in the seventeenth over and we collapsed, losing our last eight wickets for just 89 runs. It was described by impartial observers as an abject display and, to twist the knife, the cricketing gods dealt us a further blow, which Rosey confirmed with the announcement that Nick Compton would miss Saturday's T20 Finals Day because of a back injury. The Sussex openers smoothly accumulated 30 without loss by stumps, leaving them a target of 133 runs in the morning to clinch a vital victory.

Credit where credit is due: Monty took career-best figures of seven for 60 yesterday and today added another six for 77, and in so doing he surely has played himself back into contention for England's winter tours. With this classic display of the left-arm spinner's art he's also single-handedly played Sussex right back into title contention, especially as Middlesex are checking Warwickshire's progress at Edgbaston.

FRIDAY, 24 AUGUST. THE COUNTY GROUND. LVCCI, SOMERSET V SUSSEX. DAY 4

After we laboured to a modest second-innings total yesterday of under 200 it was dispiriting to see the Sussex openers canter to over 30 ahead of the clock without loss. There's rain about today and this may well have more than a walk-on part in proceedings. The stakes are high, because if Sussex can force the win they will go clear at the top of the table, as Wawks are being unusually throttled at Lord's where only two results now look possible today – a Wawks victory not being one of them.

Meanwhile injury news from the club gets even worse: Compo is out for the *season* with an acute back problem tracing to a troublesome disc. We will miss him in the last three LVCC games as he's been our standout batter this season. Roy Kerslake says he can't think of a season more disrupted by player non-availability through injury, call-ups, paperwork or seemingly divine intervention.

Sussex started the last day as clear favourites for the win, but economical and naggingly accurate swing by Tregs nicked three out and the deadly Manny claimed two more – at 115 for five the script was being torn up. Needing a further 49 for the win that would have maintained the momentum of their recent charge, they still fancied themselves to cross the line, but once again the weather gods intervened and denied anyone a result, restricting the day's play to less than 24 overs. Honours were shared and battle will be rejoined next month in Hove.

•••

I exchanged emails with Roy Kerslake and he pointed out that the avoidance of defeat today meant we are unbeaten in all competitions since 1 July, when we lost a T20 to Worcs at Taunton. As he fairly said, this is a remarkable run given all our injury problems and player unavailability. Let's hope we can still say this by this time tomorrow night!

SATURDAY, 25 AUGUST. SWALEC STADIUM, CARDIFF. T20 FINALS DAY

A change in my business schedule has prevented me from travelling back to the UK for Finals Day, so I will be following the action from our home in Spain. I'm woken by my iPhone rattling into life on the bedside table and it is none other than a very chipper Lord Archer. 'Morning, Chairman,' he booms. 'I'm thinking about coming down but was wondering what the prospects for play are, there in Cardiff.' I was able to tell him that from where I was the view was one of a cloudless sky, still wind, and bright sunshine. A perfect day for cricket, in fact. Even over the phone I could tell Jeffrey's spirits were soaring, and then I punctured his misplaced optimism by explaining I was in the Med! A stream of polite invective followed, after which we moved on to discuss the day's prospects. Before hanging up he told me he had been auctioning last night at an Olympic function and an ex-England captain has said in response to a question about KP's future that he hoped he never wore an England shirt again. We agreed that the whole imbroglio had been a great waste of talent, and had KP been better advised then possibly his career might have taken a less contentious course.

With Jeffrey's questions now being rather more usefully attended to by Guy Lavender in Cardiff, I recalled something not many people know – that in 2004 KP almost became a Somerset player. In fact terms were agreed, and so much so that he enjoyed the use of a club car for a while. Alas, somewhere between him taking delivery of it and finally signing on the dotted line for us, he changed tack. In the end he served another season at Notts and then became a Hampshire player. What might have been we are all left to ponder.

The day continued bright and cheerful with a lazy walk along the beach and games of table tennis in the shade. Tension began to mount in the very special way it does when a day's play shimmers with the hope of a trophy. Texts, emails, tweets and Facebook messages were being swapped and sent between club personnel, families, management and of course media and supporters.

My first reminder of our fallibility was when Stumpy was unplaced in the mascot's race, the ignominy compounded by the BBC race commentator calling him a dragon – when as everyone knows he's a wyvern. While Glamorgan CCC may have missed out on playing in today's game, they weren't going to lose out on the race, with their dragon sacrificing his footwear in favour of speed. The subsequent steward's enquiry was overtaken by events as the first two semi-finalists took to the stage.

I listened with dispassionate interest as the Yorkshire v Sussex game unfolded, only too well aware that my mood, manner and disposition would be totally different for the next game.

The rest, as they say, is history. We put in a wretched batting performance (save Bagel's fine individual effort) and compiled the lowest total of any side batting first in ten years of T20 Finals Day. As Compo put it while summarising for BBC Radio 5, it was highly unlikely it could be defended, and despite some heroics with the ball, so it proved. The highly experienced middle order of Hampshire steadied their ship and timed their pursuit well, putting us out of our misery with a deft acceleration in the penultimate over.

I went for a bike ride to clear my head before speaking with Guy Lavender and Roy Kerslake. While I always make a point of speaking or texting cricket management (Director of Cricket, Head Coach and Skipper) after a victory, there's no point in the immediate aftermath of a major defeat. They are always inconsolable and are best left to their own way of dealing with it. I'm reminded of Brian Clough's MO – after a win he would tear into his team and scold them individually and severally for mistakes made. After a bad loss he used to stick his head round the dressing-room door and simply say, 'See you Monday, lads.'

Our site's article explains what happened on the day.

WE WERE OUTPLAYED TODAY SAYS MARCUS – SCCC Site

For the fourth year running Somerset left the Twenty 20 Finals Day empty handed when they were beaten by Hampshire in the semi final at the Swalec Stadium on Saturday afternoon.

'It's always very disappointing to have got to this point because we put a lot of hard work into such a great day and we all know just how important it is, but we were outplayed today,' said skipper Marcus Trescothick.

'I thought that Dimitri Mascarenhas was good the way that he strangled us at the top of the order at the start and we put ourselves under pressure by losing wickets. Craig was the only one who got to grips with the pitch and worked it out. You need to get partnerships going in T20 cricket and we never did that today.'

'I thought we fielded okay and we put ourselves in with a shout, and in the middle period when we took wickets was when the game came back to us, but then those two at the end who have played a lot of international cricket between them were exactly the sort of heads you want coming in when the going gets tough.'

He added: 'We need to bounce back because we have got a big game on Monday against Surrey and another on Tuesday, so we have got to get back up and get on with the game.'

Apart from Craig Kieswetter, who batted throughout the innings, Somerset struggled to score runs against a tight bowling attack, posting 125 for six from their 20 overs.

Hampshire came to terms with the conditions and paced their reply well to reach their target with an over to spare thanks in the end to an unbroken partnership of 52 between seasoned campaigners Neil McKenzie and Simon Katich.

After being put in to bat Somerset openers Craig Kieswetter and Richard Levi took six runs off the first over, bowled by Liam Dawson from the Cathedral Road End. Dimitri Mascarenhas opened the bowling from the River End and with his first delivery had Levi caught at mid on by Simon Katich.

New batsman Marcus Trescothick soon found his T20 touch and launched Dawson high over long on, to raise a cheer from the large Somerset contingent in the crowd. Mascarenhas put an end to Trescothick's run spree when he bowled the skipper in the fourth over as he looked to work the ball to leg. Dawson followed up with another tight over and after five Somerset found themselves 24 for two.

Danny Briggs replaced Dawson at the Cathedral End and with his second ball bowled James Hildreth, trying to sweep.

Hampshire continued to exert the pressure making it hard for the Somerset batsmen to get runs on the board. It was Jos Buttler who ended the deadlock when he launched Briggs over the long off boundary off the penultimate ball of the ninth over.

Buttler brought up the 50 with a off drive to the boundary off Chris Wood in the ninth over and at the half way stage Somerset were 52 for three. However the 21 year old chanced his arm once too often and was bowled by Sean Ervine for 16 with the score on 52.

New batsman Pete Trego was next man to go, leg before wicket going for the pull shot off Ervine and Somerset found themselves 58 for five.

Kieswetter gave the Somerset fans something to cheer about when he hit Dawson, who had changed to the River End, over long on and out of the ground, which he followed up two balls later with a boundary through mid wicket.

Gregory joined Kieswetter and the sixth wicket pair rallied the situation and put on 32 in 4.1 overs until with the total on 90 Gregory was run out for nine going for a second run to the non-striker's end.

Kieswetter went to his half century with a clipped four to mid wicket, which came off 51 balls and included three fours and a six, and next delivery took another boundary this time to fine leg to bring up the hundred.

The England ODI gloveman skied the next delivery high to short square leg and almost failed to complete his run but the chance was spilled by Katich.

Somerset went into the final over 115 for six and thanks to an acrobatic four to square cover from Kieswetter they reached 125, Kieswetter unbeaten on 63.

Defending a relatively small total Somerset had to bowl tight, but it almost looked a lost cause when Michael Carberry took 12 off the first over.

Kirby replaced Thomas from the River End and last ball of his second over had Jimmy Adams brilliantly caught by Buttler diving high and wide to his right at mid wicket.

Leg spinner Max Waller came on at the Cathedral Road End for the eighth over and third ball he bowled James Vince for seven.

Next over quick work by Kieswetter who scampered into the offside to field a shot from Neil McKenzie and threw the ball to Trego, who hit the stumps from short range to run out Carberry, who had advanced a long way down the wicket for 33. At the halfway stage Hampshire had reached 59 for three.

Hampshire looked to be closing on their victory target but Lewis Gregory accounted for McKenzie leg before wicket for 10 in the 13th over to make it 72 for four.

Katich and Ervine then came together and remained at the crease until they saw their side home with an over to spare, by which time Ervine had moved onto 34 and Katich 32.

SUNDAY, 26 AUGUST.

The morning after yet another heartbreaking appearance in a Finals Day breaks with some heavy questions in the air. I would never disclose in a book like this the workings of the club's senior management team in relation to such matters. It would corrupt management integrity and could compromise the club. Suffice to say those of us entrusted to manage the club and its affairs do think long and deep about performance on and off the field of play, and the causatory factors. The following Chinese proverb sums it up: 'Deep doubts, deep wisdom; small doubts, little wisdom.' I have some deep doubts this morning and only hope my management experience will pass muster in the weeks and months ahead.

On a brighter note our magnificent disabled team have won another trophy – this time the annual challenge cup against Dorset CC.

SOMERSET DISABLED TEAM WIN CUP – SCCC Site

The youth and development team of the Somerset Disabled Cricket Club's Dragons XI took part in their annual challenge match against Dorset CC at Dorchester's ground for the Harry Pickersgill Cup.

Somerset won the toss and had no hesitation in putting Dorset into bat.

The Dragons' youthful side, drilled by team manager Jason Mayled, put pressure on the Dorset batsmen throughout their 30-over innings and restricted them to 96-8.

Star bowlers were Jack Milton and Ben Hallows, while Harry Rutter in his first season in the team also provided a spectacular direct hit run out.

In reply although Somerset lost the early wickets of Mike Contreras and Adam Snow, the ever-reliable James Mayled (14 no) and Jack Milton (40 no) saw the Dragons home to victory.

MONDAY, 27 AUGUST. THE COUNTY GROUND. CB40, SOMERSET V SURREY

The English summer weather returned and the game was abandoned after only a few overs. Regrettably this marked the end of our journey in this year's competition in spite of a remarkable run of being unbeaten in the last eight games. A return to Lord's for a third consecutive year was not to be. This season's adventures with the white ball are ending with a whimper.

TUESDAY, 28 AUGUST. THE COUNTY GROUND. LVCCI, SOMERSET V SURREY. DAY I

Phone call from Giles re Finals Day at Cardiff. He calls to pass on some observations and we have a frank chat. As ever he is wise counsel.

Meanwhile on the pitch Surrey got a move on and Kevin Pietersen left his England troubles behind and hit a superb 163 – his forty-fifth first-class century. Nevertheless, helped by four wickets from Lancashire loanee Saj Mahmood, we bowled out Surrey for 317.

At stumps we had replied with 42 for two, losing Arul Suppiah for a duck and Marcus Trescothick for 3 to Jon Lewis and the pacey Stuart Meaker. Tomorrow promises to be good, attritional cricket as the vaunted Surrey attack face our long batting line-up.

WEDNESDAY, 29 AUGUST. THE COUNTY GROUND. LVCCI, SOMERSET V SURREY. DAY 2

Summer returned and not a single ball was bowled. The only averages improved were those of some of the players on FIFA 12, I suspect. Meanwhile in the Med not a cloud in the sky as the heat wave continues unabated.

THURSDAY, 30 AUGUST. THE COUNTY GROUND. LVCCI, SOMERSET V SURREY. DAY 3

My plans to spend another idle day with the family in the Mediterranean sunshine were thwarted. The peace of the siesta was punctured by an event a thousand miles away at the County Ground. Young batter Alex Barrow has been Mankaded by none other than Murali Kartik. I unsuccessfully tried to explain to Linda why this 'within the rules' run-out was seen as probably the most heinous crime in cricket, its perpetrators damned in the annals of the game as cads. The Twittersphere exploded and feelings were running extremely high. An angry throng of Somerset *and* Surrey fans had gathered around the Caddy Shack as the teams came off for tea, and according to eye-witness accounts they positively writhed with anger. Banger had to interrupt his tea break and personally placate a Somerset member who was giving a passable impression of assembling a lynch mob.

Surrey Chairman Richard Thompson was also in the Med and his tranquillity was similarly shattered. He rang me to make a formal apology, which I accepted with good grace. We agreed in the interests of both clubs and the game to do our utmost to douse the flames and not fuel the media bonfire with more petrol. I followed that up with calls to Guy Lavender, who already had his Chief Executive's high-pressure hose aimed at the seat of the fire, and Roy Kerslake, who was there – and still had steam coming out of his ears.

Meanwhile on the pitch Tregs, who can always be relied upon when our backs are to the wall, responded with an innings of genuine quality to help us to 294 all out. By the close, Surrey had increased their first-innings lead of 23 to 81, with all ten second-innings wickets intact.

FRIDAY, 31 AUGUST. THE COUNTY GROUND. LVCCI, SOMERSET V SURREY. DAY 4

Potentially difficult conversations took place today in respect of Rosey's retirement. I called him from Spain and had a very constructive and amiable chat. He has behaved throughout with great dignity and intelligence and at all times genuinely puts the club's interests before his own.

On the pitch, after the hiatus of yesterday, neither side would countenance defeat, and so the contest gradually deflated as Surrey batted out the day to close on 305 for five. This result went towards preserving Surrey's valued First Division status, while we took a modest eight points to leave our hopes of a maiden Championship hanging by the slenderest of threads.

The article below by Richard Walsh is a poignant one and signals Rosey's reflections on a very tough season.

ROSE ADMITS IT HAS BEEN A DIFFICULT YEAR FOR SOMERSET CCC –
This is Somerset

Somerset director of cricket Brian Rose admits that this has been the most difficult year he has experienced since taking over the role in 2005, writes Richard Walsh.

But despite all of the setbacks the club has still managed to get to the T20 Finals for the fourth successive year, even though they were left empty handed once again at the weekend.

'We have suffered another bitterly disappointing day, but we have got to the finals of the T20 for the fourth year in a row as well as the last two CB40 finals,' he said.

'As director of cricket I think that this is the most difficult year I have ever had in terms of keeping a squad together because of injuries and international call ups, and recruiting overseas players.'

'The club will obviously want to do something because we are trophy-less again and the public get frustrated and the players understand that, and you can imagine the effect that it has on them.'

But Rose added: 'Directors of cricket and clubs have to look in the long term and when I took over in 2005 we were very lucky to win a competition straight away and then we were promoted in 2007 and we have gone from strength to strength since then, so we are light years ahead of where we were and people tend to forget that.'

'Where we are now compared to where we were then is that we are in space, so I think people have to temper their disappointment with that fact, and yes we will definitely look at improving what we do in certain areas and we are working on that at the moment, and one of them is definitely recruitment.'

'We will have a look at the international programme for next season but ideally I would like to have the best English qualified squad I can get and alleviate the problems of getting international Test players over for a long period, which is becoming practically impossible. For the T20 we will try to get the best available players in the world.'

Meanwhile Somerset are due to complete a championship match against Surrey on Friday and then travel to face Sussex at Hove in their penultimate four day game starting on Tuesday.

SEPTEMBER

SUNDAY, 2 SEPTEMBER. LORD'S. ODI, ENGLAND V SOUTH AFRICA

Linda and I were guests of the Surrey Chairman at The Oval for this game and we arrived in good time. The first person I bumped into was none other than our own President, Roy Kerslake. A pleasant surprise as I hadn't seen him for twenty-four hours!

The match took on another Somerset hue as Bagel set a record for an England keeper in ODIs with three sharp stumpings, all off the canny bowling of Tredwell.

Giles Clarke and Gordon Hollins were fellow guests and I took the opportunity to have another chat re the MMG's process with our application. They are due to finalise their recommendation shortly, in time for the next ECB board meeting in October.

TREDWELL TRADITIONS LEAVE SOUTH AFRICA STUMPED – David Hopps, ESPN Cricinfo

Stumped Kieswetter bowled Tredwell is hardly the commonest entry on England scorecards, but it dominated proceedings at Lord's as England took a 2-1 lead against South Africa in the NatWest series with one to play and as a result ensured they would complete the series at the top of the ODI rankings. India will have the opportunity to claim that status when they face England in January.

Three times, James Tredwell lured a South Africa batsman down the pitch and three times Craig Kieswetter completed a stumping. It was the first time an England wicketkeeper had pulled off three stumpings in a one-day international and it set them en route to a comprehensive six-wicket victory with 20 balls to spare.

Ian Bell, with 88 from 137 balls, ensured England's run chase would stay on course, a task not entirely straightforward with the floodlights piercing the gloom and mizzle causing a 20-minute stoppage. He fell with victory in sight, making room to cut Dale Steyn, South Africa's one bowler of menace, over the off side and edging to the wicketkeeper, his man-of-the-match award assured. Craig Kieswetter completed victory to cheers by depositing Steyn for six into the pavilion.

Bell's Warwickshire team mate Jonathan Trott offered grim, indeed grimacing support, in a second-wicket stand of 141 in 31 overs, batting on gamely for 48 after being struck on the hand during a fiery opening spell from Steyn, who also removed Alastair Cook lbw in his first over with a high-class inswinger. Trott, not as much a Bear with a sore head as a Bear with a sore hand, will have a hospital scan on Monday morning.

Trott took a blow on the hand in Steyn's third over and needed pain-killing spray and tablets as he batted on manfully in obvious discomfort. One upper-cut over point off Tsotsobe Lonwabo was followed by a curse at the discomfort and he settled for wise deflections thereafter. Not that it would have unduly bothered him.

Like Trott, Tredwell is a representative of an unglamorous species. His very appearance, unassuming in manner, deliberate in tread and economical of hair, accentuates the impression. He does not even deal in Graeme Swann's happy brand of kidology. But South Africa will give more attention to this thoughtful Kent cricketer after his figures of 3 for 34 gave England an advantage they never relinquished.

It was an influential toss for England to win on a murky, overcast September morning. Their catching and fielding was again sketchy, but at least the Tredwell/Kieswetter combination was working well. JP Duminy, who had looked fallible against Swann's off spin earlier in the summer, was the first batsman removed, in Tredwell's second over. Then he returned in his second spell to defeat de Villiers' expansive drive and extended the habit by finding appreciable turn past Wayne Parnell's outside edge.

Tredwell's success transformed his morning. He has the convivial air of a suburban doctor and any self-diagnosis changed from feeling decidedly poorly to tip-top condition. He began by dropping Hashim Amla at second slip, not a habit designed to make winning cricket matches any easier. Amla had 5 when Finn found the edge and Tredwell, fingers pointing downwards as the ball reached him at shoulder height, fumbled a chance he made more awkward than it might have been. England have been dropping Amla throughout the summer and have given him more than 500 additional runs since the start of the Test series. Here they also lost their review in attempting to have an lbw call overturned.

Ravi Bopara, who was unfortunate not to have Amla lbw, belatedly removed him for 45, seaming the ball back a little into the stumps as he defeated a loose drive. It was the sort of classically English late-season day when Bopara's wobbly medium pace had an influential role to play. But

Bopara's batting was again found wanting, an unfocused innings ending cheaply when Ryan McLaren defeated a lethargic drive.

Tredwell, the latest addition to a rickety England close-catching cordon, also missed Graeme Smith at slip off Finn when Kieswetter dived across him and unsettled his view, the ball striking him on the body; they were a happier couple when they were a length of the pitch apart. Smith's reprieve was not too costly for England as Dernbach surprised him with a bouncer which he top-edged through to the keeper.

Once he and Amla departed, many who followed lacked the same threat. De Villiers, with 39 from 45 balls, got himself into a position to play a decisive innings before Tredwell pushed one a little wider for the stumping, but Faf du Plessis is horribly out of form as he proved when he unwisely tried to run a ball from Bopara against the Lord's slope.

Elgar is another South Africa batsman who has been inhibited in English conditions. His 35 occupied 59 balls before he tried to pull Finn's slower-ball bouncer and gloved to the keeper. Ryan McLaren was run out the next ball, Finn's disappointment when a good appeal for lbw was refused turning to delight when Dernbach dashed around the boundary at third man and hit the stumps direct.

That South Africa made as many as they did was largely thanks to a highly imaginative unbeaten 31 from 20 balls by Robin Peterson, the highlight of which was a reverse hit over extra cover for six into the Grandstand. But South Africa's one-day side lacks the balance and certainty that the Test XI displayed so emphatically.

MONDAY, 3 SEPTEMBER. THE COUNTY GROUND.
MEETING OF THE MANAGEMENT SUB COMMITTEE

The meeting was overshadowed by the news that Brian Rose was stepping down. The discussions were sombre and dignified. No one has done more for Somerset County Cricket Club in the post-war years, and it is a matter of huge regret that all that he has accomplished could not be crowned by more trophies. It was not possible to have come any closer to the Championship (Durham 2009) and limited-overs success (T20 Rose Bowl 2010). We discussed the next steps and planning to begin the search for his successor.

We then moved on to cover ticket and membership prices for 2013, finance and the likely year-end result, and then the latest developments in relation to Phase IV and our application for Category B status. After the meeting I had time to reflect upon the change being made in DOC.

Successful organisations – whether in business or sport – strike the right balance between too much change and too little. Chopping and changing, or knee-jerking, only creates a perception of improvement and rarely achieves anything of substance. Conversely, organisations which eschew change breed complacency and calcify, and inertia sets in – they are invariably left in the wake of their rivals. Somerset County Cricket Club has been relatively successful both on and off the pitch in the last ten years and it's interesting to reflect on the management changes over the period: three Presidents; three Chairmen; three Chief Executives; two Treasurers; one Director of Cricket; eight Captains and two Head Coaches. If change is to be judged by results achieved in cricket, finance and membership levels, then this amount of change has probably been about right. Now, after eight seasons in post, the club's management and Brian Rose have jointly agreed that a change in DOC would be beneficial.

Brian's eight seasons as DOC have been very successful. The club's First XI have progressed from Second Division mediocrity, and consistent failure to reach the knock-out stages in one-day competitions, to achieving top four positions in all three competitions for the last four seasons. Although winning the T20 competition in 2005, finishing as LVCC runners-up in 2009 and reaching the semi-finals of the Champions League in 2011 were notable high points, Brian's greatest and enduring legacy will probably be the development of the club's Academy, which has identified and produced a great many players who have graduated to the first-team squad, with several also progressing to international honours. Brian's knowledge, experience and network will remain available to the club, as he will continue to advise us in a consultancy capacity.

The search for our new DOC is under way and we are confident of attracting some of the greatest talents in world cricket to apply for the role.

TUESDAY, 4 SEPTEMBER. HOVE. LVCC I, SUSSEX V SOMERSET. DAY I

Our penultimate game in what has been a difficult and challenging season. While the Championship is now Warwickshire's to lose, recent seasons have gone right to the wire as all Somerset supporters know only too well. Our fixture at Hove is intriguing because Sussex had played themselves into the outstanding position of being in the mix for all three competitions with only two weeks of the season left. Since then, unfortunately, they have fluffed their lines twice in a week, losing to Yorkshire at the T20 Finals Day and a week later missing out on the pilgrimage to Lord's by going down at home to Hampshire in the CB40 semi-final. However, they lie second in the LVCC and a win against us would put them in a strong position with one game to go – especially since Wawks and Notts meet each other this week for the second time in a month!

We are not only playing for pride – mathematically we could still win the Championship, and the kudos of a top-three finish and the significant prize money will spur us on.

Team-wise we are without a regular keeper, as Jos and Bagel are on England duty, while we have a surfeit of spinners as Manny has returned from Pakistan and Irish U19 World Cup skipper Dockrell is back from Australia. The cricketing triumvirate will have had some selection quandaries to deal with.

•••

The first day is a bright one for us as Banger bags *another* five-catch haul at first slip and then makes a serene start to our first-innings reply. Interestingly we won the toss and Sussex were inserted, although Manny would only be at Heathrow at lunchtime, having returned from international duties against Australia in Sharjah.

Even with Sussex on 96 for one, Roy Kerslake maintained we had made the right call to bowl, and as is usually is the case our President's view turned out to be correct as lively swing from Fons reduced Sussex to 184 for six at tea. They were dismissed for 221 – a total said by the Sussex cognoscenti to be 50 runs below par.

WEDNESDAY, 5 SEPTEMBER. HOVE. LVCCI, SUSSEX V SOMERSET. DAY 2

Spoke to Richard Gould today and caught up on several matters. Planning has begun for a reception and send-off for Rosey after play on the final day of the match against Worcestershire next week in Taunton. It will be announced on the club site, so that members and fans who wish to show him their gratitude and respect may attend and do so.

We also agree with Rosey to announce his retirement today. Richard Walsh's article below puts it well.

BRIAN ROSE STANDS DOWN AS SOMERSET DIRECTOR OF CRICKET AFTER EIGHT YEARS – *Bristol Evening Post*

Brian Rose revealed he decided to step down as Somerset's director of cricket in the wake of their latest Friends Life T20 Finals Day defeat – and the club will now conduct a thorough search for his successor.

Rose, who captained Somerset during the most successful spell in the club's history, has transformed the playing side at Taunton since returning to the County Ground in 2004.

But his inability to see them over the line in the major domestic tournaments in the last three years – Somerset have been beaten in five finals and a semi-final, in addition to a Champions League T20 semi-final – led him to the decision that now is the time to stand down.

Rose will continue to assist Somerset next summer, providing support in an as-yet-unspecific advisory role – but the club will now take its time over appointing a new leader they feel can guide them to a trophy-laden period of success.

'After the result at the SWALEC Stadium and another defeat on Finals Day, I have come to the conclusion that a new and fresh approach is needed at first-team level,' said Rose. 'I will continue to try to assist the club in meeting its core objective of winning trophies.'

'The success of the club off the pitch – and the real financial strength it has achieved – has been remarkable. It has allowed greater investment in the development of our cricket structure, in tandem with the wonderful transformation of the County Ground, making it one of the most atmospheric stadiums in which to play cricket.'

'The future development on the south side of the ground should ensure one-day internationals and make Taunton a unique place in world cricket. Somerset County Cricket Club is extremely well placed to prosper in the future – and I look forward to seeing this magnificent club go on to even greater things.'

Rose recently admitted that this season had been the most difficult he had experienced since returning to the club, with a host of issues such as injuries and the unavailability of overseas signings making it all the more remarkable Somerset have managed to remain as competitive as they have.

They could still end up as runners-up in the LV= County Championship, after losing in the Friends Life T20 semi-finals and missing out on a place in the CB40 semi-finals on the final day of group matches.

'I have had immense pride in overseeing the development of Somerset cricket over the last eight seasons as director of cricket,' added Rose. 'Our progress in that time from the age groups through to the first team has been outstanding, with teams competing at the highest levels across the board.'

'The cricket played by our teams has been highly attractive to watch and is reflected by the fantastic support from members and supporters. I also take a lot of pride in the development of the talented young cricketers that are now representing England, England Lions and England under-19s.'

Somerset chairman Andy Nash paid tribute to Rose's 'unique' service to Somerset – and will now, along with chief executive Guy Lavender and other top club officials, set about finding his replacement.

'Brian has uniquely served the club with great distinction as a player, captain and director of cricket,' said Nash. 'He remains the club's most successful captain, winning five trophies – and, since 2004, has transformed the performance of the first team, taking them from the bottom of the second division to one of the most consistent and competitive sides in all three competitions.'

'We are delighted that he has offered to provide on-going advice next year, which will allow us to draw on his immense knowledge and understanding of the game. This decision provides the club with the opportunity to take stock and ensure we are effectively positioned for the 2013 season.'

Chief executive Lavender said a recruitment process would now begin – but that the club was yet to decide on a formal management structure for the playing side from next season.

'We are mulling it over at the moment, so it's not something I can give a definitive answer on, apart from the fact we will be looking to recruit. There is a good opportunity now to take stock. We have got time – and we have to make sure we get it right.'

Twitter has been active in the wake of Rosey's decision becoming public. It has been exactly what we had hoped for – overwhelmingly positive, with a great many Somerset supporters and cricket lovers in general paying tribute to Brian and all that he has achieved. A selection were picked out by Richard Walsh and posted on our site. I texted Rosey, pointing out what was being said (he himself is not a great Twitterer), as he and Stevie should draw great satisfaction from the comments. Here are a few of the best:

Sad to hear Brian Rose is stepping down as Director of Cricket at #SomersetCCC. Thank you, Mr. Rose, for the years of pleasure. *Mark Gristock*

How can you replace Brian Rose? You cannot. *Chris Blackmore*

I still can't believe Brian Rose has gone... :/ *Sarah!*

Brian Rose is an absolute gentleman and wonderful asset to the game of cricket. *Barney Girnun*

Huge respect for Brian Rose. His career at Somerset had been unprecedented (Player and DOC). What next for @SomersetCCC? *GreenArmy*

Good luck to Brian Rose & ta for what he's done for Somerset. Great captain (except 1 dodgy declaration) & great leader! *Kevin Simmons*

Brian Rose is stepping down? That's very sad news. Not least because i'm named after him! *Rosie Posie*

Meanwhile at Hove our promising start on the first day proved illusory. I spoke with Roy Kerslake before play began on day two and not for the first time this season his concern proved well founded. Our batting collapsed after a promising start as the ball nibbled about in the sea breeze and on a dry track, and when it stopped seaming Monty continued his excellent run of form.

Banger still managed a milestone and it is good to see wide and generous acknowledgement of his achievement of the 20,000 first-class run benchmark. It was a significant day for Sussex supporters too, with the evergreen Murray Goodwin playing his last innings for the county as he retires in his fortieth year. He returned to form, posting an unbeaten half century in the second dig.

Having dismissed Sussex yesterday for, according to the Sussex cognoscenti, a fifty-below-par 221, we limply surrender for a deficit of 87, allowing Sussex to bat again before tea on the second day. They do so as if on a different track – Nash and Goodwin, in his last home game, extend the host's lead effortlessly to 273 at stumps.

THURSDAY, 6 SEPTEMBER. HOVE. LVCCI, SUSSEX V SOMERSET. DAY 3

The LVCC may disappoint this season as the Championship itself may not go to the last day, or even match, of the season – the excitement of which we've become accustomed to in recent seasons! Warwickshire may wrap it up today, as Worcestershire are staring down the barrels of an innings defeat inside three days.

•••

On Taunton station, while making my way to London for a business meeting, I bump into John Gannon, the Commercial Director of Brightside Group plc, the parent of eCar, one of our main and longest serving sponsors. He's wearing a tie, which either means he's in trouble (his wife's view, not mine) or he's meeting clients. I haven't seen him for a while so enjoy catching up, and in the light of recent events an interesting and wide-ranging conversation strikes up. He tells me of a friend's reaction whilst at the recent Mankad incident. It seems his friend really did overheat and sledged both KP and Kartik quite enthusiastically. KP, also not one to shy away from a confrontation, apparently responded with some colourful Anglo-Saxon of his own when it was suggested he might consider emigration as a means of solving the present impasse with Team England.

Gannon's eCar XI are due to play the Somerset CCC Chairman's XI a week on Monday at the County Ground and we both took the opportunity to engage in what the world of football calls mind games. I got the impression that Gannon's side will be a distinctly last-minute affair, and so I took great delight in letting him know that my side contains a wide range of talent stretching from a local publican (Les Biffin, of The Swan at Kingston St Mary) to an ex-Proteas wicketkeeper.

•••

At Hove we had a mixed day. Sussex's position at the start of play looked very strong and they were clear favourites to win and in so doing almost certainly secure runners-up spot in the County Championship.

A contest where batting collapses had been the norm produced yet another during the morning session when Sussex lost six wickets in 15 overs for 40 runs. Fons filed his boots, taking five for 68 – his second five-wicket haul of the season. Murray Goodwin, who fell 23 short of a century in his final appearance for Sussex, left the field to a standing ovation, accompanied by his sons, after a career which saw him score more than 20,000 runs for the county. It was announced that his number three shirt will also be retired. Without in any way detracting from the acknowledgement he deserves, I do wonder about this recent habit of retiring shirts – where will it end? It wouldn't be right to see players wearing three-figure squad numbers in the future ... would it? Or will numbers be 'un-retired'?

Chasing a daunting 396 to win, Somerset's Banger and Arul provided a glimpse of the improbable with a stand of 147 for the first wicket. However, in a classic twist of fate we lost a clatter of wickets in quick order to close on a less inspiring 155 for four at stumps, still 241 short!

FRIDAY, 7 SEPTEMBER. HOVE. LVCCI, SUSSEX V SOMERSET. DAY 4

The day breaks fine and warm and I've an early morning catch-up meeting with Guy Lavender, and before that a chat with Roy Kerslake. The opening topic is how we appear to have all but thrown away a brilliant fourth-innings start. Roy was there and related how the Aussie quickie Magoffin took heart from Banger's dismissal and stepped up a whole gear to account for three more wickets in just over an over.

While never totally giving up hope, it's fair to say we weren't overly optimistic about the day's prospects. We covered other topics in the light of Rosey's retirement.

The rest of the day passed with me taking the odd look at the score and gradually the runs were accumulated and the deficit reduced. It wasn't until after lunch that I dared to think that the unthinkable might happen after all for about the third time in this particular match! With thirty minutes to go I tuned in to BBC Radio Sussex to follow the commentator's incredulity at what was unfolding. By now tweets were flying around like confetti and the Somerset massive was awakening to events in Hove. The climax came with some mighty blows from Tregs and some silkier cuts from Hildy and we crossed the line with 40 overs and five wickets to spare. Now, tables were well and truly turned, and with Notts going down to Surrey we were second in the table, with the prospect of the runners-up honour having switched county in just a day's play. It sets up a mouth-watering finale for next week.

David Hopps' article for ESPN Cricinfo below describes the day's events very well.

SOMERSET RISE TO CHALLENGE FOR ROSE FAREWELL – David Hopps, ESPN Cricinfo

Peter Trego thrashed Sussex's bowlers around the ground as Somerset stormed to victory. Only once have Somerset pulled off a fourth-innings run chase of greater magnitude than this and Yorkshire still shudder at its memory. Sussex will feel similarly shaken after Somerset surged to a five-wicket victory which gives them the opportunity to steal the runners-up position in Division One at the last.

Peter Trego at his belligerent best, alongside a suave unbeaten century by James Hildreth, completed an outstanding win, which took them one point clear of Sussex, who must feel mugged. Warwickshire might have secured the title but the runners-up position will now not be settled until the final day of the season.

When Trego flicked Steve Magoffin, Sussex's one bowler of real threat, through square leg for four Somerset had overhauled a target outdone in magnitude only by their successful fourth-innings chase of 479 for 6 against Yorkshire at Taunton in 2009.

The loss of four quick wickets at the fag end of the third day had seemed likely to cost Somerset dearly, but Hildreth, who finished unbeaten on 101 from 180 balls, steadied matters on the final morning with Alex Barrow and then was content to tick along as Trego took command. Their partnership rattled along at more than six an over – 166 from 25 overs – and victory came with 40 overs to spare.

Trego finished unbeaten on 89 from 72 balls with 12 fours and four sixes. He is so consumed by attacking presence that bowlers can lose heart at the mere sight of him. He is surely unfortunate that England never give him a second thought in Twenty20. He could not be more dismissive of his chances. 'There is more chance of me growing a second winkie,' he said.

Trego destroyed a poor spell from James Anyon after lunch, helping himself to four boundaries in two overs from the bowler. The last was a rank long hop that he pulled for four and the previous deliveries were not much better. Three slog-sweeps for six against Sussex's spinners – the first against

Monty Panesar which took him to 50, the last two against Chris Nash – took Somerset within range. Even Magoffin was despatched over the ropes. Hildreth ticked off his hundred in the nick of time.

Hildreth's most fortunate moment was on 28 when he inside-edged Nash but the wicketkeeper, Ben Brown, failed to make contact. But, on this occasion at least, the Sussex bowling attack consisted of Magoffin and ragamuffins.

Magoffin took Sussex's only wicket of the final day. Hildreth and Barrow had taken their partnership to 80 in 32.2 overs when Magoffin, with the new ball only five deliveries old, found the penetration to have Barrow caught at first slip. But the wicket soon looked flat again, there was no swing under idyllic blue skies and Somerset reassumed control.

Barrow walked off slowly, his dejection apparent. He is only 20 and had looked composed for his 40. But you are not really a man until you have seen off the likes of Magoffin with a hard ball in hand.

'Where would we be without Magoffin?' asked a Sussex supporter at the deckchair end as the Queenslander struck. It turned out to be a rhetorical question. 'I'll tell you where we'd be. We'd be down the bottom with Worcestershire and Lancashire, that's where we'd be.'

Magoffin would be a contender for a Division One team of the season. Only a small handful of bowlers have taken more Division One wickets this season at lower cost than his 54 at 19.29. But the talk at the end was of Hildreth and Trego and, as so often in Somerset cricket, it was happy talk.

It has been a tough season for Somerset, with lots demanded of promising young players before their time. They have held together magnificently. Brian Rose, their outgoing director of cricket, might not be dreaming of another runners-up trophy, but they aim to give him one all the same, and celebrate his departure in style.

SATURDAY, 8 SEPTEMBER. CHESTER-LE-STREET. FIRST T20, ENGLAND V SOUTH AFRICA

As dusk falls on the domestic season the pace quickens with England as the World Cup in Sri Lanka draws near. Two of our finest young talents will feature, Bagel and Jos (the latter on his 21st birthday), and we all wish them well. The game, however, turns out to be a damp squib as following a run-out there's a clatter of wickets and we post a woefully inadequate total. The Proteas, with an abundance of T20 experience forged in the crucible of the IPL, barely break sweat in pursuit and run out winners by seven wickets.

Despite glorious sunshine (more reminiscent of an English winter these days) there are great swathes of empty seats at the Emirates stadium. I emailed the omnipresent Gordon Hollins and made the point that had this been at the County Ground it would have been full! He emailed back not long afterwards and accused me of being a 'fantastic opportunist'. I've been called worse things.

MONDAY, 10 SEPTEMBER. THE COUNTY GROUND

A plan has been drawn up to celebrate Rosey's reign as Director of Cricket on Friday and we will be publicising it. I'm sure a lot of members and supporters will attend the occasion wishing to pay tribute to all that Rosey has achieved since 2005 and show their appreciation in public. We are throwing open the Taunton Long Room after the presentation for all staff, players and invited guests. It will be an occasion to savour – especially if we clinch the runners-up honour for only the third time in our history.

The club's General Committee met this evening and the usual wide-ranging discussions took place. We produce an excellent monthly report along with the management accounts, which means those attending the meeting aren't there simply to learn about what's going on but to discuss the issues arising therefrom. In a cricket club, as in a business, it makes for much smoother meetings and better decision making.

TUESDAY, 11 SEPTEMBER. THE COUNTY GROUND.
LVCCI, SOMERSET V WORCESTERSHIRE. DAY 1

So here we are at the season's climax once again. For only the third time in our history we are in pole position to win the runners-up honour – which, given the plethora of problems we've had (injuries, the snakes and ladders of overseas players, international call-ups, and days lost in the wettest summer for a century) would be a remarkable achievement. In fact we've only lost one game since 1 July (T20 semi-final), and the only defeat we've suffered in the Championship was against Warwickshire, and that game spun on a sixpence. It would be a very proud note indeed for Rosey to retire upon. Let's hope we can dominate the Worcestershire game and win the honour in style.

Worcs batted, and the day's highlight was the brilliant bowling of Abdur Rehman, who took nine wickets for 65, his career best, to become only the tenth player to achieve this feat for Somerset. The last Somerset bowler to take nine wickets in an innings, way back in 1993, was none other than Andrew Caddick, who skittled Lancashire for 72 when they required only 97 for a victory inside two days. One other player in today's match witnessed Caddy's career-best performance that day – a 17-year-old from Keynsham by the name of Marcus Trescothick, who was making his first-class debut!

Manny's performance – just what spinners are brought in to do in late summer on dry English wickets – has propelled us towards an all-important victory.

While in Memory Lane I'll mention that Brian Langford, who still holds the record for the most appearances for Somerset with 504 first-class matches to his name, over a career that spanned twenty-one years between 1953 and 1974, took nine for 26, his career best, also against Lancashire at Weston-super-Mare in 1958. In the second innings Langford followed up with six for 28 in the second to end with match figures of fifteen for 54.

Below is the email sent to all Somerset CCC members announcing Rosey's retirement.

Brian Rose standing down as Director of Cricket – email to all Somerset County Cricket Club members

After almost a lifetime of distinguished service to Somerset County Cricket Club, Brian Rose has decided by mutual agreement to step down as the Director of Cricket on completion of the 2012 season. The Club would like to invite you to come along and mark this occasion at a special post-match event on completion of this match when a presentation will be made to Brian on the pitch in front of the Andrew Caddick Pavilion. You will then be able to join Brian, Club Chairman Andy Nash and Club President Roy Kerslake in the County Room for an informal drink and chat.

Brian will feature in 2013 in an advisory capacity, however Somerset Chairman Andy Nash feels it is important for all members and supporters to have the opportunity to thank Brian for his many years of service.

'Brian has uniquely served the Club with great distinction as a player, Captain and latterly as the Director of Cricket. He remains the Club's most successful Captain winning five trophies, and since 2004 has transformed the performance of the First Team taking them from the bottom of the second division to one of the most consistent and competitive sides in all three competitions.

Somerset prides itself on being a family orientated Club, and as a result we hope many of our members and supporters will come and wish Brian a fond and fitting farewell.'

EDGBASTON. THIRD T20, ENGLAND V SOUTH AFRICA

I was on business in London and had supper with my son Ed and wife Linda. We followed every ball with Cricinfo's excellent new app. Great excitement ensued over a curry in Brick Lane as Bagel and Jos took the game away from the Proteas with 48 runs brutally accumulated in just 14 balls. A very proud passage of play for all Somerset fans as the West Country dispatched the Proteas in style.

WEDNESDAY, 12 SEPTEMBER. THE COUNTY GROUND.
LVCCI, SOMERSET V WORCESTERSHIRE. DAY 2

Compo was welcomed back from injury and as the leading run-maker in first-class cricket this summer he continued where he left off in his last game, hitting an unbeaten 114 in our formidable total of 451 for seven. This took his first-class total to 1,453 at a Bradmanesque 96.86. Banger joined in, helping himself to another big century with 146. This gave us a lead of 239 over the young Worcs side with two days to go.

At lunch we were 227 for only the loss of Arul, so the pitch inspector, who had stayed on after Abdur Rehman's nine-wicket haul on the first day, was able to take his leave.

I chatted to Roy Kerslake, Guy Lavender and Rosey about plans in case the game ends tomorrow as it now looks like it might. Rosey was understanding about the fact that I wouldn't be able to join him if the game ended tomorrow but was pleased, if not a little abashed, with the arrangements that have been made for him.

THURSDAY, 13 SEPTEMBER. THE COUNTY GROUND.
LVCCI, SOMERSET V WORCESTERSHIRE. DAY 3

I have a really busy day on business in London and catch up with the latest score between meetings. We play magnificently with Compo joining Marcus with a big hundred and then Manny taking the best figures of any bowler all season with fourteen for 110!

Before I get to my last meeting at the *FT*'s building the match is over and a huge band of members and supporters gather to pay tribute to Rosey and the team's terrific achievement of the honour of Runners-Up in the LVCC.

Giles Clarke rang me to pass on the ECB's congratulations to Somerset and in turn I passed them down the chain of command at the club. Speaking to Guy Lavender it was really heartwarming to hear the celebratory noises in the background. A very large crowd, some many thousands strong, appeared at the ground, not only to witness our feat but also to give Rosey a rousing and moving send-off. I was very sad to have to miss it.

I was asked to compose a piece for the club's site and media. I found a dingy cafe under some railway arches on the South Bank and with a mug of tea for company I put pen to paper, or rather bashed out some copy on my iPad.

No sooner had I done that than George Dobell was on the line asking me about Rory Hamilton-Brown. We had an off-the-record chat and it stayed at that.

Still with time to kill I dropped a line to my counterpart at Derby CCC to congratulate them on their clinching of the Division 2 title and their elevation to the top flight. Chris Grant is slowly performing wonders at Derby and he has been very gracious in his comments about what we've achieved at Somerset in recent years – I was genuinely delighted to repay the compliment.

Andy Nash email to Chris Grant:

Dear Chris,

My heartiest congratulations on your elevation. Richly deserved and all the more given the adversity you've overcome. This is truly great for English cricket and the Counties: we have to eschew the Cat A's dominating the game.

I really do look forward to welcoming you, your squad and supporters to Taunton next year.

Enjoy your celebrations and my very best wishes for the future.

Kind regards, Andy

Chris Grant email reply:

Very kind of you to email Andy and many thanks for your kind words.

I have the utmost respect for everything you and your team has achieved at Somerset and would be delighted if we could do a fraction of what you have done.

Can't wait to see you down there next Summer.

Thank you so much Andy.

Richard Walsh's nice article below is worth savouring.

MARCUS SO PROUD OF SUCCESS AGAINST THE ODDS – SCCC Site

Marcus Trescothick was a proud skipper after his Somerset side clinched runners-up spot in the LV=County Championship against all the odds after a season ravaged by injuries.

The innings victory over Worcestershire at Taunton provided a fitting end to Brian Rose's eight seasons as Director of Cricket and a special presentation was made to him by club president Roy Kerslake at the conclusion of the game.

There was warm applause from players and a large gathering of supporters as Roy outlined Brian's tremendous service to Somerset as player, captain and most recently head of the cricketing side of the club, describing him as 'a true Somerset legend'.

Marcus revealed that he will enter hospital next week for another operation on his problem ankle, but stressed it was 'a cleaning up job', which hopefully will enable him to be fully fit for the start of the 2013 season.

The skipper told this website: 'It has been a testing season and to come out of it in second place in the Championship is something we should all feel proud of.

'I'm not sure how many players we have used, but we have finished the season strongly, with Abdur Rehman playing a key part.'

'He showed himself to be a truly world class spinner against Worcestershire. Getting 14 wickets in a game is a serious effort on any pitch.'

'Nick Compton was outstanding again, as he has been for most of the season, and we all hope he gets an England call-up as reward.'

'We have work to do as a squad and things we have to improve on. We know Craig Kieswetter and Jos Buttler are likely to be away with England a lot and after last night's performance Jos could be a target for IPL clubs.'

'Consistency of team selection is key to a good Championship season and we haven't had that. But there is clearly the potential to go one better than this season.'

Somerset chairman Andy Nash told this website: 'I have just received a call from Giles Clarke and accepted the congratulations of the ECB on Somerset County Cricket Club's considerable achievement this afternoon.'

'In turn I should like to warmly congratulate our Chief Executive, Director of Cricket, Coach, Captain, the first team squad and their back room staff on their notable achievement of Runners-up in the LVCC.

'To be the second best side of the eighteen counties is a wonderful prize in itself, but to do so when our side has for large parts of the season been decimated by injuries and non-availability makes it all the more creditable.'

'I am extremely proud of them all and I'm doubly delighted that Rosey signs off today on a high note, his head held high and yet another huge feather in his cap.'

'Lastly, can I thank all our members and supporters for their loyal and unwavering support. Their presence and passion turn The County Ground into 'Fortress Taunton' time and time again. You are our thirteenth man and all of us at the Club greatly appreciate it.'

In my absence Roy Kerslake stepped up to the plate and presented Rosey with a photo montage of his long association with the club. Rosey was understandably emotional, as we all have been about his retirement – he has been an exemplary servant of the club.

THOUSANDS JOIN IN WITH BRIAN'S PRESENTATION – SCCC Site

At the end of the game against Worcestershire on Thursday afternoon Roy Kerslake the President of Somerset CCC made a presentation to Brian Rose who is stepping down from his role as Director of Cricket from the end of this season, after eight years in the post.

Thousands of people stayed behind to pay their own tributes to a man who has been involved with the County as player, captain, Chairman of Cricket and Director of Cricket, since first appearing for the Second XI in 1967 at the age of 17.

Before making the presentation the President recalled some of the high-lights of Brian's time at Somerset.

'Brian has served Somerset County Cricket Club with great distinction for more than 40 years, as a player, Captain, Chairman of the Cricket Committee and most recently as Director of Cricket.'

'As a captain Brian Rose led the County to five one day trophies between 1979 and 1983 and during his time as Director of Cricket, Somerset has become one of the most competitive sides in all formats of the game.'

Roy summed up when he said: 'Quite simply Brian Rose is a legend of Somerset County Cricket.'

The President then presented Brian Rose with a montage of photographic images from his time as player and Director of Cricket at Somerset.

Brian told everyone: 'It has been a privilege and an honour to be involved with the club over three decades as a player and captain, and play with some world class cricketers in a time when there were many international players in county cricket. It was a great honour for me to play at that time.'

Reflecting on 2012 Brian said: 'This year we have achieved wonderful things under great adversity and it's a great testimony to the organisation and the ethos of the club.'

Brian concluded: 'I'm not saying goodbye, it's just au revoir' before joining supporters and members of the committee in the County Room.

FRIDAY, 14 SEPTEMBER. LONDON

Early morning phone call from Giles Clarke. He is calling to compliment the club on the superb send-off for Brian Rose yesterday, and then we move on to chat about some prospective player movements. Press speculation has begun and the first movements of players have been confirmed. It usually starts with those who are being released, and I note that Chris Jordan from Surrey and ex-Somerset player Neil Edwards are moving out of Notts. There will be others. The more controversial moves will follow in due course.

I'm in London on business and on the return car journey I miss a call from Giles Clarke while on the M4. I can call him later. A few minutes later a call from Guy Lavender. Too much of a coincidence! This isn't likely to be good news. I pull off at the services near Chippenham and call Guy back.

Abdur Rehman (Manny), having achieved the best bowling figures of the season yesterday of fourteen for 110, has had what could prove to be an equally notable day today; but for entirely the wrong reason. He's failed a drug test on a sample taken in August. We have no further details and are informed that protocol requires us to stay quiet until further details are known.

SATURDAY, 15 SEPTEMBER. TAUNTON

The CB40 Final takes place at Lord's between two of our recent nemeses, Hampshire and Warwickshire. It's the first time since 2009 that we haven't featured in this event. I rather enjoy watching the event on TV with no pressure whatsoever. The crowd is disappointing and there are thousands of empty seats. A portent possibly of things to come, and it will be cited by the proponents of the 50-over format as evidence that the 40 isn't so popular that it can't be changed. I disagree – based on a great many conversations and letters/emails from supporters, the 50 will drive even more supporters away.

I speak to Guy Lavender and Roy Kerslake. There's much going on, including preparation for the much vaunted contest between the Somerset CCC Chairman's XI and sponsor eCar's side. The Chief and I are extremely rusty, so have arranged for some nets and throw-downs on Monday morning.

We've also just arranged a lunch with Lord Archer next month to discuss Phase IV of the County Ground's redevelopment and our plans for a fundraising campaign which he has kindly volunteered to lead.

•••

I popped into The Swan at Kingston St Mary, which is my local, to see the landlord Les Biffin. He's been selected for the Somerset CCC Chairman's XI on Monday and is as excited as a bishop in a brothel. Apparently it's been his long-held ambition to play on our hallowed square and on Monday – weather permitting – he will fulfil it. Last year we were rained off and I think it cast a long shadow over his winter.

Such is the excitement at the pub over his imminent (and well publicised) appearance that some of the clientele are planning to come along to watch. Fred (the pickled onion man – he produces the most delicious ones which have a kick like a mule) and Mike are already armed with sick notes from work, and several others are threatening to attend. Les' wife Lil has agreed to man the fort on Monday, which means Les has a 'late pass'. Things are brewing quite nicely.

Julian Catternach has already phoned me several times about the same fixture, and this afternoon a pal of his did likewise, enquiring if we needed another player. Surprisingly we have a full complement, but it could change.

•••

Late this evening the veil begins to be enticingly lifted on the 2013 season as the draw for the CB40 is made following Hampshire's memorable triumph – a far better draw than this year, as we've avoided a 'Group of Death'. We are to compete in Group C with the Unicorns, Glamorgan, Leicestershire, Yorkshire, Gloucestershire, Middlesex and Somerset.

MONDAY, 17 SEPTEMBER. TAUNTON. CHAIRMAN'S XI V ECAR XI

After all the pre-match bravado and mind games, the time for tittle-tattle is over and we will now do our talking on the pitch. The morning breaks to the all too familiar drizzle of this summer and a sky like dirty washing-up water; but the forecast is good. Frankly, even if it rains incessantly we will play, as it is the County Ground's last game of 2012. Guy Lavender has planned the event with military precision and fine attention to detail – wish that the same could be said of my team selection!

My failings in that regard return to haunt me later in the match as we somehow contrive to snatch defeat from the jaws of victory.

The match itself was played in an exemplary spirit. No complaints at all on that front. Where things unravelled was on the technical side. I said in my welcome to both teams that this legendary ground has been graced by the colossi of the game: WG, Bradman, Hobbs, Hammond, Sutcliffe, Warne, Murali, Tyson, Trueman, Sachin, Lara, Hadlee, Bedi, Miller, Lindwall, Border, Imran, Jayasuriya, Bedser, etc ... they have all played at Taunton. But despite that fact, I confidently predicted the County Ground had probably never seen a match of the quality about to unfold today. And so it came to pass. Dropped catches, run-outs, wides, byes, played and misses, clean bowled heaving across the line (me), diving over the ball in the deep, and some of the poorest calling and running between the wickets imaginable. But we had the closest finish with the Somerset CCC Chairman's XI requiring only 6 runs off (what should have been) the last ball to win. Of course we had another delivery as eCar's death bowler managed an above the waist (in fact above the shoulder) high no-ball which was duly spanked to the boundary. Our spirits soared, but – needing only 2 to win the game off the next last ball, as it were – my batter predictably managed to fluff his lines with an agricultural play and miss to ensure victory for eCar.

The crowd on the day peaked at fourteen – excluding the hardy souls wrapped in ski wear on the balconies of the apartments behind the Somerset stand.

The paucity of talent was more than compensated for by a wealth of bonhomie and comradeship fostered by the occasion. As John Gannon's valedictory note confessed it is every cricket fan's dream to play on a first-class wicket – albeit against fourth-class opposition. We repaired to the Long Room for a curry supper, and there the game was relived – time is a great healer and we managed to gloss over the few minor technical deficiencies and focus instead on some more meritorious moments. Finally the match tea adjourned to The Plough in Station Road and the County Ground settled down for the night.

•••

Meantime the media were busy on other matters, and the article below features the outstanding achievements and subsequent awards bestowed upon Compo and Tregs.

COMPTON AND TREGO SCOOP TOP HONOURS – *Bristol Evening Post*

Somerset duo Pete Trego and Nick Compton have been recognised for their impressive seasons by each securing a prestigious award.

All-rounder Trego has been crowned the Professional Cricketers' Association's overall 'MVP' for the 2012 season, while batsman Compton was named the Cricket Writers' Club's county cricketer of the year.

The most valuable player award, which is sponsored by FTI, is updated throughout the season – and 31-year-old Trego finished 60 points clear of Kent's Darren Stevens.

Trego took 50 LV= County Championship wickets for the first time in his career and also chipped in with 600 runs, while contributing 245 runs and 15 wickets in CB40 cricket. Introduced in 2007, the FTI MVP rankings reward players for every run scored, every wicket taken and every catch held. There are also bonuses awarded to those whose runs and wickets contribute to a win for the team, with captains earning points for their command of the side.

Compton, meanwhile, amassed 1,191 Championship runs at an average of 99.25, and will today be hoping to earn a call-up to England's squad for the tour of India.

Somerset and Gloucestershire will face each other in next season's CB40, after being drawn in the same group. Also in the West rivals' group are Glamorgan, Leicestershire, Middlesex, Unicorns and Yorkshire.

New Zealand all-rounder Scott Styris won the Walter Lawrence Trophy – awarded for the fastest century of the season – for the 37-ball hundred he scored against Gloucestershire in the Friends Life T20 quarter-final at Hove.

TUESDAY, 18 SEPTEMBER. TAUNTON AND SRI LANKA

John Gannon of eCar emails Guy and me. Clearly he's still emotionally unstable after his side's unlikely victory on Monday!

Gents,

A huge thank you to you both and the staff at the club for once again providing a memorable day at the County Ground.

I am not sure if you both fully appreciate the excitement generated by our team for a chance to play on a 'proper' 1st class wicket at a ground with all the history it has – it really is a fantastic experience and the whole team just loved it. We had some very excited people I can tell you.

Nasher – thanks for sorting the team and what a great bunch of guys you bought along – thanks also for making sure that Nick (ex Hants if I am right) went easy on us – good fun – never enough sledging for my like (sorry it goes with the genes) and what a change to have some decent weather.

I am not sure if you guys were taking it easy but it was a good close game and Brightside had a rare win – I remember the last time getting pasted by the 'young guns' and last time by Auburn Wills so it was a rare taste of victory for us.

It's personally a sad occasion for me that we are not able to continue the sponsorship for 2013 but I am sure you can appreciate decisions like this are taken at board level and it's a shame we can't go on as we have – anyway I have just loved the association with the club, the whole experience and the professional way the club has gone around making sure that our sponsorship money worked as hard as it could.

You have a great club and I can only wish you guys all the success for next season – you just can't help but feel with continued hard work by all both on and off the field that success is inevitable.

I do hope that we can keep a little bit of eCar at the County Ground for next year – and as my wife thinks I prefer the Long Room to my TV room (the beer is better in the former) I do hope that I can keep in touch with the club in a meaningful way.

Good luck with the appointment of the DOC position – it's a key role and you are spoilt for choice – but a choice that is made possible by providing the club with a solid financial base – with so many clubs struggling it's a real plus that the finances continue to perform well and it's set it all up for a promising season next year.

•••

Also today our Disabled XI were appearing in yet another National final, this time against Lancashire at the County Ground, Derby. Jon Tucker's side have won the County Championship no less than three times in recent years.

SOMERSET DISABLED CC JUST MISS OUT IN NATIONAL FINAL – SCCC Site

Somerset Disabled CC finish Runners Up in the County Championship after losing the National Final to Lancashire by 3 wickets. The match which was held at Derbyshire County Cricket Club saw Kieran Cosens awarded the Man of the Match Award for his all-round performance of 2-12 with the ball and 72 runs with the bat.

In a low scoring exciting game against an experienced Lancashire side, Somerset came very close but could not take the last few wickets needed to win the trophy. Captain Jon Tucker said after the game 'I am immensely proud of my side today, who kept fighting right until the end of the game, although we are desperately disappointed, playing in a national final at a County Ground is a great experience for our young side'.

The team dedicated their final appearance to their coach Dan Hodges who passed away in April of this year. The club would like to thank their coaches and supporters who supported them throughout the competition.

•••

The advertisement for our new DOC has appeared on the net, courtesy of the ECB's situations vacant area on their site, alongside some no less deserving but less high-profile roles. Here for the record is the ad:

SOMERSET COUNTY CRICKET CLUB – Director of Cricket

Somerset County Cricket Club is one of the most consistent and successful professional teams in the country with a worldwide profile. Success on the pitch has been matched off it, with the Club being profitable in 20 out of the last 21 years, including achieving the third highest profit in the game in 2011. With a superb ground, ongoing development plans and an extremely talented playing squad, prospects look excellent for 2013 and beyond.

The new Director of Cricket will lead the cricketing affairs of the Club, setting the overarching strategy as well as directing the delivery of First Team cricket in partnership with the Head Coach and supporting staff. This is not just a strategic role but one that requires hands-on involvement in the coaching, mentoring and development of individual players and the team more broadly. Whilst the achievement of First Team success will be the Director of Cricket's core priority, they will also be responsible for the continued developing of an outstanding Academy and player pathway.

The successful candidate will be a well-established coach at first-class or international level and this will have been preceded by an excellent playing career, preferably at international level. You will need to be an exceptional leader and motivator with the capacity and breadth to span a wide range of responsibilities. In addition, you will need to display the highest standards of written and verbal communication skills.

Somerset is a Club with a unique and proud history. We have ambitious plans to develop the Club both on and off the field, and the Director of Cricket's role is an outstanding opportunity to build on the Club's success and enviable reputation as one of the best sides in England and Wales. This is a senior role and an attractive salary and bonus package will be available for the right candidate.

If you would like to apply, please send a CV and covering note to recruitment@somersetcountycc.co.uk or if you'd prefer an initial conversation, please call our retained adviser, Peter Tucker of Novo Executive Search and Selection, on +44 7970 520956.

•••

Guy Lavender rings me at 10:30 p.m. This can't be good news and sure enough it isn't! More on Manny's failed drug test. This considerable blow is softened by the fact that the drug in question is a Category C recreational one and so the club is unlikely to be penalised. Drug taking, like gambling, is recognised as a major threat to the game and any involvement – no matter how relatively minor – is a canary falling off the perch moment. A wake-up call to management that we must be absolutely on our guard against these twin threats.

On a positive note Compo has deservedly received the call-up to senior England honours and, being the sort of club we are, this results in a flurry of phone calls and social media messages. I talk to Compo and rub in the positive sentiments which abound – he has worked incredibly hard since joining us from Middlesex and richly deserves his recognition and opportunity. Having finished our chat, I have to admit I also feel a tinge of disappointment as I'm certain he will cement a place in England's top order and so will be effectively lost to us for the greater part of the seasons to come.

Conversely we are also faced with the disappointment of Bagel not being named in the squad. It had appeared a certainty (if there is such a thing in matters in cricket selection) that he would be named as Matt Prior's deputy. This setback caused a flurry of phone calls between club and player and the ECB.

Tregs has won the coveted Most Valuable Player trophy for the 2012 season. He has had a phenomenal run with bat and ball and is never more potent than with his back to the wall. Time and time again he has scrapped in games this season to keep us in contests when we were depleted by other players' unavailability. On one occasion, due to injury restricting our options, he bowled 19 consecutive overs! Always glass half full, he is a terrific asset to the club and richly deserves his prize. For the uninitiated here's roughly how the MVP is calculated: bowlers receive higher marks for among other things good economy rates, bowling maidens and for dismissing batsmen higher up the order. They can also win bonus points for five or more dismissals in an innings. In addition, batting points are handed out for high run rates and the percentage of the team's runs each batsman contributes. Fielding points are awarded for catches, run-outs and stumpings. It is, therefore, a comprehensive scoring system and has no equal in evaluating a player's performance.

COMPTON WINS ENGLAND TEST CALL UP – SCCC Site

The England selectors today announced a 16-man Test squad to be captained by Alastair Cook for the forthcoming four-Test match series in India.

The squad includes two uncapped batsmen, Somerset's Nick Compton and Yorkshire's Joe Root, and three spin bowlers: Samit Patel, Monty Panesar and Graeme Swann.

Nick Compton was thrilled with the call up: 'I am honoured to gain selection for England and have the opportunity to play at the highest level. Like all professional sportsmen, playing for your country is what you aim for and dream about so while I don't want to get carried away because it is still early days, I really hope I can contribute and become a regular in the England side.'

'I would like to thank everyone at Somerset for their support this year, particularly Brian Rose and Andy Hurry. Being surrounded by very good players such as Marcus Trescothick and James Hildreth has allowed me to develop and playing for a winning side has certainly raised my game. I would also like to thank all the Somerset supporters who have been fantastic since I arrived three years ago. It was not an easy move, but knowing I had your support then and now is really appreciated.'

National Selector Geoff Miller said: 'Nick Compton has performed well consistently for Somerset in County cricket this season, made big hundreds and shown that he has the temperament and the technique to play at a higher level.'

The selectors have also named a 17-strong England Performance Programme squad which includes Jos Buttler and Craig Kieswetter. This squad will undertake a month-long tour of India from mid-November.

A seven-strong squad has also been announced for next month's Hong Kong Sixes tournament which will be managed by Somerset Head Coach Andy Hurry.

WEDNESDAY, 19 SEPTEMBER. TAUNTON AND SRI LANKA

The ad on the ECB's site has been spotted by the Somerset massive and the first applications have appeared. Without being disingenuous, the recruitment process can be somewhat like winemaking or fine art in that the first works or samples often aren't representative of the quality which appears at a later date – or at least one hopes that this is the case. The early applicants have taken the direct approach and thrown their hats into the ring using tweets. I'm a great fan of the new media, but it is a challenge to convey one's suitability for such a post in 140 characters. Still, it's a start.

I've also penned a note to our Cricket Committee today re a certain KP! Media reports from usually well-informed sources (Nick Hoult, *DT*) suggest that rapprochement is being sought. However, the loss of a central contract transfers his salary and costs onto his county. Mindful of Durham's recent censure and points deduction for breaching the salary cap, Surrey are going to struggle to accommodate KP. But, you can't play for England without having a county contract.

With several counties unable or unwilling to take him on, the thought came to me that an audacious 'play and pay' type arrangement might possibly suit this mercurial talent. One for the three wise men on our Cricket Committee.

THURSDAY, 20 SEPTEMBER. TAUNTON AND SRI LANKA

Today is one of those enjoyable occasions where sport and business can mix productively. I have a board meeting in the Southampton area with a business called Jellyfish who provide marketing services to a wide range of clients. One client is the Professional Cricketers Association and another All Out Cricket, so this evening the MD of Jellyfish has taken a table at the PCA's annual dinner in Battersea. With Tregs having won the prized MVP award and Compo's call-up, there is bound to be a strong Somerset flavour to the evening. Last year at the same event I bumped into and caught up with the batter who topped our first-class averages in 2011 – Andrew Strauss.

The principal purpose of this glittering event is to raise funds for the PCA in order that they may support and care for cricketers who have either had their careers curtailed by injury or illness or fallen upon hard times thereafter. They provide a wonderful service, and testimony to this was the attendance – over 800 – in a rather posh tent in Battersea Park. The auction was supremely well managed and the sums raised must have been well into six figures.

The highlight of the event was the PCA's presentation of their Cricketer of the Year Award, as this is conferred upon the cricketer thought most deserving of the title by his fellow professionals. For a one-eyed county chairman like me it was doubly rewarding that this year's winner was our own Compo for his astonishing average of 99 in the first-class game. Quite a week for Compo, and it was good to see the plaudits going his way from teammates, colleagues and Somerset supporters on social media.

A good article on our site covers the award bestowed on Compo.

COMPTON CROWNED PCA PLAYER OF THE YEAR – SCCC Site

Somerset's Nick Compton has rounded off his perfect week in superb fashion – by being crowned the NatWest PCA Player of the Year for 2012.

The PCA, in association with NatWest and the ECB, hosted the Awards ceremony at Battersea Evolution yesterday evening (Thursday, 20 September). In front of players, former players, officials and guests, Nick Compton was presented with the Reg Hayter Cup for NatWest PCA Player of the Year for 2012, while Joe Root of Yorkshire was named as NatWest PCA Young Player of the Year.

Nick, grandson of England legend Denis, enjoyed a magnificent season with the bat for Somerset, scoring 1,494 first-class runs at an average of nearly 100. He was also only denied the opportunity of becoming the first player in 25 years to score 1,000 first-class runs by the end of May by the poor English weather. The 29-year-old caught the eye of the England selectors with five hundreds and seven half-centuries in 2012 and was subsequently selected as part of the Test squad to tour India this winter. This latest accolade rounds off a successful few days for the Somerset batsman who also collected The Cricket Writers Player of the Year trophy earlier this week.

The NatWest Player of the Year award remains in the County for yet another year after current Somerset captain Marcus Trescothick took the prize in 2011 to add to his previous successes in 2000 and 2009.

Somerset favourite Pete Trego was also amongst the honours last night. Having been crowned the FTI Most Valuable Player for 2012 earlier in the week, the 31 year old all rounder was named in the PCA FTI Team of the Year.

Senior Manager for NatWest Sponsorship & Hospitality Chris Long said: 'On behalf of NatWest I would like to congratulate all of tonight's winners. Our support for cricket continues across all levels of the game, from grassroots to international.'

'The NatWest PCA Awards play a key role in raising almost half of the money generated for the PCA Benevolent Fund, which helps support current and former players and their families, while our NatWest Cricket Club continues to reward our customers, fans and local clubs.'

FRIDAY, 21 SEPTEMBER. TAUNTON

The club's site today carries a first! A suspiciously marketing-led approach to raise awareness of the club, recruit more members, build fan involvement and make some more money. All good marketing led activities, which must be down to our new Head of Marketing and Sales Jezz Curwin, who has recently joined us from Bath Rugby Club.

I've included the article below as it features some special moments from the 2012 season.

PERMANENT REMINDERS OF A GREAT SEASON – SCCC Site

Somerset County Cricket Club are offering supporters the chance to own permanent reminders of what was yet another exciting season.

There were many memorable moments during the 2012 campaign and with this in mind The Club are producing completed scorecards from each of the 8 home LVCC matches.

The County Ground witnessed some fantastic cricket this season:

- Vernon Philander took 5 wickets in an innings in his first 2 games against Middlesex and Lancashire.

- 5 Somerset batsmen made 50s against Durham.

- Craig Kieswetter made 152 whilst Alfonso Thomas and Gemaal Hussain were amongst the wickets against Warwickshire.

- James Hildreth excelled with the bat whilst Marcus Trescothick took 5 catches in an innings against Nottinghamshire.

- Marcus Trescothick was back to his best with a classy 123 against Sussex which saw him reach his 50th first class century.

- There was the eventful draw with Surrey.

- Nick Compton blasted his way to 155* whilst Peter Trego took his 50th Championship wicket of the season and Abdur Rehman finished with match figures of 14/101 against Worcestershire.

These souvenirs are available at a cost of just £2 each (plus £1 p&p) and can be ordered by contacting the Commercial Office on 0845 337 1875 or by emailing spencerb@somersetcountycc.co.uk

SATURDAY, 22 SEPTEMBER. TAUNTON

The main news today is the award by the ECB of the junior contract known as an 'incremental' one to Jos. After a challenging season this is a shot in the arm for him as it demonstrates publicly Team England's faith and confidence in Jos to perform and make himself a regular member of the limited-overs squads. Jos played in nine T20s and one ODI – with five points awarded for a Test appearance and two for each limited-overs one, Jos thus notched up the twenty points required to qualify for the England contract.

SUNDAY, 23 SEPTEMBER. TAUNTON AND SRI LANKA

Today's weather reminded me of the summer just past. It began raining at dawn and was really getting into its stride by dusk. Overnight we had rain of an intensity I hadn't seen since Bangalore during the 2009 CL T20 when our match against the Challengers was delayed by a conventionally triggered downpour. How the autumnal gloom of the West Country managed such a feat I'll never know.

Fortunately England's T20 group fixture against India was to take place in Sri Lanka and the match started on time at around 2.30 p.m. BST. For England the good news stopped there. Surprisingly we fielded only one spinner, and our seamers were tucked into by the Indian batters, who amassed 170 on a wicket which looked more like a glass one at the Kensington Oval. Recent analysis has shown that nine of the top ten bowlers in the all-time T20 averages are spinners, so the bemusement caused by our team selection did have some grounding in fact.

Batting-wise England gave a pretty good impression of Somerset in this year's T20 semi at Finals Day. Only Bagel looked remotely threatening as he reminded us all of the virtues of playing straight now and again. Apart from a brief cameo where 'Tractor boys' were batting at both ends the game fizzled out as the Indian spinners ran through us with ease.

Our next match is on Thursday in Colombo on what are expected to be even drier wickets, where either the West Indies (Narine) or Sri Lanka (Mendis) will lie in wait. A thrashing might seem to beckon, but how many times this season have expectations been completely overturned!

THURSDAY, 27 SEPTEMBER. SRI LANKA

Our World Cup campaign is beginning to splutter. After a promising warm-up phase and initial group performance we have come up very short against the West Indies. England's travails aside, the competition appears to be attracting large crowds in Sri Lanka and I suspect on TV. The short format now has very few detractors left, with almost all serious commentators acknowledging its undoubted popularity and additionally the technical innovations and improvements it has brought to the game in general.

FRIDAY, 28 SEPTEMBER. TAUNTON

I met up with Guy Lavender for one of our routine catch-up meetings. As always no shortage of items to mull over. Manny's failure of a drug test and its implications loomed large, as did the forming up of the short-list for the DOC position. We also covered the projected financial results for the fiscal year which ends on the thirtieth of this month. We are on track for another above budget result and a very creditable level of profitability. The business plan, which will form the basis of the next phase of the County Ground's development, is in train and the two separate committees we've formed to progress the development plans and the parallel financial plan have now met and are under way. We are aiming for both to complete their work early in the New Year. Lastly we discussed the end of season dinner on 2 November and the presentation I would be making on behalf of the Club to Rosey. We've decided to name a pair of gates after him (the Somerset Square entrance), which means he will join the illustrious triumvirate of Jack 'Farmer' White, Sir Viv and Joel Garner – all legends of Somerset County Cricket Club.

Proposals to change the structure of the English domestic season can cause a tsunami of protest in almost the blink of an eye. Whether it's traditionalists on smelling salts over the expansion and popularity of T20 or equally indignant teenagers berating the first-class game, feelings run very deep. Given the ECB will shortly lay their eggs in respect of the structure of our season in 2014, the article below caught my eye for several reasons. Firstly it is always instructive to see how other ICC nations organise their domestic game; and secondly I found this rather energetic article to reveal remarkably little about what was actually going to change. Churchill once described our Russian friends as enigmas wrapped in mysteries – well, it seems our friends in the Pakistan Cricket Board have taken the art of obfuscation to a new level. Read the article below and see if you can work out exactly how their domestic schedule is to be improved!

NEW-LOOK DOMESTIC STRUCTURE UNVEILED – Our Staff Reporter, September 28

LAHORE – Pakistan Cricket Board (PCB) on Thursday presented a new look domestic structure to separate the departments and regions in domestic tournaments to improve the quality of the domestic cricket and bring it at par with international standard. PCB Director General Javed Miandad unveiled the structure at a press conference held here at the Gaddafi

Stadium. Intikhab Alam, Zakir Khan, Shafiq Papa and others were also present on the occasion. Miandad said the new structure would create new bench marks in domestic cricket helping the cricketers to sharpen their skills and to showcase their talent in a professional way just on the pattern of international cricket. He said the Patron's trophy has been renamed as 'President's Trophy Grade I' in which only departments would be playing and the event will be played from October 3 at various venues across the country. 'We have introduced a new structure after a thorough consideration after having input from different cricketing quarters which are related with the game and the PCB committee finalised it keeping in view the ever growing needs at domestic level,' he added. Miandad said the new structure aimed at enhancing the domestic cricket quality as the matches would be played on international standard under the supervision of qualified PCB officials. 'All the participating teams will be equipped with full coaching staff and all the grounds will be of international standard and it is going to be a domestic event being played in an international manner,' he asserted. He said doping would be conducted on a random basis during the matches and its samples would be sent abroad and anti-corruption rules would also be implemented during the matches. 'All these efforts aim at presenting an improved structure where cricket is being played in a way which ensures high quality and standards. A committee comprising Intikhab Alam, Zakir Khan, Agha Zahid, Shafiq Papa and Saqib Irfan will be monitoring the entire domestic season to put up its recommendations for further improvement. A secret committee will also be functioning to have an overall look on the domestic circuit and will also be submitting its report to the PCB.' Miandad was of the view that by improving the domestic cricket quality they would be able to produce 'quality cricketers' to serve the Pakistan cricket in a better and more professional way. He said Inter Region U-19 three-day and one-day tournaments will follow the President's Trophy after which the Quaid-e-Azam trophy will be played. 'This year, we will be having 14 teams in Quaid trophy instead of 13 as Bahawalpur is the new addition in it. We are expanding the base of regional cricket by inducting more teams to provide ample opportunity to our upcoming cricketers.' He said the PCB was striving for the cause of domestic cricket and it was hoped the new system would help in producing professional cricketers. To a query, he said: 'I want to see a Pakistan team winning the T20 Cup in Sri Lanka. Every match of the Cup is very important and I am confident Pakistan will launch its campaign in Super Eight against South Africa on a confident note by beating the rivals.'

SATURDAY, 29 SEPTEMBER. TAUNTON

Quite a newsworthy day for the club. Jack Leach, another graduate of our age-group system and Academy, is to follow in the footsteps of several other young players from Somerset in recent years and winter Down Under in Australia playing notoriously competitive Grade cricket. Jack was born and grew up in Taunton and has made a very positive impression this summer and made his first-class debut. His first wicket for Somerset County Cricket Club First XI was that of none other than one Hashim Amla, regarded by many cricket aficionados as currently the world's top batsman. Jack has a great temperament and his character and sense of humour shine through every time he steps onto the field of play.

SUNDAY, 30 SEPTEMBER. TAUNTON

Quite a busy day news-wise for the club. The Emerging Players Programme announced their appointees for the forthcoming year. This is a significant event, as these players are considered by the SCB and Somerset CCC coaches to represent the cream of the crop of the age-group players. Also, from the EPP usually stem the Academy undergraduates for the next year or so.

Adam Dibble, a graduate of our age-group and Academy system, has had a torrid season injury-wise but, having worked tirelessly on recovery, can at last see some light at the end of a rather long tunnel. Adam is a very personable young man and yet another local 'product', hailing from Devon.

KENNIS NAMES EPP INTAKE – SCCC Site

The Somerset Cricket Board, Head Coach, Greg Kennis has selected the following group of players for the 2012/2013 Emerging Player Program:

Ned Dunning U13-Millfield School and Glastonbury CC
Louie Shaw U14-Clifton College and Bristol CC
Luke Hammond U14-Millfield School
George Bartlett U15-Millfield School and Glastonbury CC
Luke Tomkins U15-Kings College and Taunton St Andrews CC
Jack Gunningham U15-Kings College and Brislington CC
Sam Underdown U16-Kings College and Taunton CC

As part of the program, the group will receive specialist 1-1 coaching from a small number of coaches, which this year will include Vikram Banerjee, who will be working with the young spin bowlers on the program.

Greg is delighted to have secured the services of the former Cambridge, Gloucestershire and England Lions bowler and said: 'In addition to his coaching ability, Vik has a real understanding of sports psychology, which he incorporates into his new career, mentoring leaders in the business world. It is a key area of the game, and I will certainly be tapping into his ideas.'

Greg has just concluded meetings with each of the players invited to join the program, setting out his expectations and planning individual schedules.

The SCB Head Coach added: 'The EPP has to be flexible, as youngsters can change extremely quickly, and other players could be added over the course of the winter, in the meantime, I am looking forward to commencing work with this talented group of ambitious young cricketers.'

•••

The article below is a significant one as it reveals how early we start planning for next season and some of the steps that are in train. With the DOC position vacant we have recalled the Cricket Committee, which is chaired by Vic Marks and includes Roy Kerslake, Guy Lavender, Andy Hurry and Marcus as captain. This will ensure that we continue to drive the cricket agenda and stay abreast of any problems or opportunities as they arise.

SOMERSET PLANNING FOR 2013 SEASON – SCCC Site

The current season may have only just ended, but at the County Ground plans are already being laid for the 2013 campaign.

With Brian Rose stepping down from his role as director of cricket after eight years in post, the Club is actively in the process of appointing a replacement, who they hope to have in place sometime in November.

In the interim however things are not standing still and a cricket management group has been appointed as head coach Andy Hurry explained: 'Our main focus at the moment is to ensure that the club keeps going forward and there has been a cricket management group put together consisting of Vic Marks, Roy Kerslake, Guy Lavender, Marcus Trescothick and myself, to make sure that until a new director of cricket comes in we are making good informed smart decisions to ensure that we keep going forward.'

Hurry went on: 'The players may have gone off for a well earned break but the cricket management group has been reflecting on another very competitive season for Somerset. We have also been reflecting on the positives and how we dealt with the adversities with so many injuries we have suffered this year and also looking at where we need to strengthen going forward as a Club.'

The head coach is relishing the prospect of a new man in charge of cricket at Somerset.

'With a new director coming in this is a very exciting time for the Club as we look to go forward in a new direction, with new fresh energy and we will be looking at things from a different angle.'

'From the Club's perspective it's important that we don't stand still. We do reflect back and look constructively at how we can get better, building on what we do well.'

Hurry talked about recruitment for next season.

'From a recruitment point of view we are looking at identifying areas where we need to strengthen for 2013. We are looking at the availability of our England players next season as well and making sure that we come up with a plan that enables us to be in a strong position next year to compete again in all three competitions.'

The management group has identified that they need to recruit a new batsman for 2013 and they are currently looking at the options available to them.

'One of the areas we are looking to strengthen is our batting and obviously with the overseas situation the way it was last year it is important we learn from that and try to get as much stability as possible throughout the season.'

'From the T20 perspective we still have the ambition to be successful and win that competition so we will be looking to recruit the highest profile player that we can who will add to the qualities and strengths that we have here already. We have got some big hitters and we have got some good bowling options available to us, so maybe we need to look and readdress what qualities and skills we require from our overseas player.'

Hurry added: 'We need to try to get the new director of cricket in place as soon as possible and embedded into what Somerset CCC is all about and embrace their fresh ideas to ensure that we are all working in one direction to make this Club have the most successful season they have had in recent history.'

OCTOBER

'It's a funny kind of month, October. For the really keen cricket fan, it's when you realise your wife left you in May.' Denis Norden

MONDAY, 1 OCTOBER. SRI LANKA
England were eliminated from the Twenty20 World Cup today. Disappointing.

TUESDAY, 2 OCTOBER. TAUNTON
The media carry the story today about Manny failing a drug test. Apart from the obvious shock and horror we were also acutely aware of the potential risk to the club – having just deservedly achieved the honour of Runners-Up for only the third time since 1875, it would be disappointing, to put it mildly, if that were wrested from us with a points penalty. Fortunately the drug in question turned out to be 'recreational and not performance enhancing', and so by the ICC rules the penalty would be confined to the player.

There was much press speculation about a ban of a year or more, so we were as relieved as Manny must have been that the tariff was set at three months. He clearly has learned a lesson, and we can but hope this sorry episode proves to be a one-off for us.

Guy Lavender called me at 10.15 p.m. with the confirmation of the above and we both drew a sigh of relief.

Gordon Hollins also called re the forthcoming ECB meeting on 18 October at which our application for Category B will be discussed. We know we've secured a positive recommendation from the Major Match Group, and so we can now hope (after some last-minute lobbying of course) that the Board will do the right thing by us.

THURSDAY, 4 OCTOBER. TAUNTON
As I've written previously, one of the strengths of the club's constitution and organisation is the Area Committee structure which provides the means for

Somerset County Cricket Club to represent itself across the South West region. Each Area Committee is democratically constituted and elects a representative to sit on the club's General Committee. Every year an area holds its own AGM and these meetings are always supported and attended by the club's senior officers. All these meetings are scheduled to take place in the next five weeks.

The dates for the area AGMs are as follows, with all meetings getting under way at 7.30 p.m.

The Weston-super-Mare area meeting will take place on Thursday, 18 October at WSM Cricket Club, Devonshire Road, Weston-super-Mare BS23 4NY.

The Devon and Cornwall area meeting will be held on Tuesday, 30 October at The Brend Devon Hotel, Matford, Exeter EX2 8XU.

The North Somerset area meeting will be held on Wednesday, 31 October at Grove Sports Centre, St Mary's Grove, Nailsea BS48 4NQ.

The Mid Somerset area meeting will be held on Monday, 5 November at The Elms, Somerton Road, Street BA16 0SA.

The Bath area meeting will be held on Tuesday, 6 November at Lansdown Cricket Club, Combe Park, Bath BA1 3NE.

The South Somerset area meeting will be held on Thursday, 8 November at North Perrott Cricket Club, Willis Lane, North Perrott TA18 7SU.

The Bridgwater area meeting will be held on Tuesday, 13 November at the Forresters Arms, Long Street, Williton TA4 4QY.

The Taunton area meeting will be held on Wednesday, 14 November at Somerset County Cricket Club.

FRIDAY, 5 OCTOBER. SRI LANKA

Anya Shrubsole has been very much to the fore in helping the England Women's team reach the final of the World Twenty20 in Colombo this coming Sunday. Anya, who is 20, plays for Bath CC and made her Somerset debut in 2004 at the tender age of 12 and her England debut four years later. Since then she has appeared in ten One Day Internationals and twenty-two T20 Internationals. Anya is a medium-paced right-arm bowler who has enjoyed particular success in the T20 format. In her twenty-two matches she has claimed thirty wickets at an average of 13.73, with a career best of five for 12 against New Zealand earlier this year. In the semi-final England inserted New Zealand and limited them to 93 for eight from their 20 overs, Anya taking one for 16 from her 3 overs. England overhauled their target with almost 3 overs remaining and now face Australia in the final.

It has just been confirmed that our strength and conditioning (S&C) coach Darren 'Dazz' Veness will be working with the ECB at Loughborough on a part-time basis again this winter. He will divide his time between the County Ground, with the Somerset team, and the National Cricket Performance Centre in Loughborough. Dazz, a popular member of our staff who has been with us since 1996, is chuffed to bits and will be working as the S&C coach with the ECB's Potential Emerging Players Programme group, which is the next group of young fast bowlers who are expected to come through as the top players over the next three or four years. This programme feeds directly into the England Lions squad, which in turn feeds into the senior England team.

The Overton twins have been selected to be on this programme, so Dazz will be able to keep an eye on them both in Loughborough.

MONDAY, 8 OCTOBER. CAPE TOWN

I arrive in Cape Town on an overnight flight from London and the emails begin to arrive as my iPhone collects a signal. Amongst them is one from Guy Lavender, seeking my approval for the awarding of a benefit year to Arul Suppiah (in our Rules for some reason the club's Chairman has to expressly approve a benefit year for a player). This I don't need to think about for long – Arul has been a great stalwart as an opener and a more than useful occasional slow left-armer, especially in limited-overs matches. I had the great fortune to be at the SWALEC when he set a new world record for bowling in a T20 game. In case you need reminding, in 3.4 overs he achieved the incredible return of six wickets for just 5 runs – a record that will probably stand for a very long time. What won't be well known is that Arul suffers from a degenerative condition in both knees and almost always plays in considerable pain – so much so that he has considered retiring from the game over the past two years. Let's hope he is able to stay match fit and capitalise on the opportunity afforded by his benefit. I know that our members and fans will be very supportive of Arul in what may prove to be his last season playing for the county.

WEDNESDAY, 10 OCTOBER. JOHANNESBURG

I'm in South Africa on business and coincidentally the CL T20 is in town. What is noticeable is the very poor attendances so far. A tight business schedule hasn't allowed me to watch a game live, but in the evening the television coverage is disfigured by vast open spaces in the stands and terraces. We drive past the Wanderers Stadium in Johannesburg and, despite strong temptation, we stick to our tasks!

The Wanderers is famous for several reasons. Known as the 'Bullring' because of its intimidating atmosphere for visiting teams, the ground has a rich history. It was the third Test ground in Johannesburg following the Old Wanderers Stadium and Ellis Park. For more than seventy-four years, it has provided the focal point of Johannesburg's sporting aspirations, whether they be cricket or golf – which between them dominate the district of Illovo, where the club is based – or tennis, squash and bowls, which can also be found tucked away in the back streets. In October 2003 the clubhouse itself was entirely gutted by a fire, which began in the kitchens and spread through the ventilation ducts, and little survived of three-quarters of a century of tradition. Among the trophies, photographs and cricket memorabilia lost for ever was the bat with which Graeme Pollock scored 274 against Australia in 1966/67. The first Test at the ground was in 1956, when England won by 131 runs, and it has gone on to witness numerous memorable moments. These include South Africa's penultimate Test before being banned from international cricket in 1970, when they crushed Australia by 307 runs. Following readmission, the ground became a lasting memory for many England fans when Mike Atherton batted for over ten hours to save the Test in 1995. In 2003 it hosted the World Cup final, as Australia waltzed to victory over India, and in March 2006, it was the scene of the most extraordinary one-day match in history, when South Africa successfully chased Australia's world-record total of 434 for four.

THURSDAY, II OCTOBER.

As the 2012 season becomes a memory, attention turns to what our players will be doing over the winter, and it's significant that seven players and support staff will be deployed with the national team. A source of great pride for the club.

In recognition of his incredible season Compo has been selected for the England Test tour to India, while Jos and Bagel will also be heading for the sub-continent with the England Performance Programme squad in November. Craig and Jamie Overton are members of the Potential Emerging Players Programme fast bowling squad and will divide their time between Taunton and the England Academy in Loughborough.

The final two Somerset representatives are Andy 'Sarge' Hurry, who will be managing the England squad at the Hong Kong Sixes tournament, and Darren Veness, the strength and conditioning coach at Taunton, who will be performing the same role with the England Potential Emerging Player Programme, where he will be working with the Overtons.

MONDAY, 15 OCTOBER.

Today I returned from a trip to South Africa too late to make the Management Sub Committee meeting, for which I had to apologise. I was at least back in time for a lunch with Compo which we arranged at the season's close.

I wrote in this book back on 30 July about Matthew Syed's excellent work *Bounce*, in which he discusses the relative merits of nature versus nurture in the creation and development of elite sportsmen. He concludes that the dominant force is the latter and goes on to discuss how practice has to be 'purposeful practice'. Listening to Compo talk about how his first-class average has increased from below 40 to over 99 in three years, it struck me that he is a classic case study of Syed's theory. He described how under the supervision of Neil Burns (former Somerset CCC wickie and now agent and coach) he has spent hour upon hour honing his skills in poor light conditions indoors facing balls at 99mph. He felt that this technical practice, allied to similarly methodical mental training, using yoga and other meditative techniques, had improved his game.

Compo also described the meticulous build-up to the India tour, including rigorous training sessions with Monty Panesar and Graham Thorpe at Lord's. Batting aficionados will be interested to note that Thorpy has identified five balls our batters will face in India which they won't have seen much of in England. He also advised that if the Indians don't get you out in the first 10 overs the fielders begin to lose interest and revert to their first love, i.e. batting. He said you should look out for them in the field going through their shadow batting practice!

Meanwhile we received sad news today that former New Zealand captain Martin Crowe, who played for us between 1984 and 1988, has been diagnosed with lymphoma, a cancer of the immune system. During his four seasons at Somerset, Martin Crowe enjoyed considerable success, playing in forty-eight first-class matches in which he scored 3,984 runs at an average of 59.46, including fourteen centuries, as well as taking forty-four wickets at 33.02. The thoughts of everyone at Somerset CCC are with Martin Crowe and his family at this difficult time.

MONDAY, 15 OCTOBER. TASMANIA

No sooner has James Regan left Kings College than he finds himself on the other side of the world playing cricket. He is the fourth student from the college to pay first-class cricket for Somerset CCC in the space of three years.

Regan, who is just 18 years old, made his first-class debut for Somerset in the opening match of the 2012 season against Cardiff MCCU. He also kept wicket for part of the game in the two-day match against South Africa in July. During the summer Regan graduated from our Academy and is spending the winter playing for Latrobe Cricket Club in Tasmania.

TUESDAY, 16 OCTOBER.

A detailed catch-up with Guy Lavender today on topics including the proposed changes to domestic cricket structure in 2014; progress towards Phase IV of the County Ground's redevelopment; our projected year end results; an update on the DOC recruitment and options; the financial performance of our Catering and Banqueting operation, and sundry other issues.

I've also been in touch with Dave of DavesSCCCNews (see Twitter account) and Mike TA1 (see Grockles) about using some of their photographs in this book. Both have amassed a very fine collection of photos which have been well catalogued. I'm indebted to them for their generosity and good spirit in allowing me to use several of their finest, and I'm sure you will agree they bring a very welcome extra dimension to this book.

WEDNESDAY, 17 OCTOBER. EXETER

Today I have a phone catch-up with Roy Kerslake, our President. We are preparing for the eight Area AGMs, and Guy Lavender – who is prone, he won't mind me saying, to producing presentations with a hint of 'military functionality' about them – has asked me to sex up his starter for ten, although he has managed a slightly more creative version as some photographs are included to lift the mood. This I've attempted to do and we hope we now have something which will be informative and interesting to our Areas and their guests.

Meanwhile in the CL T20 I note that Fons has been the pick of the bowlers for Nashua Titans with three for 13 from 3.1 overs as they end the well-fancied Auckland Aces' winning streak in Durban. The Titans are graced with another Somerset favourite in Roleof van de Merwe.

In between other items I'm also trying to complete the Chairman's Annual Report for the *Somerset County Cricket Club 2012 Almanac*, which is always a challenge as there's so much ground to cover. Roy has already finished his highly accomplished draft and I can almost feel Richard Walsh – chef de mission on the Almanac – breathing down my neck for mine. I need to get a move on.

THURSDAY, 18 OCTOBER.

Today the ECB Main Board meets as planned, and speculation is rife in the media about white smoke from the chimney with regard to the season's changed structure from 2014.

FRIDAY, 19 OCTOBER.

Yesterday will prove to be a red-letter day in the history of Somerset County Cricket Club. The ECB board approved the Major Match Group's recommendation that the County Ground be granted provisional Category B status. This is the culmination of almost ten years of effort by a lot of people connected with the club and is cause for genuine celebration.

This means the only remaining hurdle to get over before we can host England ODIs and T20s is the satisfactory completion of Phase IV of the ground's redevelopment. We've come this far with only a modicum of bank debt, which has been repaid to schedule since 2010.

We have two separate sub-committees working on the next phase: 'Finance', whose job it is to scrutinise and validate the business plan and recommend funding streams, and 'Planning and Delivery', who are separately designing the new stand and its facilities and will oversee the tender and construction process.

In the New Year we will face significant decisions on how best to proceed. What I'm clear on is that with a £1m grant on offer from the ECB, and a further £1m available at just 4 per cent from TDBC, we have a heaven-sent opportunity to complete the transformation of our ground and also to confirm Somerset County Cricket Club's position at the top table of professional cricket in the UK. We are going to have our work cut out to raise the additional £1m or so required to fully fund Phase IV, but if we don't manage it now I doubt we ever will. Lord Archer, who has been a great supporter of the club, is taken with what we've achieved to date and also with our vision to secure international cricket at Taunton – so much so that he has offered to personally lead the fundraising effort with our members. Guy Lavender and I are meeting him next Tuesday to progress these plans.

SATURDAY, 20 OCTOBER.

An article in today's *WDP* carries the news of the granting of provisional Category B status to the County Ground.

SOMERSET CAN BID TO STAGE ENGLAND INTERNATIONALS AT TAUNTON – *Western Daily Press*

Somerset County Cricket Club officials are celebrating after being granted the chance to stage England one-day internationals and Twenty20 matches at the County Ground in Taunton.

The ECB Board has granted Somerset approval to move the County Ground to the technical specifications required for international one-day cricket.

Following an extensive period of assessment by the Major Match Group, Somerset was recognised as a ground that could meet the technical requirements for England matches.

Somerset chairman Andy Nash told the club's website: 'The decision made by the ECB Board crowns a ten-year programme of the redevelopment of the County Ground, which has always had the objective of bringing international cricket to Taunton.'

'This recognises the huge improvements in quality and capacity put in place at The County Ground, which we believe is one of the very best grounds in the country.'

'I should like to congratulate all those whose vision, hard work and determination has made this possible. Achievements on this scale only come along once in a generation.'

'All at Somerset County Cricket Club can now look forward to being given the opportunity to apply to the ECB for the right to host England ODI and Twenty20 fixtures, which would bring great benefits to Somerset County Cricket Club, Taunton and the West Country.'

Somerset chief executive Guy Lavender said: 'We have now completed three out of the four key phases of our ground development and the completion of our final phase, which sees the re-development of the Old Pavilion, will bring us up to the required standard for international cricket.'

'Our core objective will always be to provide the best set of facilities we can for domestic cricket, but we are confident that with careful design and planning we can create a brilliant venue for smaller international matches as well.'

MONDAY, 22 OCTOBER.

Email traffic and several phone calls today as the short list for the position of Director of Cricket begins to form up.

We also announce that we will be offering the general public the opportunity for physiotherapy and sports injury treatment at the County Ground in Taunton. Our Head of Sports Medicine and Lead Physiotherapist, Ian 'Brewsey' Brewer, will operate the clinic from the Andy Caddick Pavilion, providing the same expert advice, support and holistic service received by the professional players. Brewsey is a chartered physiotherapist and member of the Health Professionals Council. He has extensive experience working within elite professional sport at the highest level, including with Somerset, England and Wales Cricket Board and within the rugby union.

TUESDAY, 23 OCTOBER. LONDON

Today Guy and I are meeting up with Lord Archer to discuss how he can help us raising funds from members and donors towards the cost of Phase IV and the new Somerset Members Pavilion. We coined the working name en route to the meeting.

We arrived at Jeffrey's Albert Embankment address at 12.30 p.m., in time for lunch. Earlier we were offered the choice of his local pub or a restaurant by Alison, his PA, and we decided to opt for the pub.

After a chat in his sumptuous penthouse apartment we headed over the road to his local The Black Lion. His advice, guidance and offer of support was invaluable and he explained a format he and Lady Archer used only last week on behalf of Addenbrooks hospital where £268,000 was raised at what was meant to be Mary's retirement dinner! The funds were to develop a new facility in the neo natal SCBU (Special Care Baby Unit) and donors were incentivised to donate by bidding to effectively buy various items of equipment and furniture with reference to a facsimile of what the finished faculty would contain. The idea was to do likewise on the new Somerset Members Pavilion. We also discussed how each of the 1,500 new seats in our Pavilion could be 'bought' for £100. By the time we left Lord Archer, Guy and I were convinced we had the beginnings of a plan to raise another significant sum towards the total of £3.5m required.

Over lunch inevitably the odd story arose, and my favourite is the only story the best-selling author ever wrote about cricket. It was called 'The Century' and was included in *A Quiver Full of Arrows*, one of his compilations of short stories. It was also essentially true – with just some author's licence to broaden the canvas. Mansur, an Oxonian playing in his third Varsity match at Lord's, played serenely to reach 99 and so was poised on the threshold of an achievement at HQ which would endure a lifetime. On 99 he drove the ball towards the opposition's captain and scampered off for his single. Unfortunately he misjudged his distance and the young J.M. Brearley was easily capable of throwing down the stumps and running the young batter out. Instead, however, Brearley opted to put the ball in his pocket and Mansur duly completed his hundred. Facing the first ball of the next over, Lord's latest centurion was out 'hit wicket' – so reciprocating the considerable act of sportsmanship afforded him by Brearley.

After the meeting Guy Lavender and I were heading to different locations but while sharing a taxi journey we began to make the notes which we're sure will serve us well when the fundraising gets under way in earnest.

WEDNESDAY, 24 OCTOBER.

In Manchester on business, I get a phone call from Guy Lavender following up on yesterday's meeting with Lord Archer. We also have an early chat re the forthcoming January AGM and its content, and we discuss the age-groups presentation evenings – we are keen to persuade our colleagues on the Somerset Cricket Board, who run the amateur game, to merge the boys' and girls' events. The combined event will be too large for the County Room, but we think The Brewhouse, our neighbouring theatre, could be the perfect venue.

Guy has been chosen by his peers to serve on the ECB Executive, and becomes the first CEO from Somerset CCC to do so. I'm completely unsurprised by this, as his quality was quickly spotted by his peers at other counties and by senior management at Lord's.

THURSDAY, 25 OCTOBER.

What several articles confirm today is that Compo will compete with Joe Root as an opener in the Test side rather than bat at his more familiar berth at number three. Either way I'm backing him to succeed.

FRIDAY, 26 OCTOBER.

I have a four-hour train journey back from business in Leeds during the afternoon – a good opportunity to nail my report for the club's *2012 Almanac*. Somewhere around Sheffield, I get stuck in, and by the time we've reached Cheltenham Spa – having traversed no fewer than five first-class counties – it has taken shape. I send it in by email for 'marking' by Walshy (Richard Walsh). Here is my report:

CHAIRMAN'S *ALMANAC* REPORT 2012

Based on articles, member's comments and items in social media 2012 will go down in the club's history as another successful year. In many aspects we have once again continued to set the standard to which others say they aspire; not just in the way our team performs in the middle; but also in the management and development of our County Ground and the organisation which runs it day-to-day. Let's reprise our four strategic objectives and see how we performed against them over the last year.

Firstly, we aim to compete consistently in all formats of the game. This we achieved finishing runners up in the County Championship for only the third time since 1875. In the CB40 we got off to a poor start but then were unbeaten for eight matches and missed the cut for the semi-finals by the narrowest of margins. In the FL T20 we qualified for Finals Day for the fourth year in succession. I shan't dwell on individual matches as they are covered in detail in other parts of the *Almanac*.

We also wanted to win at least one trophy which – again – we failed to achieve. Last year I wrote: 'It is important to reflect honestly on why we have fallen short in major finals and the winter months are being spent analysing and learning the lessons to try and ensure we emerge stronger next year.' We thought long and hard over the winter and tried several things differently; but once again to no avail. We concluded in discussions with Brian Rose that it was time for change at the top of the cricketing management structure and as you all know Brian retired as DOC at the end of the season. I can't think of anyone who has served the club with such distinction, loyalty and commitment as Rosey. He has devoted the greater part of his life to Somerset County Cricket Club as player, Captain, Chairman of Cricket, and for the last eight seasons as Director of Cricket. In his last role he has overseen the most dramatic improvement in our performances, elevating the first team from being THE worst team in professional cricket (double wooden spoonists) to arguably consistently one of the the best. This he's achieved with an extraordinary eye for talent (both young and undeveloped and also mature and overlooked), an ability to pick real leaders (Smith, Langer, Trescothick) and lastly an ability to set a tone and atmosphere in the age-groups and Academy conducive to the consistent development of the highest class of cricketer. In his last season no less than six of our first team squad have represented England or Ireland – a supreme achievement. Rosey will always be part of our club and we are fortunate that he will stay alongside us in a less stressful and demanding role in future.

On the playing front, while we celebrate the appearance of Kieswetter, Buttler, Compton, Craig and Jamie Overton, George Dockrell and Anya Shrubsole for International honours we had a less than successful time injury wise and with our overseas players. We were struck down time and time again by injuries of all descriptions throughout the season which on a couple of occasions left us with literally only eleven fit players. International selection depleted our squad further and often at the worst possible time from the club's perspective. We had chronic problems with our overseas players but in mitigation so did virtually every other county. A combination of bureaucracy, politics, and last minute intervention by national selectors, wrought havoc with our original plans. We've learned some lessons; but this area is going to remain turbulent for the foreseeable future.

Our second objective is to produce home grown players for Somerset and England, which we achieved. The pool of talent graduating into the First Team squad from the Emerging Players Programme and Academy once again reflects extremely well on our Academy staff, the Somerset Cricket Board and all those who work long and hard – usually without recognition – to help our young players develop. I must make mention too of all the parents to whom we owe a considerable debt for all their ministrations with laundry, food, attending to minor injuries, encouragement, travel and of course match-day support.

The age-groups annual dinners have developed into terrific occasions and we are going to work with the SCB to make them bigger and even better. To see the U11s alongside our First Team Squad, all in the same kit, all sharing the same passion for Somerset, was one of the real highlights of the year for me. In their own way, all year round, all the parties above are helping us build the Somerset and England teams of the future.

Thirdly, we are committed to continuing to ensure we improve our facilities and increase our capacity at the County Ground. The improvement of our ground began back in 2004 and the genesis was the ambition to achieve the ultimate accolade and status i.e. to elevate the County Ground to International status. In October, following an exhaustive process lasting almost a year, the ECB's Major Match Group recommended Taunton be awarded Conditional Category B status and the full ECB Board accepted their recommendation and conferred this status upon us. I've been asked many times what this means and I will take this opportunity to explain why it is of the greatest importance to the future of Somerset County Cricket Club. Firstly there is no guarantee that eighteen counties will remain, or if they do that they will continue to be treated equally. The clubs with International status are less likely to be marginalised by any such move. Secondly, we will make a handsome profit from staging ODIs and T20s for England. Gloucestershire CCC are on record as saying each fixture made them around £100,000 net profit. While we are a profitable club additional windfalls of this scale can only improve the club as we reinvest the cash into our cricket squad and facilities at the County Ground. Thirdly, players naturally gravitate towards counties which enjoy International status. Brian Rose always had to compete for the best talent with less ammunition at his disposal than other 'larger' counties. Fourthly, it will bring significant benefits to Taunton and the South West region. We've redeveloped the County Ground with terrific support and encouragement from local and regional politicians and agencies – we can now repay their faith in our club by generating economic benefits. Lastly, Somerset County Cricket Club will be bringing World Class cricket to the West Country – this will reward loyal supporters and attract many new ones. Finally let me say this too – we aren't betting the club to achieve all these benefits. It will cost us £3.5m to achieve Phase IV and build the new Somerset Members Pavilion with all its impressive facilities. We've already secured a £1m grant from the ECB; TDBC have offered us £1m over fifteen years fixed at 4 per cent; and renewal of our bank loan used to achieve Phase III will provide up to another £1m. It leaves us to raise only £500,000 from members, supporters, and commercial partners. A lot of money for sure; but far short of the £30m borrowed by Warwickshire to partially redevelop Edgbaston! I don't have the slightest doubt that our successors will look back five to ten years on and say the club did the right thing in 2012/13 in grasping the potential in front of it and creating a legacy that will be the envy of many other counties. Ten years ago people openly scoffed at the very thought of Somerset County Cricket Club hosting England international matches – we are now on the verge of achieving it.

Our fourth objective was to continue to increase our financial strength and this we have again achieved handsomely. We will shortly announce our results for the past year and yet again we will have made around £500,000 profit. The 2011 ECB report into the finances of all eighteen counties is an authoritative source and it also puts our performance into the appropriate context comparing our position with our fellow counties. We've performed incredibly well and are lauded for the consistency and scale of our financial performance. As a businessman I place the highest importance upon our financial health as without profit and cash generation we simply can't keep the club moving forwards. Someone once said, 'If your company is only about making money, you have a very poor company.' I wholeheartedly agree with this sentiment and the truly great thing about running a cricket club is it is about so much more than just making money. That said, one is well advised not to try running a professional cricket club without it making money! A weak financial position in these times would leave a professional cricket club as a 'zombie' club.

So, to the future. Our mission remains unaltered and is our guiding light. Let's reprise it: 'To win trophies and exceed our members', spectators' and visitors' expectations in order to ensure that Somerset County Cricket Club is recognised as an outstanding club throughout the cricketing world.'

Looking to 2013, achieving Phase IV of the County Ground's redevelopment is one of two stand out and specific objectives we must achieve in the year ahead. The second vital goal is the changes we wish to make to our cricket management structure need to be finalised and implemented. We are well advanced with these plans and members can expect several announcements in the near future designed to achieve greater success.

Your club is in good heart – a highly competitive and successful team; an age-group and Academy set-up that is producing many brilliant young players for Somerset, England and Ireland; an expanding membership; a democratic long-standing constitution and truly excellent facilities. I remain immensely proud of what my colleagues have achieved, and they do this by believing in the special club that is Somerset County Cricket Club, and collaborating well on and off the pitch.

I will close my report by once again paying tribute to our members and supporters. We never take your support for granted; but we do know we can always rely upon you. On big match days you are our 13th man and visiting Committee members from competing counties are invariably in awe of the spectacle and atmosphere you create for us. A sincere thank-you from all of us at Somerset County Cricket Club for that, and I know that we will do our utmost once again in the coming season to provide you with the very best cricket, entertainment and facilities that any county can muster.

I also arranged – following lunch with Compo last week – to meet up with Neil Burns, his coach. We have a chat on the phone and I invite him to meet Guy Lavender and me at the County Ground, which he readily accepts.

Two of three of our grown-up children, who now live away, come home for the weekend and at their request we eat at our local, The Swan in Kingston St Mary. As we enter the lounge, Bagel and Jos are there tucking into two of Les and Lil's finest steaks! We enjoy catching up with them before ordering our own fare. The pub has been popular with our cricketers since they discovered it during a charity evening we helped organise for Children's Hospice South West in early 2010. 'Mine host' Les Biffen dusted off his whites and appeared for my Chairman's XI in September, and, according to his pal Mike, most days he is still reliving his cover drive which crossed the boundary in front of the Caddy Shack.

SATURDAY, 27 OCTOBER.

I get up, for reasons entirely unknown, at around 2 a.m. and start bashing out on my iPad a presentation on the fundraising exercise we discussed with Lord Archer on Tuesday. Things come together well for a first draft and I send it to Guy Lavender and Roy Kerslake for their comments. We've got a compelling story to tell and are making strong progress towards the £3.5m we need to complete Phase IV of the County Ground's redevelopment. I think it was the drafting of my report in the *Almanac* that started my thought process off in the small hours. It occurs to me that once complete the County Ground will have the most fantastic atmosphere – it could become the West Country's Bull Ring – and as such it's easy to see it will be the thirteenth man for Team England in ODIs/T20s as well as a ground fit for the County Champions of England!

My enthusiasm for all things cricket today is tempered by various reports that the BCCI caused a flutter in the dovecote that is international cricket by asking for an additional sum for Sky's media room at the Test venues and a similar fee for the BBC and the *TMS* team. The media speculation is that both broadcasters will tap into Star's coverage and commentate upon that from their UK bases. One article says Giles Clarke is on the scene and is attempting to broker a solution. I can only assume he will either be equipped with an olive branch or wielding a Durston stick (the latter is a West Country club for use in a ceremony which wards off evil spirits from the cider apple crop each year).

SUNDAY, 28 OCTOBER.

The Long Room carvery is on our menu today. It is Linda's father's 82nd birthday, and there's no finer Sunday roast in this area! Recent analysis, however, has shown we are making very skinny margins on the carvery, so we are going to have to adjust pricing at some stage.

I have written recently of Compo's dedication to 'purposeful practice', and a very interesting article on the *Guardian* site deals far more eloquently with the same subject.

NICK COMPTON'S COMMITMENT COULD LEAD TO A START FOR ENGLAND IN INDIA – Andy Wilson, the *Guardian*

The Somerset batsman's unorthodox training programme has put him in contention on the tour of the subcontinent.

One of them was born in South Africa and attended the exclusive and expensive Hilton college before coming to board at Harrow as a teenager. The other has his roots firmly planted in Sheffield.

One of them is a 29-year-old man of the world who has scored almost 10,000 runs for two counties. The other is only 21, has made four first-class centuries, and only just passed 30 County Championship matches for Yorkshire.

One of them has one of the most resonant surnames in British sport, never mind cricket, as his grandfather Denis made 78 Test appearances for England, as well as 60 with a bigger ball for Arsenal – and even his father, Richard, played first-class cricket for Natal. The other comes from humbler sporting stock, although his dad achieved the notable double of winning club competitions with Sheffield Collegiate at Lord's and Sheffield Tigers at Twickenham in the space of a few months in 2000.

It is irresistible to talk up the contrast between the two candidates to open the batting with the new Test captain, Alastair Cook, when England begin the post-Strauss era this week. Yet it may also be a little misleading. Certainly, Nick Compton has had to graft for this first senior call-up, however privileged his background. And Joe Root did not exactly emerge from a mineshaft with flat cap and whippet, having grown up in Sheffield's prosperous suburbs and crossed the Nottinghamshire border to attend fee-paying Worksop College in the sixth form – a couple of years after Samit Patel, another member of this England tour squad, had left.

Richard Ibbotson, the chairman of Root's Collegiate club who also watched Michael Vaughan rise through the junior ranks a couple of decades ago, came within an injury of getting to know Compton much better the winter before last, as the pair were due to link up on an MCC trip to Japan and Indonesia. 'I was player-manager, and Nick was supposed to be my captain,' Ibbotson explained. 'We had a couple of chats on the phone but then it turned out he needed an operation, so he had to pull out and was replaced by Keith Medlycott.'

That small coincidence shows that, in some ways, Compton's rise to England contention has been as rapid as Root's – it has just come much later in his career. It's an intriguing story, too, as it has come as the result of a close working relationship with Neil Burns, the former Somerset and Leicestershire wicket keeper.

He had moved into mentoring and mind-coaching after his retirement in 2001, reforming the London County Cricket Club – for whom in 1904 W.G. Grace scored the last of his 126 first-class centuries – to work on the theories he had developed during his playing career. After enjoying early success in helping to revive the career of Darren Stevens, who has since given such good value to Kent, Burns was put in touch with Compton by Gordon Lord, the England and Wales Cricket Board's head of elite coach development.

'Nick was having a really tough time,' Burns recalls. 'He was only 20, and he wasn't sure if his contract with Middlesex was going to be renewed. Our relationship built slowly – we worked hard in the winter of 2005-06, when he came out to my academy in Cape Town. He then had a fantastic 2006 season, made an England A tour, and came back and opened the batting with Alastair Cook for the MCC against Sussex, the champion county.'

A good omen for Ahmedabad? Perhaps not. 'He nicked off for nought,' Burns adds. 'I agreed to support him from arm's length, but Nick went through a difficult spell after that. KP was all the rage, there were lots of eye-catching players out there and that became a distraction from the signature strokes he had.' At the end of the 2009 season, Burns helped to steer Compton to Somerset, one of his old counties.

'Sometimes you need that fresh start, so that people perceive you as you are today not how you used to be,' the mentor explains. 'I thought Nick was capable of being a high achiever in cricket, with leadership potential and capable of being a Test match batsman. It was a little bit now or never.'

The runs began to flow more freely in Somerset – 1,010 at 56 in the Championship in 2011 – but last winter Burns and Compton refocused, deliberately and strategically. 'I thought there was a niche in the market for what I call proper batting,' he adds. 'Nick had the capability for that, so that's where the work needed to go. That's the great thing about him, his willingness to work so hard: to do his training with Somerset, then drive two hours to me at Ascot and do some more.'

That work was often unorthodox: Burns talks of cranking the bowling machine up to full pace and turning off the lights, as well as t'ai chi, meditation and Bikram yoga at 40C. But most importantly, 'hitting an incredible number of balls for hours at a time – the whole point being to create conditions far beyond what he was going to face in the middle'.

'The challenge we set him technically was to develop the best forward defensive in world cricket, the best backward defensive in world cricket, to become the most judicious leaver on fourth and fifth stump,' Burns continues. 'We refocused goals, so instead of thinking in terms of scoring runs, it was about how many balls you faced.'

The results were impressive – only some badly timed Worcester drizzle denied Compton the chance to become the first batsman since Graeme Hick to score 1,000 first-class runs by the end of May. Now he has the shot at establishing himself in Test cricket that he and Burns have coveted for years. Will England plump for his experience alongside Cook at the top of the order, or give Root the chance to establish himself for years to come? The team selection for the opening tour match, against India A, which starts in Mumbai on Tuesday, will provide the first clue.

MONDAY, 29 OCTOBER.

Today a very interesting article appeared on the Grockles site and it spurred me to engage for the first time. While I've done so under my Twitter identity of 57deacon, I've registered in my real name and Grockles members know me from Twitter.

As I've mentioned before the overwhelming majority of those who post on Grockles are passionate supporters of Somerset County Cricket Club and have the best interests of the club at heart. The welcome I received was a warm one and I shall attempt to make a worthwhile contribution to their debates on occasion. Below is the thoughtful article which prompted me to sign up to the site.

THIS BLESSED PLOT, THIS EARTH – by Grockle

The internet comes to Taunton. Somerset starts to take notice of the ICT literate consumer and looks to become part of the information age ...

It started slow at Taunton. The ECB had this plan for a sort of 'County Hub' where they controlled all the rights and each county had its own site presence on some ECB master site. It was never going to work and some clubs had already got their web presence well and truly established (mostly the Test grounds because ticketing was so much more controllable that way) but it got Peter Anderson interested because there might be money in it.

SCCC wanted a website and had little idea what they should have on it, so as Pete and myself were the only websites they knew we found ourselves in a meeting with Peter and the Accounts Manager John Fitzgerald at the club to talk about what the club needed. They were interested in the commercial aspects: the booking of catering facilities, the ticketing of important matches, the registering of members and their membership payments and the sending out of the good word to the masses about the club and its activities. We were happy to talk about that and the possibility of linking them to a forum for supporters and access to the players for insights. That also seemed possible as they seemed to be considering that. I even offered Rivals expertise and moderation services if they wanted to do that themselves. Peter said that was no problem at all and we left the discussion feeling moderately positive about the club and our future relationship with it. They were naive days.

Days passed and I found myself in an examiners meeting in Manchester discussing the inner nuances of the AQA A Level examination for that summer when I had a phone call from a long departed Somerset coach – we'll call him 'Kieron'. He was phoning to apologise for not being able to talk to me about cricket in the county from now on. He was talking as if I had some kind of idea what he was on about. I didn't at that moment in time and I never really had it confirmed but it seems that Mr Anderson had left the meeting to compose a memo for all staff at the ground forbidding them from discussing anything with Pete or myself related to SCCC on pain of instant dismissal. We must have really urinated him off. Gosh!! How radical and revolutionary we must have been in the meeting – and there we were thinking we were helping out the club we both supported get itself the right presence on the web.

And so started the 'Coventry Years' where reactionaries like Hugh Collis, brother of John Collis the *Guardian* cricket writer and one of the most knowledgable posters 'Grockles' ever had, posted under the name of Crouchend Wyvern and really got up Peter's nose. We did our best to make that even more uncomfortable for him as players and backroom staff alike got around the 'Anderson missive' by talking very loudly about things in the bar when we were sitting there minding our own business or talking to people across our table without actually talking to us directly. It seemed even more surprising seeing as Grockles has rarely been that kind of site except when accused of it by PA and a level of paranoia it was hard to find slightly amusing. Peter had a strange and ill informed view of the media and I am also sure he heard about comments on the site rather than read them himself so we would get sort of 'chinese whisper' comments made by him about what he seemed to think was on the site. He once took Hugh on to the point that Crouchend laid down the challenge and had a meeting with PA where he surprised the hell out of the boss by a) knowing something about the game of cricket and b) having a massive knowledge of Somerset's cricket history and the club's present needs. Peter started to mellow considerably after that and the 'Coventry Years' developed into the 'Gladiator Years'.

TUESDAY, 30 OCTOBER. TAUNTON

Coffee with President Roy Kerslake in Olio & Farina's, the Italian restaurant – the club owns the freehold – which sits proudly in Somerset Square. We slalomed over a wide piste: Compo in India; the club dinner on Friday; Phase IV and Category B; Grockles; the Area AGMs and progress towards next week's interviews for DOC. Roy and Guy were attending the Devon and Cornwall AGM this evening. I'm due to attend the Bath and North East Somerset meeting next week. Either Guy or I will attend each meeting to ensure the General Management perspective is well covered, while either Rosey or Sarge will usually attend to cover cricket items and issues. The effort we've put in for several years now is paying off – at the Weston-super-Mare meeting last week attendance was over forty members.

After bidding Roy farewell I popped into the club to catch Sarge, who was 'bright eyed and bushy tailed' bearing in mind he had just arrived back at Heathrow at 6 a.m. from the Hong Kong 6's where he had managed the England side. He had greatly enjoyed it and I tried to keep the conversation on cricket, as I knew – as a diehard Reds fan – he wanted to talk about how they had turned my beloved Chelsea over at The Bridge on Sunday. I couldn't delay him for long and he enjoyed rubbing the nature of our 2–3 home defeat in. We covered some other matters and then I let him get on with his nap or whatever else he was planning to do having just had an eleven-hour flight!

WEDNESDAY, 31 OCTOBER. MUMBAI

It appears we may have put the kibosh on poor Compo, who didn't enjoy the debut he would have hoped for against India 'A'. After the Indians amassed 369 Compo was out for a duck! Being positive, Viswanath scored both a duck and a century on his Test debut – and this is only a warm-up match. Andrew Hudson and Mohammed Wasim are the only other two to have matched Vishy's feat in Test cricket – though not on their debuts.

NOVEMBER

THURSDAY, I NOVEMBER. EXETER

Tonight is the Devon and Exeter Area's AGM and the trend of higher attendances is continuing. The continued success of our First XI in the middle, together with the announcement of Phase IV and Category B status, seems to have ignited major interest amongst the membership.

DEVON AND CORNWALL AREA AGM HAILED A GREAT SUCCESS – SCCC Site

One of the best turn outs for many years gathered at The Brend Hotel, Matford, Exeter on Tuesday evening for the Somerset County Cricket Club Devon and Cornwall Area Annual General Meeting.

After the official business of the evening presided over by Area Chairman Eddie Dymond, the Club President Roy Kerslake gave a review of the season's results in all three competitions, followed by a look forward to the 2013 year. Arul Suppiah, who has been awarded a Benefit Year by the club for 2013, was also in attendance and gave his views from a player's perspective.

Chief Executive Guy Lavender then gave a very informative presentation covering many interesting topics including current management changes, the club's financial situation, membership fees, action to tackle anti-social behaviour, the club's ongoing community work, the international recognition of players and support staff, ground development matters and other ongoing matters.

After his presentation the Chief Executive, with the assistance of the President and Arul, answered a wide range of questions from the members, ranging from merchandising, car parking and overseas players as well as being asked for his views as to why the club's very own 'Stumpy' never won the Mascot Race at Twenty20 Finals day. Needless to say, that particular issue is not going to be the Chief Executive's top priority for the coming year! The evening ended with a generous round of applause for

Guy Lavender, Roy Kerslake and Arul Suppiah who had all played their part in making the evening a great success.

FRIDAY, 2 NOVEMBER. THE COUNTY GROUND. ANNUAL CLUB DINNER

Linda and I attended the traditional end of season dinner and it was, to use an old-fashioned phrase, 'a very jolly affair'. Rather than rely on my recollection through the fog of a sore head this morning I'm going to let the report below by a Grockle give an accurate summary of the evening's events.

Grockles site – post by Bagpuss

A full house – some 300 people – at the County Room (aka the CA pavilion) tonight for the Awards Dinner.

The traditional Q&A session, more of an interview really rather than a free-for-all questions from the floor, this year featured Arul Suppiah, Jos Buttler and Peter Trego.

Arul said that although he'd had some good individual performances he felt overall his season hadn't been as good as he would have hoped from the high standards he and the team set; he is honoured to have been awarded a benefit year next year although cannot really plan events until the fixture list comes out (due end of this month).

Jos is proud of having represented England at a World Cup, felt that the 32-off-10 in the T20I v South Africa was a bit of a breakthrough moment as far as his international experience was concerned, and is looking next season to improve his performances in Championship cricket, an area which he feels he has not shown his full ability. He is not expecting to get a Christmas card from (South African bowler) Wayne Parnell.

Pete Trego admitted in all honesty he never expected to take 50 championship wickets in a season during his career and now he's done so once is filled with enthusiasm to repeat the feat. He paid tribute to the younger players who came into the team as cover for injuries and performed so well. He also mentioned his award from the PCA for being the MVP – Most Valuable Pirate.

Following this there was a brief speech by Andy Hurry who also commented on the youngsters, how they had come into the team and at one point we were down to eleven fit players –all idea of fielding a 'balanced' team goes out the window in these circumstances, but they battled away, got themselves into good positions only to be denied by the weather until they got the success they deserved over an experienced Durham side at Taunton. The other match he focused on was the Warwickshire match, in particular how Gemaal Hussain came out with 9 wickets down and two runs still needed and blocked out Keith Barker cool as you like to leave Trego to score the winning runs.

Peter Trego was the first award winner of the night when Roy Kerslake chose his 50th championship wicket of the season as his 'champagne moment', although Pete observed he would have preferred it to be a 'cider moment' with suitable change of prize! Pete thanked Marcus for continuing to bowl him more than he probably should have just to give him the chance to take that elusive number 50.

Craig Overton was the recipient of the Acadamy Player of the Year. He was grateful for the chances he'd had in the first team, which he hadn't expected to get at the start of the season.

Max Waller won the Player in the Community award. Much time has been spent with local clubs, schools and with sponsors etc on match days this year, especially when he was unable to play because of injury. There was a nice video acceptance speech from Australia where he is on the beach working hard on his game.

No doubt about the young player of the season, although George Dockrell seems to have done so much already in his career you forget he is barely out of his teens. He praised the attitudes and atmosphere in the dressing room, which makes it so easy for young players to feel they fit in, and he looks forward to helping Somerset win trophies in the future.

Finally the player for the season. As with the Grockles poll it came down to two names, which were difficult to separate, but the final decision fell in favour of Nick Compton. I have to say I would agree with this; in a year when conditions rarely favoured batsmen, when only a handful made 1,000 runs in division 1 of the championship, he failed to become the first player to reach 1,000 first class runs before the end of May since Graeme Hick not because of a careless shot but because of Worcester drizzle. Marcus Trescothick, announcing the award, put it a bit more succinctly, saying, with a wry look towards Pete, 'Well, it's a batsman's game!'

Andy Nash spoke twice, once to thank the players/staff/members/supporters and to fill in those that haven't already heard the progress with the ground being cleared so far for its bid to get category B international status. The final stage of ground development on the St James Street side of the ground will take place over the next two years (no absolute time scale or start date given), there are funds in place of about 3 million with a further 500K needed, which they expect to raise over the next couple of seasons. He expects international cricket to come to Taunton probably sooner than we would expect, and wants it to be a venue where the atmosphere and crowd are the '12th man' for the England team ('Come on England, come on me babbies' maybe??). The club accounts for this year although not yet published are expected to look healthy, with a profit approaching half a million, excellent in a year of such dreadful weather which has left some other counties' finances in a sorry state.

Andy Nash returned later in the evening to announce that the 4th and so far anonymous gates into the ground – those by the flats – will be named in honour of Brian Rose. There was a short speech by Brian, which developed into a bit of a double act with Vic Marks, and that was about it unless I've forgotten anything. A fine evening out, well done the organisers and the catering staff (thanked by Guy Lavender, who also promised a fully functional scoreboard next season, so no need to remind him any more!).

SUNDAY, 4 NOVEMBER.

Today Linda and I are guests of the Lavender family at their 'farm' near Honiton. Jezz Curwin and his wife Sara are fellow guests and a very lively lunch ensues. Inevitably talk veers around to cricket now and again, but our partners are very forgiving.

MONDAY, 5 NOVEMBER.

Today Dick Edmonds, long-term friend from university, and to whom this book is dedicated, returned to the BRI to hear the results of his scan. It isn't good. The cancer has spread into his lungs and lymph nodes from the primary in his oesophagus. It was expected, but it still must be extremely hard for him and his family to bear. Another pal from the same group from university rings and we chat it over. We agree there's no point in being maudlin with Dick – we must continue as his cheerleaders and do all we can to ensure the time he has left is enjoyed to the maximum that we can provide. A good friend from Hampshire (the Burridge CC captain Rick Ankers) had very kindly arranged some VIP tickets for the Masters tennis at the O2 this Thursday for Dick, but he's decided he's not up to it after the bleak day he's just had. As John Arlott said, 'Sometimes we take cricket too seriously and life not nearly seriously enough.' Days like this show he was spot on.

Also today it is time to send off the draft manuscript to Jeffrey Archer as he has agreed to write the foreword to this book.

TUESDAY, 6 NOVEMBER.

Today the panel, which has been formed to interview applicants for the DOC post, assembled at Clarke Willmott's offices at Blackbrook in Taunton. Owing to the international nature of the short list we were exploring the frontiers of digital technology (well, some of us were) with the intention of using the law firm's video conferencing technology. I could describe the subsequent events in great detail, but a simple analogy probably fits the bill rather better. Imagine someone trying to complete a Rubik's cube, blindfolded and wearing boxing gloves. Many thousands of miles away sat an erstwhile applicant, staring at a blank screen, and in silence, as Somerset's finest grappled unsuccessfully with the kit. At one stage we managed to raise a lost soul sitting in Clarke Willmott's Birmingham office, looking as if he was in a scene not dissimilar to Brody in the serial *Homeland* awaiting interrogation in a lonely cell somewhere at Langley – perhaps he was awaiting his Performance Review! If only the lawyer in Birmingham knew how close he came to being appointed Somerset CCC's Director of Cricket! After forty-five minutes of fruitless struggle we reverted to plan B and interviewed our man 'down the line' using the telephone. As it turned out it was an excellent interview, and all the better as we had to really listen actively without the benefit of seeing him on the screen.

The next interview was on another continent but still in the Southern Hemisphere, and this time bang on schedule our interviewee appeared (albeit with a slightly frozen-in-aspic appearance) on the screen. There ensued a lively and colourful exchange with a highly impressive candidate. Buoyed up by our conversion to the digital world the panel dispersed in a state of some satisfaction. We were rudely brought back down to earth by the reappearance of the President, who announced that his battery – or rather the one in his Saab – was flat.

The Somerset County Cricket Club senior management peloton reformed in Clarke Willmott's car park and set about working out how to get Roy's car going. Guy Lavender – ex Parachute Regiment – was a likely candidate but fell at the first hurdle when he couldn't work out how to open the Vice Chairman's bonnet. The Chairman (yours truly) once drove a similar model and thanks to searching the deep recesses of my mind I remembered where the bonnet's catch was. This didn't help, as of course the battery we were searching for was actually concealed in the boot of David Gabbitas' Mercedes. By now our joint display of incompetence had developed into a spectator sport and the fee earners of the firm were enjoying a welcome break from conveyancing etc. Eventually, for the second time this morning, the management team overcame a technical challenge and managed to connect the President and Vice Chairman via the medium of a pair of jump leads. Probably a first in the history of the club. Unfortunately it was to no avail, and no matter how many combinations of terminals or engines running were tried, the Saab declined our invitation to start. With the Bath AGM appearing in the horizon there was only one course of action left open to us – the AA were called.

At 7 p.m. Roy and I met again at the Lansdown Cricket Club for the Bath and Wiltshire Area AGM. With the horrors of events in Clarke Willmott's car park expunged we got down to the serious business of the evening. Michael Davis is the Area Chairman and a more passionate and knowledgeable Somerset County Cricket Club member I doubt you will find. The Bath massive assembled and it was another excellent turn-out with around forty people forming a very attentive audience. The Bath Chairman moved swiftly through the formal business and then regaled us with some history of the host venue. Formed in 1825 (a full half-century before Somerset County Cricket Club), it was one of the oldest cricket clubs in England. However, its real claim to fame lies in the fact that Viv Richards played his first game upon English soil on this very spot. No matter that WG, his brother and father had played here many times – it was the cricketing alma mater to a Somerset County Cricket Club legend. Roy then added a wonderful twist by recalling that not only had Viv played his first-ever game here but he'd also made his debut for Somerset here, playing for the Under-25s. Our President was captain for the game and sent in young Viv to open. Viv returned very soon afterwards having scored only 3 runs. Later on in the day he also bowled a few overs without distinction. After the game, Roy admitted, he was moved to console Viv's sponsor Len Creed (a Bath bookmaker and stalwart of Lansdown CC) with words to the effect of 'Well, at least he can field, Len'!

Michael Davis also related a discovery he had made at Lansdown CC. Tucked away on a shelf were the most beautifully preserved score-books from the period 1835 to 1865 which recorded some extraordinary games. In those days cricket was effectively turn up and play, so all kinds of contests occurred and often with varying numbers per side. Some of the more memorable contests were: First Half of the Alphabet v Second Half; Under Arm v Round Arm; and Town v Country. The score-books are living testimony to the difficulties of early Round arm bowling, as in one innings total of 107 no fewer than 47 runs were extras!

Lastly it appears that Lansdown CC may have been the inspiration for Somerset County Cricket Club's wyvern. In 1825 the founders of LCC took a local aristocrat's coat of arms (he perished on a nearby battleground of a non-cricketing nature) as a starter for ten for the club badge. It featured a griffin, a mythical bird which looks a bit like a dragon. To this day Lansdown CC maintain that our wyvern is a direct descendant of their griffin.

With the history and stories out of the way we returned to more normal business and a very enjoyable evening was had. Some excellent questions from the audience had Roy and me on our metal and we left in good spirits.

Meanwhile, back in Taunton and undeterred by his failures with technology earlier in the day, our indefatigable CEO Guy Lavender was in action at Taunton Deane Borough Council's scrutiny committee. The not inconsiderable matter of them approving the long-term loan to Somerset County Cricket Club of £1m over fifteen years fixed at 4 per cent was being scrutinised and debated. Armed with a very strong case (anyone for international cricket here in Taunton?), Guy carried the day, and I received an SMS from him as I was driving home from Bath saying the TDBC committee had voted in support by twenty-eight to one. There's always one, as they say.

WEDNESDAY, 7 NOVEMBER.

Preparations are getting under way for Arul's benefit year and I've had a request to record an audio piece based upon my tribute to him on the club's website, which accompanied the news that he had been granted the testimonial. Unperturbed by yesterday's trials with technology, I've readily accepted the request and will attempt to record something suitable on my iPhone later today and email it through to Sarah Trunks, our in-house IT expert.

THURSDAY, 8 NOVEMBER.

THE LATEST FROM NICK COMPTON IN INDIA! – SCCC Site

Nick Compton greatly enhanced his chances of making his debut for England in the First Test against India which starts on November 15th when he scored an unbeaten 64 earlier this week in the drawn game against Mumbai A.

The Somerset batsman was the leading run scorer in the first class game in England last summer and set off with the rest of the touring party on October 25th.

Since then he has played in both games so far on the tour and will be hoping to get another opportunity in the final warm up match which begins on Thursday.

Talking about his tour experience so far, speaking exclusively to www.somersetcountycc.co.uk Nick said: 'The tour has been fantastic so far, everything from the support staff to the lads, everyone has been very welcoming, accommodating and professional.'

'There has been lots of hard work going on behind the scenes to get up to speed with the intensity of Test cricket and the conditions.'

'I had a disappointing first game but happy to have spent a good three hours in the middle in the second match and will be hoping to continue the work I have done this year in the next game and matches after that if selected.'

Talking about some of his experiences away from cricket Nick said: 'I went to the cinema the other night to watch the new James Bond film. It felt strange standing up to sing the Indian National Anthem as well as having an interval. People weren't shy of answering their phone calls from wife or kids just as the best part of the film was on! This is all a great experience and part of touring.'

Good luck to Nick from all Somerset supporters, we are all cheering for you back here and following your progress closely!

FRIDAY, 9 NOVEMBER.

Another routine catch-up with Guy Lavender today. Of particular note are reflections upon the recent interviews for DOC and the next steps in the process. Also of note is the confirmation that we will be announcing Alviro Petersen as our overseas player for 2013. Cricket South Africa have finally issued the NOC (no-objection certificate) required before his registration can be finalised. The cricketing management are very pleased with this acquisition, as apart from being a top-class batter, Alviro is a very popular and lively presence in the dressing-room.

We also decide to release the important news concerning TDBC's support for our plans to bring international cricket to Taunton. In business terms it is a 'no brainer' for them to support us, as ODIs and T20s will bring substantial benefits to Taunton and its hinterland. Nonetheless in this very challenging economic climate nothing can be taken for granted and we are grateful for their positive support and commitment.

The *Bristol Evening Post* covers the story below.

SOMERSET MOVE CLOSER TO STAGING INTERNATIONALS – *Bristol Evening Post*

Plans to bring international cricket to the County Ground in Taunton took another step closer to becoming reality after the community scrutiny committee of Taunton Deane Borough Council gave their backing to a £1 million loan to support the development and rebuilding of the Old Pavilion.

Over the last six months, Somerset County Cricket Club have been working closely with the council and, at a meeting earlier this week, the scheme was overwhelmingly supported by local councillors.

Somerset chief executive Guy Lavender said: 'I was delighted that the scrutiny committee decided to recommend our proposal and it will now go to Taunton Deane's full council for final approval in early December.'

'This is exceptionally good news and the council's assistance will be critical in helping us achieve our objective of bringing international cricket to the County Ground.'

'The proposal was unanimously recommended by the scrutiny committee with councillors recognising the outstanding progress we have made in developing the ground, which is a critical component of making sure we have a vibrant and successful town.'

Lavender paid tribute to TDBC for the support they have given to the redevelopment of the County Ground as part of Project Taunton.

He said: 'We have had a brilliant relationship with the council over the last ten years, where they have helped us every step of the way. Their assistance will enable us to achieve the final phase of our plans, ensuring the club can thrive long into the future.'

SOMERSET SIGN ALVIRO PETERSEN! – SCCC Site

Somerset are delighted to announce that they have signed South African Test batsman Alviro Petersen as their overseas player for the first part of the 2013 season.

The 31 year old who was born in Port Elizabeth has played in 16 Test Matches and 17 One Day Internationals and has an impressive record in all formats of the game.

In Test cricket Alviro Petersen has scored almost 1,200 runs at an average of 42.39, with a best of 182 which he scored in the series against England this summer at Headingley, as well as 437 ODI runs at an average of 31.21. In first class cricket he has scored 9,774 and has an average of 39.57.

Alviro Peterson said: 'I am very pleased to have signed to play for Somerset as their overseas player for the first part of next season. Somerset are a successful team in all forms of cricket and I look forward to becoming part of the set-up at the County Ground, and hope that I can help them to win some trophies in 2013.'

Guy Lavender the Somerset Chief Executive said: 'We are delighted to have signed Alviro Petersen and he will play for us right the way through until the commencement of the FL T20 competition next summer, when he will depart to resume international cricket with South Africa.'

'He is an exceptional player and has an impressive record as a batsman, which he demonstrated during this summer's series against England, and we look forward to welcoming him to Taunton in the spring.'

SATURDAY, 10 NOVEMBER.

Sarah Trunks, our IT supremo, has been tasked with bringing to life some publicity for Arul and has alighted upon a piece I penned for the announcement of his benefit year. She has asked me now to convert it to the spoken word, which thanks to the wonders of modern technology I'm able to do. The first two attempts are ruined by our Westie Bruce joining in and providing various background noises which detract rather badly from the fine words

I have to say in praise of our opener. I resort to bribing Bruce with his breakfast which leaves me to record the piece alone.

I'm getting itchy feet about my car, which is due for change before long, so there being no time like the present where cars are concerned I send an SMS to Banger and ask him about his Jaguar XK and where he sourced it from. Given that it's about cars he drops whatever he's doing and responds immediately and with some excitement. Within fifteen minutes I'm emailing Angus Porter, the Chief Executive of the PCA, as according to Banger it's their scheme. Within the hour Angus, his colleague Erin and some guy from Jaguar called Jos are all in touch by email and a plot is being hatched to sign up a very willing county chairman on Jaguar's 'Sports scheme'. Linda appears in her dressing gown and sees me bashing away on my iPad. 'What are you doing, Nasher?' she asks rather perceptively. 'Oh, nothing, dear – just boys' stuff.'

Meanwhile, in India, Compo is beginning to find form, and he has enhanced his Test claims with an unbeaten 54 as England close the penultimate day of their final warm-up game against Haryana at 118 for none. After beginning the tour with nought and one, Compo has now recorded 192 runs in three innings and looks certain to play in Thursday's First Test.

MONDAY, 12 NOVEMBER. TAUNTON AND AUSTRALIA

The eagerly awaited (by me anyway) foreword arrives from Lord, or rather Jeffrey Archer in this instance. I can hardly believe one of the world's most successful authors has agreed to sully his reputation by having his name adorn a book of such modest standing as mine. Still, that's cricket and Jeffrey has come up trumps.

I pick up the email and attachment while 'on the road', as it were. I have to confess to being quite chuffed to receive it, and I stop in a lay-by in Curry Rival to open the document. I wonder how the great man will start the piece … Will it be complimentary, diplomatic but quietly scathing – who knows? I start to read it. 'Andy Nash is a basket case' is the first line. Oh my God! The worst start – has my gamble backfired spectacularly? It gets better, in the second line our President is quite rightly libelled when described as 'certainly certifiable'. Jeffrey then admits to his own obsession and fallibility when dealing with the religion that is known as cricket. Phew, I finish it and it's OK. He likes the book.

I'm delighted with the foreword – it strikes for me a perfect balance and that no doubt is why Jeffrey Archer is a globally acclaimed author and I'm not. He writes simply and brilliantly.

Later I see news from Down Under about two of our bright young prospects. Both are playing in the intense competition that is Grade cricket in Australia and from the sound of it are more than holding their own.

While on a bike ride along the canal I run into – almost literally – Nigel Preston (Prezzer). I've not seen him for a while, and we hatch a plot to meet 'after work' at The Swan in Kingston St Mary. I've written before how the pub has become an established favourite with Somerset cricketers and several members, and sure enough no sooner do we arrive than Jos Buttler wanders in with an old school mate. We talk Jaguars and his imminent departure to India with the England Performance Squad.

TUESDAY, 13 NOVEMBER. THE COUNTY GROUND

I met with Julian Catternach today. He was Head of English at a school in Surrey and is one of the most knowledgeable and passionate Somerset fans I know. There can be no better person to critically appraise the current draft of this book. We meet for a 'power breakfast' in Morrisons and while away an hour talking about the religion that is cricket interspersed with Julian's deft, subtle and penetrating critique of my draft. In addition to pointing out my vast number of syntax errors, split infinitives and how I've muddled up the deities with the additive (whatever that means), we enjoy reminiscing about various moments of the season just past.

Undimmed by the realisation that my writing skills would make a proper author blush, I gather up my skirts and head into the club for a catch-up with Guy Lavender.

The menu is typically packed: Category B; players' ups and downs; latest on DOC; Phase IV and progress of the two working parties; financial year-end; treasurer's plans; and preparation for the visit at lunchtime of Neil Burns and his colleague.

I head into a well-known coffee bar in the High Street and bump into Hildy. I've known Hildy for a long time now and enjoyed his company in various places around the globe. Nowhere more so, I think, than on the beach in Barbados in September 2010 when he was on tour with the England Lions. I was there as part of Somerset playing in the Windies' T20 competition in lieu of the CL T20, which on account of its timing was not available to us or Hampshire. The ECB had arranged for us to play, as honorary islands, as it were, in the WICB's domestic competition.

Hildy immediately spots my iPad mini with all the enthusiasm of another gadget man and I take great delight in showing it off to him! In addition to that we chat about winter training and Compo's forthcoming debut.

A phone message arrives from Kevin Howells of BBC 5 Live, who is keeping his head down at the Beeb while all hell breaks loose around him in the wake of the Saville scandal. I return his call and tell him to stick it out – at the current casualty rate he could find himself as DG by Christmas. He is making a programme on county cricket for *TMS* and would like to meet up to 'do a piece' on Somerset. We diary a session at the County Ground for two weeks' time.

WEDNESDAY, 14 NOVEMBER. TAUNTON

The close season is probably considered by many cricket lovers as a time of tranquillity and rest. Today was as busy for the club, its Chairman and Chief Executive as any I've known!

Sandwiched between meetings, emails and a teleconference were another interview for the DOC position with a candidate having arrived from another hemisphere, a meeting at Taunton Deane Borough Council to progress the application for our loan over a fifteen-year period, and the Taunton Area AGM.

I send an SMS to Compo wishing him well for his inaugural Test tomorrow. I'm confident he is going to be a success and will nail his place in the England side. I've written previously of the dedication and perseverance which have been the foundations of his success.

I exchanged emails with Justin Langer congratulating him on his appointment to be the Head Coach at WA. It sounds like a 'tough gig' but his intellect, determination and strength of character will see him make a success of it. The cricketing grapevine suggests there's no shortage of issues awaiting JL's attention at the WACA.

I will have two abiding memories of today. Firstly, the intensity of the interview with the applicant for our DOC position. The candidate was passionate, and his knowledge and track record were highly impressive. We've a champagne headache now, as we've seen some very strong candidates for this crucial role. We remain on track to make our decision before the last door of the advent calendar is opened, and for the new DOC to start early in the New Year in the build-up to the new season.

My second abiding memory is of the chat I had with a member at the Taunton Area AGM. I was asked very politely by a lady while waiting for proceedings to begin if I knew when the 2013 fixture list was due. I responded that it was work in progress and should be finalised by the first week in December. Then, as cricket fans do, we began to natter, and she had some amazing stories to share. She became a member of Somerset County Cricket Club in 1948 and the first game she watched was the county against Glamorgan at Clarence Park, Weston-super-Mare, and it wasn't surprising that she became hooked after that. Despite Mo Tremlett achieving his best-ever return in first-class cricket with eight for 31 off 27, and Arthur Wellard claiming his fiftieth victim of the season, Glamorgan won the tightest of contests by 8 runs. Barbara Von Tyszka has been a committed fan ever since and even attempted to ensure her first born was delivered on Sammy Woods' birthday, but it came early, on 13 April. She had missed by a day, or rather she thought she had, according to *Wisden*. Subsequently *Wisden* realised their inexcusable error and rewound the great man's birthday twenty-four hours from the 14th, and so a conflation made in heaven was achieved.

Later, in 1964 Barbara took her baby daughter to watch the touring Australian side at Taunton.

Sammy Woods, to those who don't know of him, is still Somerset County Cricket Club's longest serving captain and not only played cricket and rugby for England, but he also played Test cricket for Australia. His legendary feats included regularly walking to the County Ground from his home ... in Bridgwater. He was an attacking captain, once famously observing: 'Draws? They're only for bathing in.' His attacking instincts did not stop him from making a fine sporting gesture when W.G. Grace became the first batsman to achieve a hundred centuries in 1895. Sammy was bowling and gave 'The Old Man' a slow leg-side full toss to help him reach the landmark!

My chat with Barbara was cut short when Peter January, the Taunton Area Chairman, got proceedings under way. The formalities were dispensed with suitably quickly and the baton passed to the formidable double act of Kerslake and Lavender, who regaled the meeting with reminiscences of the season past and a vision of the future ... including, to much acclaim, a promise of a score board which works!

One highlight of the meeting was Treasurer Brian Daw's report, which showed that Taunton Area's fundraising had almost reached £10,000 over the year, which is a terrific effort. It gives pause for thought that this amount exceeds the entire profit made by some county clubs in the whole of 2011!

Catching up with Guy Lavender after the meeting, he had good news from the TDBC meeting, where our request for a long-term loan of £1m had its latest hearing. The meeting duly approved the request with great enthusiasm and now our proposal heads for its final hurdle of the full Council hearing in December.

THURSDAY, 15 NOVEMBER. ALCOSSEBRE. AHMEDABAD. FIRST TEST, INDIA V ENGLAND. DAY 1

This extract from a piece by Scyld Berry in the *Telegraph* caught my eye – quite a colourful recollection of Compo's grandfather: 'His vitality was no less off the field, where his theme was wine, women and song. He was involved in so many japes and scrapes with his best mate Bill Edrich that Hutton used to shake his head and say: "Bill and Denis – they should have been sent home from the '46 tour of Australia." Together Edrich and Compton inspired one of cricket's finest witticisms: that Bill was best man at Compo's third wedding, and third man at his best wedding.' Magnificent.

Ted Tyler was the first Somerset cricketer to play Test cricket for England when he was selected to join the tour of South Africa in 1895/96, making his debut (which sadly was also his last Test match) on 21 March 1896. This morning Nick Compton became the twenty-second Somerset player to play Test cricket for England as he took the field in India at 5.30 a.m. GMT – watched no doubt by thousands of bleary-eyed England and Somerset fans.

Meanwhile I'm not in Ahmedabad but heading for a swift trip to our home in the Levante region, where a Spanish builder has been at work! I hope he's making more progress than our attack has in the first session of the First Test. At lunch India are 120 for no wicket.

A nice article on our site reports on Max Waller's time in Australia. As part of our evolving approach to developing our players Max is yet another of the first-team squad who is based on the Southern Hemisphere for our winter. Like all 'leggies' (and a good claret) Max will take a long time to mature into the finished article, and it is testimony to his strong character that he has shown patience and real determination as he has necessarily spent many games learning his trade in the Seconds. Many members recognise this and consequently he is a very popular young man. It's clear from his report that he's in good hands in Adelaide, and again one can see how hard he's having to work on South Australia's flat wickets. The good news for Max is that looking at Warne, Mushy and other leggies, he'll still be bowling long after his fast bowling peers have hung up their boots.

The day ends on a positive note. Guy Lavender has been at HQ today and Brian Havill, the ECB's Financial Director, has confirmed that following the scrutiny and subsequent endorsement of our Strategic Plan, the £1m grant towards our Phase IV development will arrive in our bank account by 1 February.

FRIDAY, 16 NOVEMBER. ALCOSSEBRE. AHMEDABAD. FIRST TEST, INDIA V ENGLAND. DAY 2

The news is ominous from India. The hosts are racing along and it is beginning to look as though playing only one spinner on such a slow and low deck might have been an oversight. They've scored 361 for four from 102 overs.

•••

While I drove along the Spanish motorway the English tail wagged weakly, and before long Compo was back out leading the follow-on. I was delighted when he and skipper Cook took the fight back to the Indians and dug in to see out the day. All at Somerset County Cricket Club know just how determined and limpet-like Compo can be. If they can survive the first 10 overs tomorrow a draw might yet be possible. I'm trying to stop myself thinking about Compo compiling a century in his maiden Test – but not very successfully.

Great news from the County Ground arrives in a phone call. Jezz Curwin and Guy Lavender have struck gold and signed up a new main sponsor for the club, to fill the large hole left by eCar's withdrawal after supporting us for five years. The sum is a six-figure one every season and the deal is for three years. This is a good example of success breeding success. We've never had a sponsor of this magnitude in recent times, and it's plain that our consistent success on the pitch, allied to our plan to bring world-class international cricket to the County Ground, is placing us on the radar of large national companies for the first time. This is a big bonus for next season, as our EBITDA in the draft budge,t to be discussed on Monday at the General Committee meeting, is already standing in excess of £600,000.

Lastly – yes there's more – we've also just been told we will be invited to host not one but two England Lions first-class matches next season against Bangladesh 'B'. We have accepted the invitation and will market both fixtures strongly.

SUNDAY, 18 NOVEMBER. TAUNTON AND AHMEDABAD.
FIRST TEST, INDIA V ENGLAND. DAY 4

No lie-in for Middle England this morning as Captain Cook and Compo are at the crease, having put on over a century for the first wicket after following on – an excellent start and one which has provided a glimmer of hope. Compo was eventually undone for a creditable 37, and England's top order fail to build on the foundation which has been painstakingly laid.

At 10.30 a.m. my youngest daughter, having recently passed her 16th birthday, has arranged a chat with one of our managers in Catering with a view to following her sisters into the club as a waitress during college holidays. While Imogen is chatting away to Ruth, I wait in the car and tune back in to events in Ahmedabad. Prior of Sussex has joined Captain Cook, and one of those cameos in cricket begins to unfold. As an autumnal Sunday progresses at home, these two knuckle down to the job of eroding the deficit and dragging us back into the game. By stumps the unlikely has happened and the doughty pair have not only eliminated the huge deficit but managed a modest lead. Skipper has played the innings of his life and Prior has provided magnificent support. Champagne cricket.

MONDAY, 19 NOVEMBER. TAUNTON AND AHMEDABAD.
FIRST TEST, INDIA V ENGLAND. DAY 5

Another very early start as Captain Cook and Prior of Sussex face the challenge of building on the slenderest of leads in the Indian furnace. Before

I've finished my first mug of tea the dream which all England fans had been forming is shattered as Prior is accounted for and then shortly afterwards the skipper follows him as a rejuvenated attack close in for the kill. It has been a remarkable fight back by England and three innings of the highest quality to savour in the match so far. Two other issues will have been slotted for further consideration: the relatively disappointing level of attendances (the ground never more than 25 per cent full, says Simon Barnes in *The Times*), and the Indian's continued refusal to use the DRS. Had the latter been deployed, it is being said by the commentary team, who are unofficially using it, the game would have probably been over yesterday!

Twitter informs us that Cook's knock is a historic one. He's in rarefied company. Highest score by a visiting captain in India in Tests: Clive Lloyd 242* (1975), followed by Kallicharran 187 (1978) Inzamam ul Haq 184 (2005), and now Cook 176.

A disappointing session. Our front five make 380: the last five just 66! India need 77 to go one up. Apparently India's lowest Test score chasing is 66. Tendulkar was playing in 1996 when they were bowled out by South Africa in Durban! Dare we hope?

On a brighter note, another young player who has progressed through our age-groups and Academy has been nominated for a prestigious national sports award. Tom Abell of Taunton has achieved a staggering amount of runs in the past two seasons. In eleven innings last season he passed 50 on every occasion, converting seven of those into centuries, and in total amassed 1,156 runs at an average of 193! I recall England U19 management wanting to take him to the World Cup, but his tender age and practicalities ruled it out. A name to watch, as he's another West Countryman now on our books.

Meanwhile, back at The County Ground, the club's General Committee meet in the Players Dining Room in the Caddy Shack at 6 p.m.

TUESDAY, 20 NOVEMBER.

Train to London today for three days on business. One of the day's first emails is the proposed media release on the 2013 fixture list. We went through it last night and it plays well for Somerset. Apart from a well spread Championship, our five home T20s are all on Friday evenings or Sunday afternoons, which will delight our supporters. We have the SWASHES (South West Ashes), into which we are already focusing great marketing efforts, and now in addition we are to host two England Lions v Bangladesh games. These will be very popular and well-supported.

The article overleaf summarises our fixtures for 2013.

2013 FIXTURE LIST – SCCC Site

Somerset followers have got a huge summer of cricket to look forward to, full details of which have just been released in the 2013 fixture list.

The highlights include an opening home championship match against title holders Warwickshire at the end of April and five home FL T20 fixtures in July, all of which will be staged either on a Friday evening or a Sunday afternoon.

Somerset will play a four day game against Australia in June, while in August for the first time ever the County will host two international one day games between England Lions and Bangladesh, before rounding off the home campaign with four day match against Surrey in September.

Chief Executive Guy Lavender said: 'We are delighted with the fixture list for 2013. This year we have a later start to our home matches with a fixture against County Champions Warwickshire, which is a fantastic way to open, after which we have very concentrated cricket throughout the core part of the summer.

'Particular highlights include a four day game against Australia in June, after which it's brilliant to see that all of our home T20 matches are either on a Friday evening or Sunday, which is ideal for our spectators.'

'We are delighted to have been awarded two ODI games between England Lions and Bangladesh A in late August, which will be fantastic and is testament to the way that we are moving towards hosting international cricket at Taunton.'

He added: 'We finish the season at home against Surrey on September 14th which is a great way to finish, so all in all it's going to be a packed out summer of cricket for our Members and Supporters to look forward to.'

THURSDAY, 22 NOVEMBER.

While on business in London, I attended the 'Girls on the Front Foot' fundraising dinner for the charity 'Chance to Shine'. The charity does a huge amount for cricket and has been credited with helping to achieve a substantial rise in the number of children and youths playing the game. One very special young lady named Lois, who suffers from a degenerative eye condition, explained how playing cricket had made a substantial difference to her life by ending her isolation amongst her peer group at school.

I was on a pretty lively table hosted by Sir Tim Rice and Izzy Duncan. At one stage a fellow guest had us trying to simultaneously draw a question mark in the air with one of our hands and rotate the same foot. I discovered it can't be done. Odd the things you learn at cricket dinners.

Meanwhile, in Taunton, the region has been inundated by extremely heavy rain and the new flood defences of the County Ground were tested for the first time. Thankfully, although the Tone burst its banks for the first time in fifty years, the new walls held and potentially serious damage was avoided.

The other news released today was that Banger, Somerset legend Marcus Trescothick, has signed a new three-year contract with us. To put it mildly, the news was well received by all at Somerset County Cricket Club! Banger, who made his debut for the county in 1993, is now contracted to play until 2015 – by then his career with us will have spanned an incredible twenty-two years.

FRIDAY, 23 NOVEMBER. NEW ZEALAND

Apart from the flooding resulting from almost biblical rain storms, all is relatively quiet on the cricket front in Somerset. Our new flood walls, which run parallel to the River Tone, have stood firm and protected not only the holiest of cricket squares but also a vital part of Taunton's town centre.

Meanwhile, 12,000 miles away, one of our great stalwarts and servants Tregs is preparing to compete in New Zealand's domestic T20 competition, where he will represent Central Districts. Tregs enjoyed a highly successful season, compiling 600 runs and claiming fifty wickets in the Championship as well as hitting 245 runs and taking fifty wickets in the CB40. As mentioned earlier, his achievements were recognised with the MVP award for the season.

SATURDAY, 24 NOVEMBER.

Sir Ian Botham's birthday. No book on Somerset, past, present or future would be complete without mention of Beefy, England's greatest ever all-rounder and Somerset legend. I've met him on several occasions during my time with the club, and for someone who has achieved so much he's refreshingly modest, friendly and down to earth.

Stories abound about Beefy, and the best known is surely his performance at Headingley in 1981. There are two other stories which arguably tell us more about him.

Blowers writes that he first saw an 18-year-old Botham on 12 June 1974 at the County Ground as we entertained Hampshire in the Benson & Hedges Cup. Hants were dismissed for 182 and Beefy took two wickets, including the vital one of Barry Richards. Beefy was due in at number nine and we were in trouble at 113 for seven as he took guard. A few balls later another wicket fell. Beefy faced Andy Roberts soon afterwards and tried to hook a very fast short ball but missed and it hit him in the mouth. He was soon spitting blood and help was summoned from the pavilion, but Beefy stood his ground and refused to leave the field. He composed himself and was soon in his stride with some swashbuckling strokes. He put on 63 for the ninth wicket with

Hallam Moseley. Roberts then ended Moseley's innings with a yorker. Last man in was Bob Clapp, who was said to only hold a bat because he had to! Realising this, Beefy accelerated and smashed two mighty sixes in the following over and brought up the winning runs in the next to see us home by one wicket. His fearless, match-winning display was said to be on a par with *the* innings at Headingley in 1981. After the game Both went out on the town minus a few teeth and celebrated a wonderful win.

The other story relates how he came to support leukaemia in children as a cause. After breaking a toe in training he attended our local hospital, the Musgrove Park, where he literally took a wrong turning and ended up in the paediatric ward. This made an immediate and lasting impression on Beefy, and so began his magnificent fundraising campaign for this cause. I have first-hand experience of children suffering with leukaemia and there can be no more worthy cause for which to raise money. His twelve long-distance walks have now raised over £12m for charity. Sir Ian Botham OBE – knight of the realm, Somerset cricketing legend and an extraordinary humanitarian.

MONDAY, 26 NOVEMBER. MUMBAI. SECOND TEST, INDIA V ENGLAND. DAY 5

Another early start for cricket fans as England attempt to press home their big advantage over India in Mumbai. The spinners get to work and the Indians are dispatched in short order. The first time since 1958 (when I was one year old) that English spinners have taken nineteen wickets in a Test.

There is great anticipation as the English openers set about making inroads into a very modest 57 to pull us level in the series. However, how many times has cricket confounded its devotees? It does it for fun.

I needn't have worried, as Captain Cook and Compo set a good pace, and moreover Somerset's finest shows the world his second gear by sending his first ball to the boundary and thereafter scoring at better than a run a ball. He comfortably outscores the skipper and we coast home for a crushing win.

What price now for an England series victory? Professional cricket club officers and staff are no longer allowed to bet on any form of cricket – a shame for those who might have backed England at 9:1 before the first Test to win the series.

•••

I receive a text from Kevin Howells confirming our meeting on Wednesday at the County Ground. No mention of his disappointment at being overlooked for the vacant DG's role!

A missive from Gordon Hollins arrives which updates all the counties on the status of the marathon 'marking session' taking place at HQ of our

Business Plans. Put simply, to date, two counties have passed with flying colours, others have been told to read teacher's comments and try harder, a couple have missed the deadline for handing in their homework, and one (unnamed) has seemingly refused to do it and appears to be heading for detention. I've referred in more deferential tones earlier in this book to the ECB's changing focus in the way it incentivises and rewards the counties. In short they are aiming to instil excellence and reward counties for significant achievements in the running of their clubs both on and off the pitch. There is a determined move away from rewarding all clubs equally, irrespective of their performance on and off the pitch.

TUESDAY, 27 NOVEMBER.

I exchanged early morning direct tweets with Compo (#thecompdog). He's unsurprisingly in a very positive space and enjoying the tour. He says he's had a great many messages of support and has asked me to convey his thanks to our members and supporters. Compo loves travel, and India offers any tourist a smorgasbord to feast upon. Another message from an old Somerset favourite Ian Blackwell (#Blackie37) gives Compo some tips for a day off in Mumbai. We've had terrible flooding in parts of Somerset over the past week and Compo is keen to learn that his house is still standing.

I meet Guy Lavender first thing for a catch-up and once again there are many issues to consider. Somebody once said problems never come in single file – how true! We ran through the Bath festival, Phase IV, the latest on our preferred candidate for DOC, an IPL issue with one of our senior players, the Sponsors lunch this Friday, a media accreditation for DavesSCCCNews, year-end results sign-off and our media arrangements for the forthcoming season. As a postscript I was also duly informed that our President had recently spent the night in his car after a Mid-Somerset Area annual dinner – he couldn't get through the flooded lanes! We left bidding each other farewell until Friday, and then I remembered I'd see him tomorrow – Kevin Howells is visiting the County Ground.

At 9 a.m. it's on to Morrisons for another 'power breakfast' with Julian Catternach, who has now finished ploughing through my draft manuscript. He has done a magnificent job reading the tome, and apart from spotting every grammatical error (hundreds) has embellished some of the cricketing stories and anecdotes. Julian has an extraordinary grasp of cricket facts, and by way of illustration let me describe part of our breakfast today. He has developed a cricketing mnemonic system whereby almost every number can be linked to the beautiful game. So, while in Morrisons, the total for our breakfasts was £8.50 and he immediately piped up, 'Somerset v Middlesex first innings total for eight wickets, declared.' The cashier looked very puzzled. A few minutes later the same lady who had taken our money delivered our breakfast. We were sat at table 22. She called out our table number as she placed our food on the table and Julian looked her straight in the eye and said, 'Highest number of Test centuries by an Englishman.' As the Morrisons lady returned his stare, he continued: '...Wally Hammond, Alastair Cook, KP, Colin Cowdry and Geoff Boycott.' She looked at us both with a mixture of bewilderment and sadness and returned to the checkout shaking her head. It struck me this could be the basis of an all-consuming cricket game.

Dan Whiting of The Middle Stump is also in touch today. His forthcoming book is also being published by The History Press and he suggests we might co-operate where sensible. I can agree to this instantly and email him back. If you haven't followed them, it is well worth a look, as they have some excellent articles and interviews. While their interviews are humorous in character, this belies a very shrewd reading of the game and its many idiosyncrasies.

WEDNESDAY, 28 NOVEMBER. THE COUNTY GROUND

A meeting with Kevin Howells of the BBC this morning. He wants to chat to a county chairman about 2014. I shall very happily give him my one-eyed Somerset County Cricket Club view and then twist his arm for some launch publicity for this book!

Prior to meeting him I signed off the accounts for the fiscal year ended 30 September 2012 and was pleased with our performance against the strong headwinds of recession and also the significant and adverse effect of the wettest summer in a century. Our match day income fell by over £150,000, which came straight off our bottom line as games lost to bad weather provide neither sufficient notice, nor the means, to cut costs. We have achieved a record operating profit of £409,000 and an EBIDA of £568,000. A good year's work, but we can always do better.

An interesting perspective from Geoff Cook – one of the most highly regarded DOCs in the English game. Not least his references to our squad and hunger, which are perceptive, one hopes, and to the challenges posed by Durham's financial position, together with the points penalty incurred as they exceeded the salary cap now in force.

COOK PREDICTS TOUGH START TO SEASON FOR DURHAM – *Shields Gazette*

Durham coach Geoff Cook knows his side will have their work cut out when they open their 2013 County Championship campaign at home to Somerset on April 10.

The new set of fixtures were released yesterday, with the North-East county starting with a home game at the Emirates ICG. Somerset were runners-up in the competition, and Cook believes they will have the hunger to go one better this time around. He said: 'Somerset have a very strong squad with a good mix of lots of international players past and present.'

'They also have a lot of promising young cricketers coming through the ranks, which we saw in our games against them last season. Somerset have never won the County Championship, and I'm sure they will be determined to put that right.'

Last season Durham drew with Marcus Trescothick's men at the Emirates ICG, and went down to a five-wicket defeat at Taunton. Durham will face another tough test when the two sides meet at Chester-le-Street early next year, but Cook says it will be one of many stern challenges the county faces. 'A lot of teams in Division One are strengthening their squads,' he added. 'Surrey have made some very good signings, and Yorkshire are coming back up with a more experienced squad than the last time they were in this division. It means that it will be a very competitive championship this season, and that it is going to be a big challenge.'

Cook knows that Durham also need to strengthen their squad, but constraints make that far from straightforward after they were fined £2,500 for breach of the salary cap last season. It was Durham who reported themselves to the cricket authorities after noticing the problem, and as a result of their honesty, and the fact that the breach was at the lower end of the scale, they only got a relatively small fine. However, the English Cricket Board also deducted 2.5 points from Durham for the start of the 2013 championship campaign and 0.25 points in the T20 and Clydesdale Bank 40 competitions. That means Durham must tread carefully when looking to make new additions this season. Cook added: 'The financial side of things makes it difficult when we are looking to bring people in.'

'But we know that when you lose experienced players like Diva (experienced batsman Michael Di Venuto, who retired from the first-class game before the end of last season) and Liam Plunkett then you need to replace them, and that's what we will look to do.'

THURSDAY, 29 NOVEMBER.

The news today is that Ricky Ponting is hanging up his boots. He is the only player to have won 100 Tests. As the club was trying to haul itself out of a big hole in the naughties, he was briefly our captain in 2004 and performed with great distinction, averaging 99 in three Championship matches and scoring two centuries and a fifty. He also provided the club with a transfusion of self-belief and confidence when we badly needed it. The piece below by Athers sums up his combative attitude.

Mike Atherton, *The Times*

There was a moment during the final Test at the Oval in 2009 that summed him up perfectly. He had lost a critical toss and his team were losing the Ashes (again) but there he was in the engine room at silly point, hoping for an edge from Matt Prior off his part-time spinner Marcus North.

   Prior drove and the ball bounced up and hit Ponting flush in the mouth. The batsman enquired of the Australia captain's health. Ponting spat out a tooth and some claret, folded his arms and looked Prior square in the eyes, unmoved. Bloodied and unbowed for 17 years in international cricket, but beaten now at last.'

Joanne Vickers, ardent Somerset supporter and cricket nut, tweets that she is in hospital. A false alarm – she's only there to give birth, and baby Edward has arrived safely, indeed rather conveniently in the close season. Taking a leaf out of Barbara Von Tyszka's book (see Taunton Area AGM, 14 November), the only oversight perhaps may have been missing the opportunity of coinciding Edward and Banger's birthdays!

FRIDAY, 30 NOVEMBER. THE COUNTY GROUND

Today we held our first sponsors' lunch as a thank-you to those companies who have supported us commercially. Two guests from each are invited and a complement of senior players and club officers make up the party. We have lunch in the Long Room and a very enjoyable occasion is had by all. We round off the lunch with a few words from yours truly and a presentation of signed bats in rather fetching but slightly agricultural wooden cases. Not the most prestigious or unique gifts, but as a token of our appreciation and goodwill they are very well received. We have signed a new main sponsor for next season whose identity remains a very badly kept secret! St Austell, the Cornish brewers, are heading east, and we shall be honoured to help them on their mission to capture a greater 'share of throat' in the West Country. Another highlight of the lunch was the unveiling of our new T20 shirt, which has taken some inspiration from the versions worn by our cousins in rugby. Banger viewed the figure-hugging shirt with some alarm, but a guest then volunteered to allay his fears. Maz's dad, a sheer mountain of a man, boldly volunteered to model it – and over coffee began his expedition into it. By the time the refilled coffees were finished he was snugly inside. Following the briefest of appearances on the Long Room's runway it dawned on all of us that he now had to get out of it. What followed was cricket's version of the dance of the veils as Maz's dad was extricated.

•••

I note two former Somerset captains are involved in the contest to decide the number one status in Test cricket in Perth, WA. It's a fine advertisement for the long game.

News of Ricky Ponting's retirement has caused a flurry of speculation amongst our members and supporters. All manner of positions are speculated upon, ranging from full-time DOC to part-time batsman. The reality is he would be a Kolpak player and so would be of interest to any county who could afford him. We made contact some time ago to ensure he's aware of our interest should he be minded to look towards England next summer.

DECEMBER

SATURDAY, I DECEMBER. TAUNTON

The club's physio staff are large characters in every sense of the word. The article below explains how they've enthusiastically supported Movember.

SOMERSET'S MOVEMBER MEN IN SIGHT OF THEIR TARGET – SCCC Site

Three members of the Somerset CCC support staff, Head of Sports Medicine and lead Physiotherapist Ian Brewer, Strength and Conditioning coach Darren Veness and his assistant Joel Tratt have been supporting Movember.

At the start of the month the trio set themselves a target of raising £1,000 between them, a figure they have almost reached thanks to the generous support of the players, members of staff and friends.

Ian Brewer said: 'It's been a fantastic effort and we are nearly up to £1,000 which is our main target, so huge thanks to everyone who has contributed to this very worthwhile cause. However we still need one last push to help us past the four figures so if there is anyone out there who would still like to make a donation it's not too late!'

Joel is very much the new boy of the three and only joined the Club six weeks ago as cover for Darren while he is away alternate weeks working with the England potential emerging fast bowling group in Loughborough, so he has been pitched in at the deep end.

'It's been great to have joined in with the Movember fundraising activity with Brewsy and Daz, and if we get to £1000 it will be an amazing achievement because it's a lot of money.'

'I came on board six weeks ago as assistant to Daz, and the weeks that he is up in Loughborough I work with Brewsy in overseeing things in skills weeks, and then when he is back I join in with helping to make sure the boys get all of their strength and conditioning work done so they are as fit as they can be for the start of the season.'

Joel hails from near to Ilminster and is a keen cricket follower who has been coming to watch Somerset since he was three years old.

'I'm loving it here at the County Ground and wouldn't want to be any-where else. I'm a local boy and the Club has been a big part of my family's life, so to be involved is fantastic and working here is a bit like a dream come true.'

MONDAY, 3 DECEMBER. TAUNTON, NORTH ISLAND NEW ZEALAND AND INDIA

I had lunch with our Treasurer Alex Tetley today who is stepping down at the AGM after a successful four-year spell masterminding our finances. He succeeded Rory O'Donnell, a very well-known character in the South West business community who served the club for twenty-two years. Alex had large shoes to fill but despite working full-time in the profession and bringing up three young girls he carried out the role in exemplary fashion. We owe him a considerable debt.

Jim May, the Sussex Chairman, phoned with seasonal sentiments and we compared notes on a few issues occupying our minds. Also the jungle drums are beginning to beat in respect of the election for the position of ECB Deputy Chairman – Denis Amiss is retiring after sterling service and it looks as though there may be a contested election.

TUESDAY, 4 DECEMBER. LONDON

Today is a notable anniversary in cricket – on this day in 1964 in Lahore, Pakistan Railways smashed Dera Ismail Khan by an innings and 851 runs. The biggest win in first-class history.

•••

As so often, I bump into someone connected with Somerset County Cricket Club on platform five at Taunton railway station. This time it's Richard Brice, the owner of Somerset County Sports, whose main retail outlet lies in the St James Pavilion. 'Bricey' is another stalwart of the game and our club and makes a contribution well over and above just running his business at the County Ground. He chairs St Andrews Cricket Club, one of the best clubs in the area, and is always very active supporting our players during and after their playing careers. He also helps in the design and procurement of our kit and was instrumental in introducing us to Kukri, who have been a very ener-getic partner and added considerable value in the quality of our playing kit.

After the sponsors' lunch our 2013 kit was launched to the media and the new T20 shirt took plaudits. Bricey told me that about thirty of the initial 100 ordered had already been sold. I omitted to mention we had enjoyed our own private showing in the Long Room!

I was pleased to read on our site today of the disability cricket festival held at Taunton Cricket Club recently. I've written earlier in this book about the terrific success of our men's disabled team, and it's really good to see them nurturing the grass roots of the game with such enthusiasm and strong support from us and another excellent local club.

SOMERSET DISABILITY CRICKET FESTIVAL – SCCC Site

Special schools from all over the county were recently invited to take part in a Kwik Cricket festival at Taunton Vale Sports Club.

The festival was the finale to a project jointly organised by Somerset Activity and Sports Partnership (SASP), Somerset Disability Cricket Club and Somerset Cricket Board.

Held on November 27th, the festival was attended by Selworthy School (Taunton), Elmwood School (Bridgwater), Lufton College and Fiveways School (both Yeovil). Students from Bishop Fox's school were also in attendance to help score and umpire the games.

The competition was a closely contested round robin league with the winner having to be decided by total runs scored.

At the conclusion of the event Lufton missed out by a mere 15 runs to Elmwood. Medals and prizes were presented by Somerset County Cricket Club first team players Lewis Gregory and Gemaal Hussain.

In addition to the prize giving the players also signed autographs, posed for pictures and answered the children's cricketing questions.

WEDNESDAY, 5 DECEMBER. LONDON

Up early to watch the first day of the Third Test in Kolkata, and it's a good time to finish the announcement of our financial results for 2011/12.

Here is draft 1.1.

Somerset announce a record operating profit of £409,403 for 2011/12

Somerset County Cricket Club is proud to be able to announce a profit of £409k for the 2011/12 financial year. Despite one of the wettest summers on record and poor economic conditions the Club continued to see strong attendances and once again significantly increased its Membership revenue.

The figures were boosted by excellent cricketing performances with the Club achieving Runners-Up in the County Championship as well as staging a home FL T20 quarter-final this season. Our Catering, conference and banqueting business generated substantial turnover at a healthy margin.

Finally, the Champions League 2011 campaign and the Elton John concert both made modest contributions to profit.

Chief Executive Guy Lavender has welcomed the announcement and believes that it is a testament to the efforts of everyone connected with The Club: 'This has been a very tough year and whilst we have seen some weather-related reductions in match receipts, we have been able to drive the Club's business forward in a number of different areas. It is of credit to both our playing and non-playing staff who have worked hard to make sure that we have thrived again this year. This year's results are ahead of our record profit in 2011 and considering the challenges of 2012, it demonstrates that we are able to achieve consistently high levels of profitability. Looking forward to next year, there is every opportunity for us to continue to increase the financial strength of the Club. It is satisfying to see that the Club is making progress on and off the field.'

Chairman Andy Nash believes these results are laying the foundations for the Club's future: 'Strong finances are the bedrock of being able to deliver cricketing success and to create a ground which provides excellent facilities for our Members and visitors. It is a credit to our General Committee, management and staff that our long term vision remains on track despite tough challenges being posed by the difficult economic conditions and the wettest summer in a century. Our twin ambitions are to win the County Championship and to bring one day international cricket to The County Ground. This set of results demonstrates we're achieving a consistently high level of profitability, underpinned by the strong support from our Members, spectators and our community in the West Country. We are well placed to begin preparatory work on the next phase of ground development and having consolidated and strengthened our cricketing squad for next season, we are in good shape for the 2013 campaign.'

There is some wayward discussion on Grockles about the Bath festival and the club's intentions towards it. I decide to post, making it clear we are committed to the festival and the issue is entirely one of practicalities. We rely on playing on The Rec, which for most of the year is home to Bath RFC. There is a window of opportunity for a cricket pitch to be prepared once the temporary stand has been removed. During this window, damage to the field of play needs to be made good and grass needs to grow. Mother Nature, overseen by Somerset CCC Head Groundsman Simon Lee, then gets to work to produce a playing surface fit for professional cricket and the ECB's pitch inspectors. In 2013 the window available for the gestation period is to be foreshortened as the rugby season will end later than usual. These are the practicalities which we and the Bath Area Committee are confronted with.

I place one additional post to put a brake on the rumour that one Father Christmas is to be appointed our new DOC. I do concede that the real identity will be known before the last window is opened, and chocolate eaten, on the advent calendars around the West Country.

THURSDAY, 6 DECEMBER. LONDON AND INDIA

Another pulsating Test match under way in Kolkata. During the evening session Captain Cook becomes the youngest ever player to reach 7,000 Test runs. In a peer group containing Sachin, Kallis, Smith and Jayawardene, that's not a bad list to top! Meanwhile at the other end Compo is setting about cementing his place in this side, compiling a sure-footed maiden Test 50 and bringing up the landmark with a classy pull. He looks completely at home as England progress serenely towards a first-innings lead.

Later in the day the captain continues to set records, the most notable of which was becoming the first Englishman to achieve twenty-three Test centuries, surpassing a record set by Wally Hammond some sixty-three years ago!

Meanwhile Jos and Bagel are in action for the Emerging Players Programme and both are getting runs. Interestingly, Bagel is also captaining the side, and eagle-eyed followers might note that appointment. Jos and Bagel are both in good form with the bat.

Our results are released at 9 a.m. and a frisson of pride ripples through the club. These are excellent results in a challenging environment. We are well set for 2013.

Dave Nosworthy's visit is finalised for next week. Dave is our frontrunner for the position of DOC; we are keeping this under wraps for obvious reasons. Guy Lavender has put together a varied itinerary which will give Dave and his wife a good feel for life in Somerset, ranging from housing and schools to shopping and leisure. Dave's references are exemplary. It would be inappropriate for me to identify individuals, but the recent ESPN article has prompted several ex-players, coaches and managers to email us saying what an outstanding coach and character he is.

The ECB, in the forms of Giles Clarke, David Collier and Gordon Hollins, have also emailed from Kolkata congratulating us on our financial results, which were pre-released to them yesterday.

FRIDAY, 7 DECEMBER.

Up before the larks this morning to listen to the Test match and catch the train back to Taunton after three days in London on business. The club's results have been well received.

I send Compo a Twitter message as he's received plaudits on social media and mainstream media for his solid innings yesterday.

Today we've RBS, the club's bankers, coming in for what Peter Cook and Dudley Moore used to call 'a bit of a chat'. Our bank has indicated to our CEO that, despite the club being around for 137 years, always repaying its previous loans, being cited as the modern game's 'model club', having made a profit in twenty-two of the last twenty-three years, repaying our existing loan to schedule and now having the chance to stage England internationals, they don't feel we are the sort of outfit that they would like to do business with.

Guy Lavender and myself might feel obliged to point out that because of their own reckless behaviour they had to be baled out to the tune of some £50bn and are in some difficulty for financial wrongdoings; but apparently they still think doing business with a county cricket club is no longer what they are looking for. So we are going to have 'a bit of a chat' with the gentlemen from RBS.

We had our 'bit of a chat' with the bankers and it remains to be seen whether our long-term relationship will survive. The ball is in their court; as incumbents they are well placed to retain the business if they wish to.

FINANCIAL BOOST FOR SOMERSET – ECB Site

Somerset have once again announced extremely impressive financial figures, revealing a record profit of £409,000 up to September 2012.

That total represents a marginal improvement on last year – something that is all the more impressive given how much cricket was ruined by inclement weather last season.

Developing Taunton represents the next phase of Somerset chairman Andy Nash's plans as he looks to bring ODI cricket to the stadium.

Chief executive Guy Lavender said: 'This has been a very tough year and while we have seen some weather-related reductions in match receipts, we have been able to drive the club's business forward in a number of different areas.'

'It is of credit to both our playing and non-playing staff who have worked hard to make sure that we have thrived again this year.'

Chairman Andy Nash is not content with Somerset's outstanding financial efforts and has already set his sights on further success – on and off the field.

He added: 'Our twin ambitions are to win the County Championship and to bring one-day international cricket to the County Ground.'

'We are well placed to begin preparatory work on the next phase of ground development and having consolidated and strengthened our cricketing squad for next season, we are in good shape for the 2013 campaign.'

SATURDAY, 8 DECEMBER.

I was a guest of Dick Macey, Chairman of the Friends of the Taunton Titans RFC, for their fixture against the Worthing Raiders. Dick is a passionate sports fan and also finds time to be part of our commentary team at Somerset. He is a font of wisdom, stories and jokes. Today he regaled us with several over lunch and then went on to entertain the entire crowd by switching roles and becoming the announcer on the PA system during the match. I too was asked to multi-task by saying a few words, presenting a prize for their raffle and then auctioning the same item off!

On our table was Jeremy Brown MP, who I hadn't seen for a while because of his frenetic and endless globe-trotting as Minister of State in the Foreign Office. He's obviously been spending more time at home of late, as his partner Rachel was positively blooming in her third trimester. Jeremy has always been a strong supporter of Somerset County Cricket Club, and he was very positive about the County Ground achieving its Category B status and keen to learn more about the proposed new facilities and timescales. Having covered all these aspects I asked him about how cricket had crossed his path while on tour, as it were, for the FCO. He had a fund of stories including meeting the Chinese Premier, Hilary Clinton, Arabic Royals, etc (which might be another record in a year for a Somerset member), but the one which really resonated with me was a memory from Barbados. While in the Caribbean he had met Joel Garner at a function. Once they had dispensed with the diplomatic niceties they got down to proper business – and discussed where the best cider could be found in Wiveliscombe. Jeremy then recalled how another player, who shall remain nameless, had told him how inconvenient it was back in the days when the official players' cars used to have the players' names emblazoned upon the doors. Apparently this caused no little embarrassment on more than one occasion when said cars were found outside various homes in the town on Sunday mornings!

...

What is the secret of Somerset County Cricket Club's financial success? It's a question people sometimes ask me, out of simple curiosity or even bewilderment. The answer of course is that there is no simple answer, but one key element was visible tonight as I 'walked the ship' that is the Colin Atkinson Pavilion.

Our management accounts tell us that 'catering' turnover in a year is in excess of £1.5m. It doesn't explain why. Walking into the County Room tonight provides the answer. Sam Safe, manager of events, tells me, 'We've only 300 in tonight, so it's not too busy. Last night was 430.' The room looked simply stunning – the design, lighting and decorations couldn't fail to ignite the festive spirits in guests out for a memorable Christmas party tonight. So there's one answer. Then came another one. An hour previously the glass washer in the Long Room had malfunctioned. It left the Long Room bar and kitchen under two feet of water, threatening the event. So while Compo, Bagel and Jos were in India and Fons was in Oz for the Big Bash – plus Tregs in New Zealand, Max and Mesch in South Africa and young Regan and Jack Leach in Tasmania – around twenty members of the catering staff, armed with mops and buckets, baled out the Long Room and saved tonight's event. This commitment is born of the pride they have in the family and the enterprise that is Somerset County Cricket Club. You can't grow this on trees and you can't just buy it with money.

On the way out I had a quick chat with a waitress I recognised from long ago. She explained she was glad to be back working at the club. She had left us to work for a well-known pub in town, but they had treated her badly. She had come back to be part of a team that is valued and treated with respect. This is the fabric of our club, and this is undoubtedly another reason why we are making a good living in these challenging times.

SUNDAY, 9 DECEMBER. KOLKATA

Another early start as the coffin that is the Indian team has only one nail left to go in it. Or so one hopes. With the hosts' final wicket taken fairly smartish, we only need 41 runs to win the Test and complete a historic turnaround from the disaster of the first Test less than three weeks earlier.

In almost the flash of an eye cricket reminds everyone it can make a fool of the pundit and fan. We are 8 for three, with Captain Cook, Trott and KP back in the hutch and the wicket now very much Mr Hyde after several days of being Jekyll. Compo is still there, though, and with Bell at the other end they overhaul the target. Thankfully we weren't chasing 175, which might well have been a target too far. I wrack my brains to remember when a Somerset County Cricket Club batter was last at the crease when England won a Test match, and then I remember – it was last week! Compo received the ultimate accolade as victory drew nigh – the Barmy Army sang a newly composed number in his honour.

An article by Richard Walsh on our site captures the moment.

NICK IS A HAPPY BUNNY! – SCCC Site

There was celebrating back in Somerset when Nick Compton helped England to a second successive victory over India in Kolkata this morning to give the tourists a 2-1 lead in the four match series.

Nick was at the wicket when England beat India in Mumbai in the second Test to level the series last week, and once again the Somerset batsman was there to see them through to victory today.

Batting for a second time England found themselves 8 for 3 before Nick and Ian Bell saw them to 41 without further loss and a well deserved victory.

By the time that the tourists had won Nick had moved onto nine not out from 30 balls including a four.

Shortly afterwards Nick said: 'Two Test wins in India makes me one very happy bunny. I am really glad that I could contribute towards it and I can tell you everyone in the changing room is dead chuffed.'

Nick went on: 'I thought that second session on day 4 changed the game with Graham Swann and Jimmy Anderson particularly impressive.'

'My heart was going pretty hard when we lost a few wickets and there were a few chirps coming from the close in fielders.'

He added: 'I'm glad I managed to see it through, and to again walk off having the Barmy Army chanting your name is something I won't forget. We are off to Nagpur tomorrow.'

Thanks Nick and well done on seeing England through to another victory out in India.

MONDAY, 10 DECEMBER. TAUNTON

'You can learn more about a person in an hour of play than in a year of conversation.' So said Plato, and he was pretty wise, so we are taking a leaf out of his book. Tonight Guy and Leisa Lavender, Linda and myself are at play with Dave and Monique Nosworthy in the Pink Garlic – a very homely Indian restaurant tucked away in the Taunton suburbs. The Nosworthys are in town for what we hope will be the last step of our search for the club's new DOC.

First I have to travel to Gatwick and back for a board meeting in the deepening mid-winter gloom.

Walking to the station from the County Ground I hear a strange scraping noise. It's coming from the other side of the wooden fence along Priory Bridge Road. A few minutes later as I walk past, the source of the sound is revealed. It is none other than Simon Lee and Rob Hake, two of our ground staff. They are multi-tasking by making some repairs to our boundary fence rather than being in their more familiar environment tending Taunton's fabled square. We have a quick chat and exchange seasonal greetings.

Simon has been our head groundsman for about four years, and with guidance from Rosey has overseen a huge improvement in our pitch. Not only has he achieved a better balance between bat and ball but also the quality of the outfield and its drainage properties has been transformed - and he performs what is a demanding role with a very sunny disposition and positive attitude.

In the evening we arrive at the Pink Garlic at 7.30 p.m. and it proves a real pleasure to meet Dave and his wife Monique in person. They have had a long day being introduced around the club and meeting many staff members. Tomorrow is a 'cricket day', where he will spend more time with Head Coach and Captain, observe squad training and meet with the Academy and age-group coaches and students. They will then spend time visiting local schools and areas to give them an idea of the options for housing. It is a huge move for them, as not only are they uprooted from their home in SA but their daughter will also be relocating, while their son will board in Joburg.

WEDNESDAY, 12 DECEMBER.

Anya Shrubsole has been selected for the World Cup in India. She's worked extremely hard on her game and thoroughly deserves her call-up. An article is posted on our site congratulating her on her achievement.

Taunton Deane Borough Council met in full session this evening and formally approve our £1m loan over fifteen years. While we expected this to be approved, we were pleased to see an amendment which sought to increase the interest rate being charged us voted down!

We run an article on the site which explains how our profits will be reinvested into the club for its future benefit.

PROFITS TO GO TOWARDS DELIVERING SOMERSET PLAN – SCCC Site

Somerset announced a new record profit of £409,403 (EBITDA £563,332) at the end of last week confirming that the Club enjoyed a successful season all round in 2012.

Over recent years Somerset has become one of the front runners in all formats of English cricket and last season saw them end as runners up in the County Championship for the second time in three summers and also win a place at T20 Finals Day.

The profits from 2011-12 will enable the Club to continue to realise their ambitions, something which all fans will want to hear, as Chief Executive Guy Lavender explained.

'The generation of decent levels of trading surplus each year are really important to us because of the plans we have for the Club.'

'We want to move forward on the re-development of the Old Pavilion as well as making sure that we can invest heavily in cricket. For us to achieve these aims and ensure that the Club thrives and develops, generating surpluses is critical.'

'After what has been a difficult summer this is a great opportunity for us to make sure that our plans are on track to enable us to complete the final phase of development of the County Ground which will allow us to bid for international cricket; a hugely exciting opportunity.'

The Somerset boss went on: 'We also need to make sure that we address areas that were not satisfactory this year; in particular the scoreboard and public announcement system which were unacceptable, and we are investing resources to make sure that there is a dramatic improvement for the 2013 season.'

He added: 'It is important to re-emphasise that as a Members Club we invest all of our surpluses back in to building the success of the Club for the future.'

There was further good news for Somerset on Tuesday evening when Taunton Deane Borough Council gave their full backing for a £1m loan to the Club to enable them to continue their development of the County Ground.

'The loan from Taunton Deane Borough Council is magnificent news and we are delighted that they have chosen to play a critical part in the development of the Club, which we believe contributes significantly to the prosperity of Taunton.'

The Chief Executive added: 'When this loan is combined with the support we have received from the ECB, as well as good levels of profit, it means we are exceptionally well placed to achieve the re-development of the Old Pavilion and make sure we have the cricketing resources to achieve success.'

•••

12 December is John Daniell's birthday. Daniell was quite a character, being an international rugby union player for England as well as being a Somerset cricketer and an administrator of some note. He captained Somerset for thirteen of the fifteen seasons in which first-class cricket was played between 1908 and 1926, and acted as occasional secretary and general organiser for the county over many years. He was also a national selector for the England cricket team.

1907 was a year of some difficulty for Somerset, and at the end of the season, with the county club's finances in disarray and fixtures with several other counties under threat, Skipper Lionel Palairet told an acrimonious club AGM that he was not willing to continue any longer, and so it appeared possible that the unthinkable might happen – i.e. the county could be wound up.

Daniell, recently returned to England, and back as the protégé of Sammy Woods, who remained county secretary, agreed to take on the captaincy for the following season.

Drastic action was taken; the professional staff was cut to just three and Daniell embarked on the policy that was to serve Somerset well for many years: recruiting players from far and wide, from the public schools and universities and also overseas. The policy did not bring the county any great successes, but it is said that Somerset cricket was rarely dull, and of course the club stayed in business.

There were many stories of John Daniell, who was clearly a formidable fellow. I love this one, which featured in the *Guardian*'s obituary of Mandy Mitchell-Innes. 'His [Mitchell-Innes'] favourite memory was of sitting alongside Daniell at Taunton. Suddenly, Frank Lee, the batsman, was hit in the box. "The box, you say," thundered Daniell, a former England rugby captain. "What namby-pamby nonsense is that?" A few minutes later it happened again and Daniell exploded: "What does he need a so-called box for? In my day, we hit fours with our private parts."' As I say, a formidable fellow and another great character from Somerset's past.

THURSDAY, 13 DECEMBER. LONDON

I'm a guest at Nigel Gray's testimonial lunch at the Royal Garden Hotel in Kensington. All Somerset supporters will know Nigel! You may not think you do – but you do. Play at the death of the 2009 T20 final was held up and he featured prominently in the nail-biting delay: we all had to wait for the last ball of the match while Nigel repainted the popping crease. The scores were level, meaning Hampshire needed one run for victory. If we bowled a dot, Somerset would be victorious ... we all know what happened.

There were 350 guests at the lunch, which, bearing in mind that one for Matt Prior next week has just been cancelled due to poor take-up of tickets, reflects very well indeed on Nigel, his testimonial organising committee and Hampshire CCC.

The guest speaker was Dusty Miller. He was on cracking form and told some terrific stories of past and present which had some guests splitting their sides. One such tale offered a contrast to the posse of specialists who now accompany Team England: fitness coach, strength and conditioning coaches, a lifestyle coach, team psychologists, fielding, batting and bowling coaches, security co-ordinator, etc. Geoff said that while he was at Derbyshire CCC one bloke, 'Fingers Fred', did all these tasks.

The auctions (silent and loud) raised a more than tidy sum for Nigel Gray, and afterwards I left for Leeds reflecting on how good a thing it was that a club should hold a testimonial for a groundsman. They are all too easily overlooked, as they only really come into the public eye when there's a problem ... or a hold-up in a final.

FRIDAY, 14 DECEMBER.

The article below refers to an annual lunch which resonates with me because I used to work at Taunton Cider with Harry Burden's mother Denise. Harry's dad Richard is a keen cricket fan. Harry was a sports nut and while at a tender age was struck down with leukaemia. He battled bravely and the family carried themselves throughout the terrible ordeal with great dignity and composure. A great many people did what they could to support the family. I wrote to Kevin Keegan, then manager of Newcastle United, and explained the situation. KK invited Harry and his mum for breakfast with the team before they played Bristol City, and also to watch the match from their box at Ashton Gate and present him with his own miniature kit. Harry lost his battle, but the spirit he showed in fighting it made a lasting impression, and his annual lunch which raises funds for youth cricket in the West Country, and incentivises young cricketers with awards and bursaries, commemorates his love of cricket and his fighting spirit.

HARRY BURDEN LUNCH A GREAT SUCCESS – SCCC Site

The Harry Burden Memorial Lunch that took place in the County Room of the Colin Atkinson Pavilion at the County Ground earlier this week has been hailed as a great success by all concerned.

With improved support this year in the region of £2,000 was raised to help the development of youth cricket throughout the South West of England.

After a most enjoyable festive lunch, former Somerset favourite Keith Parsons hosted a lively Q&A session posing questions to Somerset players Arul Suppiah (beneficiary for 2013) and Lewis Gregory.

The Harry Burden Award was presented to Will Godmon of Millfield School for an exceptional innings of 173 not out for Somerset Under 17s which featured a last wicket partnership of 231 in an innings total of 332.

The Harry Burden Bursary went to Karla Rose of Taunton who played for Somerset at Under 13, Under 15 and Under 17 levels as well as for Somerset women's team during the summer. The awards were presented by Richard Burden, Harry's father.

Thanks go to Somerset County Sports, MJ Baker, Taunton Vale Golf Club, Porter Dobson, House History Somerset, Alan Hembrow Meats, Tony Pryce Sports, Wessex Malthouse, Monkton Elm, Somerset Cricket Board and Somerset County Cricket Club for their support of the event and all who attended to make the event such a significant success.

SATURDAY, 15 DECEMBER. INDIA

In India today Bagel played a captain's innings of 63, but it wasn't enough to save the England Performance Programme from a four-wicket defeat in the second of their 50-over matches against the Netherlands Lions in Pune.

Nick Compton spent the whole of the third day of the final Test match between India and England in Nagpur out in the field. By the close India had reached 297 for eight in reply to England's first-innings total of 330 all out. All three results remain possible at close of play.

MONDAY, 17 DECEMBER.
Brian Langford's birthday. 'Langy' holds the record for the number of appearances for Somerset at 576 in a magnificent career spanning twenty-one seasons between 1953 and 1974. At only 17 years and 5 months, a ten-wicket haul made him the youngest Somerset player to do so in the County Championship, a record that stood until May 2007, when James Harris completed the feat a few days after his 17th birthday. His career tally of 1,390 wickets ranks him third in the county's history, behind only Jack White and Arthur Wellard. In 1969, he had the following extraordinary analysis in the John Player League against Essex at Yeovil: 8 overs, 8 maidens, 0 runs, 0 wickets.

Brian has been bravely battling cancer and his appearances at the County Ground have been understandably limited this season. Everyone involved with Somerset County Cricket Club will wish him the strength to try and turn the tide against this awful disease.

•••

The Test fizzles out to a draw and England win a historic series in India. It's a supreme achievement, and I email the ECB with congratulations from Somerset County Cricket Club.

Jos is added to the ODI squad as Jonny Bairstow withdraws for personal reasons. Now for two T20s before Christmas and the ODIs in the New Year.

WEDNESDAY, 19 DECEMBER.
Abdur 'Manny' Rehman is announced today as one of our overseas players for next season. He took twenty-seven wickets in four championship games, including a career-best nine for 65, during his stint with us this season. He is currently serving a twelve-week ban after testing positive for cannabis. He failed a test following day two of our game with Nottinghamshire on 8 August – his first four-day match. His suspension, enforced by the England and Wales Cricket Board, runs until 21 December. Manny said, 'I am happy to be coming back to England to play for Somerset, I really enjoyed my time there last year and will look to play with the same intensity and passion. I would also like to thank the Somerset management and fans for their support in what has been a difficult period for me.'

Adam White is the Chairman of the Somerset Visually Impaired Cricket Club and he has been in touch with news of their considerable success this season.

Despite challenges posed by poor weather they played ten games and won eight of them. They currently play in the Southern Development League and they were crowned champions of it. They are going to receive their trophy at our Centre of Cricketing Excellence in January. Adam has been thinking how they can raise their profile, and following discussions with Guy Lavender we are going to arrange for them to parade their trophy at the County Ground before a one-day fixture next season and enjoy our hospitality for the day. With more support from the SCB, Adam is planning for the SVI Cricket Club to progress further and establish themselves, attracting more players and members.

FRIDAY, 21 DECEMBER.

Tonight Linda and I are out for dinner with Wayne and Belinda Kieswetter. They are here for Christmas with Bagel and younger son Ross and then returning to South Africa for the New Year as Craig joins up with the ODI squad for the series in India.

I send an SMS to Tregs, having noticed his fine run of form for Central Districts but also an injury. It's a niggling calf which shouldn't keep him out for long, hopefully. He called Banger a 'tough old goat' during his ankle injury, so I also use a farmyard analogy for him.

The club is settling down for Christmas. The last of the Christmas functions has taken place and a seasonal hush begins to descend on the County Ground. The club post a Christmas message on our site.

Merry Christmas from all at Somerset County Cricket Club – SCCC Site

The Club Offices at Somerset County Cricket Club are now closed until 9am on Wednesday 2nd January 2013.

We would like to wish all our Members and Supporters a very Merry Christmas and Happy New Year.

If you a still looking for that last minute Christmas present, membership can still be purchased online by clicking here. Although membership cards will not be sent until the New Year, a confirmation email will be sent to you which you can present as a gift.

Finally, this is Joel Garner's birthday. A Somerset legend, he was an indispensable part of the great side which enjoyed a golden period in the 1980s. At 6ft 8in (2.03m) he is one of the tallest bowlers ever to play Test cricket, appearing in 58 Tests between 1977 and 1987, taking 259 wickets at an average of barely above 20, which makes him statistically one of the most effective bowlers of all time. However, in limited-overs cricket he was deadly, using his height to devastating effect: in 98 matches he took 146 wickets. He is the only player with more than 100 ODI wickets to average under 20, while his economy rate of just over three runs per over, and average of less than 20 runs per wicket, are also the best ever for any bowler who took more than 100 wickets. His five for 39 in the 1979 Cricket World Cup final against England remains the best-ever performance by a bowler in a final; it included a spell of five wickets for four runs, and he was on a hat-trick twice. I met Joel while watching England at the Kensington Oval in 2009 and on behalf of the club invited him to open gates named in his honour between the Trescothick and Somerset stands. He readily accepted and in front of a media circus and a large crowd of supporters, he and his beautiful daughter Jewell (a former Miss Barbados) enjoyed the ceremony in May of that year.

SATURDAY, 22 DECEMBER.

Jos plays in the second Twenty20. Chasing 176, he's there at the end as we win on the last ball.

SUNDAY, 23 DECEMBER.

Dave 'Nos' Nosworthy arranges to have his own message posted on our site. It's a nice touch, and a sign of his style and gift for communication. He's going to do the job in his own way.

Dear 'Somerset County Cricket Club Members,'

I trust this short note finds you all well and that you are well prepared for Christmas and have completed all of your shopping by now?

I am sure that by now you have all heard that I have been appointed to fill the rather large boots of Brian Rose as the new Director of Cricket at Somerset County Cricket Club. Brian has clearly over the years done a superb job and I look forward to continuing on from where he has left off …

This appointment is an absolute honour and a privilege for me and I can't wait to join the structures and to meet all of you in Taunton in the early New Year.

The process to get to my appointment over the last few months has been extremely thorough I believe – as I have been through various one on one discussions and an intensive interviewing process along the way.

I also had the privilege to touch base personally with all key management at the Club itself, before I eventually got the very exciting news from Guy Lavender the CEO that I was Somerset's preferred candidate and was then officially offered the position.

The decision from my side of things to accept such a position was pretty much a no brainer – as in a funny way Somerset is in my blood! Yes, my ancestors left the shores of the United Kingdom in 1820 from 'Sidbury' and 'Widdecombe on the Moor' in Devon – to travel to the Eastern Cape in South Africa where they were part of establishing an outpost and a small village they named 'Sidbury'. Also somewhere down the family tree on the other side of the tree, I am believe it or not told that I am the 28th cousin of Prince Charles! ... I'm not too sure if I should claim such just yet or not?

Having the opportunity to coach and to hopefully add value on the cricket side of things within the United Kingdom, which is for me undoubtedly the home of cricket, has always been a dream – so for me to be joining Somerset County Cricket Club is just totally amazing and is a dream come true!

As such, I humbly cannot wait to get started. I am sure many of you like myself remember well all the many cricketing greats that have passed through the hands of the Club, and I am as such so looking forward to playing my small part in polishing and producing a few more such greats for all of us to enjoy well into the future.

My first few months will be spent very much 'sponging' as much information about all the players, the staff, the structures, and the whole culture of the Club. I don't believe in trying to fix something that is not broken – and as such believe that a few small strategical changes and plenty of polishing will ensure we are on the right track.

As we all know there is unfortunately no magical switch and I am by no means a magician who will be able to ensure that our trophy cabinet is full of silverware by the end of the season, but rest assured this is a major focus area for us all – which from a worst case scenario may even mean we will have to go one step to the side to then go two steps forward.

As a Club and as supporters we all need to just believe in the processes and try to relieve the players of as much pressure as possible so that they are able to express themselves and play their natural games in an unshackled manner.

It's exciting times ahead for Somerset County Cricket Club I believe, and I personally am looking forward to hopefully blending in with you all as easily as possible.

Please feel free to stop me if you see me around to introduce yourself and to make known your allegiances – otherwise I'll take it for granted that you are another team's supporter and shall thus just politely ignore you ... Many thanks too for all the recent support and messages of goodwill since the media release went out – I have been overwhelmed and humbled by the kindness and excitement around my appointment.

That's all for now – I thought I would just write a short note to greet everybody and to assure you of my best intentions and excitement about joining the Club.

Have a very Happy Christmas and may 2013 be an awesome year for you all and for Somerset Cricket as a whole!!

'We Are Somerset'

Kind regards,

Dave

TUESDAY, 25 DECEMBER.

Christmas Day and of course the anniversary of the birth of two important men – Marcus Trescothick and Dave Nosworthy!

Facebook tells us the club still isn't entirely quiet as Simon Lee, our Head Groundsman, was called out in the early hours – ground staff multi-task in the winter. An errant driver has creamed the Jack 'Farmer' White gates while attempting to drive between them and found them to be more than a match for her vehicle.

John Cornish White, known as 'Farmer' or 'Jack', hailed from Holford in Somerset and is one of Somerset's legends. He was named Wisden Cricketer of the Year in 1929 and played in fifteen Test matches, captaining England in four of them.

He was a classic slow left arm bowler who used accuracy and variation of pace rather than spin to take wickets. He made his debut for Somerset on the eve of WWI in 1913 and played regularly until 1937, managing an incredible 100 wickets a season on no less than fourteen occasions. He could also bat, and in the seasons of 1929 and 1930 he scored more than 1,000 runs.

He set and still holds several county records. His total number of wickets at 2,165 and total number of catches at 393 remain extant. He was club captain between 1927 and 1931.

Jack made his England debut in the 1921 series against Australia and was also selected for the 1928/29 winter tour Down Under when he was Percy Chapman's vice-captain. In the Adelaide Test he bowled 124 overs, taking thirteen wickets for 256 runs as England won by just 12 runs. In the final Test of the series, he stood in as captain for the injured Chapman.

He captained England in the series against South Africa in 1929,winning once and drawing twice. Further Tests followed against Australia in 1930 and the following winter in South Africa, again as vice-captain to Chapman. Farmer White became a selector for his country in 1929 and 1930 and was President of Somerset County Cricket Club at the time of his death.

Not entirely surprising then that the gates named in his honour proved more than a match for a modern car!

WEDNESDAY, 26 DECEMBER

An interesting and well researched article by Matthew Sherry describes matters probably on Nos' mind over the Christmas holiday.

NOSWORTHY KNOWS SIZE OF TASK – by Matthew Sherry, ECB Site

Dave Nosworthy is relishing the pressure of vanquishing Somerset's bridesmaids tag after being appointed director of cricket.

The 44-year-old was handed the reins following Brian Rose's departure and takes over a club desperate to end their recent run of being runners-up.

This year and in 2010 they came second in Division One of the LV= County Championship while 2011 saw them runners-up for a third straight season in the domestic Twenty20 competition and for a second consecutive campaign in the Clydesdale Bank 40.

Nosworthy, who has previous experience coaching New Zealand's and South Africa's A sides as well as other roles, was named Rose's successor amid glowing praise from Somerset's cricket committee chairman Vic Marks.

Marks said Nosworthy was the outstanding candidate – something that does plenty to fill the new man with confidence.

Speaking exclusively to ecb.co.uk, he said: 'I am really excited to be joining a club that is steeped in a massive amount of tradition and has done especially well in the last few seasons.

'There are some really good people at the club with integrity. Vic is one of those and it is a privilege to have come out as the preferred candidate. I know there were plenty of other guys interviewed and looked at.'

Marcus Trescothick, 'a real stalwart in the Somerset structure' according to Dave Nosworthy, has overseen some near misses.

'The reputation that Somerset has is right up there as one of the best clubs in the world. The main objective is to try and get across the line; there has been a lot of talk about that with whoever I've spoken to.'

'That adds to the pressure, but my key has to be to take the pressure off the players. Far too often, your eyes are focused on the end result rather than the natural processes. If people are able to play day by day and follow those basics, they will be able to play with more flair and far less pressure.'

As he aims to ensure that mantra is put into place, Nosworthy will benefit from being assisted in some capacities by his predecessor.

'Hopefully I do not disappoint,' he added. 'There are a couple of big boots to fill given Brian Rose is obviously a legend at the club, but he is still around and has a contract in place in an advisory role.'

Coming from South Africa means Nosworthy does not have the familiarity with Somerset's players that other candidates may have, albeit with a couple of notable exceptions.

He revealed: 'I've got a good knowledge of every individual player's performances, even if I have not seen them all in action. The player I am closest to is Alfonso Thomas.'

'I helped bring him through in South Africa when at the Titans and brought him in at the Lions recently as an overseas player for our T20 competition.'

'He is the player I have got the closest knowledge of. But I also spent some time with Marcus Trescothick recently while I was across in the UK, so that is important to have some sort of idea.'

'But it is going to be a couple of months of what I call sponging; taking in as much information as possible before really acting on too much. I think that's important as there is a process in place that is working. There is nothing broken and I think it's just a case of polishing for me.'

It is the relationship between head coach Andy Hurry and Trescothick that Nosworthy feels will be of most importance as the trio look to steer Somerset in a new era.

Nosworthy said: 'Any head coach's relationship with the captain is of the utmost importance and Marcus is a real stalwart in the Somerset structure. He is going to play a key role in the way I operate. I am looking forward to working with him.'

•••

The brouhaha with the Farmer White gates is rather diplomatically understated.

PARKING AT THE COUNTY GROUND – SCCC Site

Unfortunately the St James Street Gates have taken a knock over the festive period and to ensure the safety and stability of the gates, we have had to shut and lock them.

However, our car parks are open as normal and entry can be gained via the Priory Bridge Road Gates. Please take extra caution for pedestrians when entering, driving through and leaving the County Ground.

We hope all our supporters have had an enjoyable Christmas and we wish you all a happy and peaceful New Year.

FRIDAY, 28 DECEMBER.

I was in Taunton shopping with family members when I received a call from Guy Lavender. I knew him to be overseas, so this wasn't going to be something trivial. He called to tell me that Noel Lock had taken his own life

over Christmas. I was deeply shocked, and the many people who knew Noel
will be greatly saddened to hear of his passing.

SOMERSET MOURN THE LOSS OF NOEL LOCK – SCCC Site

It is with deep sadness that we inform Members of the death of Noel Lock.
On behalf of all of the Club our deepest sympathies are extended to Jill and
all of Noel's family at this sad time.

Noel was a very active Long Room Member and hugely supportive of the Club
travelling the length and breadth of the country with Jill to follow Somerset.

He was immensely popular with the players for his unconditional support regardless of whether we had won or lost and he will be deeply missed
by Somerset County Cricket Club.

Noel's funeral service will take place at Taunton Deane Crematorium on
Wednesday 2nd January 2013 at 10.30am. Family flowers only by request
but donations in memory of Noel for Depression Alliance may be given at
the service or sent to E. White & Son Ltd, Funeral Directors, 138/139 East
Reach, Taunton, Somerset, TA1 3HN.

SATURDAY, 29 DECEMBER.

The day breaks with news of the loss of another passionate Somerset
member. William Rees Mogg dies aged 84. He was a lifelong Somerset supporter, establishment figure and self-confessed cricket nut.

The Keeper of the Scorebook – Ivo Tennant, *The Times*

William Rees Mogg's lifelong interest in cricket was forged as a boy at
Charterhouse school, where he was scorer for the first XI.

John Woodcock, the cricket correspondent of this newspaper, was to
describe him as 'keeper of the and, later, *The Times*.

Rees-Mogg's particular interest was his home county team of Somerset,
which for much of his life were a feckless side in terms of their standing in
the county championship. As Editor of *The Times*, he would walk across to
the sports desk in quiet moments and ask how Somerset were faring.

His occassional articles on the game were invariably laced with nos-
talgia for the County Ground at Taunton and venues such as Wells and
Weston, which were no longer used for first-class cricket. Rees-Mogg was a
life member of his beloved club and, writing in The Independent in 1986,
supported the retention of Viv Richards and Joel Garner before a highly
charged special general meeting at Shepton Mallet. Nevertheless, the two
famous overseas players were not reinstated.

In recent years he could be seen at Taunton with his family, sitting in front of the pavilion or in the public seats. He had a poor opinion of the Twenty20 version of the game, describing it as 'a decadent, dumbed-down, third-rate formula for sub-prime cricket.' In 2006, on a perfect July day, he saw Graeme Smith, the captain of South Africa, score a triple century. It was two days of the London bombings. 'What right did we have to be so happy, so exceptionally happy at such a time?' Rees-Mogg wrote. The answer? He was watching his favourite sport in a treasured place.

Our site carries a story of another product of our age-group and Academy system which is a counterpoint to the sadness of two lives ending. It is an interesting account as it covers some training and development methods as well as how a talisman like Banger can motivate young players learning their craft.

WILL SOBZAK ENJOYING HIS TIME AT THE ACADEMY – SCCC Site

Will Sobzak is one of the new members on the Academy at the County Ground which has been back in full swing since early October. The 16 year old top order batsman who plays his club cricket for Sidmouth talked about his first couple of months on the Academy.

'In September I was asked to join the Academy at the County Ground, after spending the previous two years on the Emerging Player Programme, and I was delighted to accept the invitation. Since then time has gone very quickly and I have thoroughly enjoyed my initial Academy experience.'

Will explained about what is involved with being part of the Academy. 'We have had One to One coaching sessions every week and a group session every Sunday. During the One to Ones I have a session of batting, bowling and go into the gym, each for an hour. Each of these aspects of my game has greatly improved in these first six weeks. '

'In the group sessions we have explored welfare and social media. One of the most memorable sessions was our "Dragons Den" presentation, in which we had to sell our attributes and explain why we should be invested in as players. This made us think about our strengths and our areas of improvements, as well as looking at our presentation skills. Later in the sessions we move on to batting and fielding and end with a fitness session.'

Will talked about the highlight of his time on the Academy so far. 'A real highlight has been having Marcus Trescothick come in and talk to us about playing world class spin. Being able to watch and listen to him was an amazing thing to do and I gained a lot from it.'

On Sunday the Academy had their last group session before taking a break for the festive period about which Will said: 'After Sunday we pause for the Christmas break, but I can't wait to continue with the programme in the new year.'

Certainly Will is highly rated by Jason Kerr the Director of the Academy. 'Will has now been on the programme for a couple of months and has been really impressive in his attitude and has embraced what the Academy is all about and certainly made the most of his opportunities both here and at school.'

The Director added: 'He is working tirelessly week in week out trying to improve and we are seeing huge improvements being made in the first two months so from his point of view he is getting everything out of it and max-imising the opportunity.'

•••

Meanwhile having enjoyed a very brief respite at home with his family in Taunton over Christmas, Fons was back among the wickets out in the Big Bash to help Justin Langer's Perth Scorchers to a 51-run victory over Melbourne Renegades at WACA ground. Fons repaid his former skipper's faith in him with a career best of four for 8 from his 3.1 overs.

SUNDAY, 30 DECEMBER.

A third death is reported in as many days. Tony Greig has succumbed to cancer and cricket has lost another great character and servant to the game. Mike Selvey's piece below is a fitting tribute.

Tony Greig – showman, salesman, charismatic leader and cricketing great –
Mike Selvey, *Guardian*

Tony Greig was without question the most inspirational captain I played under and deserves more than an epitaph written around one unfortunate word .

Tony Greig's strength as England captain was not in his tactical acumen, or even man-management skills. Instead, it was rooted deep in charisma.

His epitaph will be written around one single unfortunate word, and his major participation in the initiative that was to change the face of cricket for ever, and not for the worse. But this is to do him a disservice for he was so much more than these things: Tony Greig was a great cricketer, a fantastic captain, a showman and salesman.

I can still see him now, standing in the middle of a heaving Indian cricket stadium, a beacon of leggy burnished blondness rising above everyone else around him, collar up, white neckerchief, directing the traffic of his

England team. We knew him as Washie, short for the old fashioned wash-peg that his peers at school in South Africa said that the gangling youth resembled. Personally, the way in which his legs splayed out as he stood at slip reminded me of the Eiffel Tower.

He had his lieutenants alongside him, lucky man that he was, some of the wisest men in the game in Mike Brearley, Keith Fletcher and Alan Knott. Any cricketer would be a fool not to draw on that well of knowledge and nous. Greig's strength as England captain was not in his tactical acumen, or even man-management skills. Instead, it was rooted deep in a charisma like none since Denis Compton was Brylcreeming two decades before, and unmatched since except by the remarkable Ian Botham. To a man, his players would do anything for him.

Certainly, he was without question the most inspirational captain under whom I played. When England won the third Test in Madras to take an unassailable lead in the five-match series, we hoisted him on our shoulders and carried him triumphantly from the ground, in a more restrained age a spontaneous gesture of the respect and affection in which he was held by the team.

The progress he made round India on that memorable historically successful tour 36 years ago, and the esteem and celebrity he generated in that country was a remarkable achievement in itself. Kevin Pietersen is finding that now. Greig recognised the value of his personality, not in financial terms (that was to come later, although he had already started to market himself successfully in England, of which his white Jaguar, result of a sponsorship deal, was testimony) but as a weapon to be used in his campaign against Bishan Bedi's formidable side of batsmen and spinning magicians.

Other visiting captains have gained immense respect in India, but Greig achieved what none has done in managing to turn the massive crowds to his advantage and get them onside. To help win them over, the entire team would, before a match and at his behest, put on the touring blazers and walk round the ground, waving.

It was a simple enough exercise but not only did the crowd respond positively towards the visitors during matches, but at times, as Greig gained a stranglehold on the series, they appeared actually to turn their support away from India. I think that was a considerable element in the success of the campaign.

Throughout he played the showman in an environment made for him. If a game started to drift and the crowd (always huge) became restless, he would encourage Derek Randall to turn some cartwheels or do some trickery in catching the ball. Once, Randall, not playing in a match, assembled a squad of police, donned one of their hats himself and marched them round the ground.

If he was batting and a firecracker exploded, Greig would clutch his chest and stagger as if shot. Slapstick worked. It brought to mind the way in which he hammed up to the West Indian crowd at The Oval the previous summer, grovelling in front of them as his team were destroyed.

If his ill-judged, offensive comments at the start of that summer (never intended maliciously but with an appalling lack of sensitivity in his choice of words: he just didn't engage brain first) sparked the fire in the West Indies team, endearingly he could make a virtue even out of that vice. Today it would be seen as undignified or plain crass.

None of this though should mask the fact that first and foremost he was a cricketer of great ability, a brilliant allrounder whose Test match batting average of more than 40 and bowling average of around 32 fulfilled the first criterion in defining the best, that the former average should exceed the latter.

For England, Botham could better him, but none other, and his ability as an allrounder, from almost the same loping run, to bowl both medium-fast swing and properly spun offbreaks (not cutters, as some inaccurately and to his lasting irritation, suggest) with equal facility to a high standard has been matched only by Garry Sobers.

His massive hands made him as near infallible a catcher of the ball as England have possessed, whether in the slips or, for Derek Underwood, perched ridiculously close at silly point where, as a distraction to the batsman, he would hang his right arm down and gently move it around, while at the same time cudding gum very loudly.

In the cauldron at Eden Gardens over new year of 1977, suffering badly from illness and grey with fatigue as a result, he willed himself to one of the greatest centuries ever scored by an England batsman, a match-winning innings of total self-denial in a team cause. Two years previously, his off breaks had brought him 13 wickets in a win over West Indies in Trinidad, match figures bettered only by Jim Laker of England offspinners.

The advent of World Series cricket cut short his captaincy and ultimately his international career. But although his pact with Kerry Packer ensured his own security in perpetuity, and change, no doubt would have come at some stage anyway, there is scarcely a professional cricketer today who has not benefitted in some way from the initiative he took.

For England international cricketers the impact was immediate. For each Test match I played in 1976, I received £210. The following year, too late for me, the fee had almost quintupled to £1,000. As ever, Greigy had led from the front.

All-rounder Lewis Gregory's winter training programme has received a big boost with the news that he will be heading to Cape Town early in January to play cricket and coach for three months. Lewis is a highly talented all-rounder and captained the England U19 side, making his first-team debut in the one-day game against Pakistan in 2010. He went on to make a great impression taking wickets regularly in the limited-overs game as well as some useful contributions with bat in the middle order. In 2012 he suffered from some injuries which checked his progress. The period he now has in South Africa is an excellent opportunity for Lewis to find match fitness and return for the 2013 season and press his claim for a regular First XI position.

MONDAY, 31 DECEMBER.

I am in London with family, which is where I was almost exactly a year ago when I started writing this book on New Year's Day. The year has been another extraordinary one for its variety and richness of content for Somerset County Cricket Club. It draws to a close with players, coaches and staff scattered all over the globe, who will form up once again in March and begin writing the script for 2013. It will be Somerset's 138th year, and who knows what it might bring. Whatever it brings, or doesn't, it won't be for the want of effort from a very special and gifted array of individuals, teams and groups who make this club the incredibly special and unique institution that it is.

HAPPY NEW YEAR FROM ALL AT SOMERSET CCC – SCCC Site

With 2013 fast approaching, senior players Marcus Trescothick and Steve Kirby along with Andy Hurry the Head Coach have shared their New Year wishes for 2013.

The Somerset captain, who missed four months of last season with an ankle injury, said: 'Personally I'd like to make sure that I keep my ankle in good shape so that I can play throughout the 2013 season in all formats of the game, which is my first challenge.'

He went on: 'However I would want to get my hands on some silverware which is what everybody who is part of this Club is really aiming for in 2013. I want to score big runs in big games and take Somerset across the line and win a trophy.'

'I would just love to be the first Somerset captain to lift the County Championship. That is a major goal of mine to achieve in the time that I have got left playing.'

He added: 'To be part of the sorts of crowd scenes from the times that we have won trophies would be an amazing achievement, so that is what I wish for going into 2013.'

Fast bowler Kirby said: 'In 2013 it would be just amazing if we could bring that championship home to Taunton. All of the supporters here have been dreaming of winning it for so long, so if we could bring the title back to the County Ground it would be fantastic. We want to do well in the T20 and win the trophy and get back to the Champions League if we can, but I think for me it has to be the championship that is my number one dream for 2013.'

'Kirbs' added: 'I'd like to be able to stay really fit and strong all of the year, stay in the team, take some wickets, and contribute on a big scale, they are my ambitions looking to 2013.'

Head coach Andy Hurry said: 'There is no doubt that we have put together a very competitive squad for 2013 with the acquisition of two quality high performing international players. Alviro Petersen in early season will provide us with a lot of experience and depth into our batting and later on Abdur Rehman, who showed what he was capable of last year, will be coming back to join us.'

'The exciting thing for me is that this squad is starting to gain maturity, and a key area we are going to be looking at before the start of the new season is the players' ownership and responsibility for their own game and how they are going to look to perform in critical situations of the game.'

Hurry went on: 'We have got some really exciting and talented young players who have gained some experience in 2012 who will now be challenging the more senior Somerset players in the squad and fighting hard for a place in the first team.'

The Head Coach added: 'I am focusing on making sure that we are the best that we possibly can be on every single day. We are fully aware of our game and delivering our game plans, and for me 2013 will be judged by how well we perform to the best of our potential.

APPENDICES

LVCC RESULTS

Division One final table

1	Warwickshire	16	6	1	9	43	45	0.0	211.0
2	Somerset	16	5	1	10	32	45	0.0	187.0
3	Middlesex	16	5	4	7	33	38	0.0	172.0
4	Sussex	16	5	5	6	28	41	0.0	167.0
5	Nottinghamshire	16	4	2	10	26	43	0.0	163.0
6	Durham	16	5	5	6	18	45	4.0	157.0
7	Surrey	16	3	4	9	26	40	2.0	139.0
8	Lancashire	16	1	5	10	25	35	0.0	106.0
9	Worcestershire	16	1	8	7	17	42	0.0	96.0

Match by Match

Somerset v Middlesex, Taunton, 5–8 April
Somerset won the toss and fielded. Somerset (22 points) beat Middlesex (3 points) by six wickets.

Warwickshire v Somerset, Edgbaston, 12–15 April
Somerset won the toss and batted. Warwickshire (20 points) beat Somerset (3 points) by two wickets.

Somerset surprisingly elected to bat in bowler friendly conditions and poor shot selection saw them dismissed cheaply inside 40 overs with Chris Wright taking four wickets. Warwickshire batsmen showed more application in their reply and gained a lead of 96. Somerset's second innings was built around a sixth wicket partnership between Nick Compton and Jos Buttler and a career best of 43 from Adam Dibble. Warwickshire were set 259 to win and were coasting at 190 for three when Peter Trego took four wickets in 23 balls to reduce them to 207 for eight. Jeetan Patel then adopted the long handle to hit 43 from 36 balls and secure a two wicket victory.

Somerset 147 (39.5 overs) and 354 (105 overs) N.R.D. Compton 133, J.C. Buttler 93.

Warwickshire 243 (85.2 overs) and 262 for 8 (77.5 overs) W.T.S. Porterfield 84.

Nottinghamshire v Somerset, Trent Bridge, 19–22 April
Somerset won the toss and fielded. Nottinghamshire (3 points) drew with Somerset (11 points).

Somerset v Lancashire, Taunton, 26–29 April
Lancashire won the toss and batted. Somerset (6 points) drew with Lancashire (9 points).

Durham v Somerset, Emirates Durham ICG, 9–12 May
Somerset won the toss and fielded. Durham (6 points) drew with Somerset (8 points).

Somerset v Surrey, the Kia Oval, 16–19 May
Somerset won the toss and batted. Surrey (10 points) drew with Somerset (11 points).

Somerset v Durham, Taunton, 22–25 May
Durham won the toss and batted. Somerset (24 points) beat Durham (7 points) by five wickets.

Worcestershire v Somerset, New Road, 30 May–2 June
Worcestershire won the toss and batted first. Worcestershire (9 points) drew with Somerset (7 points).

Middlesex v Somerset, Lord's, 5–8 June
Middlesex won the toss and fielded. Middlesex (10 points) drew with Somerset (4 points).

Somerset v Warwickshire, Taunton, 18–21 July
Somerset won the toss and fielded. Somerset (21 points) beat Warwickshire (8 points) by one wicket.

Lancashire v Somerset, Liverpool, 1–4 August
Somerset won the toss and fielded. Lancashire (6 points) drew with Somerset (6 points).

Somerset v Nottinghamshire, Taunton, 7–10 August
Somerset won the toss and fielded. Somerset (7 points) drew with Nottinghamshire (6 points).

Somerset v Sussex, Taunton, 21–24 August
Somerset won the toss and batted. Somerset (7 points) drew with Sussex (8 points).

Somerset v Surrey, Taunton, 28–31 August
Surrey won the toss and batted. Somerset (8 points) drew with Surrey (9 points).

Sussex v Somerset, Hove, 4–7 September
Somerset won the toss and fielded. Somerset (19 points) beat Sussex (4 points) by five wickets.

Somerset v Worcestershire, Taunton, 11–14 September
Worcestershire won the toss and batted. Somerset (23 points) beat Worcestershire by an innings and 148 runs.

T20 RESULTS

Friends Life T20 final table
Midlands/Wales/West Group

Teams	Mat	Won	Lost	Tied	N/R	Pts
Somerset	10	5	2	0	3	13
Gloucestershire	10	4	2	0	4	12
Worcestershire	10	4	3	0	3	11
Warwickshire	10	4	3	0	3	11
Glamorgan	10	2	3	0	5	9
Northamptonshire	10	1	7	0	2	4

North Group

Teams	Mat	Won	Lost	Tied	N/R	Pts
Yorkshire	10	7	1	0	2	16
Nottinghamshire	10	5	1	0	4	14
Durham	10	4	4	1	1	10
Lancashire	10	3	4	1	2	9
Derbyshire	10	2	6	0	2	6
Leicestershire	10	2	7	0	1	5

South Group

Teams	Mat	Won	Lost	Tied	N/R	Pts
Sussex	10	6	1	0	3	15
Hampshire	10	5	2	0	3	13
Essex	10	5	4	0	1	11
Kent	10	4	5	0	1	9
Middlesex	10	3	7	0	0	6
Surrey	10	3	7	0	0	6

Quarter-finals
Somerset beat Essex by 27 runs
Sussex beat Gloucestershire by 39 runs
Hampshire beat Nottinghamshire by four wickets
Yorkshire beat Worcestershire by 29 runs

Semi-finals
Yorkshire beat Sussex by 36 runs
Hampshire beat Somerset by six wickets

Final
Hampshire beat Yorkshire by 10 runs.

Match by Match

Somerset v Warwickshire, Taunton, 13 June
Warwickshire won the toss and fielded. Somerset (2 points), won by 63 runs.

Gloucestershire v Somerset, Bristol, 14 June
Match abandoned. Gloucestershire (1 point), Somerset (1 point).

Somerset v Northamptonshire, Taunton, 17 June
Northamptonshire won the toss and batted. Somerset (2 points), won by five wickets.

Warwickshire v Somerset, Edgbaston, 21 June
Warwickshire won the toss and fielded. No result, Warwickshire (1 point), Somerset (1 point).

Somerset v Welsh Dragons, Taunton, 22 June
Welsh Dragons won the toss and batted. Somerset (2 points), won by four wickets.

Northamptonshire v Somerset, Northampton, 26 June
Somerset won the toss and fielded. Somerset (2 points), won by seven wickets.

Somerset v Gloucestershire, Taunton, 29 June
Somerset won the toss and batted. Gloucestershire (2 points), won by nine wickets.

Somerset v Worcestershire, Taunton, 1 July
Somerset won the toss and fielded. Somerset (2 points) won by 54 runs.

Welsh Dragons v Somerset, SWALEC Stadium, Cardiff, 6 July
Match abandoned. Welsh Dragons (1 point), Somerset (1 point).

Worcestershire v Somerset, New Road, 8 July
Somerset won the toss and fielded. Somerset (2 points), won by seven wickets.

Somerset v Essex, Taunton, 24 July – Quarter-final
Essex won the toss and fielded. Somerset won by 27 runs.

Hampshire v Somerset, SWALEC Stadium, Cardiff, 25 August – Semi-final
Hampshire won the toss and fielded. Hampshire won by six wickets.

CB40 RESULTS
The Clydesdale Bank 40 final table

Group A

Teams	Mat	Won	Lost	Tied	N/R	Pts	Net RR
Lancashire	12	9	2	0	1	19	+0.050
Middlesex	12	6	3	1	2	15	+0.778
Gloucestershire	12	5	5	0	2	12	+0.995
Netherlands	12	5	6	0	1	11	-0.910
Essex	12	4	6	0	2	10	-0.185
Leicestershire	12	3	6	0	3	9	-0.732
Worcestershire	12	3	7	1	1	8	-0.011

Group B

Teams	Mat	Won	Lost	Tied	N/R	Pts	Net RR
Hampshire	12	7	3	0	2	16	+0.754
Surrey	12	6	3	0	3	15	+0.466
Somerset	12	6	4	0	2	14	+0.385
Nottinghamshire	12	6	5	0	1	13	+0.101
Durham	12	5	5	0	2	12	+0.262
Glamorgan	12	3	6	0	3	9	-0.971
Scotland	12	1	8	0	3	5	-1.359

Group C

Teams	Mat	Won	Lost	Tied	N/R	Pts	Net RR
Sussex	12	7	1	0	4	18	+1.012
Warwickshire	12	8	3	0	1	17	+0.660
Kent	12	7	2	0	3	17	+0.870
Derbyshire	12	4	5	0	3	11	-0.438
Yorkshire	12	4	7	0	1	9	+0.006
Northamptonshire	12	1	6	0	5	7	-0.568
Unicorns	12	1	8	0	3	5	-1.545

Semi-finals

Warwickshire beat Lancashire by 23 runs

Hampshire beat Sussex by eight wickets

Final

Hampshire beat Warwickshire by losing fewer wickets

Group B Match by Match

Surrey v Somerset, the Kia Oval, 4 May

Somerset won the toss and fielded. Surrey (2 points) won by 105 runs.

Durham v Somerset, Emirates Durham ICG, 13 May

Somerset won the toss and fielded. Durham (2 points) won by 14 runs.

Somerset v Hampshire, Taunton, 27 May

Hampshire won the toss and fielded. Hampshire (2 points) won by nine wickets.

Nottinghamshire v Somerset, Trent Bridge, 4 June

Nottinghamshire won the toss and fielded. Nottinghamshire (2 points) won by five wickets.

Welsh Dragons v Somerset, SWALEC Stadium, 12 July

Match abandoned. Welsh Dragons (1 point), Somerset (1 point).

Somerset v Scotland, Taunton, 15 July

Somerset won the toss and batted. Somerset (2 points) won by 60 runs.

Somerset v Durham, Taunton, 22 July

Durham won the toss and batted. Somerset (2 points) won by eight wickets.

Somerset v Welsh Dragons, Taunton, 28 July

Welsh Dragons won the toss and batted. Somerset (2 points) won by three wickets.

Somerset v Nottinghamshire, Taunton, 12 August

Somerset won the toss and fielded. Somerset (2 points) won by five wickets.

Hampshire v Somerset, the Ageas Bowl, 14 August

Hampshire won the toss and fielded. Somerset (2 points) won by 50 runs.

Scotland v Somerset, Uddingston, 19 August
Scotland won the toss and batted. Somerset (2 points) won by 53 runs (D/L method).

Somerset v Surrey, Taunton, 27 August
Somerset won the toss and fielded. No result, Somerset (1 point), Surrey (1 point).

BATTING AVERAGES
Division One

Player	Matches	Inns	N/O	Runs	High Score	Average	100	50	Catches	Stump
N.R.D. Compton	11	18	6	1191	204	99.25	4	7	7	0
C. Kieswetter	11	17	4	654	152	50.31	1	2	28	1
J.C. Hildreth	16	25	3	946	120	43.00	3	5	16	0
M.E. Trescothick	9	13	0	506	146	38.92	2	1	26	0
P.D. Trego	16	21	3	600	92	33.33	0	4	12	0
A.V. Suppiah	16	25	0	728	124	29.12	2	5	9	0
J. Overton	3	4	2	55	34	27.50	0	0	1	0
J.C. Buttler	12	16	1	400	93	26.67	0	2	12	1
C.A.J. Meschede	6	6	0	135	62	22.50	0	1	2	0
A.J. Dibble	1	2	0	44	43	22.00	0	0	0	0
C.R. Jones	5	7	0	150	50	21.43	0	1	2	0
G.M. Hussain	5	7	4	55	29	18.33	0	0	0	0
A.W.R. Barrow	9	15	0	186	47	12.40	0	0	14	0
C. Overton	7	8	1	75	50	10.71	0	1	4	0
V.D. Philander	5	6	0	62	38	10.33	0	0	2	0
L. Gregory	4	4	0	40	18	10.00	0	0	0	0
A.C. Thomas	9	11	1	96	39	9.60	0	0	1	0
G.H. Dockrell	10	10	4	54	13	9.00	0	0	4	0
S.D. Snell	2	2	0	18	10	9.00	0	0	8	0
A. Rehman	4	5	0	43	17	8.60	0	0	2	0
M.T.C. Waller	2	3	0	24	17	8.00	0	0	4	0
S.I. Mahmood	3	4	1	25	13	8.33	0	0	1	0
S.P. Kirby	9	11	5	20	6	3.33	0	0	4	0

Also played two matches: M.J. Leach 0*

CB40

Player	Mat	Inns	NO	Runs	HS	Ave	BF	SR	100	50	0	4/6s	Ct
A.W.R. Barrow	5	3	1	108	72	54.00	124	87.09	0	1	0	8/11	2
N.R.D. Compton	6	6	1	237	81	47.40	306	77.45		3	0	19/1	1
J.C. Buttler	10	8	1	289	71	41.28	319	90.59	0	2	0	36/1	4
M.E. Trescothick	5	4	1	118	87*	39.33	109	108.25	0	1	0	14/1	5
C. Kieswetter	7	7	0	236	103	33.71	192	122.91	1	1	0	29/9	7
P.D. Trego	11	9	0	245	81	27.22	188	130.31	0	2	2	34/6	3
C.A.J. Meschede	6	5	1	102	33	25.50	117	87.17	0	0	0	8/4	2
A.V. Suppiah	7	7	1	144	56	24.00	169	85.20	0	1	0	14/2	3
C.R. Jones	3	2	0	48	24	24.00	73	65.75	0	0	0	4/1	0
A.C. Thomas	5	3	2	23	16*	23.00	29	79.31	0	0	0	2/0	0
J. Overton	3	3	2	19	10	19.00	30	63.33	0	0	0	2/0	0
L. Gregory	10	6	0	103	39	17.16	137	75.18	0	0	0	8/0	3
J.C. Hildreth	11	10	2	102	26	12.75	144	70.83	0	0	0	10/0	4
C. Overton	2	2	0	25	20	12.50	21	119.04	0	0	0	2/0	3
M.T.C. Waller	8	4	1	30	13	10.00	45	66.66	0	0	0	1/0	5
A. Rehman	3	2	0	17	9	8.50	23	73.91	0	0	0	2/0	0
G.H. Dockrell	6	4	1	21	18	7.00	36	58.33	0	0	1	1/0	3
M.J. Leach	3	1	0	2	2	2.00	10	20.00	0	0	0	0/0	0

Also played: G.M. Hussain, three matches, 1*, DNB, 18*; S.P. Kirby, six matches DNB; R. Mutch one match, DNB.

FL T20

Player	Mat	Inns	NO	Runs	HS	Ave	BF	SR	100	50	Ct/st	4s	6s
C. Kieswetter	4	4	1	134	63*	44.66	111	120.72	0	2	4/6	12	4
J.C. Hildreth	9	8	3	223	107*	44.60	167	133.53	1	1	3	30	2
A.C. Thomas	10	3	2	28	11*	28.00	30	93.33	0	0	3	3	0
J.C. Buttler	10	9	2	195	58*	27.85	168	116.07	0	1	4/1	19	3
L. Gregory	7	5	2	83	22	27.66	65	127.69	0	0	0	7	2
R.E. Levi	7	7	0	179	69	25.57	111	161.26	0	1	3	18	11
N.R.D. Compton	8	7	2	120	42*	24.00	123	97.56	0	0	2	10	2
J.A. Morkel	5	4	0	81	38	20.25	72	112.50	0	0	1	6	3
A.V. Suppiah	7	5	2	55	18	18.33	48	114.58	0	0	1	5	0
K.J. O'Brien	6	4	1	52	22	17.33	51	101.96	0	0	4	6	1
M.E. Trescothick	2	2	0	31	19	15.50	22	140.90	0	0	1	4	1
C.A.J. Meschede	3	3	1	19	19*	9.50	16	118.75	0	0	1	2	1
P.D. Trego	8	8	1	52	16	7.42	77	67.53	0	0	4	3	0
S.D. Snell	2	1	0	4	4	4.00	4	100.00	0	0	0	0	0
G.H. Dockrell	7	2	1	2	1*	2.00	9	22.22	0	0	4	0	0

Also batted: S.P. Kirby, eight matches, one innings, 4*; M.T.C Waller, seven matches, DNB.

BOWLING AVERAGES

Division One

Player	Overs	Maidens	Runs	Wkts	Average	Best	5w	10w
A.J. Dibble	13.0	2	42	3	14.00	3-42	0	0
A. Rehman	174.0	50	383	27	14.19	9-65	3	0
V.D. Philander	181.1	42	491	23	21.35	5-43	2	0
M.J. Leach	20.0	4	43	2	21.50	2-37	0	0
A.C. Thomas	252.4	50	740	33	22.42	6-60	2	0
G.H. Dockrell	309.5	67	950	34	27.94	6-27	2	0
G.M. Hussain	92.4	17	353	12	29.42	5-48	1	0
S.I. Mahmood	66.1	10	241	8	30.13	4-62	0	0
C. Overton	113.1	23	363	12	30.25	4-38	0	0
S.P. Kirby	225.1	47	735	24	30.62	3-34	0	0
P.D. Trego	508.5	123	1554	50	31.08	5-53	2	0
L. Gregory	24.0	2	127	4	31.75	2-22	0	0
C.A.J. Meschede	98.0	18	350	10	35.00	3-26	0	0
J. Overton	66.0	7	229	6	38.17	2-61	0	0
A.V. Suppiah	73.0	18	211	3	70.33	1-8	0	0
M.T.C. Waller	19.0	2	83	1	83.00	1-78	0	0

Also bowled: C. Kieswetter 3-0-3-2; C.R.Jones 2-0-17-1; J.C.Buttler 2-0-11-0; J.C.Hildreth 2-0-30-0

CB40

Player	Mat	Overs	Mdns	Runs	Wkts	BBI	Ave	Econ	4w
A. Rehman	3	20.5	2	73	9	6/16	8.11	3.50	0
J. Overton	3	17.0	1	100	6	4/42	16.66	5.88	1
C. Kieswetter	7	2.0	0	19	1	1/19	19.00	9.50	0
S.P. Kirby	6	40.3	1	175	8	3/19	21.87	4.32	0
C.A.J. Meschede	6	35.0	0	198	9	4/27	22.00	5.65	1
A.C. Thomas	5	27.0	3	112	5	2/13	22.40	4.14	0
R.G. Mutch	1	8.0	0	46	2	2/46	23.00	5.75	0

Player	Mat	Overs	Mdns	Runs	Wkts	BBI	Ave	Econ	4w
P.D. Trego	11	61.4	2	372	15	3/26	24.80	6.03	0
G.M. Hussain	3	18.2	0	104	4	2/29	26.00	5.67	0
L. Gregory	10	28.4	0	195	6	2/25	32.50	6.80	0
M.T.C. Waller	8	34.0	1	180	4	2/29	45.00	5.29	0
A.V. Suppiah	7	18.0	0	99	2	1/32	49.50	5.50	0
C. Overton	2	11.0	0	72	1	1/35	72.00	6.54	0
G.H. Dockrell	6	28.0	1	168	2	2/32	84.00	6.00	0
M.J. Leach	3	19.0	0	90	1	1/30	90.00	4.73	0

FL T20

Player	Mat	Overs	Mdns	Runs	Wkts	BBI	Ave	Econ	4w
J.A. Morkel	5	11.5	0	89	5	3/30	17.80	7.52	0
G.H. Dockrell	7	26.0	0	169	9	2/17	18.77	6.50	0
L. Gregory	7	17.3	0	120	6	4/39	20.00	6.85	1
M.T.C. Waller	7	21.0	0	148	7	4/16	21.14	7.04	1
S.P. Kirby	8	26.4	0	171	8	3/37	21.37	6.41	0
A.V. Suppiah	7	12.0	0	88	4	2/10	22.00	7.33	0
A.C. Thomas	10	33.0	0	282	8	3/17	35.25	8.54	0
P.D. Trego	8	11.0	0	72	2	2/23	36.00	6.54	0
K.J. O'Brien	6	8.0	0	63	1	1/15	63.00	7.87	0
C.A.J. Meschede	3	4.0	0	39	0	-	-	9.75	0

Also bowled – C.A.J. Meschede, 4 overs, 0 maidens, 39 runs, 0 wickets.

SOMERSET COUNTY CRICKET CLUB FINANCIAL
RESULTS F2011/12

	2012	2011
Turnover	**5,528,128**	**5,354,758**
Income		
Subscriptions	693,202	675,473
Match Receipts	615,593	750,188
Commercial Income (net)	41,891	227,318
ECB Pool	2,007,922	1,942,784
Catering (net)	265,965	282,336
Car Parking, Rents, Lettings etc	298,331	300,321
Interest Received	1,812	386
Elton John	20,310	0
Miscellaneous Income	98,796	17,527
	4,043,822	**4,196,333**
Expenditure		
Regional Academy	104,732	127,929
Playing Costs	2,326,866	2,234,108
Ground Maintenance	439,443	453,137
Match Expenses	241,275	265,966
Administration	357,399	455,879
Finance Charges	96,059	99,324
Depreciation and Profit		
on Plant Disposal	114,541	110,777
	3,680,315	**3,747,120**
Trading Surplus for the Year	363,507	449,213
Fund Raising and Donations	103,284	32,582
Surplus for the Year before Taxation	**466,791**	**481,795**
Taxation Charge	-57,388	-73,208
Surplus for the Year after Taxation	**409,403**	**408,587**

SLIDES FROM 2012 AGM

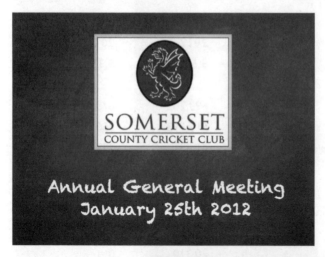

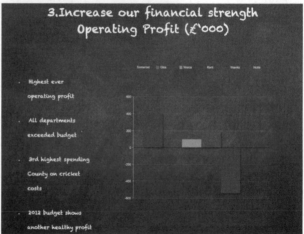

Morgan Review

- ECB board to consider next steps in March

- decisions will affect 2014 season and Media Agreement

- Counties need certainty to be able to plan eg Players' contracts, Ground development

- ECB / Counties have tinkered for years and fixture list largely ignores fans' needs. Strong Leadership required!!!

Somerset CCC

VISION

'To win trophies and exceed our members, spectators and visitors expectations in order to ensure that Somerset CCC is recognised as an outstanding Club throughout the cricketing world'.

Summary

- Your Club is currently THE best Club in England

- Success on and off the pitch

- Trophies a top priority

- Change is a major challenge

- International cricket will secure our long term future

- Foster the Spirit of Somerset

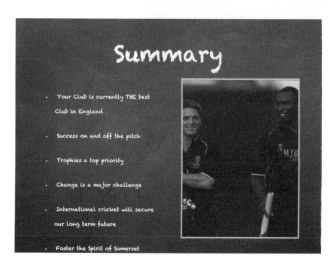

2011 highlights

- One of the country's best teams but disappointment at no silverware

- Three players in senior England squads

- Academy produces more talent and young internationals

- Record profitability. All Depts beat budget

- Richard Gould succeeded by Guy Lavender

FOUR Major Objectives

- Compete in ALL forms of Cricket

- Develop our OWN Players

- Increase our FINANCIAL strength

- County Ground - improve facilities & increase capacity

2. Develop our own Players